s t i l l   m i l l

Poems, Stories & Songs
of **Making Paper**
in **Bucksport, Maine**
1930 – 2014

edited by **Patricia Smith Ranzoni**

Distinctive realms appear to us when we look and hear by poem-light.
And these realms clearly are needed – there is no human culture that
does not have its songs and poems.

– Jane Hirshfield

The reason we tell stories,
to judge from what I have seen
among traditional people,
and what I believe was already
well worked out by Cro-Magnon
people, is to keep each other
from being afraid.

– Barry Lopez

Poetry is just the evidence of life.

– Leonard Cohen

Editor, Patricia Ranzoni
Project Partner, Ed Ranzoni
Editorial Intern, Joey Ranzoni, Unity College Student
Student Assistant, Michael Shaw II, Buksport Recreational Department
Technical assistance: Patricia Newell, Gina Tapp, Joe Ranzoni, Dan Ranzoni, John Graveline

All inquiries and requests for permissions to reprint should be directed to:
pranzoni@aol.com or   Patricia Ranzoni
                       289 Bucksmills Rd.
                       Bucksport, ME 04416

Published with gratitude through a generous SpiritWords Fund grant from the
University of Maine Foundation with all proceeds to benefit:
                       Bucksport Historical Society
                       P.O. Box 798
                       Bucksport, ME 04416
for the purpose of locating, protecting, and exhibiting materials relating to the
history of making paper in the Bucksport region.

COVER: Emily Newell photograph of oil on board painting, worked from a 1964
photograph, by esteemed Maine artist, Harriet Fisher Hill (1915–2004), and loaned
by Bucksport artist and businessman, Larry Wahl.

The images collected here, and the perspectives and memories recounted, are those of
the individual authors and may or may not represent those of the editor, other authors,
mill owners, mill workers, Town of Bucksport, Bucksport Historical Society, University
of Maine Foundation or others associated with this publication. PSR

> *Truth is the shattered mirror strewn in*
> *myriad bits; while each believes his*
> *little bit the whole to own.*
>
> – Sir Richard Francis Burton (1821–1890)

in honor of ourselves
and each other,
still papermakers,
and this singular history
we have lived
and now leave
and which it is our duty,
we believe, to save

Anne Stevenson
Northumberland, U.K.

from PAPER

Paper,

the beauty of it,

the simple, strokeable, in-the-handness of it,

the way it has of flattering ink,

giving it to understand that

nothing matters

until it is printed or written down

to be cherished on paper.

The way old paper levels time,

is the archive's treasure,

is evidence talking to your fingers. . . .

Born in England in 1933, **Anne Stevenson** *moved between the United States and United Kingdom during the first half of her life until claiming British citizenship in 1962. In 2007 Stevenson was awarded the Lannan Life-time Achievement Award for Poetry and the Poetry Foundation's Neglected Masters Award. She has authored more than a dozen books of poetry, several of prose, and has edited two anthologies. Although Stevenson says that her poetry comes first from sound, she slowly lost her hearing years ago. In a 2007 essay she wrote: "poems still come to me as tunes in the head. Words fall into rhythms before they make sense. It often happens that I discover what a poem is about through a process* *of listening to what its rhythms are telling me. Ever since I can remember, I have been aware of living at what E.M. Forster called 'a slight angle' to the universe. I have always had to create my own angular environment or perish. But that's the whole point about borders. It's the best place from which to be able to see both sides." Her poem, "Paper," excerpted here, is from her 2005 collection,* Anne Stevenson, Poems 1955–2005, *published by Bloodaxe Books, Northumberland, and is reprinted with the author's generous permission.*

CONTENTS

VI. GRATEFULLY EVER AFTER
Knowing Who We, Still, Are   302

VII. MORE
   Of Our Voices   418

VIII. AUTOGRAPHS
   Of Papermaking People Who Shall Not Come Again   419

IX. APPENDIX   420
   Call for Submissions
   SpiritWords Publication Grant
   Preview Exhibit: Bucksport Area Poetry Route
   Directory
   Letter of Thanks

X. THE ARTISTS   428

XI. THE EDITOR   431

I. THE SHAPE AND SOUND OF IT

An Introduction and Invitation

Once, for the better part of a century, at the mouth of the Penobscot River watershed halfway up the coast of Maine – called "Downeast," – there was a small town about which it was said that chances were high that a day didn't pass in the life of an American reader when he or she didn't touch a piece of paper turned out there. It was accurately and pridefully boasted that every day more than 1,000 people employed from the area produced more than 1,000 tons of the finest lightweight, coated, publication papers available on the world-wide market. (From undated St. Regis publication, probably 2007, the mill's 75th anniversary.) And it took just about everything we had to give for four generations of our families alongside uncountable others from the forests to the ocean routes and railroads of Maine and beyond.

For the rest of my life I shall remember our first ride across the Bucksport–Verona bridge after the sudden news that our multi-million-dollar paper mill was done. Not only done but to be immediately and irrevocably destroyed and sold for scrap. Scrap! And how my usual scan, to enjoy our shipshape waterfront all the way west to the mill at the mouth of the River, brought tears with a mind of their own.

Before reaching the Island side of Doc. Thegen's memorial, the words, STILL MILL, rose over the Bay showing me what I must do. Remembering in a flash the innumerable poems I had written through the years relating to the mill and our lives as mill families, based on the belief that while I alone am not important, my people are, my first thought was that I would put together a booklet of these. We Mainers are a poetry, story, and music loving people. From First Native Peoples and earliest European settlers, anything of consequence to our lives here has been expressed accordingly, in our own languages. So it seemed natural when the idea of inviting others to join their words with selections of mine for a community collection occurred. I can't consider the title anything but a gift. STILL in that it would soon be quieted. STILL in that as long as we live and after, as long as stories are told, the mill and the people who made it what it was—with all its flaws and wonders—shall live on, will still BE.

In the days and weeks to come, it became evident to me that this was to be one of the greatest shocks this place has known since the attack on Pearl Harbor drew us into WWII. Born upriver during the build-up to that war and moved by our mother down to Bucksport for work at the mill upon my father's return from battleship combat, my first sister's and my early childhoods were spent in apartments on the waterfront and Central Street praying every day for his survival. And, under our mother's instruction, keeping patriotic faith, following the rules of austerity, conservation, pitching in and

1

making do, and self defense on the home front. News of the mill closure felt like the greatest cultural emergency and threat to our town since then. Of course, the loss of one mill in one village in one New England state could not equal world-wide all-out war but there would be reminders. We were again at the mercy of powerful forces beyond our control. We would have to fight to ensure our future and it would take everyone's commitment. There would be death and dislocation. "Salt of the earth" people would disappear, never to be seen again. There would be the necessity of self (if not federally) regulated rationing in the face of financial insecurity. Fear and anger. Sacrifices would have to be made. Now, as then, our well-being would depend on mutual caring and assistance, respect for our heritage and identities, community. Hope, determination, future-directed intentions. Belief in strengths derived from who we have been as a people–our history, coupled with visions of possibilities for life here during and after this struggle. We knew how to do this because we had done it before on a much harder scale. And we would.

But as paper and electronic news media covered various aspects of this insult, it became evident that not all Mainers felt the same. That what was happening in the Bucksport area was part of a larger, state and country-wide loss of industry just as the coming of our paper mill had, in the first place, for better or worse, contributed to the industrialization of the Penobscot River, of the State of Maine and of the United States. Not our story alone. We've stood through the years in solidarity with the papermaking people of Augusta (Statler), Millinocket and East Millinocket (Great Northern), Old Town (Penobscot Chemical Fiber), Lincoln (Lincoln Pulp & Paper), Brewer (Eastern Fine Paper) and Madison (Madison Paper Industries), whose towns and cities have also held on in the face of their mill closures. And others suffering severe cutbacks and on again – off again uncertainties on the verge of the collapse of what the Maine Department of Labor has designated our "heritage industries." (Courtesy of Glenn Mills, Chief, Economists Center for Workforce Research, Maine Dept. of Labor.) Internet searches of these companies through their various ownerships provide a shattering history of and for those who lived the stories between the lines, of which young people and newcomers know little.

One needed only walk downtown or stop by the market to hear contrary views. Some were overcome with shock and grief. A number passed away. Others were philosophical. Others upbeat. Some, all of these, in waves. It was not unusual, day after difficult day, to hear conflicting viewpoints from radio talk shows, electronic newspaper comments, and in the necessary arguments demanded at times like this. To dwell on it would be "negative," some said. We needed to "accept it," "get over it." Some media commentary was brutal and often from people without relationship to our or any mill. So were some Main Streeters. It wasn't uncommon to hear, "Thank God we won't be a mill town anymore." When it soon became apparent how close such judgments felt to "Thank God we won't be a town of people like you anymore," with its class implications, I stopped saying "it felt like a death." It wasn't like a death, it was a death. But we could forgive, believing that neither mean-spiritedness nor classism was intended. That all were wrestling to come to terms in their own ways as we all have had the need and right to do, trying to make sense of it.

Get over it? "We get over the measles. And we need to make that distinction" wrote the distinguished American poet, Albert Huffstickler (1927 – 2002) in his "The Cure" (from Walking Wounded, *Backyard Press, 1989) in a fine example of how poetry matters in the universal struggle by humans to make sense.*

2

"We think we get over things. / We don't. . . / Or say, we get over the measles / but not a broken heart . . . The things that become part of our experience never become less a part of our experience." We get over life when we die, he wrote. "Short of that, you move with it, / let the pain be pain, / not in the hope that it will vanish / but in the faith that it will fit in, / find its place in the shape of things." Thus, this book – a striving to identify the shape of what we have experienced. "Wisdom is seeing the shape of your life / without obliterating (getting over) a single / instant of it." ("The Cure") And, I would add, the __sound__ of our lives. For every place and human and nonhuman activity has sound. Mill towns certainly do. Our very location in or near town was, in fact, figured by our proximity to the mill and the blessed or cursed –depending on one's point of view – sounds of industrial papermaking. We knew where we were by what we were hearing. See what our mill workers, especially the machine tenders, and others midst the roar and whistle of it, have said about the noise. Listen to this book, good readers, and you will hear what I and the other authors mean and why I have introduced their, our, images as shape and sound.

So, "Get on with it," we know. Move ahead without delay to one or more of the no end of visions for what could work in the mill's stead – a distinguished school, an enterprise carrying on our maritime heritage, a giant water slide and Disney-like park, for some examples. A permanent scrap-iron salvage site since it would be that on the way to the mill's demolition. An accessible retirement or multi-generation community with condos on the River, another. A haven for artists, for still another, kindled by Matthew Foster's powerful granite sculpture, "Before the Wind" that we were able to bring to Bucksport through the Schoodic International Sculpture Symposium putting us on that trail in 2014 (http://schoodicsculpture.org). But the mill land, that storied Indian Point edging our western horizon, was not ours to do with as we might. And it would be years before we would know what new owners would put there, shaping our reality. The most we could hope for was to try to influence development decisions, manage with care our town fund established years ago for just such a fiscal emergency – the disappearance of our tax base – and tap all of our native and newcomer strength more than ever.

Several groups formed to tell us what they thought we should think and feel, what we value, and where we should go from here, even what language we should use speaking about it. Some found pre-packaged agendas developed outside Maine and installed over and around us comforting. Others, including our steadfast Town Council and officials, were determined to do both – express the full range of our response to this trauma, honoring our paper makers – while at the same time contributing to problem-solving and thoughtful consideration of what steps we should take in a natural and logical way, as people here in the birthplace of what would become America have done for centuries, many of us their descendants. It would be up to us to assert who we are if we are to survive as a people. This book would be one way we would. Our own way of saying we know who we are, thank you, what we value, and what can be counted on from us.

Hereabouts, we hold remembrances and celebrations of life for the departed. This book is that – our refusal to agree to bid goodbye as easily as some seemed to expect us to. For as long as any of us are alive and stories still told, we are still, unapologetically, mill. And that has always meant that, in addition, we are so much more (than the mill).

3

My method was to publicize a call for submissions in local, regional and far-reaching newspapers and networks of families, friends and neighbors, schools, churches, clubs and organizations. At the same time, I tapped into my own lists, following where they led, network to network, from next door to country- and world-wide. While I do not do "facebook" and other "social media" online, our young people were helpful, indeed, spreading the word on theirs. I applied to the University of Maine Foundation for a publication grant which was funded, making it possible for each contributor to have a free copy. And turned much of our downstairs over to STILL MILL for the two plus years (unbeknownst to us) it would take. I couldn't have guessed it would be so long in its realization but had to work around my own and others' limitations, much of the work accomplished from my daybed, making me all the more grateful to all who helped in any way. And I would not have wanted to miss one bit of it. I asked school children to elders for – and got – both the good and the hard. The realistic as well as the romantic. Both schooled and unschooled evidence of how the mill as a town presence as well as workplace shaped our lives. The table of contents is evidence of the extent to which groups and individuals responded.

When submissions began arriving, I saw how the biographical statements I asked contributors to include magnified the content of their offerings, showing the rich and diverse lives we have lived here and beyond, which had been my goal, and decided to put each one on the page with each author's composition rather than in the back of the book as is typically done in anthologies. I have found that bio notes are most often read when placed near, rather than far from, the author's work. And these are so interesting, varying considerably, as we have ourselves through the years, because contributors interpreted my invitation individually, sharing as much or as little about their lives as they chose. Their addition doubled the work and they are not incidental.

In order to honor one another's stories, and sound most like ourselves, I've kept the text faithful to the writers' and speakers' wordings, editing only for clarity, to document our voices as authentically as I could. Any errors or confusions are mine. Likewise, any failings or absences. I am not an unbiased, removed and objective editor. I am one of you whose story this is, in the spirit of Dr. Martin Luther King Jr.'s "Beloved Community." I have listened as hard as I could for as long as I could – my whole life – and I am more than grateful for those who gave of themselves and their poems, stories and songs to this document beginning with those exhibited in the BUCKSPORT AREA POETRY ROUTE preview exhibit we mounted along the main streets and outback of Bucksport, Orland, Verona and Prospect to introduce the collection from Spring to Fall the first year after the closing. The directory for this exhibit can be found in the Appendix. At once, the STILL MILL project proved itself as contributors transformed and transcended their realities into powerful and artistic expressions of historic consequence. It is offered as representative of what's out there to be found, but not exhaustive, not yet complete. We hope you, dear readers, will find them of value for your own family treasure and add to them, especially in your copy's section entitled "MORE" in the back. Keep telling and singing it. And keep writing it down before you go. Our echoes.

One of the most marvelous revelations from this material, has been the far-reaching diversity of world-wide roots represented in our mill family voices – a humble, multi-cultural comradeship our schools never taught, let alone celebrated. We knew about our Native American, Scots, Irish, English,

Canadian, and Franco neighbors but lucky those who knew the ones from Russia, Sweden, Newfoundland, Italy, India and Asia, among others. Those years before and after WWII were years of quiet homogeneity, assuming we were all alike, like the new white store-bought bread. We weren't. We've been, since the coming of the mill, a more ethnically rich place than we were ever given credit for. Looking back, we see how, in addition to wood pulp, the tons of world-class paper shipped out of Bucksport also contained the fiber of thousands of strong, dedicated workers from near and far. Made with their bodies, it contained their spirits. Imagine how and where it is archived around earth.

Another way of looking at our history in relation to the mill is "The Life and Times of..." as one mill mother entitled her family's contribution. If I were a painter, I would create a huge panel showing images of the workers, those early years, leaving their homes in all directions for miles around, heading to the mill on foot every shift change, drawn as by a magnet. The dignity of work. Of providing. Earners of their families' liveli-hoods. Story after story tells how they walked through all kinds of severe weather at great risk, even loss of life. I hope someone will, maybe four panels showing the mill walkers through the seasons. And everyday heroes like Horace Wardwell and Henry Whitham who drove up from Castine picking up Lawrence Mann and Donald Soper in Orland to work in the Electrical Dept. at Seaboard which became St. Regis.

What we <u>were</u> taught, in the elementary grades here, was how to make paper. St. Regis supplied our schools with kits containing instructions and materials. We learned the wonder of how trees get converted to paper by hand and on an industrial scale, what most of our families were doing. Sad, hearing how that ended years ago.

Early in my organizational process, I envisioned naming one section, "In Harm's Way," but it soon became apparent that just about every aspect of papermaking put its workers in harm's way, from working in the woods, cutting and hauling mountains of it out, to loading and shipping paper by the gigantic ton.

At the end of the last shift, as Bucksporters and neighboring townfolk gathered at the mill gate to thank and bid our final paper making workforce farewell, I saw the biggest teardrop of my life–like a crystal pendant– well up and splash down from young Dan Wentworth's uplifted eyes to his work boots as we spoke in the parking area. Being from one of many four-generation families of Bucksport papermakers, he would become one of the most articulate spokesmen during the hardest time. For a number of the elder contributors, this was some of their last telling before passing away. Evidence of their lives. Their testaments. How could we not hold it to us?

By this work, this book, we join hands and hearts with hopeless and hopeful humanity around the world who've faced culture shock and disrespect on this kind of scale, and survived by transcending and transforming our expressions of loss, anger and fear into artful written and visual images of what only we have known and felt. Not imposed upon us from without, but welcomed and honored from deep within ourselves. As Sandra Lynn Hutchison, editor of the electronic journal, e*lix*ir has put it: "The processes of personal and social transformation are inextricable. We heal the world by healing ourselves. We heal ourselves by healing the world. Art, that well-crafted instrument of change as well *as joy, thrives at the heart of both processes...let it change you, let it bring you joy!" May this book change you and bring you joy as it has me.*

Yes, it hurt us to read the Boston Globe *headline, "Closing the Book on a Mill and Its Town" because although we were in mourning for the loss of all the mill had been to us and our identities as papermakers, we were refusing to accept that that meant the very loss of our town and all else we've been. Maybe our town the way it used to be, yes, but we never doubted that the Closing of the mill also meant the Opening of a new book, not just chapter. Bucksport is many books, only starting to be written. We need only consider the generations of our children who have grown up here and stayed or returned for the love of it, growing it, or gone out around the world making significant contributions from what they've learned and become here – both, carrying aspects of who we've been in their hearts for safekeeping, celebrating, and repaying. Validating that we've been and remain all the more a community of worth, of creative, welcoming, strong people of hard-earned heritage and vision.*

"2017 is the 225th anniversary of the town of Bucksport, the 130th anniversary of the Buck Memorial Library and the 20th anniversary of the Bucksport Bay Festival. Plans are underway for a spectacular combo event that incorporates all three milestones this summer. The biggest things that Bucksport has going for it as it moves into the future are its momentum and community spirit. The positive energy of its residents and businesses and their willingness to work together for the future of the community is the foundation on which all community success is based."
– Susan Lessard, Town Manager

Because we have done this – listened to and saved these "once upon a time" voices – never have we been readier to celebrate. And we know how!

Now when we turn, crossing the Bucksport –Verona bridge, coming or going, our eyes are drawn to the new compass pocket park at the (former) mill end of the waterfront walkway where, thanks to the vision of Jeff Hammond and his co–creators, we can refresh and show off our local facts and pride from interpretative panels showing where so much of our country's remarkable narrative took place. Right here! With luck, should you accept our invitation to turn in our direction, you might sit a spell and envision Penobscot Indians from their ancient homeland upriver paddling their birchbark canoes by or actually engaging in a world-class modern canoe race. Long ago river drivers balancing their massive log booms with cantdogs, peaveys, and pickpoles, or see an honest-to-God present day papermaker with his family or buddies (for a while longer), or his or her descendant (years to come). Just close your eyes and listen. And remember what they have shown you in this book. Then, with good fortune, you might sense the spirit of the mill, still, all around you.

Pat Ranzoni

II. LONG AGO HERE

As Only Our Elders Remember

1929: CITY OF WOOD, BUCKSPORT ALIVE

BANGOR DAILY COMMERCIAL, December 18, 1929

Bucksport Alive With Action As Its New Ten Million Dollar Industry Draws Nearer

PRELIMINARY WORK ON BUCKSPORT'S BIG MILL IS NOW AT ITS PEAK;
250 WORKMEN ARE CONSTRUCTING A CITY OF WOOD

By a Staff Correspondent

At the right of the highway, as one enters Bucksport, is a scene mildly reminiscent of California's El Dorado in the golden days of '49. Only, this time, it is an industrial El Dorado – the preliminary steps in construction of a great plant that will bring millions to Bucksport, to Bangor, and to Eastern Maine.

Salmon Point – still called Indian Point by some of the older residents – is now alive with activity. Huge shovels bite into the frozen ground. A ribbon of steel, 2,500 feet long, is being laid – the spur track leading from the Maine Central's main line. A derrick with a 105-foot mast, and a 95-foot boom, begins to loom against the sky. The staccato symphony of electric drills, mingled with the pounding of what seems countless hammers is incessant.

Although it is only a few days since the first of fifteen car loads of lumber arrived, a city of wood already is taking form – a city that will have its far-flung bunk-house, its commissary department, its many smaller buildings. All of this is preliminary to the beginning of permanent construction: the erection of the great mill to be operated by the Maine Seaboard Paper Company. But detailed plans for this mill have not yet been received by the general contracting firm, which is the Morton C. Tuttle Construction Company of Boston. At present this preliminary work, which includes the clearing and grading of Salmon Point, is at its peak. It will continue about ten days. Then, probably, there will be a lull before the start of work upon the mill proper.

Specifically, there are now about 250 workmen. Just what percentage come from Bucksport, representatives of the contractors, when questioned, could not say off-hand; but Bucksport men have been given preference whenever possible. The others are largely Orland, Belfast and Machias, with some few from Bangor. In other words, they are State of Maine men – the majority born and reared here, and in sharp contrast to the "drifters" who are utilized on so many big-city construction jobs.

"Could you read the payroll," said one of the officials, "I think you would be impressed by the fact that so many are plain, old-fashioned American names. It's often very different in the big cities, where so many just over from Europe are employed."

These workmen range from common laborers, who get 40 cents an hour, up to carpenters – the highest paid – who get 75, all on a nine-hour day. They are of a clean and steady type, as intimated, and most of them have families. Some, it has been found, are surprisingly versatile. One man, asked what he could do, replied modestly: "Well, I'm a truck-driver; I'm a time-keeper, and I run a jackhammer." He paused a moment and added: "I'm a stenographer, too." They tried him out, and sure enough he made good – he was an expert at each. And, although he obviously was an exception, a great many have been found proficient at more than one line of work.

Work now is being rushed upon the bunk-house. It is shaped like a letter H, the sides being 72 feet long and the cross-section about 30. Here will be a hundred beds – an individual bed for each man – toilets, shower-baths and so on. It rather resembles an army barracks and will be fully as comfortable. The commissary department in a building adjoining will feed the same number – 100. Whether it will be conducted on a straight cash basis, so much per meal, or whether credit will be extended and the amount deducted from the pay envelopes each week, has not been decided. Probably it will be the former, for deducting from pay envelopes means extra bookkeeping and some confusion.

Thus, food and lodging will be assured to a hundred of the workmen – those who desire them under the company's immediate auspices. Most of the others have found boarding places about town; a few go to near-by points, and the Bucksport men have their own homes.

Another building, 160 feet long – and like all of them, steam-heated – will be utilized as a field office, with separate compartments for the more skilled trades. Here carpenters, bricklayers, etc., will gather and keep their tools. A building 100 by 25 feet will be divided, half being used as a tool house, the other half as a machine shop and blacksmith shop. Rather ingenious is the "heating shed", into which carloads of sand and gravel which require heat before being made into concrete are run over new-laid tracks. Heat flows through pipes from a boiler adjoining, and the ends of these pipes are buried in the material.

Then, taking form, is an "aggregate bin" of 85 tons capacity, from which the "aggregate" – meaning sand and stone, the inert components of concrete – will be fed to the mixer. The 2500-foot spur track is well under way. Over it will be run cars of sand, gravel, brick, steel and lumber. A giant derrick – more than 100 feet high, as has been said – is a black and aggressive smudge against the landscape. A steam shovel and three gas shovels make the air scream – here on this age-old point where only a little time ago a perpetual silence reigned. One of these shovels is making the railroad cut for the temporary track; the others are on general excavations.

This preliminary work will continue a week or ten days; then, probably, there will be a lull before actual work upon the great mill that is to revolutionize industry in this part of Eastern Maine. Detailed plans for this mill, which will come from the Maine Seaboard Company's engineers, have not yet been received by engineers of the contracting firm. When they are, undoubtedly Bangor houses will be prominent among those who enter bids. But this is in the future – the immediate future, perhaps, but still speculative. Not until the plans arrive will definite schedules of work be made out, and then only after a great deal of thought and study. It is believed – that the peak of the permanent construction, the really big job, will come next June.

It isn't possible to say as yet what effect the beginning of this permanent construction will have upon the number of workmen employed. Possibly there will not be so many more, the aggregate, but they will be of a higher class – more carpenters, steel workers, and other skilled mechanics.

There is a little touch of sentiment, too; for it is recalled that some 35 years ago, an Indian mound was opened on the shore near the Blodgett tannery – which is directly in the pathway of the great development, and will be razed to make way for it. Here were relics of the "Red Paint" Indians* who roamed the valleys of the Penobscot when the world was happier and younger – several thousands of years younger, in fact. Stone hatchets, arrow and spearheads, all steeped in a pigment known as red paint, but which in reality was an almost indestructible mineral of some kind, were unearthed, and were given to a number of museums. For the point was once an Indian camping-ground.

If, anywhere upon the point, other priceless historic relics have been struck up by hurrying drills and spades of the workmen, there is thus far no record of the quick passing of another trace of old-time glory – 50,000 feet of pine. This was the property of the tannery, was cut by the workmen, and is now piled along the railroad tracks. Burning the brush and cutting away the undergrowth has been a substantial job, too.

– Newspaper clipping courtesy of Buck Memorial Library

*Editor's note: Present day researchers and scholars now refer to the term "Red Paint Indians" or "Red Paint People" (which we grew up hearing in school and community) as a misnomer, so-called solely on the basis of red ochre found in burial sites. These ancient people, rather than being a "vanished race," as some erroneously concluded earlier, are now known to be ancestors of today's federally recognized Wabanaki tribes, known collectively as "People of the Dawnland," especially the Penobscot Nation whose ancestral homeland includes the Penobscot River Valley and the site of the Bucksport paper mill. For more, including accurate archaeological documentation, see "Ice Age to Borderland, 13,000 BP–1790," *HISTORICAL ATLAS OF MAINE,* edited by Stephen J. Hornsby and Richard W.

Judd (University of Maine Press, 2015); www.penobscotnation.org; and www.abbemuseumorg/research/wabanaki/index.html. Grateful acknowledgement is due consultants: University of Maine history faculty member and Wabanaki scholar, Micah Pawling, and John Bear Mitchell, Penobscot scholar, storyteller and Interim Director, Wabanaki Center, University of Maine.

Polly Bayer Lally
Bucksport

THAT FIRST BLAST OF DYNAMITE

"the legs and arms of our stories"

I was born in 1926 on Third Street near the old ball field next to the Oblate Seminary and would go down to visit my Grandmother Eldridge on Main Street near the canning factory overlooking the mill site. When I was a little girl I saw everything. Some complained but I thought all the activity was very interesting, all the truck work. When they came they came fast so we knew something big was happening. The sound of heavily loaded trucks hauling. I remember that first blast of dynamite well! I told my father that was the first time I remember feeling frightened by noise from above.

When I was old enough, I worked as a secretary in the mill where I met my husband-to-be, Herman "Tuck" Bayer, a UM chemical engineering pulp and paper student working in Bucksport for the summer. There were three or four of them, several from India. We all became friends. We used to go swimming at Craigs and they were fascinated that my mother was a "Saturday-night-baked-beaner." "What are these baked beans?" they wanted to know. I thoroughly enjoyed this aspect of meeting people from all over the world who came to work here.

After Tuck graduated we married and began following "the paper mill route" to Wisconsin, upstate New York, and so forth, a very happy life with our sons who were learning the system. Wherever we went in the papermaking world there were nice people, like here. We came home when he became mill manager from 1977 through November 1981. Our two boys enjoyed participating in sports here and I loved all my activities through the years. I remember how mill people would call to ask if they could come to the house to talk about mill problems. All of them wanted to make things better. I might go out shopping to give the men space.

Of course there were "incidents" that only a very few know, about the strikes, for example, and mill visitors partying on the lakes. But these memories make the history real.

Approximately 15 years ago, some of us made a movie about the mill's coming and people who came at its startup and their encounters. Some of the filming was done here at home, some at my camp and people contributed who had been involved in the mill's earliest weeks. This movie was shown at the Alamo Theater to a full house, and, of course, was free.

These tellings are so important. I call them "the legs and arms" of our stories.

Pauline Eldridge Bayer Lally *served several terms on the Bucksport Town Council and as head of the Conservation Commission which she reports she delighted in. "We had a wonderful committee of volunteer workers who, like the people here today, were interested in making our town look pretty. We planned all winter for spring plantings, both trees and flowers. I especially enjoyed swapping ideas--where we could get the best buys, and so forth-- with the Blue Hill folks who do such a good job, too."*

Phyllis Soper Wardwell
Bucksport

GODSEND

"Even the cows were happier."

My earliest memories were when the mill was built. It was a godsend for my parents. They had inherited my grandfather's old, run down farm – no running water, no electricity and only a lonely little "outhouse." (Brrr – those winters were brutal!) AND the pipeline was to be built! It would run nearly two miles across hay fields and woodlots owned by my parents. AND they were to be paid for this! I don't remember, if I ever knew, how much they were paid but it was enough that they could put in a "real" bathroom AND running water – as they were allowed to tap into this pipeline. No pump required – plenty of pressure! (And electric lights, too!) Even the cows were happier. No more hiking nearly 1/2 mile to the nearest brook for a drink. A big tub – always full – right next to the barn! And mother's wash day was so much easier for all concerned. No more lugging pails of water pumped from the well to the house. Usually my job.

My father – Herbert M. Soper – was one of the first hired at the mill when it was built. He had been gassed during World War I when he was in France and something about the atmosphere at the mill irritated his lungs. But he continued to supply the mill with pulp wood until he retired from farming.

I worked at the mill the summer after I graduated from Bucksport High School in 1939. My job was wrapping reams of paper. I don't remember just what kind or the name of the department.

My husband, Don, went to work in the mill in Sept. 1946 after returning from two years in Belgium and Germany in World War II. He worked in the boiler room of the power plant for 37 years, retiring in 1982. Along with this work, he had his own pulpwood business cutting, selling, hauling and supplying pulpwood to the mill during those years as an extra job. My son, Joel, also worked summers in the boiler room with his father while going to U of M, in the early '70s. He and our son-in-law Wilbur Wilson, daughter Donna's husband, were the third generation of our family to work at the mill, and their son, Greg Wilson, who lost his job when the mill closed, the fourth.

I don't have much to tell about the "great" years of the paper mill. Maybe I just can't remember. That's what you get for getting old. The mill provided many livelihoods for hard working families. We had a good life with our four children except for the heartbreaking loss of our son, Eric Michael, a Marine, in Vietnam in 1967.

After her summer at the mill, **Phyllis Soper Wardwell** *took a course in library administration and worked at the Buck Memorial Library for nearly 17 years off and on. In 1968 she was hired as assistant librarian at Bucksport High School. When librarian Ellie McGraw retired in 1985, Phyllis took her place until she, herself, retired after a total of 17 years, calling it "a very interesting and rewarding experience." In her "spare" time, she was an assistant leader of the Pine Tree 4-H Club and the Pine*

13

Cone 4-H Riders horse club, being an accomplished horsewoman. She was also a den mother for Cub Scout Troop 26 and a Sunday school teacher, remembering fondly how her two youngest, Jeffrey and Joel, participated in these organizations along with her. Phyllis will also be noted in local history as one of the saviors of the Duck Cove one room yellow school-house (next to the golf course) which generations of her family and neighbors attended, and a faithful supporter of the County Extension Homemakers Club that met there through the years.

Tin lunch pail of the kind used in the 1930s by railroad workers, miners, and Phyllis Soper Wardwell's father, Herbert Melvin Soper, working in the woods cutting pulp to haul and sell to the paper mill. It carried a cup upside down on top, a tray on the inside for the food, and the makings of tea in the bottom. He would hang it over his campfire when he worked and while the tea was brewing it warmed his dinner. As told by Phyllis.

SMOOTH AS A SMELT

*"Father taught me the necessary skills to handle a ship
and to master the currents at Bucksport Harbor."*

In 1929 a dock and terminal was built above Bucksport near Harriman Cove under the name of Maine Coal and Dock Inc. Since the port of Bangor was closed during the winter months, coal ships could use this dock year around. Locally, this became known as the Coal Pocket. My father's records show that he piloted the steamship *RUTH* in to the Coal Pocket on Dec. 11, 1929. This could have been the first ship into this berth. Bulk sulphur was also discharged at the Coal Pocket. Discharging bulk sulphur was a hazardous operation. Sulphur would catch fire easily. The unloading bucket or the endless belt could set the sulphur on fire. In fact, the terminal burned down three or four times. I can remember coming down from Bangor with my mother and the firemen stopping us. The white smoke from the sulphur fire was so thick that we had to wait to get by. In time the boiler plant was built on shore and a cement tower was built to hold the sulphur.

In 1930 Maine Coal and Dock bought the tug *WILBUR DUBOIS* of New York, an oil-fired steam tug. She worked under the Penobscot Towing Company and was renamed the *PENOBSCOT*. She was bought to make sure the coal steamers into the Coal Pocket had tug assist. A lot of steamers did their own docking, so to make ends meet, the *PENOBSCOT* went into competition with the *WALTER ROSS*.

With oil replacing coal, the later coal shipments to the Coal Pocket, now Maine Coal Sales, were by Sheridan tugs and barges.

Sulphur, an important commodity for the paper mills, was being shipped into Bucksport. In the late 50s the mode of transporting it changed from bulk to liquid. By heating the sulphur to 365 degrees, it could be pumped and thus carried in tankers. One of the advantages of the liquid sulphur was the time saved in discharge. Whereas a bulk ship would take 2 or 3 days, the tanker would dock one day, sail the next. One trip I remember, we docked on the high water, pumped two hours and then sailed on the same tide. All good things seem to come to an end. The paper mills changed their pulpmaking process so the end of sulphur tankers came about with the last ship sailing July 4, 1977. The plant was bought out in 1978 or 1979 by Elden Corporation who built another tank using this and the other tank for number 6 oil storage by Belcher Oil Company.

In 1987 the terminal was bought by C. H. Sprague & Sons to add to their oil tank storage in Bucksport.

Boom times arrived for Bucksport and surrounding towns in 1929 and 1930. Maine Seaboard Paper Company built a mill in 1929 and the state built the Waldo Hancock bridge in 1930. A dock with a paper storage shed was built so as to bring in bunker C oil by ocean-going tankers for the mill's steam plant. Also the dock could be used to ship out newsprint. The berth was dredged to 26 feet, and the flats next to the shore were dredged for a pond to bring in pulp wood by schooners and ships. The oil contract seemed to alternate between Standard Oil and Pan American Petroleum. From my father's records, I believe the first tanker into Seaboard mill dock was the *S.S. NORMAN BRIDGE*, November 28, 1930. Merle had to go to Monhegan Island to board these ocean-going tankers and pilot them to Bucksport. Mother used to take him to Port Clyde. If she were late getting home, Manley Abbott, who ran the ferry, would wait to bring her back across the river.

Now let's return to the tug *PENOBSCOT*. Docking the tankers at the mill dock was kind of tricky. At first there was only one tug, the *WALTER ROSS* to assist. When the tug *PENOBSCOT* was available to help, berthing became much easier. On February 12, 1931, father was piloting the tanker *S.S. FREDRICK ERWING* up the Penobscot River to Bucksport with the tugs *WALTER ROSS* and *PENOBSCOT* assisting. Just above Gunlow Cove or about a mile north of Odoms Ledge, the *PENOBSCOT* caught fire in the boiler room. The crew quickly abandoned ship and rowed ashore in a dory they had for a lifeboat. The crew of the tanker cut the tug's lines to the ship. The *PENOBSCOT* was left afire and drifting in the river. On the ebb tide she grounded out on Gunlow Cove ledge. As she lay there burning, the smoke stack canted back causing the whistle to blow for an hour or more. I can remember this because it was across the river from our house. When the tide flooded, she drifted off the ledge and up to Bucksport Harbor. I also remember that evening starting up the road with mother and father for Bucksport when there was a big flash in the sky, it being dark now. Apparently the boiler or bunker tanks had blown up as she drifted up by Verona Park. Linwood Abbott says she hit the western pier of the bridge. From there she drifted around Bucksport harbor. The crew of the tanker had its fire hoses run out and ready in case the *PENOBSCOT* drifted close to the ship. The *WALTER ROSS* was running around the burning tug and using its wash to keep the *PENOBSCOT* from hitting the docks or tanker. Eventually, by low water she landed on John Whitmore's shore on Verona Island. On the low drain of tides you can still see her remains.

There were other vessels into Bucksport. Capt. Merle Abbott's book shows he piloted the generator ship *S.S. JACOMA* to Bucksport. Apparently the power lines were not completed to the mill. She lay on the inshore part of the dock parallel to the shore. Special piers were built for her to lay to as she generated electricity for the mill. From Bucksport the *JACOMA* went to Portsmouth, New Hampshire, where she was used for many years. Some pictures of the mill show her at the berth.

Since a good dock and warehouse existed at the mill, Seaboard chartered the steamship *MALANG* from Mallory Steamship Company to carry newsprint. She arrived at Bucksport January 9, 1931. *MALANG* made her layover dock at the Seaboard taking on paper. After a week or two, with a load of newsprint, she would sail for one of the ports of Boston, New York or Philadelphia. This routine went on for a number of years. *MALANG* ended her days as part of a breakwater constructed of old ships on the Normandy shore during the invasion of France in World War II.

During the 30s potatoes were shipped out of Bucksport. Using the old Eastern Steamship wharf, which the mill now owned, potatoes were trucked or railed to the warehouse on the dock. Ships would load potatoes and carry them to ports along the coast.

The winter of 1934 was very cold so the river froze over. One of the Mallory ships was stuck in the ice at Fort Point Cove. I can remember walking out on the ice with mother and father to buoy #4 so they could take her picture, which I still have.

Maine Seaboard had dredged an area making a pond that was boomed on the outside and with piers for hips to dock and discharge pulpwood into the pond. In 1931 records show that Merle piloted the ships *SHOOTERS ISLAND*, *T.A.D. JONES*, *PETER CROWELL* and the Norwegian ship, *HEIN* in with wood. I believe the wood came from ports in New Brunswick. Every summer a couple of these little Norwegian ships would come over here carrying pulpwood to Bucksport and Brewer. The wood was loaded right up even with the pilot house.

Along with these ships, coastal schooners also brought in wood from the islands. Some of these schooners were: *MERCANTILE, MATTIE, LYDIA M. WEBSTER* and *STEPHEN TABER. STEPHEN TABER* was about the last of these schooners to bring in pulpwood.

In 1941 Seaboard bought a steam tug and named it the *SEAWOOD.* She was 125' long with 600 HP. Along with the purchase of the tug, the schooner barge *HELVETIA* was acquired. This combination was used for a few years to bring in wood. Needless to say, it wasn't long before the *SEAWOOD* got the nickname *SEAWEED.* After WWII the mill bought some flat scows and used a big motor boat to tow them to bring wood from the coastal islands. The last of wood coming in by water was by Canadian tugs and barges, and small vessels. Captain Molly Kool was Captain of one of these vessels. Molly, the first woman granted a captain's license in the Maritime Provinces, came ashore in Bucksport for good. She made a delightful addition to the town.

The feasibility of bringing in wood by water went by the boards. Today, the wood pond has filled with mud as has most of the berth alongside the dock. Only the tugs *VERONA* and *MACK POINT* use the dock to lay over to undock ships. Another era gone by.

After WWII some newsprint was shipped out to foreign ports. Some of this paper was shipped to South American ports and a few Argentine ships arrived at the mill's dock for news-print. There were a few more shipments, but this export was short lived.

Time Inc. bought the mill from Maine Seaboard during WWII to guarantee a supply of paper for its magazines. Time Inc. built a special barge to carry paper from Bucksport to Chicago via the Hudson River, Erie Canal and the Great Lakes. The barge was the *N.C. WALLACE.* Moran towing Company did the towing and the tug *ANNE MORAN* was on this run. The operation was so successful that a second barge was built, the *STILLMAN,* also towed by Moran tugs. The barge transport of paper continued until the construction of the St. Lawrence Seaway diverted Great Lakes water traffic to the Welland Canal. Due to the delays in passing through the locks, the barge operation was discontinued. Paper was also shipped to Rouen, France, for Life Magazine. It was shipped in small, 200-foot, two-hatch diesel ships with house aft, under the Danish flag. When loaded they had special steel plates to cover the forward windows in the deckhouse so that seas coming on deck would not break the glass. Basically, shipping paper by water ended when the runs to Rouen and Chicago were dropped.

* * *

The present oil dock, the last to be constructed in Bucksport Harbor, needs a little review as to why it was built. The winter of 1947 and 1948 was cold and the port of Bangor was closed for a couple of months. Eastern Manufacturing Company had always kept enough #6 oil storage to last through the winter months. February 1948 found them low on oil. By the time that the Coast Guard Cutter *SNOWHOMISH* had broken a channel through the ice for the barge *SEABOARD 99,* pushed by tug *AGNES MORAN,* the Eastern mill had only enough oil left for eight hours running time. To remedy this situation, a search was made to find a spot on the Penobscot River where ocean going tankers could be berthed year-round and the oil railed or trucked to the Eastern mill in Brewer.

A good site for the dock was found just off shore from the old Eastern Steamship dock. St. Regis Paper owned this dock so a deal was made and Eastern constructed the present dock. The dock was designed to accommodate a T-2 tanker. These tankers were built for WWII and at this time, many were available for charter. A storage tank was built just northwest of the mill to hold 4,000,000 gallons of #6 oil. At the time it was the largest storage tank in New England.

Another milestone in shipping occurred when Webber built a tank farm in Bucksport. Two pipe lines were run to Eastern's dock, one for gas and the other for heating oil.

During this time new tankers were being built even larger than T-2s. These came under the class of super tankers at that time, although not by today's standards were they "super." It was a big event when the new and larger tanker *S.S. ESSO NEWARK* arrived at the oil dock which had been designed for a T-2 tanker. On December 3, 1958, she carried a cargo of oil for Webber Tanks and I had the privilege of doing the docking. With the help of tugs *CLYDE B. HOLMES, SEQUIN* and *SECURITY*, docking went off as "smooth as a smelt" as Captain Gamache would say. Father taught me the necessary skills to handle a ship and to master the currents at Bucksport Harbor. The *ESSO NEWARK* was captained by Harold F. Blytt and welcomed by a committee consisting of Webber Tank officials, Frank O. Smart and John Carlisle, Esso's Port Captain, Frank I. Shaw, and Bucksport Selectman, Russell Meigs, and Town Manager, Lester O. Conner.

As St. Regis' berth was shoaling up, it was not too long after the construction of Eastern's dock that St. Regis hooked up with Eastern's pipe line and used the new dock for its tankers.

In the fifties C.H. Sprague & Sons bought out Eastern's facilities in Bucksport and continued to bring in oil. As tankers increased in size, Sprague updated the dock and still continues to do so.

The ships visiting Bucksport bring many different and interesting cultures to the port. The crews like to visit here as the people are very friendly and the dock is right in town, offering recreation facilities. Also, their men give the economy a good boost. Let's hope that the future continues to see numerous ocean-going vessels visiting the great port of Bucksport, Maine.

From "The Age of Steamship" by Capt. William E. Abbott, *Bicentennial Edition History of Bucksport: 200 Years and Counting*, Ben Craig, Editor. (Bucksport Bicentennial Committee, Town of Bucksport, Maine, 1992). Reprinted permission of his daughter, Beth Abbott Place of Verona Island.

Capt. William E. Abbott (1922-2014) *was born on Verona and attended the one room school at the head of the Island. He graduated from Bucksport High School in 1941, then attended the University of Maine at Orono, transferring to the Maine Maritime Academy and graduating in 1945 with a Third Mate's license of unlimited tons. He shipped out on tankers as a second and third mate. Late in 1946 he returned to Verona to work with his father as a first class pilot on Penobscot Bay and River. He continued in the piloting profession for 54 years, founding the Penobscot Bay and River Pilot's Association and being appointed by Governor Curtis as one of the first members of the Pilot Commission. He was a leader in many marine-related networks and systems including Camden Marine Radio (connecting ship radios to the mainland telephone system), Portland Marine Society, The Propeller Club of Searsport-Bucksport, Penobscot Chapter of the MMA, the Maine Retired Skippers Race and U.S. Coast Guard Auxiliary as well as numerous civic and fraternal organizations. His brother, Richard Hopkins, worked at the Bucksport paper mill.*

Richard Rosen
Bucksport

THE BRIDGE, THE MILL, & ROSEN'S DEPARTMENT STORE

My grandparents Rosen were Jewish immigrants, Robert from Russia and Sarah from Poland, escaping the Russian pogroms. In 1892 Sarah was twelve years old arriving in Bangor with her siblings and parents. My father and his siblings were born in Bangor, lived on Hancock St. with the other European arrivals. My grandfather was a peddler finally settling the family in Woodland (Baileyville), Washington County, opening a general merchandise clothing store and trading with the paper mill families. My father Lawrence and his siblings David, Daniel and Ida graduated from Woodland High School. In 1929 construction of Seaboard Paper Mill and the Waldo Hancock Bridge began. That year my grandparents Robert and Sarah moved to Bucksport, relocated Rosen's Department Store to Main Street here, and bought the house at 3 Main St. where my parents and my brothers and I lived and grew to adulthood. Growing up, I think we were the only Jewish family in Bucksport.

My grandparents ran the business, my Aunt Ida was a third-grade teacher at the Luman Warren school (George H. Jewett was her Superintendent and Ralph, his son, was her student). My father graduated from the University of Maine in the spring of 1929, went to work on Wall Street in New York City that infamous year of the Stock Market "Crash" ushering in the Great Depression, and stayed 10 years. In 1939 my grandfather Robert died and since dad was the only single child, he left New York and came to Bucksport to help his mother with the store. When WWII drew the U.S. into the fight Dad joined the Army Air Corp and served for the entire four years of the war in the South Pacific (mostly New Guinea). He was discharged with the rank of Captain. During the war years Ida and Sarah ran the store. Ida told me a story of the resentment of some of the long-established Bucksport families with all the immigrants descending on Bucksport searching for work and opportunities. She said some told her that in the winter they eat snowballs. Ida responded that if that's what the townspeople eat then that's what they will eat too. Shortly after dad returned to Bucksport he met and married Lillian Meade.

My mother, Lillian, was born in Bucksport. Her mother, Alice Meade, was a Harriman from Prospect. Her father froze to death in the Penobscot River leaving her mother to raise the young family on her own. Alice married Frank Meade and they raised their four children – Leslie, Madeline, Lillian and Kenneth – in Bucksport. My grandfather, Frank, worked in the tannery and Alice took in people's laundry to wash, starch, and hang on the line to dry well into her eighties.

My mother graduated from the Seminary and was the first woman hired at the paper mill. She was a switch board operator working in the front building while the mill was being built. She worked at the mill for twenty years, and at the time she left the mill to marry Dad and work in the store, she was working as the administrative assistant to the mill Superintendent. Mom talked of occasionally catching a cabin on the ship that transported finished product from Bucksport to New York City.

My parents transformed a struggling family retail store into a vibrant and successful operation that provided a living to our family and to longtime co-workers as well. My parents provided house charge accounts to multiple generations of the same families and loyal customers. They quietly helped scores of people when they faced tough times and times of struggle. They were also quiet, but generous and dependable benefactors to many local projects and initiatives, many times working with mill employees and personnel. Examples include the redevelopment of the downtown riverfront, the construction of the "new" Catholic Church, the establishment of the Bucksport Regional Health Center, the demolition and cleanup of the Blodgett Tannery on Franklin St, and many individual and personal kindnesses.

Mom's brother Ken, brother-in-law Eugene Lally, and many nephews, nieces and cousins enjoyed long careers working at the paper mill.

The clothing store was operated from 1910-2013, 103 years of continuous operation and family ownership from the Woodland paper mill to the Bucksport mill. Mom and Dad both worked full time until each died at the age of 86.

Editor's note: *Among other generosities, when we were required at school to have white shirts for band and chorus, the Rosens let us "pay on time," whatever small amounts we could. Not layaway, either. We could get them when we needed them. We never forgot.*

1930 Waldo-Hancock Bridge sketched by Edward DesJardins, donated to the *Still Mill* project.

Bucksport area benefactors, Lillian and Lawrence Rosen in the 1940s. Courtesy of Richard Rosen.

Richard Rosen *was born in Castine and raised in Bucksport, graduating from BHS with the class of 1973. In 1977 he received a B.S. degree in Business Finance from the University of Maine, "married Kimberley Clark from Aroostook County and settled in Bucksport to raise our two children, Rachael and David (both BHS grads). Three grandchildren! We owned and operated Rosen's for 35 years." Rosen's was named the 2002 Maine Retailer of the Year. In 1998 Richard was elected as a member of the Maine House of Representatives representing Bucksport and Orrington for three terms (6 years) then elected to the State Senate representing 22 towns in Penobscot and Hancock Counties for 4 terms (8 years). In 2012 Governor LePage appointed him as the first Director of the Governor's Office of Policy and Management. In 2014 he was appointed Commissioner of the Department of Administrative and Financial Services (DAFS). The DAFS Commissioner serves as chief financial advisor to the Governor and Legislature, prepares the state budget and manages nine state bureaus and approximately 1,000 employees. Richard's activities include volunteer board member, Northeast Historic Film, Bucksport Regional Health Center, Retail Association of Maine, Acadia Hospital. "Along with George McLeod, Beth Roderick and others," he helped establish the Bucksport Bay Area Chamber of Commerce and served as first President. "I also volunteer on Kim's legislative campaign."*

Ruth Hutchings Gray
Bucksport

TEN MILES A DAY IN ALL KINDS OF WEATHER

My father, Nathaniel Hutchings, was a school teacher for a year in Hardscrabble (Orland) before going to work at the mill in Bucksport. I was told he might have helped build it but that's hearsay. He lived on the Upper Falls Road and walked ten miles a day, five over and five back. Sometimes he waded in snow up to his armpits 'cause he was only 5' 4" and weighed only 140 lbs. and the side roads were very seldom plowed. When he got to the main road he made better time as they were plowed. In summer he threw pulp wood into the Penobscot River. In the winter he worked in the magazine room where he filled holes with wood to be ground into paper. He sometimes would get up at 3 o'clock in the morning, get his breakfast, and strike out walking in all kinds of weather. He worked there until they made him retire at 65 but he could have worked until 75. He also worked in the stock room so his clothes and shoes were covered in white papery things.

His two grandsons, Dorance and Nathaniel Gray, whose father, Leroy, worked there from 1942 to 1945 in the magazine room, both worked in the mill many years. Dorance, until he lost part of one of his legs, so he had to get done. He also served many years as an EMT. Nat, his namesake, worked in the mill while still in school and right up until it closed, as maintenance man. If there was an opening in the mill, he always put his name in so always advanced. He went back to school after the mill closed to be a finish carpenter.

The mill was our livelihood. The only jobs they ever had.

Ruth Hutchings Gray *was born in 1927 down on the Lower Falls Road, the only child of Nathaniel and Elizabeth Fergeson Hutchings. "I grew up on the upper falls road in an old farmhouse that H.O.M.E. Co-op used for sheep then tore down. I cried when they did that. I attended the one-room schoolhouse located in front of where the new one which all of my kids attended got built. I grew up going to the 'Gypsy' dance hall in Orland where I met my husband. I remember the 'Whip-Poor-Will,' too, but never went there dancing. They even had a zoo there once. For a while I had piano lessons from Olive Peavey until the woman who loaned us her piano took it back. Ours, a great big thing I called 'an acre and a half piano,' it was so big, didn't sound right so I had to give it up. I was getting ready to have my third child when I got my 8th grade certificate. I had a brood of six altogether. I have* *taken care of kids my whole life and everybody else's. Once I went to a country-western show starring Lone Pine up behind the mill on the River Road. Then up to the first old wooden Bangor Auditorium to see Johnny Cash. In 1991 my girlfriend, Annette Prosser, took me to the Grand Ol' Opry in Nashville for a birthday gift. I worked at Maplewood Poultry in Belfast for six years more or less and at Penobscot Nursing Home as a CNA for six years after my husband died. I worked at the Ellsworth woolen mill about two years and cleaned house for people quite a while before going to work at the Jed Prouty Tavern as dishwasher, then cook. And I cooked at Anna's Restaurant by the mill. My last job was as Senior Companion for fourteen years. I've got a plaque they gave me. I served on a lot of committees through the years until I couldn't drive anymore. I love country music, dancing, knitting and crocheting for gifts, and my family and friends. And my earring collection, almost a thousand!"*

Jeannine Hall Peters
Bangor

ODE TO THE ROAD COMMISSIONER

Gayland Redman of thee we sing
    As Commissioner of Roads you are
        the King.
The snowdrifts melt when they see your
        plow,
    The voters elect you because you know
        how.

But things aren't rosy all the time,
    When you need a dollar they give you
        a dime.
Of favoritism you are often accused
    And outlying districts feel they're
        abused.

Even the weather must give you pains,
    You plow one day and the next it
        rains.
You sand the roads and then it snows –
    Whether people or weather, you have
        only foes.

But when in after life you sit with a
        crown upon your head,
    And all your earthly enemies are wish-
        ing you weren't dead,
That they hadn't skinned you and taken
        your hide,
    You can look back on your work with
        pride.

But until you reach that celestial state
    Behind St. Peter's pearly gate,
When kicks and complaints set your

nerves ajar,
Just light up another five-cent cigar.

—Fuller Clay (Owen K. Soper)

From a 1946 *Seaboard Bulletin*

*Courtesy of his granddaughter, **Jeannine Hall Peters**. "Owen K. and Laura Soper were my mother's parents. Because the first fifteen years of my life were lived in New Jersey and New York, I spent relatively little time with my grandparents in Orland. However, the one-week trips to Maine every two years are the source of some of my most treasured memories. My grandmother who had been postmistress in Orland for many years died in 1954. My parents, my younger brother and I moved to Old Town in 1955 to be closer to my grandfather. I graduated from Old Town High School, went to work, got married and had two wonderful children. I went back to work in 1975 as a secretary in a school system where I enjoyed over 28 years working with staff, students, parents and the public. Since my retirement in 2004, it seems I am busier than ever! I have always enjoyed writing, mostly poetry. Gee, I wonder where that comes from?? Another strong interest is genealogy. Although I research my family history in a sporadic manner, I find it fascinating. The Sopers were among the earliest settlers of Orland. In recent years I have become a Reiki practitioner and enjoy sharing healing energy as a volunteer at Eastern Maine Medical Center and the Bangor Veterans Home and with others in need. I also volunteer at the Salvation Army soup kitchen in Bangor. As a member of the Bangor YMCA I participate in fitness classes and several social activities available there for seniors. I also belong to two garden clubs and tend two raised vegetable beds at the Bangor Community Garden. My greatest joys come to me from my children, grandchildren, extended family and friends. I consider myself to be very blessed and am always grateful."*

Ben Craig (1920-1995)
Bucksport

SWEARING WOMEN, FOREIGNERS & THE MILL

With the advent of the age of steam, shipping and shipbuilding gradually lost their importance in the industrial affairs of the town. Fishing, always vital to subsistence and trade in coastal towns, surged under the influence of the Tom Nicholson Fish Company and, near the middle of the nineteenth century, dominated the waterfront and the affairs of the town. Around the turn of the century the fishing industry literally collapsed.

The town of Bucksport limped into the Great Depression without the support of any large business activities. The town "fell upon hard times" as did the rest of the country, but Bucksport was already there when the depression began.

* * *

Section 1: NO CORPORATION, UNLESS EXPRESSLY AUTHORIZED SO TO DO BY SPECIAL ACT OF LEGISLATION, SHALL TRANSMIT OR CONVEY BEYOND THE CONFINES OF THE STATE FOR THE PURPOSE OF FURNISHING POWER, HEAT OR LIGHT, ANY ELECTRIC CURRENT GENERATED DIRECTLY OR IN-DIRECTLY BY ANY WATER POWER IN THIS STATE; . . . .

The foregoing preamble to Chapter 244 of 1909 Maine Laws, was signed into law on April 2 of that year. Introduced by Ex-Governor Percival Baxter, the "Fernald Law," named for the governor who signed it, set into motion a series of events leading to the construction of the paper mill in Bucksport.

An attempt to repeal the Fernald Law resulted in the Smith Bill being passed but it was vetoed in 1927 by Governor Owen Brewster. Again, in 1929, a bill was presented to repeal the Fernald Law and that bill had a referendum clause. On September 9, 1929, the referendum, by a vote of 54,583 for repeal and a vote of 63,312 against, sustained the law. Maine public Laws, Chapter 402, repealed it outright on August 20, 1955.

Ex-Governor Baxter was a man of vision who loved the state of Maine. When he presented the Fernald Law in 1909 he was well aware that the technology required to transmit electricity out of the state was nonexistent. Twenty years later, however, the technology was in place and Central Maine Power Company (CMP) began construction of their Wyman Dam at Bingham, Maine and its generating facilities.

The Fernald Law was still in effect but the legislature was expected to repeal it. The political and business climates were ripe in expectation of the law's demise – the country was in the depth of the Great Depression and Maine was a poor state. Pressure on the Legislature forced the issue to a public referendum where it failed. The legislature, along with other civic-minded prominent leaders, could envision the state as being one huge hydro-electric plant with its energies being carried south on high-voltage highways. Without the Fernald Law this likely would have happened.

A final, and successful, attempt to repeal was made in 1955. By that time the ecological and environmental climate in the state made it virtually certain that no new power dams would be built. The law had served the will of the visionaries who enacted it nearly half a century ago.

Back to 1929 and CMP's Wyman Dam – water power to generate electricity can be stored behind a dam, but only to the point where the water level rises and dam spills over. Electricity cannot be stored at all in any significant amount, but must be used within a fraction of a second of being generated. Being unable to export the power the dam was capable of producing, CMP was driven to find or create a demand for their product.

The paper making industry uses large amounts of energy. The flexibility of design allows a paper mill to be sized so its energy requirements match the output of a generating plant. The Maine Seaboard Paper Company mill was built in 1929-1930 to use the power generated at Wyman Dam.

Without the Fernald Law Maine would have become a generating station for the nation. A chain of pristine man-made lakes would drop from dam to dam down the Kennebec River Valley from Moosehead Lake to the Atlantic Ocean. The same scenario, but for Great Northern Paper Company, would have been seen in the Penobscot River Valley as well as on the St. John and Androscoggin rivers and any other flow of water with sufficient volume and head to generate power.

* * *

The Maine Seaboard Paper Company was formed to build and operate the paper mill at Bucksport to use the energy generated at Wyman Dam. Following completion of the necessary groundwork, engineering and acquisition of land and water rights, construction of the papermill on Salmon Point began in 1929. The tannery bought from the George Blodgett Company had to be torn down. A thrifty note of interest – some of the "tacking boards," boards upon which the wet hides were fastened while drying, are still visible as roofing boards on the townsite houses.

"Just a year from the day," the old timers say, the first paper rolled off a paper machine. It was on Thanksgiving Day, 24 November 1930. Maine Seaboard purchased the tannery in November of 1929.

The two paper machines, built and installed by Rice Barton and Fales of Worcester, Massachusetts were, at 1400 feet per minute, the fastest in the world. To illustrate the point, the newsprint production on these two machines exceeded that of Great Northern's 11 machines at their Millinocket mill.

The machines were ready to run before the mill steam plant was operable and while the high voltage power line was still snaking its way through the woods from Bingham. Maine Seaboard chartered the generating ship *S.S. JACOMA* to furnish power to turn the machines and steam to dry the paper. The *JACOMA* burned coal and, without the virtue of a hundred-foot smokestack to carry away soot and smoke, she early on became the scourge of the town's housewives. A sudden windshift would send groups of swearing women scrambling to snatch clean laundry off the lines. The arrival of the Central Maine powerline and the departure of the *S.S. JACOMA* were well received.

One of the concessions granted by the town fathers to lure the paper mill to settle here was a forgiveness of property taxes for the first twenty years of its existence. With the increased demand for schools and services brought on by the influx of workers, a heavy burden was placed on the shoulders of local tax payers. The citizens, both old and newcomers, "paid" for the mill.

* * *

Blessed with ample amounts of papermaking ingredients, water, wood, and power, Maine Seaboard began to claw its way into the marketplace. The mill could ship paper by road, rail, or water to markets worldwide. The *S.S. MALANG* was chartered for ocean shipping, delivering newsprint to New York harbor where it was sold dockside for "$10.00 a ton under the going market price." Survival was the goal and Maine Seaboard Paper Co. survived.

* * *

The Mill brought with it a melange of cultures in the families that came here from away to build and operate the plant. These "foreigners" wedged their way into the local community and, not without some trauma, melded with the whole into a society stronger than any of its parts. The migration trickles in and out even today, while the town quietly absorbs the flow. Bucksport still retains the way and quality of life pretty much the same as it was before the Wyman Dam and the Fernald Law.

Book publishers during and after World War II were plagued by paper shortages and uncertainties of delivery. Many publishers bought into papermaking companies and some actually built paper mills to ensure a supply of paper for their printers. Time Inc., for these reasons, purchased three paper-mills: The Bryant Paper Co. at Kalamazoo, Michigan; The Hennepin Paper Co. at Little Falls, Minnesota; and The Maine Seaboard Paper Company at Bucksport. Time Inc. engaged St. Regis Paper Co. to operate these mills with St. Regis having an option to later buy the mills.

Time Inc. sold the mills to St. Regis after the war in December 1946. St. Regis shortly disposed of the two other mills.

From this period on St. Regis began a program of modernization and expansion that continues to this day under the banner of Champion International.

In time it came to be called, "The Mill," an entity as well as a physical plant. "'The Mill' says...," became an easily recognized phrase in the idiom of household gossip. The Mill could and did do many wonderful things for and with the town, although at times it raised its ugly head of corporate insensitivity – labor strife and layoffs being the usual cause. We get along with The Mill. Generally they are good neighbors and, let's face it, some of these things live for a hundred years or more.

From 200 Years and Counting, The Story of Bucksport, 1792 – 1992, Bicentennial Edition, *courtesy of* **David Keene**, *Mayor, who "put in 23 years of service at the mill, the last 10 as the manager of utilities." A member of the Bucksport High School Class of 1968 and the Maine Maritime Academy class of 1973, "I sailed for 16 years before going to work in the mill's power plant."*

Ben W.D. Craig *was a member of the History Sub-Committee of the Bucksport Bicentennial Committee, serving as editor of their publication (cited above), from which this essay, originally entitled "The Mill" comes. Of his father and his writing, son Gerry L. Craig of Craig Publishing, Carthage, N.Y. wrote in 2009 for Ben's story collection,* Comfort Cove, *which he edited:*

"Ben W.D. Craig was born Wellington David Craig in the town of Millinocket, Maine in 1920. He served in the U.S. Army Corps of Engineers during WWII mainly in

Alaska. Ben settled in the small coastal town of Bucksport, Maine where he and his wife, Carolyn raised ten children (and many neighborhood kids as well). Following his retirement from the local paper mill in 1985, Ben pursued his interests in writing by enrolling in classes at a local community college and participating in a writers group. During this time he wrote many short stories on a wide variety of subjects from wood-stoves to brinkometers to Manly the cat. One subject Ben especially enjoyed writing about was life in Maine and he wrote many short stories about the characters in one small town, Comfort Cove. Some of these stories were purely Ben's imagination, some were loosely based on actual events in his life and some were born from tales told around the woodstove in the kitchen of the big house on Franklin Street. Unfortunately, Ben passed away before he could realize his dream to finish and publish *Comfort Cove*."

Both this essay and the above author note are published with the family's permission.

As Told By Henry Bourgon
Buscksport

WHAT WAS AND WHAT IS: THE TOWN SITE

Henry Bourgon grew up in what was and continues to be known as the Town Site. Thanks to him, we have a record of how it was when the mill built the houses for employees, all at once, in 1935. A few more were built when he was in high school. There were two sizes according to square footage, he recalls, all alike, but they could be turned in different directions.

As time passed, the houses have been sold, but the high quality with which they were built and maintained by the mill as long as the mill owned them, resulted in their lasting into the present. A summer crew of mill employees was assigned to maintain the houses. Every year you could choose a room to be wallpapered. And every ten to fifteen years they got new roofs and paint.

The whole town has benefitted through the years from the recreation area with ball field that was included in the Town Site neighborhood. In fact, the mill used to be well known for the ways it lent equipment and personnel to many town projects and activities. For example, when the boys wanted to go to scout camp, the mill sent trucks and employees to load the kids' camping stuff, took them, and stayed. "I went myself! Such a difference from what was and what is."

Henry Bourgon, *a life-long resident of Bucksport, is the son of Nelson Bourgon who began working for Maine Seaboard Paper Company in Bucksport in 1930 as a papermaker, putting the first paper on the roll at about 3 a.m. some morning early in the winter of '30 - '31, and eventually working his way up to superintendent of the mill. Dr. Bourgon and his wife, Nancy, of Bethel, raised their family in his home town where he practiced dentistry for forty years. In addition to many other civic contributions such as serving as Co-Director of the Bucksport Bicentennial Steering Committee, he was elected as a Town Councilor for three terms.*

The Town Site under construction, 1935, from the collection of Freida and Dick Chase, Published in *Narramissic Notebook* #6, 2005.

"Town Site" housing development built by the mill in the early thirties for lease by upper level employees. Published in *Paper Talk, Seaboard Edition*, 1988, and used here with the magazine's permission.

Ruth P. Shook
Bangor

FOLLOWING FATHER'S WORK

I have been pondering about my brief time in Bucksport and have remembered a few things. I lived there for a few months, less than a year, when I was 8 or 9, in the mid to late 30's. My name at that time was Ruth Fernald. We lived in an upstairs apartment of a house on Main St., across the river from Fort Knox. There was a garage next door where cars were repaired. The building is still there, #108 (I checked when we drove through Bucksport recently). I would walk down to the edge of the river. There was a wooden pier a bit further down the river from where we lived, where ships tied up regularly and unloaded supplies for the mill. I would walk out on the pier, and it surely was not a safe place to be! There was no sidewalk on our side of the street. I was very shy, had one friend who lived on McDonald St. I can't remember her name, the name of the school I attended, nor much about school. It was on a street that was off the Main St.

My father was a bricklayer/mason and was working on an addition to the mill. It could have been the first of many additions. He took his lunch to work in a lunch pail.

I remember the department store and how this Christmas they had a drawing for a doll and I didn't win! Strange things we remember.

Clothing well-remembered was the long underwear we had to wear in the winter and the ugly brown cotton ribbed stockings we wore over the underwear and they were fastened to a garter belt. As the weather became warmer, I shed the long underwear and rolled the stockings down below my knees. Of course, this was not approved by my parents. Most of my clothes (cotton dresses) were made by my stepmother or ordered from the Sears-Roebuck catalogue. And I was lucky when I was given hand-me-downs. These were depression days and we wore whatever we could get.

I lived in several towns in Maine where there was work on buildings for my father.

Ruth Shook, then **Mitchell**, *became the first executive director at United Cerebral Palsy of Northeastern Maine in 1958, and together with a Board of Directors, began developing programs and services for children with disabilities and their families and held that position for 34 years, retiring in 1992. She currently serves on the Board of Directors of Camp Capella at Phillips Lake, Dedham, a camp serving children and adults with disabilities, and she enjoys Senior College classes.*

Sharon Bray
Orland

PEARL HARBOR DAY

the day a war set my mother free
from life on the farm
though she loved the farmer, not the cows.
He went off to war,
came home a grown-up, almost
father and provider,
went into the mill,
traded paid labor for hours on his land,
for house and food and shoes for five children,
who, unlike him, went on to college
on their own as tough in core
as two determined Americans —
the newly wed couple at 22 and 15 —
hearing news of Pearl Harbor
on the truck radio
while they harvested Maine trees
for the Boston Christmas market.

Previously published in the "Will We Remember" section of *PUTTING POEMS BY* by Sharon Bray
(A *Narramissic Notebook* Project, 2014).

Her father Richard Bray went to work as an electrician apprentice at St. Regis paper mill in Bucksport the week **Sharon Ann Bray** *was born in 1945. "Over the years my brother and former husband worked on the 'spare' list at the mill. Dad retired after 35 years to resume his true passion: farming. We lived in the townsite between 1949 and 1954, which my mother Anita loved. She preferred in-town to the isolation of a farm on the Castine Road. I am fortunate to love farm life." A member of the Bucksport High School Class of 1964, Sharon went on to study at U. Maine Orono, Indiana U. Bloomington, U. Mass Amherst, and Rensselaer Polytech, receiving her bachelor's degree in 1968 and master's in 1978.*

"I have lived mostly in towns along tidal Penobscot River despite many moves since high school, including Toronto, Boston and East Machias. My family roots are in Hancock County, Maine, and the west coast of Newfoundland." When Sharon *"failed to become an actress,"* she turned to activism as a community health educator and a writer/editor. *"My work in women's health and spirituality spans more than 4 decades."* She founded and edited the area newspaper, The Enterprise, *in Bucksport and published local history and poetry collections in 11 issues of* Narramissic Notebook, *"fitting in time to write hundreds of poems, stacks of prose, and to make thousands of photographs."* Her work has also been published in numerous journals, anthologies and newspapers, including regular freelance writing for the Castine Patriot *and other newspapers throughout Hancock County and beyond. She self-published the book,* Putting Poems By *and several chapbooks "and continues to spend more time helping other writers than submitting my own work."* In addition to the Salt Coast Sages writing group, Sharon *is a member of Maine Writers & Publishers Alliance, Maine Poets Society, Great Pond Mountain Conservation Trust, Orland Fire Department and other local organizations. "Inspired to answer a question from a recent strip in the* Bangor Daily *funny papers – 'In one sentence, can you justify your existence?' – my footprints on the garden amount to no more than a clam hole in the river's flats mud; I have no justification."*

Sandra Bowden Dillon
Philadelphia and Orland

A LOT OF PRIDE IN ALL THAT HARD WORK

Part I

My grandfather, Emery Bowden, worked at the mill in the 30's and 40's, periodically, in the yard when the mill needed help to unload large quantities of wood that sometimes arrived at the same time. The extra money would always "come in handy" for a major project. He didn't want to work full time at the mill or to be bound by anyone else's rules and schedules as he loved the outdoors and the seasonal life of a Maine farmer and fisherman.

On the Castine Road in Orland, Maine, one of the winter jobs for men was cutting wood; firewood for home heating, sometimes for sale; logs for Herm Austin's saw mill in Penobscot for lumber for sale or for personal use; and pulp wood to sell to the St. Regis Paper Co. in Bucksport. My grandfather, Emery S. Bowden, and my father, Donald Bowden, manned the two-man saw, axes, wedges, and horse hauling sledge to harvest the wood. They hauled out the wood on the sledge; put it in one of the appropriate three different areas of piled wood, alongside the "Detour" woods road that ran behind their big chicken houses, all convenient to the Castine Road to be taken to the various mills. Don and Emery split their own firewood, to be seasoned and eventually stored in various woodsheds. There was a lot of pride in all that hard work.

Living on Hardscrabble Hill with its rocky shore and mud flats had some advantages. One of which was that the Penobscot River current, coming around the northern end of Verona Island brought daily treasures to our shore with each tidal change – bottles, dishes, logs, pots, toys, wood, balls, parts of buildings – even buildings themselves, especially on flood tides. The best part was the pulp wood that escaped from the various mills along the river. All the people who had shore property would retrieve the logs and pulp wood to sell back to the mills.

SPRING WALK ALONG THE SHORE

The first spring walk along the shore reveals
The changes made since fall. The plank that led
To fish-house is askew, and where that house
Once stood, there's just the view of facing shore.
The bank is raw, exposing rock and root
To Nature's forces. Gale, gravity, tide
Will take them, too. Amid the shore-grass lies
A broken wharf, while over stones are strewn

Brown chips and straw. Among the trees beyond
The bank rest logs once meant for paper. Just
Ahead, a tree-trunk, smooth and gray floats in,
Retreats. The gulls still glide and scream,
And hawks still fish the tide. It's hard to tell
If they are new or old familiar friends.
The tang of seaweed, salt-spray, open-earth
Absorbed with breath endures beyond the spring.

– Minnie E. Bowden

First published in *PEOPLE POEMS* (Hillside Publishers, Orland, ME 1978).

Unfortunately, two dead bodies were also discovered on our shore. One was a Canadian sailor who fell off his ship that was anchored in Bucksport. A few bottles of whiskey were found in his pockets so everyone joked he died a happy man. The other man was a friend of Emery and Don. He had slipped while helping to unload a barge at the mill. He had hit his head as he went underwater. The current was too swift and murky for anyone to rescue him. Emery and Don would go to the shore daily on the tidal changes to check for the body. A week later, they found him. Even though it was very difficult for them, they handled everything with quiet dignity and care that Maine men do for one another and their families

When Don came home after serving in the Army Air Corps in WWII, he wanted to continue what his father was doing for the family farm and shore. With the GI Bill, he took "agi" courses at night at BHS to learn how to "do it all" better. He loved it in spite of the hard work and undependable weather. When my mother, Minnie, stopped teaching due to poor health, he felt the family needed a consistent paycheck and benefits, so he joined the St. Regis Paper Co. After going through the probationary period of being "called in" anytime – day or night, in any weather, doing any job, he finally was put on the paper machines as a 6th Hand. It was very difficult to balance shift work with the changing weather and tides in trying to farm and fish.

It was a big treat when Don would come home, open his lunch box in front of the family and distribute paper from the mill to each member. It was the first time they could use all the paper they needed for various projects as well as scrap paper. The construction paper was the best as it had many uses – school projects, book report covers, birthday and Christmas cards (or cards generally), decorations, May baskets, etc. Most of the mill men brought paper home to their families. The mill turned a "blind eye", allowing this wonderful generosity, within reason, to its employees.

After a few years of mill employment, Don took his family on a tour of the mill so they could understand what he daily endured. When the family first felt and heard the tremendous heat and noise in the dark, dirty paper machine area, they felt that they were seeing a man-made version of hell. To see all the big open holes in the floor with no rails or warning labels around them, was very scary – especially when the family learned that the "grinders" were directly underneath the holes. They were a quick, convenient way to dispose of any scrap paper or mash that occurred around the paper machines. All of a sudden a huge respect and appreciation was gained for all the men who were putting their lives and bodies "on the line" every day when they went to work – just to make paper.

In the winter of 1962 there was a record blizzard that blasted the Bucksport area with a lot of snow and intense high winds. The mill rule was that one couldn't go home until the man on the next shift "relieved" you. Don, working on the 4-12 shift, coming from 7 miles away on the Castine Road in Orland, barely made it to the mill. The man he relieved lived "in town" and was very grateful for my father's efforts. Even though he lived fairly close to the mill, it took him a lot of effort and time to get home – which he safely did. From midnight on, no one could safely come or go from the mill. Because of the terrible winds, there were a lot of power interruptions – thus a lot of "breaks" in the paper stream and wind. It was awful! The men took turns sleeping and manning the machines. Eventually all the food the men had brought and all the food in the canteens was gone. The mill contacted the Bucksport Police to see if they could round up some food and get it to the mill. After a while Bucksport snow plows brought food to the men in the mill (don't remember what it was or where they got it). On the afternoon of the first day, Bob Harper, who lived on Orland Hill in Orland, was very worried about his family so decided to try to make it home, braving the deeply drifting snow, ice, and terrible winds. He was given a ride part way and let out on top of the hill on Route One, walked across the field, but never made it. He was found frozen, sitting beside their dog house.

Meanwhile at the mill, the machines were running, no matter what obstacles were happening, thanks to the dedicated men who were stuck there. On the morning of the 3rd day, Don's "Day Shift" replacement had arrived. He lived near the mill and had walked – actually "snow-shoed" in as nothing had been plowed. Don could now go home if he wanted to go. Even though nothing had been plowed, he felt he had to try to make it home, as his farm animals and poultry birds hadn't been fed or watered in 3 days plus he was worried about his family. The phone lines as well as the power lines were down. Ralston Grey who lived further down the Castine Road also wanted to go home. A fellow worker said his skis and boots were in his car in the parking lot, of one of the men wanted to use them. Don didn't want to "bother" as he wanted to get home as fast as he could by his own power. He knew he could do it as he had walked the 7 miles to high school every day, even when he had stayed for football, basketball, and baseball practices and games. However, he had never seen so much snow outside the mill in his life! He was very worried about getting over the huge drifts. He soon discovered that huge drifts were made by big winds clearing a lot of the land of its snow – so he could just walk around the drifts! It was a beautiful sunny day – a nice day for a walk! As it turned out, Don was the first person anyone had seen on the road for 3 days. Everyone would ask him to come into their house for rest and food but he would thank them and say that he had to get to his animals and family. Once in a while, he would accept some water. Everyone was very impressed by his efforts so he felt like a celebrity. As soon as he arrived home and saw that his family was fine, he tended to his animals and birds and did all the necessary shoveling. Ralston finally walked by the house, carrying the skis. "I couldn't make these damned things work! It was easier to walk!" Don finally ate, slept and was back to the mill, luckily on the new week shift which changed onto the 12-8 shift for him. By that time the main roads were plowed, his wife gave him a ride to the mill so he could come home in his car the next morning.

Minnie Brown Bowden (1915 – 2000) *was born in Fairfield, Maine. She graduated from Waterville High School and received an Associate's Degree in Education from Gorham Normal School, teaching in Sidney, ME at age 16. She then earned undergraduate and graduate degrees at the University of Maine. Because of challenge and opportunity, she taught in many places--the last of the one room schools in Sidney, Penobscot and Orland, plus regular schools in Castine, Winterport, Orland, Bangor, Milo and Belfast area schools as Reading Director. When federal monies for reading programs became available to public schools, the Belfast district had the first Title I and Title II reading programs in the United States. She was a mother who helped start the momentum to build the Orland Consolidated School, copied by other towns in Maine. She served on the Orland School Board. Her father was a farmer as was her husband who held many other jobs as well, also serving on the School Board and as Selectman. She lived on Hardscrabble Hill in Orland with her father-in-law and his housekeeper for much of her life. She was an active member of the Maine Poetry Society which gave her a diverse writing style. She had many poems published individually in anthologies, magazines and papers and was the poetry columnist for the* Rockland Gazette *for many years. Because of her interesting life she had many stories to tell which she did through three books of her poetry –* People Poems, People Poems II, *and* Hardscrabble *– now out of print but available through Fogler Library at the University of Maine in Orono. In 2000 she was honored with the first* Spirit-Words Maine Poetries Collaborative Award *for her poetic voice and contributions to Maine literature.*

Patricia Ranzoni
Bucksport

THESE ARE THE DAYS / *from* ANOTHER LONG (15.)

These are the days of blankets over doorways.
These are the days of shutoff rooms.
These are the days of frost on wallpaper.
These are the days of sinkcupboards open to the stove.
These are the days of washbasins chilling faster than you're done.
These are the days of using water again and again.
These are the days of trousers under skirts.
These are the days of throbbing toes and wearing boots inside.
These are the days of chapped hands in dough.
These are the days of mopwater freezing on the floor.
These are the days of not going out but for the animals, the well, the woodpile,
                 the sloppail and the mail.
These are the days of men dying in blizzards walking home from work at the mill.
These are the days of accidents in the woods.
These are the days of nothing but working to keep warm.
These are the days of chimneys roaring for a family meal.
These are the days of children and old people going up in awful sorrowful smoke.
These are the days of tomorrow's flaming lips.

Excerpted from a numbered Fall–through–Winter–to–Spring cycle entitled *"Another Long"* first published in *SETTLING Poems by Patricia Ranzoni* (Puckerbrush Press, Orono, ME, 2000).

III. WHO WE BECAME IN THE WORLD

Ton by Ton, Generation after Generation

Carolyn Osgood Levensailor
Mobile, Alabama

OUT FOR A RIDE, ENDING UP IN THE BUCKSPORT MILL

Where in the world do I begin? I have been receiving the Ellsworth paper for quite a few years since I sold our cottage there. I read the write-up about your book project and became very interested.

I have lived here in Mobile, Alabama for almost 50 years. My husband and I moved here from East Millinocket to make paper for International Paper. He has been gone for 30 years. He was born in Waterville Maine and I was born in East Millinocket.

Back in the '30s – as the story goes, my mother (Mary Osgood) and father (Vaughn Fitzherbert) and we two girls were out for a drive. At the time he worked for International Paper in East Millinocket. We ended up in Bucksport – talked to people at the new mill – he was offered a job. Probably machine tender.

We moved – I remember the house (revisited years later). Best friend Betty Taylor. Remember the Main Street – hotel – mill – river – bridge. Stayed there five years until a Frank Silver offered my father a paper mill super job at a new Bowater paper mill in Corner Brook, Newfoundland. We lived there for eight years.

Back to Maine – my father built a dance hall and cottage while we were there, on Pushaw Lake. "Villa Vaughn." It is on the Maine map now. I still have chairs from it!

My grandfather – Al Osgood – had a snow shoe mill in Milford. Shipped snow shoes to the troups in first W.W. Their home that he built is still there in Milford.

I am most interested in what you are doing – God's Peace,

Carolyn Osgood Levensailor *stays "very busy" keeping the archives in her church, St. Pauls and Christ Church Cathedral. Also at Wilmer Hall, a home like Goodwill, and St. Paul's School, the largest Episcopal school in the United States. Her sister, Mary Dustous, lives in Lincoln, Maine.*

Betty Arey Kirk
Bucksport

DADDY'S MILL

"He was a very kind, patient and fair man."

Most of my mill memories go back to childhood. My parents were Lavina and Francis Arey. Dad started working at the mill in 1934. I turned to my sister for the date. She remembered! He retired in the early '70s. Most of those years he worked as a millwright.

They had just moved from Southwest Harbor (where my mother grew up along with her 12 siblings). At first they lived in East Orland and my father walked to work....but often would be picked up by a kind soul along the way. My sisters would have been about two and four then.

Later they bought a house on Franklin Street in Bucksport which had been partially destroyed in a fire. He used what materials he could salvage, bought whatever else was needed and built their home. Then I arrived on the scene in 1945.

Every kid thought of the mill as "Daddy's mill." There was that sense of pride of ownership. The mill gave me and my family a sense of security. For me personally it gave me a college education....which, of course, I didn't really appreciate for a few years! I remember having treasures come home in my father's dinner basket.... a ream of colored construction paper, half of a candy bar, etc. What magical gifts! There was usually a humorous tale to tell....he loved practical jokes!

Later memories were not so joyous....he limped coming out of the mill after his shift....his feet hurt. Perhaps a legacy of walking on the cement floors for all those years. Later, it was suggested that his pancreatic cancer may have been at least in part caused by chemical exposure....who knows. He retired early because of the foot pain. Fortunately he was able to enjoy several trips with my mother and summers at Toddy Pond before his passing.

Years after my father was gone I was chatting with a mill worker at a social gathering....he asked my father's name....he said my father had taught him so much about his job. I remember feeling so happy that someone remembered him in this way. He was a very kind, patient, fair man.

Betty Kirk was *born and grew up in Bucksport, graduating in the class of 1963. She attended Husson College, earning an ABS degree in secretarial science (medical), and worked at various hospitals and medical practices mostly as a transcriptionist. Now retired, "I enjoy spending time at camp, our grandchildren, sunsets, knitting teddie bears and other creatures, cooking, basket weaving and whatever else interesting that crosses my path! My husband is a skilled wood worker, carpenter, and enjoys car projects with many household projects in process so there is never a moment when we lack for something to do!"*

Among earliest lunch and dinner boxes, pails, buckets or baskets carried by Bucksport mill workers were the classic ash baskets woven of pounded brown ash splints by Maine's Indians. They had two moveable handles and various–styled lids, woven or of solid wood, attached with small metal or hand-cut leather hinges. Sometimes they were carved or painted by or for their owners as an expression of individuality. Cloth napkins or dish towels typically lined the baskets, enfolding waxed–paper or cellophane–wrapped food and utensils. Usually, these prized possessions were passed down for use by younger generations, some even in evidence being carried by workers leaving the mill on their last day in 2014. These baskets, featured in many of our STILL MILL stories and poems, are treasured family heirlooms to families who know what they are and what they represent. The work of today's most accomplished Native traditional and contemporary basketmakers can be found on exhibit throughout Maine and beyond, and through the Maine Indian Basketmakers Alliance (maineindianbaskets.org/artists/).

I'M ON MY WAY TO KINDERGARTY.
BYE, BYE MAMA. BYE, BYE MARTY.
I GOTTA GO NOW OFF TO SCHOOL
SO I WONT BE A STUPID FOOL;
SO I WONT BE NOBODY'S MULE.
BYE, BYE MAMA. BYE, BYE MARTY
I'M ON MY WAY TO KINDERGARTY.'

Courtesy of Jeannine Hall Peters. "My grandfather wrote that poem specifically for me in honor of my first day in kindergarten in 1945. 'Marty' was a nickname for my younger brother, Marshall, who was named for my Uncle Marshall (Owen and Laura Soper's son) who was killed when the merchant ship on which he was a junior engineer was struck by a torpedo from a German warship in 1942."

OUR MASONIC MILKER

Yes, my father worked in the mill from 1946 til retirement. He was a welder, having been taught by his brother-in-law. He had worked on submarines during the war in Portsmouth N.H. He would come home from work and start right in doing the farmer chores.

Yes, he rehearsed his Masonic speeches while milking the cows. What a great sense of humor?

I have heard from several people along the way that he was a cracker-jack welder. No doubt. He never worked shift work although he would get called in occasionally.

I am getting through this brutal winter. I have had a generator installed. My children can rest easier now knowing that I am "snug as a bug in a rug". It gives me peace of mind.

After graduating from Bucksport High School in the class of 1958, **Evora Bunker Mattson** *went to Boston Children's Hospital School of Nursing, finishing in 1961. She worked there until marrying Don Mattson whose father Henry, Uncle Nelson Bourgon, and brother Perry would all, like her father, retire from the mill. Don was in the Navy so they lived in many places including Norfolk, Virginia, Brunswick, Maine, Kodiak, Alaska, Long Beach, California and Middlebury, Connecticut before returning home to Bucksport. They have four daughters--Kristine, a pharmacist in Las Vegas; Cindy, a florist in Massachusetts; Heidi, a wife and mother of three and a writer; and Rebecca, a wife and mother of three and a nurse. Evora retired from nursing in 1997 after 19 years in the Newborn Nursery at Eastern Maine Medical Center, enjoying golf, tennis, needlework and traveling to see the "kids." Don passed away in 2012, having retired from the service, being active in the VFW, and participating faithfully with the renowned "Troop Greeters" at the Bangor International Airport. For a time, he participated in a Civil War club, portraying Sgt. Heghi in encampments at Fort Knox. Among their many contributions to the community, they delivered Meals on Wheels to shut-ins in the Bucksport area.*

Jeannine Peters
Bangor

FIRST SNOW

How beautiful the snow
That now all nature clothes
The whisper of a blanket
From out the heavens lowers.

How beautiful, how silent
How radiant white the sheet
That now so gently covers
The flowers so fast asleep.

The gentle mantle falling
Covering each blade of grass
Hiding their sturdy spirits
Until spring shall come to pass.

Would that the peace of heaven
So kindly cover me
Make my slumbers quiet
E'en to Eternity.

--"The Poetic Paper Maker", Owen Soper

"My grandfather, **Owen K. Soper**, was born in Tremont, Maine and received his education in the Orland and Bucksport schools. He went to work at the Bucksport mill November 7, 1946 in the Raw Materials Mixing Department, from a clerical job with the Sprague Coal Company, and worked for a year in the Finishing Department before transferring to the Mixing Department. He was well known for his artistic ability and spent several years as an artist for the mill's monthly publication, and was known as "The Poetic Paper Maker," among other pen names. He wrote to me when I was a baby/toddler. Some are long letters, all in verse. He did a lot of his writing on a Smith Corona portable typewriter and used a double stripe ribbon – red and black. I have that typewriter which is one of my prized possessions. I remember watching him type as he sat at the oak dining room table which I also have. Owen had what I as a child thought was a huge vegetable garden. He loved animals and was known to have rescued a few from unqualified owners."

46

Patricia Ranzoni
Bucksport

WHEN WINDOWS

If we didn't cover the panes ice did
in sash rotting inches. Tar paper years

then papermachine felt
(what didn't get used on our beds)

over the front door funnel from The North.
Ragged sheep-colored windings hoarded

from the mill still roaring *Saturday Evening...*
and *Life...* wrapping our houses

in scraggly scarfs pounded ritualistically in place
through roughsawn laths each fall. Bits of wool

still surface screaming in cellar-edge soil. Next,
cloudy plastic coverings closed us in. How I wished

to see out our windows all those years dreading
the annual bracing and blanketing that took the light:

the long *out there* light. Now we worship at broad
glass breakthroughs east and south. Even the north,

with lowered case, dares look upon snowheaped nests.
Curtains don't get closed until dark. If then.

First published in *CLAIMING, Poems by Patricia Ranzoni* (Puckerbrush Press, Orono, ME 1995)

Leland Bowden, Sr.
Blue Hill

HOURS OF POEMS & STORIES

That's how his daughter, Susan Ellis, put it in her forward to his collection of poems entitled, *Wild Violets for Mother and Other Reflections.* How she and her brother, Leland Bowden Jr., "his #1 SUN," listened through their childhoods to stories in verse, prose, and songs born of his deep appreciation for a life he considered blessed, sorrows and all.

Leland Atkins Bowden Sr. telephoned one day after reading about our *Still Mill* project in the *Ellsworth American.* "I've got something I want you to have," he announced in that familiar Yankee voice I'd heard through the years at my mother's Castine High reunions. Driving her was such a privilege, both to hear her stories and those of Leland and other characters of the last living alumni from the days before high schoolers went out of town. Back when boys and girls had separate stairs to their upstairs classrooms, and promises not to tell who put the skunk in that desk went to graves. The building now housing the Castine Historical Society. I always considered these folks VIPs and could never understand why their yearly gatherings weren't celebrated in *The Patriot* and why the Society wasn't there recording all the local knowledge being exchanged each time before it would be gone forever, as my mother's tales and precious ways of saying are, now, except in family archives.

Now, here I am with the privilege of listening to Leland and his gracious wife at their place on the way to Blue Hill, apologizing that we are out of his favorite bread 'n' butter pickles 'til Ed's new summer batch. But I didn't come empty-handed. Being early May, I made my only Maybasket of the season for him, the old-fashioned way, dreaming fudge the way his and my mother's generation would have and he recognized the memory right away with gratitude. He is 90 and requires oxygen the way we require voices like his.

"75 years of quality papermaking, 1930 – 2005" the postage stamp size bronze-like plaque hinged to a bark-colored leather watch fob or key chain proclaims. What a thrill to hold this in my hands, knowing the thousands of people it represents. To the extent any daughter of the mill can know. The very reason for this book. In the fullness of time I will give it to the Bucksport Historical Society with other treasures surfacing from this project to be protected and exhibited along with other proof of what our families did here.

"People came from as far away as Canada to work at that mill. In 1947, after the war (army field artillery), I had no car so rowed from Verona Island to Dr. Thegen's for a physical so I could work there. Went first in construction for some Massachusetts outfit, building rooms for supers # 2 and 3, then the core room and lab. Rode with George Harris. One day near the end of that job we heard there was a fire on company property in Whitneyville so we went down to see if they needed help. Sure enough, Perly Farrington said they could use all the help they could get so I sent word for someone to tell my wife I'd see her when I get there and Ralph Remick and I worked fighting that fire for about a week. Then one day I saw Perly talking with Bobby Brooks and Bobby came over and asked, "Want a job?" "Sure!" So after that I worked on a Quonset hut, then they sent me to work inside. That's how I started there, from the woodland division up to B man on the supercalendar. It was hot and loud. I hated that mill. Nerves weren't cut out for it. Plus I was doing lawn work and building on the side. Did too much. Once, putting up a splice I got awful headaches."

"Lot of people got hurt in that mill. Worried myself sick about the rolls getting stove up being down 4-5 hours. And about snap offs. One time, bringing 3-ton rolls of paper over, I noticed something wrong with that crane and protested. They still wanted me to go under it but I told 'em I ain't goin' -- you go!" So the riggers were found and said it was broken in six places. One of the workers hurt there had to have his fingers grafted to his chest."

All the while Leland is telling this, as I'm telling you for him, his accomplished wife is bringing out bag after bag of handworked afghans and spreads the rich colors of a sweet shop and the seasons. They point out his service medals and her paintings around the living room, a gallery of their clearly colorful lives. And his pride-filled scrapbooks from his time in the military. I can't get it all down but will begin again at this year's Castine High reunion we've been invited to attend in Mama's honor, yes, with a mason jar of bread 'n' butters in hand, and where we'll find a seat near his so as not to miss the stories and laughter as long as we can of this true Yankee -- a man of God with a devilish twinkle. His poem, "Happiness", puts it this way:

> One day I walked along the beach
> in a place I'd never seen before. And I saw the
> great green waters wash something upon the shore.
> It was a barrel of happiness enough for everyone.
> So smile, laugh, and be merry
> until your time has come.

We stay as long as their and our energies hold out, leaving with a flowered gift bag looking for all the world like a Maybasket in its own right. In it, along with the commemorative 75th token he'd wanted me to have, is a signed copy of his *Violets for Mother* poetry collection brimming with preserves from his memoried mind. Like his mother walking them across the road to the nearest church in Castine so they wouldn't get hit by a car, though there may have been just two in town. More likely to be struck by a horse and buggy, he writes. "Then we had to dodge golf balls the rest of the way." This is a history book. *He* is a history book! A memoir, testament of his faith, generosity of spirit, sense of humor, love of family and place, inner strengths, musicianship and literary and artistic core as evidenced in his poem, "Gone Is My Castle" written at age 14 expressing the fictional loss of an only brother in child-hood and just a half year later, his beloved mother. What an imagination, for his mother lived into her eighties.

On our refrigerator door are two painted and collaged shore village scenes made on old plastic cassette tape boxes looking for all the world like miniature canvases and signed inside, "Made 2013 by Alice Spencer, unique folk artist" he wanted us to know, and maybe we could ride out to Deer Isle some nice day and look her shop up.

But lest you think this is all I have to tell you about this former papermaker, survivor of the mill, here's this c.d. in my gift bag with three songs he's composed: "A Year and a Day" in which mermaids and zephers play, "Open Your Heart," and "Golden Stairs", recognized from his booklet. Wish you could hear them, dear reader. With luck, some Historical Society will know enough to treasure them, thankful they didn't get drowned out by the roar of the paper machines.

from A PRAYER

So when my life on earth is done
and we leave earth's grassy sod
Great and good is man who knows
the righteousness of God.

– Leland Bowden, Sr.

The son of Ida Belle and Charles Bowden of Castine, **Leland Atkins Bowden Sr.** *was born April 4, 1925 "down in a house on Windmill Hill." He lived there "all his life" growing up, graduating in the class of 1943 from Castine High School, which now houses the Castine Historical Society. After returning from World War II, he lived in Verona, Castine, West Penobscot and Searsport until settling in Blue Hill for forty-two years, raising two daughters and a son. Castine and other historians are now seeking him out to record his voice in print and sound.*

1947 ST. REGIS WAGE SCHEDULE

My mother and father were Frederick and Beryle Ames. My dad worked at the mill and my mother worked at Bucksport Hardware. On my father's side, my grandmother was Guida Ames and my grandfather Maurice Ames. My grandfather used to own HF Ames store on Main St. near where Pop Hills store used to be. My mother was a Snowman – her father was Burleigh Snowman and her mother Josephine Snowman. My brother is the genealogist, Tim Ames.

– Robert F. Ames

NO. 3 MACHINE

Machine Tenders	1.42
Back Tenders	1.25
Third Hands	1.17
Fourth Hands	1.08
Beater Man	1.17
Helpers	1.04

CONVERTING

Press Cutter	1.15
Ruler	1.15
Rotary Cutter	1.15
Rotary Cutter Helper	1.07
Pony Winder	1.04
Finisher	1.08
Checkers	1.22
Finishing Girls	.91-.93
Helpers	1.04
Marker Helpers—Girls	.99
Cartons and Pads—Girls	.97
Marker	1.14
Core Man	1.18
Core Helper	1.04

KAMYR MACHINE

Operator	1.12
Tailer	1.06
Bailer	1.04
Loader	1.04
Kamyr Tester	1.06

MISCELLANEOUS

Two yard trucks (Individual rate F. Gross truck)

Truck	.97
Driver	1.08
	2.05
Stevedoring Gang Foreman	1.49
Stevedore	1.39

Overtime rates paid in accordance with all Government regulations.

ST. REGIS PAPER COMPANY
SCHEDULE OF WAGE RATES
Effective May 1, 1947
International Brotherhood of Paper Makers
Local 261
International Brotherhood of Pulp, Sulphite and Paper Mill Workers, Local 88
and
International Association of Machinists
Local 1821

PAPER MILL

Machine Tenders	$2.17
Back Tenders	1.99
Third Hands	1.60
Fourth Hands	1.26
Fifth Hands	1.18
Sixth Hands	1.09
Broke Man	1.07
Spare Crew Clothing Foreman	1.52
Asst. Crew Clothing Foreman	1.26
Oilers	1.17
Elec. Crane Operator	1.13
Cleaners	1.14
Rewinders	1.23
Rewinder Helpers	1.13
Head Decker Operator	1.39
Decker Operator	1.29

FINISHING ROOM

Elec. Truck Operators	1.23
Checkers	1.20
Weighers	1.16
Finishers	1.12
Car Stowers	1.12
Roll Pushers	1.09
Wrapper Cutter	1.09
Header Man	1.07
Head Cutter Man	1.07

DOCK WAREHOUSE

Elec. Truck Operators	1.23
Roll Pushers	1.04

SCREEN ROOM
Wet Machine Operators	1.08
Screen Room Operators	1.15
Screen Room Helpers	1.08

SULPHITE MILL
Cooks	1.43
Acid Makers	1.23
Cook Helpers	1.12
Blow Pits	1.12
Blow Pit Helper	1.04
Chip Loft	1.04

GROUNDWOOD MILL
Sharpeners	1.18
Grinder Operators	1.08
Magazine Loaders	1.06

LABORATORY
Paper Testers	1.16
Paper Testers' Helper	1.10
Laboratory Helpers	1.10-1.12-1.14
Pulp Testers	1.08-1.10
Paper Inspectors	1.30

CLAY BUILDING
Clay Tank Man	1.12
Alum, Size & Glue	1.12
Clay Helper	1.04
Silo Operator	1.10

WOOD ROOM
Switch Operators and Oilers	1.08
Drum Operators	1.04
Conveyor Operators	1.04
Head Sorter	1.09
Sorters	1.04
Chipper Man	1.07
Splitters	1.08
Basement Cleaners	1.04
Hand Barkers	1.09
Streambarker Operators	1.12
Wood Pecker Operators	1.09

BOILER ROOM
Boiler Operators	1.38
Asst. Boiler Operators	1.26
Pump Operators	1.23
Turbine Operator	1.29
Turbining Tubes	1.23

MECHANICAL & ELEC. DEPARTMENTS
Foreman			1.47
Machinists			
Millwrights			
Carpenters	Class	A	1.37
Blacksmiths	Class	B	1.32
Welders	Class	C	1.29
Painters	Class	D	1.23
Roll Grinders			
Masons			
Pipers			
Helpers			
Mech. Helper			1.13
Elec. Helper			1.15
Starting Rate			1.04

MISCELLANEOUS
Asst. Storekeeper	1.16
Janitors	1.04
Head Watchman	1.17
Watchman	1.07
Stock Boys (Stores)	1.07-1.10
Head Oiler	1.28
Laborers	1.04

YARD
(Including Wood Storage & Wood Reclaiming)

Rake Crane Operators	1.32
Labor Pushers	1.08
Shift Foreman	1.16
Laborers	1.04
General Yard Foreman	1.45
Rigger and Calendar Stacks	1.13
Oiler	1.08
Sulphur Loading & Unloading	1.14
Truck Drivers Sulphur Loading and Unloading	1.18
Truck Drivers	1.08
Bull Dozer Operator	1.16
Scoop Truck Operator	1.16

NO. 3 MACHINE
Machine Tenders	1.42
Back Tenders	1.25
Third Hands	1.17
Fourth Hands	1.08
Beater Man	1.17
Helpers	1.04

CONVERTING
Press Cutter	1.15
Ruler	1.15
Rotary Cutter	1.15
Rotary Cutter Helper	1.04
Finisher	1.07
Pony Winder	1.08
Finisher	1.22
Checkers	1.08
Finishing Girls	1.04
Helpers	.99
Waler Helpers—Girls	.97
Cartons and Pads—Girls	1.14
Marker	1.18
Core Man	1.04
Core Helper	1.04

KAMYR MACHINE
Operator	1.12
Tailer	1.08
Boiler	1.04
Lender	1.04
Kamyr Tester	1.06

MISCELLANEOUS
Two yard trucks (Individual rate F Gross truck)

Truck Driver	.97
	1.08
Stevedoring Gang Foreman	
Stevedore	

Overtime rates paid in accordance with all Government regulations.

"Noses to the grindstone" by Owen K. Soper. August 1948, *Seaboard Bulletin*.

Owen K. Soper
Orland

DUST AND SUCH

I'm back again from a safety talk
Where I heard some good advice
As to how a fellow shouldn't walk
When he's stepping on thin ice.

It's well to think about things like
    that.
There's a lot of thin ice in a mill.
Watch your ring or a loose cravat

Around gears that are quick to kill!
Around machines, there are many ways
For a pass to beyond the pale.
Watch where the juice electric plays!
Look out for an upturned nail!

Beware of the warning tag in red!
Watch your step, your fingers and
    toes!
It's bye-bye, chum, when Death holds
    your head
With an ether-cone on your nose.

Yes, I'm back again in deepest
    thought,
Up under the roof, on the tanks;
Breathing clay-dust, and sizzling hot
While the sweat drips down my
    flanks.

I'm back in my stuffy cloud of dust,
And gasping a wheezy prayer

That some day, someone kind and
   just,
Will give us a breath of air.

       − Fuller Clay
Owen K. Soper, "The Poetic Papermaker"
August 1948, *Seaboard Bulletin*

"As you can see, this pen name came from his occupation. Clay, usually China clay, was used to en-hance the quality of the paper. I cannot find a precise definition for "fuller clay." Perhaps someone who worked there would know."
        –Jeannine Peters, granddaughter

Rick Doyle
Bucksport

THE WOODS

Cantdog, pulphook, pickaroon,
unloading cars in any weather.
The wages were decent, but still
all the time he was up in the woodyard

Lawnie Harper was driven hard.
When Lawnie said he was going to quit
if they couldn't find him
an easier job, Bobby Brooks

laughed and promised he wouldn't:
"You'd never get another job like this one!"
But Lawnie knew the woods, and so,
except for his time in North Africa and Sicily,

the woods is where he lived his life.
He could trap and fish. Hunt bear, line bees.
Hunters from all around the country
sought out his services as a guide.

Doctors, lawyers, politicians,
all of them looked up to Lawnie.

First published in *Crosscut, the literary journal of Husson College.*

Rick Doyle *was raised in North Orland, graduating with the Bucksport High class of 1976. Several members of his family worked in the Bucksport mill. His paternal grandfather was hired by St. Regis around 1940 as a carpenter; he eventually became a machinist in the wood yard, where he worked until his retirement in 1970. Great-uncles on his father's side also worked for St. Regis, one as a mechanic, the other as an oiler: Other great-uncles worked at mills in Brewer and Millinocket. His mother was a secretary in the Bucksport personnel office, in the long low brick building by the main gate,* *where she worked right up to the Saturday he was born, June 1958; later she transferred to Woodlands, where she was an office administrator. His brother started out as a spare laborer at the stud mill in Costigan, then got into the mill at Bucksport, where he worked in the instrumentation department and eventually in Information Technology. As a college student Rick worked summers in the spare labor pool at St. Regis.*

Brenda Locke as told to Linda Smith
Bucksport

HOGS HEAD CHEESE, CORNED BEEF & PIE

My father, Frank Ames, worked in the wood yard running the crane when they first opened. He had sold fish from a truck before he worked at St. Regis. After a while he worked his way into the paper machines. They used to tease him that he was "not all there" because he had lost a finger to infection from a fish bone. We lived on Second Street which is now Franklin. He carried a basket lunch box with handles like a picnic basket and lugged it on his arm. Sandwiches, like hogs head cheese, and desserts like my mother's pies. Apple, rhubarb, whatever she made. Thermos of coffee. I remember one time she took a can of cat food from the shelf next to the tuna by mistake and he called her up and asked why she'd done that! Once in a while he carried a crossword book. Sometimes he'd walk to work or take the car. When he took the car he'd forget and walk home and have to go back after it. He retired in 1974 at 63 and died at 83.

Editor's note:
Sadly missed by her family and friends, Brenda passed away November 16, 2016.

Brenda Ames Locke *was born in 1948 at the Stinson Hospital in Bangor and was adopted by Frank and Arlene Ames, her grandmother. Her great grandfather was Herman Bowden, a carpenter. She grew up in Bucksport where she attended schools with the class of 1966. Through the years she waitressed at Millett's Restaurant on Verona Island and the Iron Kettle, Lee's Pizza, and Chaisson's Restaurant in Bucksport. She worked as a stitcher at Viner's Shoe in Bangor, Bass Shoe on the air base, and for Baugher Canadian Skates in Bangor, and stitched soles at a slipper factory in Brewer. After earning her CNA (Certified Nurses Aide) credential, she worked at Brewer Rehab, Stillwater Healthcare, and Ellsworth Convalescent Home, now Courtland Rehabilitation & Living Center. She worked at Bangor Mental Health from 1988 to 2000 when she became disabled. In addition to starting off in Bucksport, she has lived in Prospect and Vinalhaven before returning to Bucksport where she has lived at Knoxview Apartments since 2004. She loves playing BINGO and doing crossword puzzles and is known for having been a master crocheter of baby sets, afghans, scarves, hats and mittens. A* *favorite activity is going down on the waterfront and sitting by the river. "It's relaxing." But she can't leave the third floor now unless someone takes her. She and a "little group" of friends who keep an eye and support each other get together daily for coffee and share meals, holidays and birthdays. "I used to do a lot more when I could. I used to make homemade corned beef and cabbage (cutting and corning the beef myself) for our monthly pot lucks downstairs. Ernie Smith came and played his bagpipes. Here's my grandmother, Arlene Bowden Ames's recipe:*

BRENDA'S HOMEMADE CORNED BEEF AND CABBAGE

Spread salt in bottom of glass dish. Put beef on top of it being sure to salt the sides and top. Pack it right in. Let set all day then rinse off and rinse the dish. This draws off the blood. Repeat that night. Next day it will be ready to cook. Boil with veggies – cabbage, potatoes, carrots, turnip. Beets and onions? You can. Whatever veggies you want.

Albert Bunt and Dick Chase
Bucksport

LUNCH BASKET COMPLAINT

I carry a lunch basket to and from the mill
I haven't any choice so I guess I always will
Sandwiches and sauerkraut and a little bit of cheese
Sometimes a piece of pie or a cold dish of peas.

Nothing appetizing so to make you fat
Just a few left overs, a little this and that
Put up in a hurry to catch the 8 to 4
Thrown into the basket as you go out the door.

Sometimes no spoon to eat with, no knife to cut the cheese
But maybe in tomorrow's basket an extra pair of these.
Everything as cold as ice to cool your appetite.
Cold meat, cold slaw and sometimes cold tripe.

Sandwiches and sauerkraut and maybe applesauce
Or anything the cook can come across
Laying there so neatly, wrapped in cellophane,
Tasteless as all getout to give your gut a pain.

No wonder I look poorly when I meet you on the street
No pep, no vigor, just a-draggin' at the feet
Just a shadow of my former self – how thin can you get
Eating sandwiches out of a lunch basket?

From the *"Paper Room"* column of the *VOL. 14 SEABOARD BULLETIN* published by St. Regis Paper Co., February, 1952. Richard O. Chase, Editor. All of the material that was drawn from the SEABOARD BULLETIN for republishing in this collection appears with Dick Chase's permission.

Dick Chase *would turn 90 in April of 2017. After graduating with the Class of 1945 with the Bob Redmans and Goldie Adams, he served in the U.S. Army, then worked 36 years at the Bucksport paper mill "from clerk to personnel manager," including many years as editor of the* SEABOARD BULLETIN, *a small magazine containing every aspect of working for the mill, in the logging camps* *upcountry, and living in a papermaking region. Departments had their own reporters of facts and figures, and would submit news of the work, itself, shutdowns and repairs, facts and figures, records set, union news, regional goings on, school activities, sports, mill family weddings, births, illnesses, injuries and recoveries, local service people and veterans, hunting stories, parties, jokes and pranks, travels of mill people, fashions and fads, photos and original cartoons and poems. Copies are treasured wherever they are still to be found for the history in them. Dick's wife, Freida Emery, was from St. Francis up in The County between the Allagash and Ft. Kent. "We read a lot and take little trips. He calls me 'the cleaning lady', in an affectionate way, of course. We enjoy going to camp at Alamoosook and we winter close to home."*

Editor's note:

Although we could not locate anyone with knowledge of what job(s) **Albert Bunt** did at the mill, and his department and job class was N/A, his employment date was listed as 8/28/45 in the Champion International Corporation Employee List. The following obituary provides a glimpse into his interesting life with another mill employee:

In Memory of Pauline A. Bunt (April 20, 1931 – May 15, 2016)

*Pauline A. Steinarson Bunt was born April 20, 1931, to Sigurd A. Steinarson and Doris Varnum Steinarson in Bucksport, Maine. She met **Albert Bunt** when they were both in high school. She was very active in sports and academics, and was a member of the National Honor Society. She was a cheerleader. She married Albert R. Bunt, Jr., on September 9, 1950. After high school she worked in the office of the St. Regis Paper Company in Bucksport until February 1953 when she joined her husband in Bedford, England. She sailed to England on the* Queen Mary *to be with him. Pauline and two new friends sat on a curb all night waiting to see the coronation parade of Queen Elizabeth. Albert enlisted in the U.S. Air Force in October 1951 and they spent 22 years traveling the world and various bases in the U.S. While in Anchorage, Alaska she worked for the Bureau of Land Management in the homestead division. In 1969 she accompanied her husband in Brindisi, Italy where they lived for two and one-half years. After retiring from the Air Force they continued traveling and camping. Pauline loved sports. She was an avid bowler and bridge player earning many awards in both. She had a sharp mind and excelled as a statistician. She and her husband spent their retirement years in San Angelo, Texas.*

Patricia Ranzoni
Bucksport

MAKING MAYBASKETS

for the Centennial of the Ellsworth Public Library's Festival of Poets, April 1997

CONTEXT: APRILS 1947 TO 1957, HANCOCK COUNTY MAINE
                    (with remnants of songs, riddles, chants, and rhymes
                        from our schools and buses, churches, families, and outbacks)

(sung)   *"There's Been a Change in Me"* by Cy Cohen.

You've saved small pasteboard containers all winter. Match-
boxes the size of the holder on the wall behind the stove.
Round Quaker Oats ones cut down. A sweetghosted box from chocolates
if you had one kept from Valentine's. The rooster running his prerogative 'round
'n' 'round the thawed yard his showy crow riding the bullish brook
chasing   kissing   chasing   kissing.

Your mother trades her eggmoney for pleats of tissue
and crinkled crepe paper at the 5 & 10 the colors of arbutus trailing
on the ledges where handsome young Lyman and Joannie Hutchins from your mailman's
family drive *head on* one after the other exploding into those cliffs missing the turn
off the Waldo-Hancock Bridge where Bill Carpenter will someday come to write and run
come to live and *breathe in* what people imagine you girls imagine about those sailors
off those tankers and barges come to load and unload. Don't go down town
there's a boat in come straight home there's a boat in your father and mother and teachers warn
lest you pick all Bucksport's rare wild rose yarrow on the way to the wharf,
encounter rainforest you don't know about emotions, become women right there on the dock
emerging with foreign flowers between your souvenir breasts for the rest of your life.

> You don't know Robert Lowell is learning sailing
> and kissing a few miles downriver summers
> you don't know about, *classic summers* Elizabeth Bishop
> names it in North Haven poems. You don't know E.B.
> has been crossing the river on the Prospect-to-your-town ferry years
> before that stanzaed bridge is spun, his domestics scared

for where they're being taken and Lowell's help is right.
These are dinky roads.

Paper the color of shadblossoms you don't know roof and rug Ruth Moore's
writing place down back of her place in Tremont where you don't know she's come home
to claim her poems you don't know will someday seize, and kiss your heart like an ancestor
handing you something she wants to make sure you get, the color of wild pear
sprinkling your openair playhouse of fruit-crate furniture and broken dishes from the farm
and its antique dump in the woods rainsmocked and flocked with pollens and insect wings, laced
with webs, feathers, salamander tracks and *remember this!*

You don't know there's any such thing
as a slick magazine called The New Yorker
though its paper could've been made right here
by your father and uncles and neighbors,
or that One Man's Meat is anything but all
a war-horrified boy home from the Pacific wants
for the rest of his life--a page of pasture
with a job at the mill to make sure.

Paper the color of forsythia you won't see
until your first trip out of state on this chartered bus
to Jack Wyrtzen's Youth for Christ Rally at Boston Garden,
returning with a bargainbible with leaves thin as spent narcissi
(you know from oldest farms) from answering the invitation
to come forward.
(sung)   *Just as I am....I come, I come.*

Not crocuses, snowdrops, hyacinths from bulbs
you don't know about needing planting at closin'-in
time, who'd *have* the time or money to spare, not for sale
anywhere you've seen anyway you don't know anyone
who actually has daffodils. But pussywillows, dandelions
(a food not weed), skunk cabbage, maple and chokecherry
flowers, fiddleheads, and
(sung)   *There was a little man standing in the wood.*
He wore a purple cloak and a small black hood.
Tell me who this man could be
standing there so quietly
with his purple cloak and his small black hood.
Oldtime daylily shoots clumpin' up 'longside cellarstones
facing south. What grows on homesteads bequeathed by creation
and relatives and oldtimers wantin' you to have some.

Paper the colors of those layers in your Grammie Dunbar's *what is it* riddle:

> *Within a hall as white as milk,*
> *within a wall as soft as silk,*
> *within a fountain crystal clear,*
> *a golden apple doth appear.*
> *No doors there are to this stronghold*
> *yet thieves break in and steal the gold.*

[an egg]

Paper the colors
of all the leaves in Jacob Buck valley!

> You don't know anyone who writes
> for a living or that there's any such thing as that kind
> of living working to get words right for printing
> though your mother knows and always wanted to
> but women don't. Wins a dollar
> in the WABI contest with a poem they read on the radio
> about the well in winter freezin', in the summer
>   goin' dry, after that song Life Gets Tedious Don't It.
>   Always bringing up Thanatopsis from her classic Abbott
>   School education how anyone so young
>   could know to write such a thing! Doesn't know
>   before her life is through that poem will name any such thing
>   as a heavy metal band. Reads you Mother West Wind How,
>   Mother West Wind Where, Mother West Wind When
>   stories not poems exactly still they sing in your mind
>   the same way you tease her to recite Little Orphant Annie again.
> *You better mind yer parents, an' yer teach/ers fond an' dear, ...*
>   Going right along with the naughtygirl tale
>   in the children's book your warbrideaunt Gabrielle Joan
>   Pendred Lockwood *oo* ...brings you from England
>   where a young girl falling asleep at the shore
>   is bound 'round her wrists by creatures she doesn't know about,
>   pulled with cords to the clouds down skystreets she
>   doesn't know about where people *shame shame*
>   to work for Mrs. Do As You're Told and Mrs. Mind
>   What I Say her sorrys and tears to no avail until sufficiently
>   improved she's allowed back through those approving now
>   faces, waking in the dunes to be forever, now, good.

> You learn there's a Bar Harbor and Mount Desert Island

64

when the radio says your town's sending engines, scared
sparks will cross to the mainland, then the truckride there,
eyes watering to see up close the loss you don't know is instruction
for the decades: how the most amazing greens
spring from burnt ground no matter how tall
and fog-blurred the ghosts or how long they insist
like those charcoal spruce and fir. How seeds come through fire
flare into their best destiny after all.

Paper the tints of new growth nerving
against granite pinks old as earth.

And your father never does anything without some
colory words probably got from his Scottish granddad, the voice
teacher come over, and going with his sisters Beulah and Hazel
with their great aunts to drive the cows home to verse.

You admire the sound of Tojo
the name your father with an ear for Longfellow
gives the Husky puppy he brings home after his discharge
not knowing you're loving the name of the prime minister
of Japan the arch enemy he reduces to a dog
before he is hanged.
Under a spreading chestnut -tree
The village smithy stands....
he orates between lovesongs and The Old Rugged Cross,
beholden to Henry:
And looks the whole world in the face,
For he owes not any man..... flexing his muscles
shaving in the mirror, delighted or distraught with himself
as Robert Lowell who could be shopping right next to him
for his own gallon of cheap wine
to quiet or reward his own warring mind.

You plan which little boxes will be which shades and designs.
Daffodil cups, lavender-trimmed rectangular ones. Which
fringed snowy and which for grass. Cones, and lantern ones
from cutting pastel tissue folded justright then unfolded
into lace, corners joinedup to a braided loop. Imagine Hattie Grindle's
paper parasols-- miniature closed umbrellas
with candy in their creases. Anita, Barbara, Jean, known
for their stunningest--or--depending on your tongue--cunnin'est
kind.

They could be brothers you don't know
you'll be jolted to see, Cal Lowell looking so familiar
In books baring his soul they could be brothers
but their worlds will never
touch that they'll know about good thing too no doubt
though they might've found something to admire in the other
if they'd dared find their common ground, until,
one proud he went to war
for his family and country the other proud he didn't,
they'd've come to blows sure as hell, Lowell
coming for these tennis summers (which is not to forget his
kind of elbow grease in his kind of barn), your father
never owning playclothes his whole rich life
when he plays he rolls up
or takes off.

You don't know you'll someday bet they might
in rare thoughts
have been proud to suppose themselves friends
but in the end when they couldn't forgive themselves
or each other who they were and were not,
they'd've given up, missing the glimpse of themselves
received from the other at their best all
of their fallingstar years.
But doesn't Lowell make your mother's
people's cemetery and our skunks famous (not the other way around
the way your father's people wore skunkoil against the croup)
seeing his own moonstruck eyes in theirs confessing his own
wild taste for cultured trash? How Hancock County serves
his genius these days freeing him to loosen and swivel his
aesthetics no less, you may never be forgiven
for proposing, than Elvis, and *shush...*

what's this Howl!

You've heard of Luzon and Mog Mog Island
in the Philippines but don't know there's any such place
as Brooklin Maine or Eggemoggin Reach except for the skit
Mr. Mac has each 6th grade do called The Lighthouse
Keeper's Daughter where the tallest boy gets to be the light
so Bobby Terrill is yours and how you all split
when Alfred Kettell like Barnacle Bill

(sung)   *Who's that knocking at my door...cries the fair young maiden.*
              It's only me from over the sea, I'm Barnacle Bill the sailor

66

        chases Judith Cropley you don't know will die so young
        losing her leg, 'round and 'round Bob you don't know
        will die so young working maintenance at the mill
        no connection they'll say. Gangly he stands while all roar
        in the gym but you'll hardly be able to smile
        his last reunion his face turning back into that light
        he's leaving on and *Dear Christ*
        you hope you kissed him goodbye.
This is the forest primeval   you memorize with voice sad
               (and not unprophetic) for Rena Grey in 7th or 8th and
...he tapped with his whip on the shutters, but all was locked
and barred;/He whistled a tune to the window/and who
should be waiting there.../.../.../ Plaiting a dark red love-knot
into her long black hair.

You cut across wrinkles of your women's art the way you've been taught
playing sepalous garlands and corolla strings like paper dolls, pressing petals
and leaves out round with your thumbs.

You make boiled flour-and-water paste.

        You don't know E.B. these years calls the management
        of his desk paste a # one problem.
        You don't know George Oppen is pasting words
        over words (because neither he nor Mary type) but loosely
        so they can be tried and untried
        like where to stick the right bud and leaf on what handle
        or ruffle, floating discrete words over Penobscot waters you
        don't know about from their island-bobbing boat. You
        don't know you are learning alliteration from waons
        on depths just as capable of drowning. Not the rhythm
        of trimming sails exactly but *build that load, walk that hay,*
        trimming, trimming, your father's chants teaching you *that*
        ballet where to tread to an edge to balance and not fall off,
        your own sweat your own salt, chaff
        an inland sting and after full days after days of it not
        foxtrots you don't know about over any harbor
        you don't know about but The Barbara Polka, the *schottische,*
        and Irene Goodnight at the Gypsy or up to the hall, spitcurls
        on your cheeks, blackest ponytail the Methodist minister
        calls a sin down to your waist swingin' in squares and rounds,
        not chintz and linen you don't know about but cotton broomstick
        skirts (you don't even need a pattern for) twirling

over net petticoats starched in sugarwater dripped outside to dry
so stiff they scrunch like iceout from the racing brook
that spicy old scent of life wanting to chase and kiss itself.

So you turn out Maybaskets for the Willis kids
and Johnsons and Conners and Smiths. Allisons, Bridges, Grindles
and Hurds. Winchesters, Gowans and Whites planning which for which
keeping the old promise to chase and kiss
and always give the new
people the best.

Last of April you make the fill. Your mother's divinity, sister's
peanut butter, your
cocoa fudge keeping the old secrets of the full rolling boil
to the soft ball stage you keep testing for
with drops in cups of cold water
'til the syrup gathers in your fingertips
like a nipple at rest
then waiting, waiting, to let it cool
before beating out its shine
having waxed paper to turn onto that *instant* it sets.

May First it goes like this: you've picked through dreams
through days and nights where
you'll deliver, which
heart where, not by moonlight

        but after school after supper after chores before dark.
        After rings on the still-party line all agreeing to fake,
        listening for who'll be home when. *I'll come to thee* [before]
        moonlight, though hell should bar the way.

        Across the valley youngsters watch who's where, when.
        Baskets behind their backs, they walk or bike
        to each house, those inside pretending not to notice.
        Not since Una Wardwell's day when from eggshells
            fancied with wallpaper have most Maybaskets
            been light or right enough to hang from knobs, so you nest
            them on granite and wooden steps quiet as birds
            setting down. *Knock* and *run!* Cheeks flushed to russets,
        you *chase   kiss   chase   kiss   remember this!*

           You don't know someday you'll wonder why, living here,

your paths never crossed, all these late great poets
along your coast, although you could have waited
on them not knowing, not allowed to talk.
You don't know how some shocking day
owning your own voice, you'll re-see
serving people like that not joking with them or fraternizing
like that crewcut Kitchen Boy Phippen
you don't know about tryin' to be good over to Hancock
you don't know about, but with one arm locked bent
across your waist behind your back as required in your
station, *deferential*, and how that will someday bend
how you say what you say. Too bad
they missed what you might've held in that hand
back there.

You don't know the Philip Castine come home
to honor his and your ancestral grounds here most of all
will come to own the path your family takes to the shore,
and harking some slanted day for his own life's work you
don't know about may hear heart caught there,
and thrashing, from a noisy child never shown how to swim right
but figuring it out enough to make her own claim
wrestling saltwater and riding that bigol' slippery pulp trunk
rolling in ThatTime's tide.

Sally over the ocean
Sally over the sea
Sally broke a beanpot
and blamed it onto me
I told ma
ma told pa

Sally got a lickin'
so ha ha ha holding hands treaddancing and bursting as high
          out of the water as you can on the ha's, crashing back
          into the waves 'til your bottom bounces
          on the water's floor or hear where a Mainechild cried,
          teaching herself her legacy (Amy Clampitt will come here to learn
          and Minnie Bowden already knows) and none
          too soon how neither tears nor words are anything
          to an ocean.
          You don't know when or where in any world off
          or near, poets Little and Mancuso are. D'Angelo,

Shepherd, Blair. Or Hanson. Or Thomas, Kestenbaum,
Greenberg, Stover, Shetterly, Hubbell, Pollet. Or
how you will *will* to come some
time *in time* to find *their* spirits here. Nor have they had,
these years, any way to grasp the neighbor you are,
nor to guess, if they slipped quietly out into your valley
hanging a paperformed grocery hope
on your May door
how you would *soar* for the poem
in kissing them!

Author note:
This collage poem was composed, read, and sung for the invitational Festival of Poets commemorating the Centennial of the Ellsworth Public Library in 1997, curated by Marion K. Stocking (1922–2009), Editor, from 1954 to 2003, of *Beloit Poetry Journal*. Inspired by my wish to honor some of the poets, past and present, who have written in Hancock County, it was first published in *Puckerbrush Review* and *SETTLING, Poems by Patricia Ranzoni* (Puckerbrush Press, 2000) and has been excerpted in numerous collections. Though many of these noted authors have passed away or moved elsewhere, their work can be found in area libraries and on the internet.

Alfred Kettell
Souderton, PA

DANCING WITH THE DEVIL & PUTTING HER BEST FOOD FORWARD

I remember the woven lunch baskets nearly everyone carried. Not wicker but flat woven wood strips. Once in a while a small pile of paper sheets would find its way home in the basket and my brother and I would have something to write on as we wished.

On Thursday paydays, my mother would sometimes catch the bus from home on Hurd's Brook Hill to town, meet my father at the gate at an arranged time to get the paycheck for that week, and take the family car from the lot to do shopping. She would return at quitting time to pick him up. Thursday night supper would be some-thing special on those days–maybe even a steak to share.

The economic class divisions between the families of the ordinary workers and the families of managers were evident in the lifestyles but, in my experience, not in relationships. My mother belonged to a bridge club (The HI-Neighbor Club) with 12 members who met monthly to play cards. The venue rotated with each member hosting once a year. I was too far removed from those ladies to dredge up any names. I do remember as a child up in bed thinking they talk awfully loud. More than half smoked as well so my mother had to air the house after it was over. Each member hosted one of the monthly meetings. Creative appetizer competition was fierce. I'm sure there was some amount of angst my mother felt when she was the hostess, but didn't exhibit it because she knew everyone would be more than gracious. I recall helping her with the food prep for such an event, and she certainly put her best food forward, but everyone did. I don't suppose there were any poor cooks in the group!

When the club met at the home of one of the more economically advantaged members, they may have had a bit fancier accoutrements and roomier setting for the three card tables and folding chairs that were loaned about, but no envy was ever expressed that I heard. At least until later in high school when some class pressure evolved, I had friends across the economic landscape. As usual, we made friends most easily with the people who lived near us and resembled us in most ways. Most of us were 'poor folks', if the truth be told, but we were proud of what we had.

One other memory is the daily train that ran between our house and the river. It would have pulp wood in the earlier years until trucks became more prevalent and always tank cars full of the necessary mystery liquids that helped make the paper. More than any really bad smells from the mill I more remember a musty woodpile smell that probably mostly came from the bark dump a bit up the Shore Road.

My father always hated his time at the mill and it was short compared to most at about 15 years. After quitting the mill he tried to eke out a living by various farming ventures and those, although with some sense of freedom, were poor alternatives to a steady paycheck. A quote, "It's hard to dance with the devil on your back," may express what those who work at places they dislike feel, but do so out of necessity.

Alfred Edward Kettell *was born "at home on William's Pond Mountain in Bucksport in 1940. Lived in several homes all about 7 miles from town on the River Road/Shore Road (Rte 15)." He graduated with the Bucksport High School class of 1958 then the University of Maine class of 1963 with a Bachelor of Science degree in Mechanical Engineering. His work history includes Bethlehem Steel, Buffalo, NY and Bethlehem, PA from '63 to '83; James River and Jefferson Smurfit, Chambersburg and Philadelphia, PA from '83 to '97; and Sealstrip Corp., Gilbertsville, PA from '97 to the present. "I'm still working full time. Lisa and I have had the opportunity to travel to Great Britain 7 or 8 times. Three of those trips were to the Highlands of Scotland. Our last trip we went with a group (Lehigh Valley Chapter of The Hardy Plant Society) to North England and Wales, visiting gardens. That was the first trip with a bus involved. Other trips I drove, typically 1000-1200 miles, on 'the wrong side of the road'. I enjoy folk, Irish, and bluegrass music and still play guitar. We support environmental causes and nature organizations and love to hike, albeit shorter distances, in peaceful woodlands and other quiet places."*

Irene Bridges Atwood
Bucksport

THE MOST HANDSOME MAN IN BUCKSPORT

After we were married in 1956, my husband, Herb Atwood, worked at several jobs during the summer. In the fall, he applied with Mr. Chase to work at St. Regis as a spare employee.

In order to be assured of work, Herb would arise every day and be in the outer office of the mill very early. He wanted to be readily available if a spare was needed that day. Some mornings, he did not get work, so he would repeat the process in the afternoon. He worked many jobs during this time, many of which were quite demanding. That first winter, he sometimes would arrive home after midnight, completely soaked and nearly frozen because of the ice-covered pulp he had unloaded from the train cars.

Before long, however, Herb obtained a job in the train shed. Though this was an outdoor job for the most part, he enjoyed the work and the crew, even participating in a "fork lift derby." The steering handle, one day, unfortunately accounted for a broken wrist, which was his only injury during his many years at the mill.

When Herb was offered a job in the Coating Department, he accepted it happily and remained there with a great group of co-workers until his retirement, having gone from handling pulp wood to operating a computer.

Our children's favorite mill memory is that, upon their Father's return from work, they would rush to open his "lunch basket" (used by most of the men in the mill) to see if Herb had visited the canteen machines and dropped some M&M's into the basket for them.

On occasion, since we were a one-car family, I would need to take Herb to work in the morning, returning with the children to pick him up later. There were always groans as I consistently said to them, "Now when you see the most handsome man in Bucksport walk out through the gate, then of course that will be Dad."

Though sometimes the shift work could be difficult, the mill provided a good living for us and many other Bucksport families. Herb enjoyed his work and co-workers there, first for St. Regis, then Champion and ultimately retiring from International Paper. We were all heartbroken when our beloved Herb dropped suddenly on September 22, 2016. As was written in his obituary and often repeated by his family and co-workers: "Herb was a kind and gentle man who never made an enemy in his whole life." He is sorely missed.

Irene Bridges Atwood *grew up in the "outback" Bucksport farming community at the foot of Jacob Buck Mountain known as Millvale. "Proud am I to say that I have lived all of my life in the 'mill* town' of Bucksport. For me, growing up in the Bucksport 'suburb' of Millvale was an idyllic life. We were happy to perform farm chores, and enjoy winter sliding and skating parties followed in summer by participating in the neighborhood baseball games, pretend carnivals, etc. The lack of traffic on the Millvale road in the 40's and early 50's, because most of the vehicles were at the mill, allowed the young people to use the main road for part of their recreation. In winter almost everyone gathered on 'Bridges Hill' for the sliding, followed in summertime by coasting down the same hill on one of the 'gigs' that had been built by the boys in the neighborhood with a pair of wagon wheels and an axle.

After we were married we chose to make a home for our family in the same area, as did many of our child- hood friends. The neighbors knew all the children and gave them communal support, and, indeed, a 'talking to' when necessary. Though as adults many of the children raised in this way have traveled away from their home- town of Bucksport, they acknowledge that growing up in Millvale was truly idyllic.

Being a member of a remarkable family of 13, my husband was taught as a child to be humble and grateful for the little things in life. He said that it was wonderful at Christmastime to receive a visit from the local fire- man who brought fresh fruit and little gifts to the family. Also, he remembered the family outings as his Dad took them all in the family car for a trip around Verona Island, with him riding in the rumble seat.

As a former 4-Her it was gratifying that our own children became 4-Hers themselves and were taught lessons that have followed them into adulthood, along with Bucksport's small- town ethics.

Having traveled extensively to visit our children who did move away, and to see the country, we were always happy to return to our 'mill town' and our roots in Millvale."

Patricia Ranzoni
Bucksport

OUTBACK BALL

In the fifties we felt the pull
from Turkey Path and Silver Lake,
Jacob Buck Mountain and Charlie Cole way,
across brooks, *yes marm* roads and hills.

We went every night when night
started at the four o'clock whistle
ending the dayshift, and papermakers
made their ways home to the valley.
Across Millvale, newfangled pressure cookers
helped get meals to tables on time. Nothing
on the few t.v. sets in the neighborhood
but snow from the first station upriver
in Bangor. Dishes done, to the field!

To the game!
To chickenwire backstop, hay stubble, mud.
To hand over hand who picks first from men,
women, kids. Everyone gets to play, little ones
to grands. Every night after supper. To play
after dark in pasture park and hike home
under star-seeded skies to the singing of frogs
and friends. When families played ball outback
after supper.

First published in *CLAIMING, Poems by Patricia Ranzoni* (Puckerbrush Press, Orono, ME 1995.)

Nancy E. Wasson
Orland

GIB: FROM BASEBALL TO FOREMAN

In the late '40's Gilbert "Gib" Snowman (1921-1982), a World War II veteran of Patton's Army, was playing baseball for the champion Brewer AA's when at a game he was approached by Ted Gross of Bucksport and asked "When are you going to play ball for Bucksport?" To which Gib replied "When I get a job in the mill." Needless to say a job was forthcoming and Gib moved his family to his wife's homestead on the Castine Road in Orland. He played several years, as a catcher, a little tall for the position at 6'4" and first baseman for the Bucksport AA's which was sponsored by St. Regis. He had the ability to hit some of the longest balls out of the field at Luman Warren Field. He played baseball with the Nickless brothers, Wally Thomas, Artie Wight, Bucky Jones, Charlie Gravelle, and Winnie Weston, along with numerous college students who were working part-time during the summers at St. Regis, just to name a few. After his playing days he coached and umpired baseball for several years.

With his good work ethic and being a quick study, about 1950 Gib was given the opportunity to go to the Deferrit, New York plant to train for the coating process. At this time one was still able to take the train from Bangor to their destination. After two weeks of training, he returned to train the Bucksport crews. Some of the men he worked with were Sparky Nickless, Harold Willis, Kelsey Gray, Kelsey Patten, Bill Clifford, Zeke Paige, and Otis Hanscom. Gib had the reputation of being a fair and just foreman well respected by all his crews. In later years he was transferred to the Finishing and Shipping Department from which he retired due to illness. At the time of his retirement he was the longest serving foreman in the mill.

> *The May-flowers are blooming.*
> *Daylight Time is here again, the alewives*
> *are running, dandelion greens are large*
> *enough to dig and the chief topic of conversation*
> *is fishing, all sure signs that Spring is here again.*
> *Gib Snowman has been acting a bit*
> *dumpy of late. Upon inquiry, he informed me*
> *that there wasn't a thing the trouble with him*

*that a good feed of fresh alewives and dandelion
greens wouldn't cure. Must have been a touch
of spring fever.*

– Reporter unknown
Coating Dept. column
Seaboard Bulletin
May, 1957

Historian **Nancy E. Wasson** *was born New Year's Eve 1936 at the Wasson Farm, in Bucksport. "My elementary education was basically in one-room schools in Orland, Franklin and Eddington with a short period at the Luman Warren School, graduating from Bucksport High School in 1954. In high school I had the opportunity to attend Girl State, increasing my interest in the political process." In 2001 Nancy held a most successful reunion of the one-room schools of Orland with over 190 in attendance. For this project she received the Hans Honder Community Service Award from the Bucksport Chamber of Commerce. "After working at a variety of jobs and raising three sons, Randy, Regan and G. Eric Brown, I decided it was time to pursue higher education and earned my Bachelor's Degree in Personnel from Husson College in 1980. While at Husson I worked as a Work-Study student responsible for the entire Work-Study Program from freshman year until graduation, learning all the Federal Student Financial Aid Programs and regulations, enabling me to become Financial Aid Director and Continuing Education Director at Beal College. In 1983 I was offered a position with the State of Maine Department of Education to administer the Maine Student Incentive Scholarship Program, a position I held until retirement in 1997." Nancy then became employed by Sharon Bray at 'The Bucksport Enterprise,' first selling advertising then interviewing and writing about World War II veterans, starting with her father, George "Hornet" Wasson and his brother, Fredrick "Bim" Wasson (a mill retiree) who were united at Normandy Beach. "Honoring these men was an experience that we all should enjoy." After a second retirement, Nancy became involved with the Orland Historical Society serving as both Secretary and President several times, and as chair of the 50th anniversary committee. She has worked on family genealogies for years, "both Snowman and Wasson, trying to keep the descendants included as they come along." She is currently working to record the genealogies that OHS has in their files. In 2013 and 2014, with the assistance of Brian Barker, Nancy compiled two books encompassing the cemeteries and private burial grounds in Orland, "which proved to be both educational and gratifying experiences for both of us." Nancy served as a member of the Board of Gardner Commons apartments for two years and on the Orland Planning Board for several. She has been active in the United Methodist Church of Orland and has worked on the free community luncheons, falls through spring. As a member of a mill family, her stepfather, Norris Deans, retired from St. Regis, two of her brothers, and her uncle "who raised me through my teenage years" all worked in the mill. Her brother, Dana Deans, transferred from Bucksport to St. Cloud, MN where he retired; and her brother, Leroy, retired from the Bucksport mill. However, "my major connection to the mill was through my uncle Gib Snowman, the first man St. Regis sent to New York to train for the coating process. Of course, his connection with St. Regis came from his ability to play baseball in the days when Bucksport had several years of great semi-pro teams, sponsored in part by the mill."*

Editor's note: Unbeknownst to her, **Nancy Wasson** purchased her great grandparents'–Capt. William Livingston Snowman and Ethel Minerva Gray Snowman–homestead on the Cross Road in Orland in 1994. "The story goes that when I walked in I could see it needed a lot of work, but I got a comforting feeling that I was home. I didn't know anything about the house until my mother came a couple of months later when I was scraping tiles from the floor and told me to be careful as there were hardwood floors. When I asked how she knew she replied, 'It was my grandmother's house.'" Home, indeed.

Seaboard Bulletin
May 1957

EITHER TWO DAYS BEHIND OR A DAY AHEAD

*I came back from my day off last week
and for a minute I was lost. Man, alive,
they sure had changed everything over
in the wet-end of the paper room. They
had ripped out half of the cement, put in
a new decker, changed over the water
and steam system, and it took me two
days to find all the valves. Of course I
have been either two days behind or a
day ahead ever since we changed over
to Daylight Saving Time. "Tennessee"
Ernie Ford says that Daylight Saving
Time is like cutting off a foot at the
bottom of the sheet and sewing it on
the top to make it longer.*

– Reporter unknown
Paper Room column

IV. HARD AND MASTERFUL YEARS

Of Devotion and Pride

Black tin lunch pails were considered modern for decades, their domed lids
carrying Thermoses of hot beverages or soups.

Philip Edmund Booth (1925-2007)
Castine

from THAT CLEAR FIRST MORNING

I was where they were.
There were men waking to coffee
and lunch boxes, women

tending the coffee and making
lunches. They were me.
I was there, being young.

Although born in New Hampshire, the distinguished American poet, **Philip Edmund Booth** *(1925 – 2007), wrote a substantial amount of his work from his ancestral home in Castine and Penobscot Bay, papermaking territory, where he grew up and brought his family. He studied at Columbia University and Dartmouth College where Robert Frost was one of his teachers and he, himself, taught at Dartmouth, Bowdoin, Wellsley, and Syracuse University where he was a founder of the graduate Creative Writing Program. Viking Penguin published his first book,* Letter from a Distant Land, *the 1956 Lamont Selection ("for the discovery and encouragement of new poetic genius") of The Academy of American Poets, which in 1983 elected him a Fellow. Other collections published by Viking Penguin include* The Islanders *(1961),* Weathers and Edges *(1966) ,* Margins *(1970),* Available Light *(1976),* Before Sleep *(1980),* Relations: Selected Poems 1950 – 1985 *(1986),* Selves *(1990),* Pairs *(1994) and* Lifelines: Selected Poems, 1950–1999 *(1999). The University of Michigan Press published his book of essays,* Trying to Say It: Outlooks and Insights on How Poems Happen, *in 1996. His work has been published in distinguished periodicals, widely anthologized, and honored by Guggenheim, Rockefeller, and National Endowment fellowships; by Colby College, The Theodore Roethke Prize, The Maurice English Prize, and an award from The National Institute of Arts and Letters. Although he declined Maine's first Poet Laureateship, those who know his work still think of him as such.*

Hazel Smith Hutchinson
Manhattan, Kansas and Bucksport

WHEN THE FOUR O'CLOCK WHISTLE BLOWS

rhubarb stalk in hand
I run out from behind
the falling down barn
to see him

not expecting
a hug
only a look
into his black metal dinner pail
just in case
there's anything left

First published in *PlainSpoken*, Weary Woman Press, Kansas, 2000.

Hazel Smith Hutchinson *was born into a St. Regis family, her father, Percy Smith, being a rigger. Hazel worked in the office of St. Regis during one summer break and received a St. Regis scholarship upon graduating in the Bucksport High School Class of 1969. She graduated from Husson College with an Associate Degree in Legal Secretarial Science which she applied in a variety of public and private professional settings through the years before and while raising her family. She has had a number of poems published in journals and anthologies, including* Begin Again, 150 Kansas Poems, *edited by Caryn Mirriam-Goldberg, Poet Laureate of Kansas, celebrating the spirit of Kansas in its Sesquicentennial year, 2011; and is a SoulCollage™ facilitator. She lives in Manhattan, Kansas with her husband, "Hutch", where their two sons and their wives settled. "We are now blessed with seven grandchildren and are happy to have a camp on Jacob Buck Pond in my childhood neighbor- hood in outer Bucksport to escape from those long, hot Kansas summers."*

Gene Sanborn
Orland

THE RIGGERS' SHACK

The Riggers' Shack consisted of an area of the maintenance section in the mill basement. The area was divided into two rooms, one being the office where Reg Howard and Kit Gross could be found. Reg was the time keeper and Kit was the foreman. Of course I am talking in your father's days.

The other area was where the men congregated, ate their lunch, had coffee breaks, and waited for the orders. It had an old stove and refrigerator where the men kept their lunches. Off to the side were two narrow alleyways each about 16 feet long. The one nearest the office was cluttered by cables, slings, rope falls and chain falls. In the very back was a wooden cabinet where the comealongs and other small tools were kept. The other held rain gear, coats, shovels, picks, and the like.

Usually a crew was made up of a lead man and two helpers unless it was a big operation and then it was a lead man and however men it would take to do the job. Your father [Percy "P.D." Smith] was a lead man with the knowledge to do any job assigned to him whether it be to clear snow, move a ten ton load, or fill an ocean going ship's hold with massive rolls of paper.

Hope this sheds a little light on the riggers. You know you are taxing my mind to remember some of this that occurred over fifty years ago, but it all seems to come clear in my mind as I relive my earlier years.

It seems nice to remember those early years. Thanks.

Also, the original unions at the mill were Pulp and Sulphite, United Papermakers and Paperworkers, International Association of Machinists, International Association of Electrical Workers and Long Shoremen's. The Long Shoremen's Union dissolved at the Bucksport mill around 1960 after they stopped shipping paper to France. Your father, being in the rigging crew, belonged to the Pulp and Sulfite Union and, because of shipping, had to be under the Long Shoremen's charter. The original charter hung in the Riggers' Shack.

*After graduating from Bucksport High School in the class of 1958, and finding that neither teaching nor business colleges were for him, **Eugene Sanborn** went to work in the Bucksport paper mill as an apprentice pipe fitter and after a short time was awarded a Journeyman's position. After gaining a permanent position, he married and started a family, sons Daniel and Brian. "Along with working at* *the mill, I worked part time for the Bucksport P.D. for about five years, and also was a call fireman for the Fire Department. In 1964 we bought our first house on the Shore Road. After quitting the Police Department I was elected to be the new training officer at the Fire Department and a short while later moved to the position of Captain. I remained with them until retiring with twenty years of service. During that time we built a new house on the Bucksmills Road. Divorce and remarriage brought a new love, Joanne Soper and sons Richie and Lee into our lives. And about that time I became the president of my local union. This lasted just a few months and I was elected to the International Association of Machinists. From that point things moved quite fast and I was appointed to the Board of Directors of the Maine AFLCIO for which I served eight years. In that time, I was also appointed by Gov. John McKernon to two terms on the Board of Directors of the Maine Workers Compensation Commission, to the Hillary Clinton Committee for National Health Care, and to the Board of Directors of the Machinists' Non Partisan Political League. Joanne and I have had the opportunity to travel a great deal with my work and feel very fortunate to have had so many wonderful experiences, including a trip to Japan and, for a few years, spending cold months in Fort Meade, Florida. We live in Orland in a house we built ourselves and where I have worked our mountain woodlots. Our hobbies have been gardening, camping, and taking part in living history reenactments in which we portray the period of 1776 to 1840. Our family now consists of four sons and their wives, 10 grandchildren and 4 great grandchildren."*

GRADUATING ONE DAY, GOING INTO THE MILL THE NEXT

One never knows, meeting oldtimers around here, what they have to tell. Like meeting stories, them- selves. That's what it was like when I met Parker Carter in the elevator of Knoxview Apartments in Bucksport a while ago. One pleasantry led to another, and it didn't take long before we were discovering connections. How he worked with my father, P.D. Smith, at the paper mill, for example, as a rigger. So it was that we made a plan to visit again, when we could, to exchange more of our stories.

I had remembered his wife of 61 years, Beverly Plant, and her younger sister, "Tita" (my own nickname) as glamorous upper classmen at Bucksport High. We laugh, remembering how we sewed clothes from grainbag cotton.

Parker graduated in 1950 and the day after, started right in working at the mill. "Those days, you knew when you got out of school you were headed for the mill." "Yes," adds Bev from their welcoming round dining table. "And it made a good living for me and our three kids."

Parker started his 43-year career working mostly for St. Regis that June with the riggers as a temporary spare until Christmas, unloading sulphur, driving truck, whatever jobs needed to be done. "Your father was a 'hellova' rigger. He was a team leader, what they called a "lead rigger," and often chose me to work with him. He was 'happy go lucky', an awful nice guy to work for. He liked to jingle change in his pocket and would loan a fellow worker a quarter for coffee even if he knew he wouldn't get it back." [*Editor scribbling through tears.*]

After the riggers crew, Parker went to the woodroom as a spare working "all over the mill doing regular mill work." In the woodroom that involved "cleaning the wood and sorting it out. If it had bark left on it it had to go back to the barking drums to get it all off, then it would come back around. I was running a chipper the last of it. A big dish with knives in it that chipped wood to send up to the sulphite mill to be processed into pulp. A man could fall into it but I never knew anyone who did. The wood came on 4' flat chain conveyors where men worked with pick poles to sort it. I had a pulp hook pulling wood off the chain and putting it on the chute going to the chipper."

"From there I went to the sulphite mill and unloaded lime rock, big chunks, put it in the towers and melted it for the acid-making process. Then it was up into the chipper loft to fill the bins from the chippers. Yes, that wood smelled good. Then downstairs to the blow pits where, after the chips were cooked in acid, you had to wash the pulp out to get the acid out."

"I bounced around a lot. Not into the paper machines much but the other end. They done away with the acid machines and sulphite mill and I was working part time in the bleach plant and went from the sulphite mill to the groundwood mill, while still working part time in the bleach plant. I became a steady operator til they shut it down, then I went to the wastewater treatment plant when that was started up and worked there til I retired in 1993. I never worked for Verso."

85

"What gets me is that eventually you had to have two years beyond high school or college. There were guys working there that couldn't read nor write. They'd come up to me to ask their schedules. Lots of men who built that mill and worked there couldn't. But I'll tell you who was one smart man—Jack Caroll. I think he was superintendent. He was an awful good man to work for. And smart. When others were figuring with slide rules he'd be way ahead of us figuring with his head and a pencil, that's how smart he was."

– With Pat Ranzoni

Parker Elwin Carter was born on March 8, 1932, at the Carter place on the River Road in Bucksport which his parents, Clarington and Vivian Carter had built in his grandparents' pasture. He grew up in Bucksport. He enjoys joking how his mother in recent years still thought he liked to wear white shirts to school. "No such thing. I wore white shirts because that's what she bought me to start school with every year – three white shirts, a pair of pants and a pair of shoes. I wore them because that's what I had, not because I liked them." He and Bev's families had been friends "all their lives so it was natural," she says, "that we became close and married in 1955, the same month of my birthday, and graduation. Our son was born in 1957 and daughters in 1959 and 1961." From his youth, Parker enjoyed making things out of wood. In high school he made a classic cedar "hope chest" he shows with pride. Their cozy apartment at Knoxview, to which they moved a couple of years ago, and which they like very much, is furnished with other pieces he has crafted through the years including a fold-down pine ironing board cupboard, and an elegant fancy pedestal table with hinged top that folds up to make a backsplash against the wall. And the frames he makes for her vivid expert colorings of animals and Native American symbols on paper and velvet make their walls a gallery honoring the life they have created together. At the time of this telling, "I'm making Christmas scenery" for our son – Santa and his Mrs. riding motorcycles!" For recreation, Parker still enjoys hunting and fishing, "mostly around here and Moosehead. He has a lifetime of stories, especially of families "who wouldn't have had food if not for game brought them," stories that won't be told. Relationships with wardens and so forth. And how a teacher on lunch duty could smell venison and would ask "who's eating deer meat?" Volumes about "the way it used to be years ago, how people fed themselves and 'the hard up' by hunting and fishing" both inside and in spite of the law. Stories that will never be heard except by the lucky who get to sit and listen to the likes of Parker Carter.

George D. Bearce (1888-1977)
Bucksport

THE OLD YEAR AND THE NEW

The St. Regis Management as usual starts the new year confident that the many problems which may be encountered will be met and solved with the assist– ance and cooperation of the entire St. Regis family. This optimistic feeling for the future is based on the record of accomplishments in the past. The year 1951 presented many problems, some seemingly insurmountable and yet they were solved. Production and safety records were established of which we can well be proud. These records did not result from the efforts of any one man or any few men but the result of cooperation and team work of everyone connected with the St. Regis Paper Company, Bucksport plant.

May we continue our present associations to the mutual benefit of all during 1952.

– Geo D. Bearce, Mill Manager
(1888 – 1977)

From *SEABOARD BULLETIN, VOL. 14* Published by St. Regis Paper Company, Bucksport, Maine, January, 1952. Richard O. Chase, Editor.

Alfred Conners [of Bucksmills] owned and ran a shingle mill for a few years in the late 1940's. At that time, only a few men had jobs downtown and none of the women were employed outside of the home. He worked on the rake in the yard at St. Regis before that. In the early1950's he was hired to work in the lab at the mill which he did until he retired in 1976. Some of the women, like his wife Shirley [Coombs], began to work downtown. In the early 1950s she worked a couple days a week as a cook for Mr. Bearce, the mill manager, and for Mr. Walker, the assistant mill manager.

From *HISTORY OF BUCK'S MILLS COMMUNITY BUILDING 1947 – 1960,* by Christine Conners Gray, 2004. Courtesy of Raymond Bishop.

LEWISTON EVENING JOURNAL August 10, 1977

"Bearce Services Are Scheduled"

 Bucksport, Maine (AP) – Funeral services are scheduled for Friday afternoon here for George Bearce, a former member of the governor's executive council.

 Bearce, who was a member of Maine's 100th Legislature, died Monday while visiting in Norway. He was 89 years old.

 He was manager of the St. Regis Paper Co. here from 1935 to 1956, a former trustee of the University of Maine and former president of the Maine Chamber of Commerce.

 He is survived by his widow.

Paul Corrigan
Millinocket

SHIFTWORK: A SEQUENCE

I. THE PULP AND SULPHITE BROTHERHOOD

My hands have lost their gritty shine
but still have the timing and the touch
to spear a raft of pulp
and float it to a grinder sluice.
Few leave this town without such skill.
I thought of staying on, letting
the years spin like grinder wheels,
the rhythms of work settling
into my sinews. Lifers
treated me well, called me Curly,
bought me rounds down at Sonny's.
I saw them all as a kid
shuttling to and from the mill,
going in circles, their women
cool and aloof at the center,
sending them away with a kiss
to work the twelve to eight,
greeting them with a kiss next day
at the gate. They never saw me.
. . . .
Poling wood those summers, I felt
the rhythms catching in my blood,
my hands callused and quick
with a pole, the shift passing swiftly,
each hour like the last. And when I
smelled trout frying on lunch break
or shared a chunk of someone's venison steak,
I would drift off into the balsam airs
of unbroken forests, into the world
of which we all partook beyond the shift,
where the eye could rest on a spruce
horizon or a windswept lake,

and the seasons lend their fare
to each man's freezer.
It would only last a moment,
that sense of the quiet landlocked
enfolding the factory which
enfolded us all, then the racket
would swell up around me, the pulp
would thud, the grinder presses hiss
and I would again be part of the crew,
just someone else with the stains
of pitch on his palms, that
balsam balm that had worked itself
into the grain of our lives.

St. Regis Paper Co. Long Log Drive on Machias River, Washington County, Maine. 4/28/51, photographer unknown. River drivers using peavies working on the log jam at Carrick Pitch. A total of 1.5 million feet of logs were tied up in the jam. River drivers working from dawn until dusk broke the jam in one day. Courtesy of the Forest History Society.

II. OLD WOODPOLERS

Their forearm veins are thick as nylon cord.
They have calluses the size of quarters.
Their poles are sandpapered smooth,
the points honed sharp on an emery wheel
so a light poke embeds the steel
half an inch through pulp logs
passing on the current.

All the men are old tonight and quiet.
Stooped next to the troughs,
they arrange logs
in groups of threes and fours.
Their spare quick motions
have a fierce regularity
that never slackens.
They let the water
work for them, never going
against the current.

III.   THE BOSS MACHINE-TENDER AFTER LOSING A SON

When paper snaps in machines,
he pokes through greasy alleys, flashlight
beaming among clamoring wheels
and huge whirring belts.
He'll run himself ragged
getting sheets back on the reels,
shelving time for moments
when the clock ticks like a dream
of flawless paper. Then he smokes
his pipe in the office, and recalls
the smooth glide of his Old Town canoe.

He moves through waters
that sustained father and son-in-law
between slender, canvassed ribs.
The two drift leisurely, machinery roaring
like distant whitewater
inside his throbbing temples,

while somewhere back of his mind,
hidden like jagged river rock,
lies the night he shut down
machine number nine
to pull out his boy.

IV. A LIFER

Tonight the August moon hangs
above the wood chip silos. Soon bark
will harden on the logs. Seasoned hands
will gripe as half-peeled wood spills from the drums.
This job's a bitch when pulp peels hard each fall.
Men bust their butts skinning logs
while silo volume drops. Except for spot checks
by the boss, I hardly care
if bark stains paper brown.

. . . .

Those few that leave
for easy bucks out in "Timbuctoo"
can't stay away, are back before
too many dawns come gray and cold
to wood yards where pulp piles up.
Before I punch a week of work they're back
it seems, itching to pick up this cold routine.
You'd think, the way they talk, they had more reason
than the moon for coming back around.

Editor's note: Grateful acknowledgment is made for the author's permission to include these poems from his book, *At the Grave of the Unknown Riverdriver, Poems of the Upcountry* (North Country Press, 1992) in this collection documenting papermaking in Maine. Drawn from the realities of Millinocket's Great Northern Paper Co. (1877 – 2014), they are offered by Mr. Corrigan in solidarity with the Bucksport mill's people.

As well as being a writer, **Paul Corrigan, Jr.** *is a teacher and outdoorsman. He holds a Masters Degree in Creative writing and Literature from Brown University where he won the 1976 Academy of American Poets Award. His poetry, often about his native Maine, has been published nationwide and his essays* *on teaching poetry in a maximum security prison and on ways of involving students in a classroom writing apprenticeship have appeared in the journal,* Blue Line, *and the national education journal,* Voices in the Middle. *His most recent project is a memoir about being a wilderness therapist and instructor for at-risk teenage girls. "Before settling down to become a high school English teacher in central Maine, I was an itinerant poet in the public schools in New York State. In the manner of an old time circuit preacher I brought the good news of poetry to school districts from Long Island to the Adirondacks and west to Buffalo. I found ways for students who had never written poetry, particularly boys with little interest in writing and literature, to create their own body of work which they read aloud to gatherings of family and friends. For years, I was a participant in the Maine Touring Artist Program. My life-long love of the outdoors was handed down to me by my dad and by other woodsmen from Dad's generation. He and I fished, canoed and hunted together and I was an enthusiastic listener to stories told and retold around the fire at night in the family cabin in Millinocket. Over the years, I mastered woods skills such as fire building and emergency shelter construction, became an experienced fly fisher, hunter, canoeist and bird watcher, worked as a whitewater raft guide for several summers, and am a Registered Maine Guide. Most of all, my years as a wilderness instructor deepened my belief in the wild as a place of healing."*

Janet Mercer

SEARS, MONTGOMERY WARD, J.C. PENNEY, *LIFE* AND *TIME* AT MOPANG

My mother, Pat Edgecomb, started her career at the Woodlands Office working for Herb Weller in 1953. Tuck Bayer, the manager, hired her in 1956 to be his assistant at St. Regis Paper Co. She also worked for managers Gerace, Pollard and Bob McDonald.

She remembers that men could smoke at their desks, but the women had to smoke in the ladies room. She retired after 32 years.

Homer Edgecomb ran Mopang Lodge owned by the mill. At the lodge, clients Sears & Roebuck, Montgomery Ward, JC Penney, *Life* and *Time* magazines, among others, enjoyed the surroundings while negotiating contracts with the mill associates.

Janet Edgecomb Mercer *is a member of the Bucksport High School class of 1966.*

Editor's note:
According to the Maine Dept. of Inland Fisheries and Wildlife, Mopang Lake is a moderate size, clear, scenic water located north of "The Airline" road in Washington County with an area of 1,487 acres and maximum depth of 76 feet. Access is gained by a "good gravel road" which leaves "The Airline" about two miles off the Mopang Stream bridge, a good boat launch being maintained by owners of the Bucksport paper mill through the years. Its principal fishery has been landlocked salmon, white perch and splake when they were introduced in the '90s. Containing a moderate volume of cold, well-oxygenated water suitable for coldwater sportfish, the winter fishery was especially popular with anglers for both stocked and wild salmon. The outlet, Mopang Stream, further along, was reportedly one of the best trout streams in Downeast Maine. From time to time, a vintage classified ad for Mopang Lodge has appeared on the internet auction site, "e-Bay."

STOPPING FOR LL BEAN BOOTS ON THE WAY TO BUCKSPORT

Fred Goodwill, along with sons Bill and Dave, came to Bucksport in the summer of 1954 - that is of course after stopping at LL Bean to buy "new boots." My Dad was transferred from the St. Regis Paper Mill in Kalamazoo, Michigan to the St. Regis mill in Bucksport.

We – Dave and I became fast friends with the locals in no time – that being the Redmans – Rod and Frank, Jim Swenson, Dale Hanson, and others. We both attended Bucksport High School – I graduating in 1956 and Dave in 1958. And we both participated in sports – I running track for 2 years and David playing football. We remember our father as a decent and fair role model parent which contributed to our upbringing in the wonderful town of Bucksport. He had many good friends and loyal men and women that contributed to his success as mill manager.

My father retired from the mill in 1961 and upon his retirement he and my mother moved to Newfane, Vermont and while living there he continued his involvement in the paper industry as a consultant to paper companies traveling to Russia, Spain and Argentina. Upon his retirement as a consultant they moved to Vero Beach, Florida where he lived until the time of his death in 1983.

*After finishing school in Bucksport, **William Goodwill** graduated from the University of Maine with a degree in biology. "As far as places I've lived - it would be New Hampshire and Maine - but living in Maine is the best! Karen and I have travelled quite a bit since we have been married - mostly to 'warm' places - and my love of birding has taken us to those places. At the top of the list would probably be Trinidad and Tobago and Belize although we have spent time in the US birding also. We have also done all the Spanish Virgin Islands and the British Virgin Islands and those trips were on a sailing adventure aboard a Windjammer. Pleasures and hobbies would be birding. I have been active with Audubon Societies in both NH and Maine and for the past 30 – 40 years have taken part in the annual Christmas Bird Counts in both states as well as in the Annual Breeding Bird Survey for the US Dept. of the Interior." Bill presently sits on two boards – The Board of Trustees of the Maine Audubon and The Board of the Friends of Maine Seabird Islands. He has conducted programs in the local area for*

Mid-Coast Audubon of which he is a former Director, and independently for SAD 40 and Adult Education Courses at Camden High School. As a Consultant to The Rush of Wings Seabird Rehabilitation Center *in Friendship (www.ontherushofwings.org), Bill is cited as "a lifelong birder and ever curious naturalist" that they are "honored to have in their midst," his service also including Past President of the Capital Chapter and Nashua Chapter of the Audubon Society of NH, as well as Past President of the Mid-Coast Audubon of Maine. He also "takes enormous pleasure spending time with my grandchildren - 3 girls and 2 boys plus spending time on the tennis court both in summer and winter (indoors). My church is also a big part of my life - having been born into the Episcopal Church, we now attend St. John Baptist where I am a lay reader - former vestry and Eucharistic assistant."*

Jean Smith (1916-2014)
Bucksport

5 KIDS, NO RUNNING HOT WATER, PAPERBOATS, PIES & CAKES & ROCK 'N' ROLL

Lines from the journals and letters of a rigger's wife between innumerable pies and cakes for Bucksmills Community Club, 4–H, East Bucksport Methodist Church, Victory Grange and other benefit suppers and sales.

(excerpts from her journal, handmade with cardboard and storm-window plastic cover)

Friday, April 5, 1957
Cold. Snowed most of the day. Turned to rain and has rained steady for about 8 hrs. I did not go out town last night as Percy went up to the hall [Bucksmills Community Building] to work. He brought home some groceries so I didn't have to go out after all. What a nasty mess it is. It is 12 o'clock midnight and it has poured since about 3 this afternoon. I have slept most of evening in chair like I did last night so I didn't see much TV.

Sunday, April 7, 1957
Sunny and cold and windy. Got the kids all up as I had to take them with me when I went to the mill with Percy. Got a lot done this morning. Got dinner started before I took them to Sunday School. I made 2 pies before dinner and Linda made muffins which were very good. After dinner I cleaned up the house and Loretta and Patricia got home at 3 o'clock. Went after Percy at 4. The ones who went to All State Music Festival in Augusta with our two were Peter Leighton, Rod Redman, Jimmy Swenson, Sandra Bowden, Georgeane Harris and Caroline Turner.

Monday, April 8, 1957
Windy, sunny, not so cold. Took Percy to the mill so I could have the car again. I've got to get Ernie some pants, shoes and tie for the operetta tomorrow night. Did up the work and went out town. Glenroy [sister-in -law] gave me a cup of coffee and I did some shopping for her. Got shoes for Hazel, shoes, pants, tie and socks for Ernie at Rosen's and paid $15. on bill. Ate lunch at Glenroy's. Oh yes, paid light and tel. bills. Watched stories and came home. Hazel's shoes were too small so when I went after Pat (Loretta came on bus) exchanged them for size 9 ½. Shampooed Hazel's hair. Watered and fed the barn animals. Percy worked on paper boat til 9 tonight. Went after him at that time. Busy busy day believe me. Percy was up at 4:30 this morning – got breakfast and called me at 5 so it has been a very long day even though it went fast. 11 P.M. right now.

Tuesday April 9, 1957

What a snow storm. It started snowing just about the time the school bus came. The old snow plow didn't get around til after dinner. There's about 6 or 7 inches of wet snow, and getting colder. The operetta was cancelled. It's going to be tomorrow night instead and the supper Thurs. night instead of Wed. Both girls came home on bus. Percy went up to Ernie Cole's after supper and I slept in chair all evening.

Monday April 22, 1957

Weather warm sunny with some wind. Did a big wash. Mary Gross was over and Bea Mercer spent the afternoon with me. Percy took Pat practice driving then he went after Loretta in town. She had practice for senior pageant. I was over to Hazel Gross's for a few min. to return potatoes I borrowed Sunday. Made a cake and frosted it after the kids went to bed. It's 8 p.m. I'm going to bed. Percy is up to Ernie Coles I guess and the girls are studying, washing hair, dancing and singing ~

Monday April 29, 1957

Weather sunny and cool. Made 2 pies for 4-H supper. Percy went to auction alone with car. Cleaned up house. Carlton Willis brought Loretta and Pat home about 4:30. We all went up to the hall to supper. Percy got back in time for supper. It was delicious. Linda had to work but the rest of us walked back. We also walked up as Percy hadn't gotten back by then. She rode home with Vernice White.

Tuesday April 30, 1957

Cloudy and cold. It rained most of the night but has cleared off and very windy. Percy has gone to the dump and to see about a spare tire. Glenroy was going to ride out on the mail but missed Alton [Hutchins] and started walking and got a ride. Got here before the mail came. Percy has been working on his fences all day. He got a spare tire and had the car greased and oil changed. I took Glenroy out about 3. Mrs. Patton called about 10 or 10:30 and said Linda wasn't feeling very well. I couldn't go after her as Percy had the car. Took Glen home around 3 and came home and got supper. Loretta came home on the bus but Pat had to stay to work for Junior Prom. After supper Ernest and Glen and kids came out and spent the evening. TV was the best I've ever seen, especially Panic and Jane Wyman shows. Linda went to bed. She's not going to school tomorrow. Percy took Glen and Ernest home.

Wednesday May 1, 1957

Sunny and cool. I haven't done much. Linda stayed home and feels better this afternoon. Percy went out and got 3 prs. sneakers for the little kids. Loretta is staying at friend's in town tonight. Pat came on bus and finished making the pizzas I'd started. Linda took the shower gift up to Dottie's and I went in to see Dr. Thegen. He gave me a thorough examination and I'm in perfect health outside of the pain in my leg and arm which is a pressure on a nerve and I'm over tired. Stopped in to Bea's and she made me some coffee. Dr. T. gave me a shot and some pills and told me to come back next week if I didn't feel better.

Thursday May 2, 1957
Windy and very cold. I nearly froze all day. Temperature is 34° over news at Bangor. Washed all day. Put the machine [wringer] away at 3:30 p.m. Percy and Ernie Cole went to the auction in his truck.

Friday May 3, 1957
Windy and quite cold – not so cold as yesterday. We went out and got some groceries then took a ride down to Camden. Beulah is home from hospital and looks fine. Saw Fred at store and he gave us 2 jump ropes. Stopped at Belfast on way home and bought some things for the kids. Percy bought Patricia a nice big record of hymns and Loretta a big popular hit record. We ate supper at Ernest's and Glenroy's. The girls went to bed early as they go to a music festival at old Town tomorrow with the band. The bus leaves at 7:30 or 7:45. They can ride out on it as Maynard Gross is going to drive.

Saturday May 4, 1957
Weather clear – sunny and windy. The little kids dug some dandelion greens. I wasn't up when the big girls went but they looked fine and happy. They don't know how lucky they are. They are having the time of their life and don't realize it. I feel so rotten it isn't funny. Did I mention that Mary Gross is working at 5 & 10. p.s. Both girls went to Salisbury's in the Town Site to a pajama party tonight.

Sunday May 5, 1957
Windy – clear – The girls didn't come home until about 5 p.m. So just Hazel and Linda went to Sunday School. Ernie has the croup. It was bad this morning and not much better today. The girls had a good time at the pajama party. Hazel, Linda and Ernie dug greens yesterday and we had them for dinner today and were they good. Believe me I haven't done much today. My foot aches pretty bad and I've had a sore eye besides everything else. Patricia is 17 today!

Monday May 6, 1957
Sunny and warm. I was so sick I didn't get up except to get Ernie some dinner as he couldn't go to school. Loretta is busy nearly every night now with the senior pageant.

Tuesday May 7, 1957
Sunny and warm. Did the washing and took my pills as ordered and became very sick after dinner and had to go to bed after Ernie ate. He is good to take care of alone. He has been very good to me while I've been sick and minded very well.

Wednesday May 8, 1957
Sunny and extremely warm. They said 100° on Main St. in Bucksport. Last night the girls went to the Thespian Banquet at Jed Prouty Tavern and had a nice evening. I have felt better today but the work is discouraging. I sent out most of the graduation announcements. A few more left to do. Ernest came out and helped Percy. Loretta and Pat were both out. Ernie went out this afternoon for the first time. I think he can go to school tomorrow. I have just finished the dishes and it is 11:10 p.m. And I've just taken 2 Anacin and am going to bed.

Thursday May 9, 1957

Warm and cloudy. I think Ernie has measles. He's all broken out with a red rash. No I guess he hasn't. I rubbed musterole on his chest and neck and it was quite strong so I guess that is what it is unless it's heat rash and he's quite warmly dressed. There's not much to write. I got a nice letter from Percy's mother.

Friday May 10, 1957

Warm and sunny. Went in town and got groceries and things for Pat's party. Loretta went to Connie Baker's pajama party and Pat went to a Rock and Roll dance at Colon and Hazel McDonald's Promenade In under the bridge. It's raining hard tonight. I feel terrible but we took Ernest and Glen and our kids over to Fat's [Crosby's] and got an ice cream.

Saturday May 11, 1957

Sunny and warm. Made yeast bread, baked beans, made 2 orange cakes, 1 choc. Cake and a extra big white birthday cake. I had Ernest and family to supper. Percy got me a doz. beautiful mixed carnations and a lovely card for Mothers Day. They are lovely. Pat and I went up to the hall with the cake, napkins, spoons and plates etc. Percy brought the ice cream about 8 p.m. They had a fine time. Pat, Loretta, cousin Beulah, Christine Conners, Janie Grunwald, Jane Harvey, Beverly Mercer, Georgeane Harris, Patti Millet, Ruthie McAllian, Joan Guse, Evora Bunker, Jackie Willette, Sandra Salisbury, Judy Cropley.

Sunday May 12, 1957

Cloudy and cool. Took Percy to the mill and washed dishes all forenoon. Gave Ernie, Linda and Hazel their baths, etc. Sunday School was at 1 p.m. this afternoon. I never felt worse. I slept in the car until church time. I took 4 Anacin today. Ruth Wardwell came with the kids to have their piano lesson. After supper Bump and Margaret [Smith] came and I had such a headache I had to take 2 more Anacin. Ernie has 3 tickets to sell for church supper next Sat. night.

Monday May 13, 1957

Cloudy and misty. They all went to school. I feel like I'd been sick a month in bed. Went to bed at noon and stayed until 3:30. Did the washing. Ellen was here for 4–H. Percy worked on the paper boat.

Tuesday May 14, 1957

Sunny and warm. Did most of ironing. Hazel did not go to school. She has a bad cold. Got a letter from Percy's mother with his brother Leo's and Maurice's addresses. She told me about [his cousin] Barbara's husband getting hurt so badly. And [his cousin] Irene has a baby boy, no details. Both girls came home on bus and we all ate early. Percy planted his potatoes and I dug dandelion greens. Loretta has a bad cold. Pat went to work on Junior Prom and also worked on her dress. She was initiated into the National Honor Society in chapel this morning!

Wednesday May 15, 1957

Pouring rain storm. Percy got his garden in just in time. He has worked awfully hard. Hazel and Loretta did not go to school. Their colds and coughs are bad. Barbara [White], Julia and Linda were here to-night.

Thursday May 16, 1957

Cold. Got groceries early this morning and zipper for Pat for her gown. Glenroy came out with me and we watched stories. Went back about 3:15 – picked up Hazel, Ernie and Linda and took Linda to library where she returned book and got another. Parked in front of 5 & 10 and they all went shopping. Came home made fudge and they filled the Maybaskets they had made. Percy worked on paper boat but came home earlier than I expected so he took them to hang Maybaskets while I made supper.

Friday May 17, 1957

Percy's mother's birthday. Cool and sunny. Percy, Loretta and I went to Bangor to get Percy a suit, Loretta a suit and dresses and something for myself for graduation. Made the car payment and came home and Percy worked in garden and trimmed hedges. Patricia pressed her gown and looked wonderful when she was ready to go to the Prom. She went with Donnis P. Loretta went to movies with John C. Linda stayed out to [cousin] Ellen's. Linda has been out town 2 nights this week selling tickets for the church supper Friday night. We all had chicken for supper and when she got home she was so pleased.

> **Post card of May 17th:** *Mrs. Percy Smith, Star Route*
> *Will you give 2 pies and 2 cakes for Community Club supper on May 25th?*
> *Also will you help wait on tables (also one of your girls, if possible)?*
> *Thank you – Ginny Gross*

Saturday May 18, 1957

Cloudy and cool. Beulah came home with Pat. They had a wonderful time at the Prom and afterwards went to Bangor to Millers to eat. Well I made 2 pies for church supper, bread for dinner and doughnuts. This afternoon I did the washing and got supper for Beulah, Loretta and I. Percy, Ernest, Glenroy, Ellen, Linda, Ernie and Hazel went to the supper and Pat worked on it and came home with Mary. I didn't get through work until 8 p.m. Loretta ironed 3 hrs. Loretta and Pat were both asked to go to movies but I decided they'd better stay home one night especially Sat. night. They were both tired. Pat took Ernie out with her and Beulah this p.m. to the track meet and he had a good time.

Sunday May 19, 1957

Cold – sunny, windy. Cleaned up kitchen and washed some more dishes. Hazel Gross took the kids to Sunday School. Washed again this p.m. Ernie and Hazel ran away – down the brook to the crossing.

Monday May 20, 1957

It has rained hard all day. I took 2 of the pills Dr. T gave me, as ordered and I became very sick so that is one thing that ails me. I felt just as bad today – I took them yesterday. I must get to him as soon as I can and tell him – perhaps he can give me a tonic and make me feel better. Made 2 pies and a cake for

Percy to take to the Community Club meeting tonight. Linda is sick tonight. Pat went to a church supper and discussion tonight. Cat had 2 kittens.

Tuesday May 21, 1957
Sunny and cool. Linda and Hazel were very conveniently sick when they found out about the kittens so they didn't go to school. They feel quite well this p.m. And are out playing. Sister Charlotte called up. I am so sorry. It's too bad Stan had to hurt his back. I know they don't want pity because we didn't when we were up against it. People were wonderful to us. It's a hard situation these days.

Wednesday May 22, 1957
Beautiful day. Warm and sunny. The sounds and smells out of doors are just out of this world. Didn't get off to a good start but Percy brought the car home so I could have it this p.m. Called for oil and had 1 barrel filled. The girls looked wonderful when they went to Athletic Banquet tonight. Mama called from Belfast about 5. Her voice sounded real good.

Thursday May 23, 1957
Foggy and damp this morning. I had the car today. Got the rest of my groceries. Watched stories at Glenroy's Stopped at Bea's for awhile and had coffee. Haven't done much today. Ellen and Dianne Libbey were here to supper. Ernie went to Susanne Billing's birthday party. After the party Patricia and the girls went up to 4–H practice. The Clairs were here and we had coffee and talked. They brought a graduation present to Loretta. It was a gift of money from all the family. It was very nice of them. After they went Mrs. Libby came after Dianne and the kids all played out of doors til dark. I went to bed shortly after she left. Loretta was so pleased with her present she didn't know what to say.

Friday May 24, 1957
  A lovely day. Did the washing. After the stories were over Percy and I went over to Bump and Margaret's [Smith] in Millvale. Their house looks lovely. I went into town and got the girls or rather Loretta. Pat had to stay out. Wilbur Wilson went out with us when we went to high school. Glen went with me. It was Exhibition Night and very good. After it was over Pat & Loretta went over to Promenade In. When I got home Percy said Ernie had jammed his finger pretty bad and it was. All the kids were up. Linda and Percy have just arrived from taking Ernest and Glenroy home.

Saturday May 25, 1957
Beautiful day. I went back to bed after Percy went to work and did not get up until 9:45. Made 2 cherry pies. Loretta and I went to work up to supper at hall at 5 and I worked until about 7:30. I tended biscuits and Linda and Loretta waited on tables. Ernest and Glenroy came out and they, Percy and kids went up there to supper. Loretta went over to Marjorie Mann's to stay all night and go to the dance. Pat went to the movies in Bangor.

Sunday May 26, 1957
Beautiful day. I took the kids to Sunday school and stayed. They practiced their pieces for Childrens Day. We went over to Fat's and Tita borrowed Ruthie's notes and then over to Orland and got Loretta and came home. Linda went with 4-H to church in Bangor (National 4-H Sunday), They visited the

new Mormon Church. Sandra Bowden came to study with Patricia. Winnie Stanley and another fellow came from N.E. Harbor.

Wednesday May 29, 1957
Nice day. Got groceries. Pay Day. Loretta went to Sweetheart contest with F.F.A [Future Farmers of America] to Brooks. She was chosen Sweetheart at B.H.S. A girl from E. Corinth or Corinna won.

Thursday May 30, 1957
Beautiful day. Had the car. Took the girls to bus at 7:45 to go to Blue Hill to Parade. Went after Percy at the mill at 4 and stayed out to Parade.

Friday May 31, 1957
Beautiful – Percy's day off. Did Loretta's pressing – got my neck clipped, got ready and went to Senior's Last Chapel. I never went before. Pat came home with us and Loretta changed and stayed out to go to Banquet in Rockland. Percy and Pat went and got chicken baskets for us out to Fat's. Percy took Pat out at 4:15 so she could parade in Orland. She went to dance after.

Saturday June 1, 1957
Beautiful day. Took Percy to work came home and got Loretta and took her to the bus to go on class trip. Came home took the kids to get haircuts. Came home – lunch – Mrs. Johnson came with Pat's things. I ordered lipstick for myself and she gave me a sample. Went out and got Percy. Got home Mama, [brother] George and Gail were here. She brought us all some nice things from Florida. Gail gave me a box of Candy's old clothes. They stayed to supper. Pat did all day's dishes, made a cake and cleaned up the house and took care of the kids while I was at the mill for Percy. Willie was over and gave Loretta a graduation Present. George and Gail gave her a lovely pen and Mama gave her a necklace. Jeannette, [brothers] Richard, Ernest and Glenroy were here.

Sunday June 2, 1957
Cloudy and misty. We all got to bed early last night. Took Percy to work. Hazel Gross took the kids to Sunday school. Got lunch and took Loretta and Pat to Baccalaureate Sermon at high school. It has poured all the afternoon. Went after them at 3. Went after Loretta at 5 at Mitty Keene's [lunch shop on Central St.]. Percy called at 4:30 and said he'd have to work overtime. At 6:30 I left for Castine – got some groceries first. Stayed at George and Gail's until about 8. Got kids' clothes ready for school. Mama came back with me to stay for graduation. Percy worked until 11 p.m. Went after him. I'm tired.

Monday June 3 1957
Nice day. Last day of school for little kids. Put up cold lunches for them and they were happy. Percy came home to dinner. I washed. Mama mended for me. Dress rehearsal.

Tuesday June 4, 1957   Graduation Day

Weather cold, rainy at times – cloudy. The kids acted awful. Mama mended about all day. I pressed and ironed most of the day and got a very easy supper. Percy took Ernie and Hazel, Loretta and Patricia out first about 6:15. Then Ernest's family. Then we left at 7:15. Our seats were center front. Mama and Linda sat together and Hazel and Ernie sat with Ernest and Glenroy. Pat with band. Loretta did a wonderful job in the pageant. She sang with Rod Redman and also did a solo. Percy and I were both so proud of her. Graduation is so sad but I developed such a head ache I couldn't cry as much as I felt like it. Loretta had some pictures taken. She went to Bar Harbor and Pat to a party – I was glad to get home.

Wednesday June 5, 1957

Sunny and cold. Hazel is very croupy. Loretta and Cynthia Leach came about 9:30 and took off again for Bar Harbor for the day. Patricia went to Bar Harbor with Terry Brooks, Connie and Wilbur. I took Mama down to George's. Picked up Percy at mill. Ernie and Hazel are both sick. Willie came over. He has a new car – Ford. I've been to bed twice and had to get up for company. Mary Gross was over. Percy and Linda went up to Ernie Cole's. What a miserable head ache I have and I feel awful. Mama was the only one on my side of the family that came to Loretta's graduation and she looked so nice and did her part so well. She had so many lovely presents and lots of money, and a wonderful time. At least she has been on the go continuously all week day and night. Hazel and Ernie are both sick tonight.

Thursday June 6, 1957

A beautiful day. Both girls were home last night and today. I finally got rid of part of my headache. Percy worked on paper boat today and tonight, late. Keith and Sharon Gross were over most of the day. Ernie went fishing twice down to the brook.

Friday June 7, 1957

Rainy most of day. Cleared off and sunny at supper time. Loretta cleaned her room and did dinner dishes. Pat cleaned bathroom and got dinner. I did the rest of upstairs and washed the floors up there. Patricia also did kitchen and breakfast dishes. Percy went to Esso and I got some groceries. I had a nice talk with Mr. Ernest [principal] today. I will be glad when I know what Loretta is going to do. Mr. Ernest said he'd help her get in any school if she'd only let him know. He thinks very highly of her.

(from letters to daughters working at summer hotel on Mt. Desert Island)

Bucksmills, Sunday July 8, 6:30 p.m.

Dear Loretta & Patricia: While the kids are still asleep I will write a little to you and some time today I'll have them each write a little letter to you. I'm sorry about last night but neither one of us would have been able to make the drive down there and back. Your father had Dr. Thegen examine his chest and heart and he said he had torn a ligament in his chest. (by coughing so hard) His heart is o.k. Leo came out here about 9:30 and I was washing as usual. I had the down stairs work all done and most of the washing done. We had a cup of coffee and then he mowed part of the lawn and ran out of gas. Well Hazel stayed out to Ellen's night before last and had a wonderful time. I missed her something awful especially at bed time. Ellen took her to the swimming pool yesterday and she came home when your father came home from the mill. The paper boat hasn't come yet. I picked peas yesterday for supper with Ernie's help and Linda stayed at the house so she could answer the phone if it rang. Patricia, Mr. Craig is working in your father's crew and he and Daddy had quite a talk about you two girls! He seemed so pleased to hear how the teachers felt about you both. I saw Pearl Cunningham and told her you got your license and she said "good – I know how I felt when I got mine!" By the way Patricia if you have those Methodist books that Richard Gross sent over will you please either send them to him (be sure to put the address on and address it to Mrs. Thomas Gross, Bucksmills, Bucksport, Me) She was asking me about them yesterday and told me how much they cost etc. If you don't get a chance to send them put them where you can find them in a hurry so if and when we come down we can bring them back with us. I looked for them here but couldn't find them so decided you took them with you. Did you get the shoes you sent for from Spiegels catalog and how did they fit? Loretta how much do you want to pay on your bill at Rosen's? I have paid $5. on Dr. Gould's bill so all there is left is $5. We are paying on Eastern Maine Gen Hospital, Rosens and Dr. Gould's bills at present. Then we have to start on your father's surgeon It's going to take quite a while but a little each week will all add up. I've got the house pretty well cleaned up. I am anxious to get started on it now. I want to do so many things it's hard to decide where to start. I guess the big front room will be first so we can get it settled as I'm anxious to use it. We miss you girls awful. Every night about 11 p.m. Percy and I say it seems like its time for you to be coming through the kitchen door and saying "hi". The porch light is left on every night out of habit! Oh yes, your record is here Loretta. I didn't open it I just put it high up in the cupboard just as it came. Do you play the records much or do you have time? Daddy was very pleased and quite surprised I think when he read about your 2 outside jobs! Patricia let me hear about your job etc. You haven't said very much about it as yet! I hope you girls don't mind me writing to you together. I can write more that way and I don't like to bother writing 2 letters when I can say the same things in one. I hope you'll answer all my questions and each of you write a nice long letter etc. Did you have a good 4th? Have you had much mail? Have you met a lot of kids? How do you all get along? Monday morning. Just as soon as I go out town again I'll pay your bill at Rosens Loretta with the money you sent up and put the other $7. away which I've already done. Thanks for sending up the books Patricia. I took them right over as soon as I got them. Leo and Billy were here yesterday around noon. They didn't stay very long, maybe an hour. It was at dinner time and Percy came home to dinner. It seems awful without you two here. Well Billy left in their car when Percy went and Leo took the kids for a ride on the turkey path then left. He looked just the same as ever and the kids were excited to see him as usual. I understood him to say his ship might be going to Norfolk, Virginia. Well I've got to get this in the mail. Linda has just made a pan of muffins. She is going to make them every morning she says. Please write. Love from us all God Bless you both Mama XXXX I'll send your things you asked for Pat as soon as I can get them together. It will be a day or two before I can get in town for needles and thread as Daddy has the car and paper boat is in today.

Thursday a.m.   July 11, 1957

Dear Girls: Just a line to let you know I am thinking about you and hope you are getting along good and like your work. Ernie wrote a song called "Blouse Blues" the other afternoon while it was raining. Daddy got quite a kick out of it. Please don't let anything happen to it as I'd like to keep it!

[in his printing, enclosed]

> Way are The clouDs
> So Blue. IS it because
> It was raining. Oh.
> I wish It wouldn't.
> Rain at all. BodaBom.
> Bom Bom. Blos Blues.

                    Ernie Smith age 8

Yesterday was quite a day. I left the car lights on until the battery was dead and had to call the garage and have them come out and start the car. Ernie plugged in the radio and blew a fuse and bent the plug so I can't use the radio til he gets a new plug in. The TV has gone again, but Mr. Freeman fixed it last night. I had to cook for food sale and the frosting wouldn't harden and it wasn't ready when they came after it. Keith and Ernie had a little misunderstanding – and I guess Daddy and Tommy did too —— ? ? ? ? ? ? ? Well anyway I've had a lovely time. Believe it or not. I hope next time I can write something a little more pleasant. I'm so sick of this rain I could <u>screech</u>! There isn't much to write. I'll send your things as soon as I can get the thread and needles. I am going to have a couple hours to myself tomorrow I hope so I can do some things in town I want to. Please write both of you. So long and love from us all Mama X X X X

Saturday July 13, 1957

Dear Girls, Just a line this morning. You won't get it until Monday but I'll send it out anyway. How are you getting along and how is your health? Your little brother got hurt again. He tried to break a big rock and a junk of it bounced back and struck him halfway between his eye and mouth. It drove his tooth almost through the flesh and made a gash a good inch inside his upper lip. That was Wednesday night. No I guess it was Thursday night and he couldn't eat and threw up all day yesterday. He feels a little better this morning. I guess he's over the worst of it as the cut is healed over this morning. There's quite a bruise on his face. Boy I hope he don't kill himself! He sure has his troubles. He'll probably write a song "Big Rock Blues" now! Well I've made yeast bread and got the washing [wringer machine] nearly done. Keith is over to play. I've got to make 3 pies for the supper yet, get the kitchen cleaned up before Mrs. Johnson comes and this p.m. I've got to pick peas and get supper. I am not going to work up to the hall I just can't do it. When night comes I'll be ready for bed I guess, at least that's what I'm going to do whether anyone likes it or not. Please please write.

Thursday July 25, 1957

Dear Loretta and Patricia: I didn't hear if you got back Mon. nite or not but presume that you did. Say "hello" to those two nice girls you brought with you also the boys. They were very nice. Wish you could come every week! Try to make it again soon as it is something to look forward to. We enjoyed your visit so much but the kids were so tired. They were so afraid you weren't coming then they didn't want you to go back! Linda got over her spell after awhile. She wanted to go back with you so bad! Hope you had enough to eat! Daddy and the kids went blueberrying on Mt. Olive last night and got 3 qts. I made 2 doz. blueberry muffins. Ernie ate 5 and Hazel ate 4. We also had beet greens from our garden and he says that if nothing happens to them we'll have lots of cucumbers! Here come the mustard pickles! I've got the bantam chickens in the big hen house in the stable and they are happy I guess. They have grown nearly an inch in just 2 or 3 days. Well I've got to get busy. I'd like to finish my dress. I have made so many mistakes on it that it will only serve as a housedress now. It's a hard pattern to make if you don't know much about sewing! I'm going to get another pattern tomorrow if I go in town by myself. I don't think we'll be down to see you tomorrow but maybe next week as we want to work on the front room. It's all ready to paint now and I do want to get it done and get the piano in there. I don't have much time and when I do I'm usually too exhausted and I mean exhausted. Well girls, so long for now and God Bless you both. Please write to your loving Mother & Dad X X X X

August 13, 1957
49° in Bangor at 6 a.m. How are you both and what is the latest? I'll be glad when you are both home again so we can have a talk. Daddy worked on the paper boat all day Sunday until 9 p.m. And yesterday until 9. He is very tired. After he got home last night I took the kids over roller skating. They skated until 10:30 so they had some time to skate after all. There was a big crowd. Walter Thompson took Ernie and Hazel around in the outside a number of times. They are doing good also Linda. She goes on the outside by herself now! They have so much fun. 2 weeks from last night they are going to skate for the last time and I expect they'll be there early! By the way have you bought any new records?

August 16, 1957
Here it is Friday again. How are you and what are you doing? Anything exciting and how's your health holding out? Who are some of your [Kimball House] guests etc.? Any new girls or boys working there etc.? I took Mama over to Aunt Wilma's yesterday. Cousin Frances's girl Dianne [moved here] is taking her road test next Tuesday morning down to Ellsworth. She was talking to Ruthie out to [Crosby's] ice cream place and Ruthie said "Oh Pat's my best friend!" She is very anxious to meet you girls and Sept. 9, the day school starts, is her birthday. She is anxious for you to get home. She has been raking blueberries the last 2 weeks down to hard scrabble. By the way, Glenroy told me last night Grammie Smith is buying a trailer to live in next to their house and is going to Bangor tomorrow to pick one out. I don't know any more news but will write a long letter over the weekend as I hope to have some time to myself. God Bless you both and be nice girls and take care of yourselves. The kids will be awful glad when you are back home! So will we. 3 more weeks to go. The busier we all are the quicker the time will come. We miss you and love you! MA and PA [surrounded with hearts and exclamation points]

Wednesday, August 28, 1957
Dear Loretta and Patricia: Rec'd both your letters and very happy to get them. You have $142. Loretta plus the 93¢. First I'll ask some questions. How are you both and are you happy? How is [cousin] Beulah? Are you coming home together and do you know what day yet? There isn't much to write except I have been sick since last Sat. and in bed most of the time. I feel better this morning. Linda has

really done some work this week. She was up at 5:30 yesterday morning and she never stopped until supper. Percy had to work on the paper boat last night so they didn't get over to roller skate. It was the last time and they were pretty disappointed. Your father has put in a lot of hours this week. His back is getting worse all the time. I am pretty discouraged. I've got to close and start the stove. It isn't very warm here and I can't breathe very good yet.

Editor's note:

*My mother, **Dorothy Jean Young Smith**, was born in Bangor and grew up in North Castine at her stepfather Duncan Dunbar's dairy farm known as Meadow Farm and Dunc's Meadow. Dunc, my grandfather, delivered milk and produce by horse and wagon throughout the Castine peninsula. His wife, my mother's mother, was Hattie Snowman Young Dunbar, daughter of Ethel Leach and Capt. William Livingston Snowman of Orland. As a girl, Mama loved books and playing school with her younger brothers, George and Bennett Dunbar, who worked at the paper mill as adults. She met our father, a young Canadian-American and mixed Native woods-man, while visiting her mother's sister, Berenice Snowman Applebee, upriver in Enfield when he was home on leave from the Army. They married soon and after working for a time for the future governor of the Penobscot Tribe at his lodge on Cold Stream where they boarded with the Penobscot Indian, John "Old Buck" Andrews, moved us to a cabin my father built for us on the Dodlin Road. He continued to work in the woods, cutting and hauling, until Pearl Harbor when he enlisted in the Navy and she brought us (two toddlers) home to the Dunbar farm while looking for a place for us to live in Bucksport hoping he would find work at the mill after the war. She worked briefly, while he was gone, wrapping blocks of paper at St. Regis until childcare became a problem. My father's naval skills did prepare him to be a rigger at St. Regis which he did along with tending small subsistence farms with woodlots and fields in Millvale and Bucksmills as long as he could. Along with his mill job he was a cattle and antiques dealer. Also a poetry lover and reciter, he was always bringing home old books to Mama from which she would often read to us. When we were little she wrote our words in books she stitched by hand. Throughout her adult life she wrote daily in humble notebooks, documenting glimpses of a true Yankee–Native life. In later years she turned to writing poetry, filling notebooks and totebags with hundreds of images of nature, history, travel, philosophy, even politics. Her children and grandchildren frequently begged her to read or recite to them. In her honor, my sister, Hazel Smith Hutchinson and I established One Water Press to publish a collection for her 90th birthday entitled SCATTERINGS From OffNeck, drawn from her beloved Meadow Farm in North Castine. As she had taught us when we were young, haying on our places, "scatterings" are the bits of hay missed by the rakes on their sweeps along the windrows. No self-respecting farmer worth his salt would leave many, she'd point out on rides through the countryside to the end of her days, with a disdainful judgement, "look at that!"*

Master Musicians Hard at Work

Music at the annual Woodlands get-together April 26 was furnished by the following musicians: L. to R. — Dr. Edward Thegen, St. Regis physician at Bucksport; Clifford Lambert; Dick Maley, superintendent of super-calenders; Bobby Brooks, safety director; Roy Stairs, superintendent of the finishing room.

In the foreground is Ed Lowell, superintendent of the steam plant at the Bucksport mill.

Owen K. Soper
Orland

GOD AND DR. THEGEN

If you're feeling lousy
And your belly's achin'
Just say a prayer to the Lord
And send for Doctor Thegen.

If you've had a drop too much
Of the brew you're makin'
Just lay off the cuss words
And send for Doctor Thegen.

He is the greatest doctor
That helps us, you and me
Our own beloved surgeon
That's Thegen, our M.D.

He doesn't operate upon
Your purse, or scare you silly
He laughs and jokes and makes you well
With a humor that is witty.

So if you feel at low ebb
And ready to be taken
Just pray to God a little prayer
And send for Doctor Thegen.

– "The Poetic Paper Maker"

Editor's note:
This is the work of **Owen K. Soper** *who also had his work accepted for publication in the* Seaboard Bulletin *under the pen name "Fuller Clay." Courtesy of his granddaughter, Jeannine Hall Peters, who remembers that "He had a great sense of humor as evidenced in much of his poetry and he was also a deep thinker. I wish I had more of his poetry. Who knows where it all went, and because he signed it with so many different names, it can never be tracked down. At least we have a few examples for this collection."*

Carrie Mott Doyle Bragdon
Bangor

WOMEN AT THE MILL – IN REMEMBRANCE OF WILMA BROOKS

In July, 1957, right out of college, I was fortunate enough to get a job at the Bucksport Mill. I say fortunate, because I met so many wonderful people who will stay in my heart and memory forever. Wilma Brooks was the first.

I began my career in the Human Relations office, with Frank Larrabee as my boss. Wilma worked in the Personnel Office, which was in the same building, with Dick Chase. She was the kindest, sweetest person, who knew every single person working in the mill, and we all loved her. After a few years, I moved to a position in Personnel and worked with Dick, Wilma, and Phyllis Gross. We became very close and enjoyed all the meetings and parties the mill put on, as well as the never-ending work keeping personnel and education records up to date.

Wilma and her husband, Shirley, were great dancers and went dancing often with her niece, Marilyn and Ralph Jewett (my BHS basketball coach). Marilyn also worked at the mill. Wilma adored her family – two sons, Terry and Dan– grandchildren (who lovingly called her "Bum") and all of her siblings and their families.

Wilma did many home projects and loved to visit with my Dad, Jerry Mott, at the Bucksport Hardware Store. She told me several times that all she had to do was ask and Dad would tell her just what she needed to do the job and how to do it!

A year later, I had my first son, Rick Doyle. I remember Dick and Frank telling me that I couldn't have any time off to have this baby, but that they would set up the conference table on which I could give birth. It was a Saturday, June 7, and I was scheduled to work that day. Needless to say, I called in at 7 a.m. and Rick was born at 7 p.m. – at Stinson Hospital in Bangor, not on the conference room table! Of course, they gave me six months leave and all were delighted with my new baby boy. I can still see the beautiful blue baby sweater that Wilma knit for Rick.

Five years later, I was transferred to Woodlands Division at St. Regis Paper Company and enjoyed a wonderful thirty-seven-year career, working with Herb Weller and Bob Cope.

Wilma and I remained friends until her death and I have many memories to cherish.

Carrie Mott *was born in Millinocket, Maine, "in my Nana Moore's home, then moved to Connecticut at age four for a year while Mom and Dad worked at Pratt and Whitney. We then moved to Boston where I attended grammar school and Girls' Latin School. With much pleading from Sister Jalaine and me, we moved back to Maine. We settled in Bucksport so Dad could manage the Bucksport Hardware Store." Carrie started as a Freshman at BHS and graduated in the Class of 1956 with second honors. She then attended Husson College and graduated 4.0 from the Secretarial Science course. "My two sons, Rick and Kevin Doyle, were and are the light of my life. Russ and I loved camping with the family and went to Prince Edward Island, Halifax, Nova Scotia, Hawaii and lots of picnics in the beautiful state of Maine. We also taught round dancing and traveled to Canada many times. Les and I also traveled to visit my siblings in Florida, California and Arizona. We also loved to hunt and had a great hunt in Colorado, where I got my Mule Deer. Dad loved to tease Les because he came home empty handed! He is now in Alaska guiding hunts." Now that Carrie is retired after 50 years of work, she enjoys volunteering at the Next Step Domestic Violence Group in Ellsworth, at The Shoestring Thrift Shop and her church at North Brewer-Eddington United Methodist Church, "where we have many suppers, pie sales and holiday fairs." Her favorite hobbies are going to plays, the Bangor Symphony Orchestra, reading and meeting monthly for lunch with the "Old Grads". "Of course my very favorite hobbies are my three grandchildren and four terrific great-grandchildren. The Lord has blessed me profusely!"*

Sharon Bray
Orland

WILMA SHARES HARDSCRABBLE MEMORIES

ORLAND – Wilma C. Brooks, 94, died Tuesday, Dec. 20, 2011, in her beloved home in Hardscrabble, where she was born Oct. 25, 1917, to Adelbert and Maggie Marks.

– Bangor Daily News
12/22/2011

Wilma Marks Brooks lives in the Orland house where she was born. On the small farm on tidal Penobscot River, Adelbert (Del) and Maggie (Bowden) Marks raised five children. "Some people prefer to call it South Orland, but we always and still do call it Hardscrabble," Wilma said in November 2009.

Starting in 1931, Wilma attended Castine High School for three years. To get to school in Castine, Wilma and a few others walked – "we always said it was four miles" – to Frank Devereaux's to catch a ride to the school on Castine Common (now Castine Historical Society). She remembers one winter trip when she "froze my fingers and ear."

In 1935 she changed to Bucksport High School, "tired of the long walk" and finding the chance to get a ride with near neighbor Reg Howard driving to work at the paper mill. The high school was located at the former East Maine Conference Seminary before the town built the Walter Gardner High School. Her classmates included Donald Bowden, Frances Soper and Dorothy Davis. Her brother Milford, 15 months younger than Wilma, dropped out of high school to cut wood and provide for the family in other ways. He lives a short distance from the homeplace just across the town line in Penobscot.

After graduation Wilma worked briefly as a waitress, "not a very good one," in Bucksport before going to work in an office at Seaboard paper mill. At the mill, she met and married Shirley Brooks. Their first house was the 14 ft. by 16 ft. building that stands between her house and the South Orland Church of God.

When their first child Terry was born in 1938, Wilma took some time off, went back to the mill in 1944, and worked there another 44 years until her retirement in 1988.

Dan was born a couple of years after she returned to her job.

Her life of hospitality and generosity has made Wilma popular in the immediate and wider community. For years she was in charge of soliciting casseroles for Orland Methodist Church suppers, making as many as she needed if she couldn't find enough volunteers.

When Bucksport Bay Healthy Communities set up a bus and taxi system for Wednesday trips around town, Wilma became a favorite passenger in the taxi that picked up folks in outlying areas to

113

connect with the Bucksport bus. When voters at Orland town meeting had to decide whether to help fun the transportation system, they only had to hear that Wilma Brooks used it regularly before they voted unanimously to support the project.

Excerpted from *Narramissic Notebook #10*, 2009, with permission of editor and author, Sharon Bray.

Patricia Ranzoni
Bucksport

COMES BACK A DARK / *from* ANOTHER LONG (13.)

                        Comes back a dark
before the 4 o'clock
shift lets out. Comes back
the deep freeze
safe to slaughter in, safe
to hook the year's beef
critter from a north porch
rafter in, just the right
sensed degrees
barring too great
a January thaw, to keep
raw meat too expensive
to grain to its prime in.
Pasture time done. Enough
field feed to hang lean
suspended months
in crystal state for children
to whittle chips from
to fry after county basketball
games in town while friends
sip Coke at Pop Hill's.
For a wife's hands chapped
from outside work
or work inside in a house
cold in as out
for a wife's chapped hands
to carve stars from
ragged slices of *the-sky's-
the-limit* to fry in that rugged
castiron pan that is his entire
universe raised on salt pork
and biscuits the tenathem
swearin' his family'll never
go to bed hungry, for a wife's

chapped hands to have on the table
by the time P.D. comes through that door
from unloading hundredpound
bags of tapioca for test-coating paper
from that day's #2-machine's run.
Rigger. Before his pie.
                    Shaved to the bone
checked the winter long
for telling smell watched
for dreaded iridescent swatches
'til nearing March.........*disappears*
drug into the woods down back
no doubt. A steering clear of those
who'd be shocked to hear it said
hear it told straight out.

                    Comes a dark
brought back
of a half frozen people's meat
shining in leaky sheds
of a memory shared with rodents
of starved late-February popula-
tions snarling over such lucky
spoils along the crusty Turkey Path
all the way back to Pickle Ridge
where old Percy was born in Webster Planta-
tion. Of that still steering clear require-
ment it not be told not straight out.

Author note: This poem is a segment of a long, numbered cycle from Fall through Winter to Spring entitled, "Another Long", published originally in *SETTLING, Poems by Patricia Ranzoni* (Puckerbrush Press, 2000), used as a textbook in writers of Maine courses at the University of Maine.

ON RETIREMENT

The ringlets, I'm told, are fast leaving my head,
  And the luster is gone from my eyes;
No more do my cheeks have that bright, rosy red;
  My condition seems quite a surprise.
But of course I am not such a stupid myope
  That I can't see I'm no more a child–
That far from the pink of my youth I have stope,
  Yet, withal, I am quite reconciled.
Here and there, I am told, is a pale silver thread–
  My shrubbery is turning to gray.
It's because of the way I have lived, it is said,
  That I am beginning to fray.
So perhaps I should now be a sorrowful mope;
  Perhaps I should worry and fret
Because of the way I am going aslope,
  Yet, somehow, I have no regret.
If tomorrow the doctor pronounces me dead,
  Let no one sob, sigh or shed tears
'Cause short was the way in the life that I led;
  You can't measure life by the years.
I know I am nearing the end of my scope,
  I know there is gray in my hair;
But I've found more of living within my short rope,
  Than have many with fathoms to spare.

Editor's note:
Fuller Clay is the pen name of Owen Soper, who contributed items to the Seaboard Bulletin. *He also signed his writings "The Poetic Paper Maker." He retired August 1, 1957. This poem and information was contributed by his granddaughter, Jeannine Hall Peters who notes "His oldest son, Keith, also worked at the mill for many years."*

Julia Bowden
Castine

BOX SOCIALS

I go way back with box socials at the old school house at the four corners by Charlie Cole's farm in Jacob Buck Valley in Millvale. Later we went to the Bucksmills Community Building, and Colin Mac-Donald, our square dance caller, played washtub with string and his wife Hazel sang. Sometimes my uncle Roland White and others played. I remember the box socials well. We decorated shoe boxes something like covered Maybaskets with colorful handmade crepe paper flowers and ruffles, and filled them with food! Maybe pie. Everything was made by scratch in those days, even the yeast bread. The auctioneer would describe them in delicious ways to tease everyone. Men bid on these then ate the meal with the woman who had made the box. It was a fun way to raise money for the Community Club and other causes, especially to help neighbors who were out of work from accidents at the mill or other hard luck.

Another thing I remember is Aunt Nellie's [Willis] hill on the side of Jacob Buck Mountain across the brook. Evenings going there, sliding down that big hill in back of Uncle Harold's and Nellie's. Just one slide since it took us awhile to walk back up the hill! Then we visited them and played Ping Pong on their dining room table.

Julia White Bowden was born "on Grampa White's farm on outer Silver Lake Road. Grammie White delivered me. Who does this now? When we were young, my father and mother, Kenneth and Barbara, and Uncle Vinnie and Aunt Hildred, moved us Whites and Conners to Portland for work at the Portland Ship Yard. Then the war broke out and our fathers were drafted. Luckily the war ended before they reported for duty. We returned to Bucksport and both worked at the Mill. Uncle Ross Allison and Uncle Harold Willis also worked at the mill. My cousins, Barbara, Helen and Gloria Conners grew up at that White homestead where I was born. We loved swimming in the stone-lined swimming hole that the family had made in the brook. I grew up in the outback Bucksport community of Millvale, next road over. We used to sing a lot, including harmonizing, on the bus going to and from school. And going to pick beans which some of us did as quite young children. We would meet at the four corners in the valley by the old one-room schoolhouse between Charlie Cole's fields, with our jars of kool-aid and peanut butter sandwich lunches and a big truck would pick us up. We'd ride standing up and holding on in the back and go to Orrington to pick string beans all day for 25¢ a bushel. Most of us were in 4–H doing projects for demonstration in Ellsworth, a big deal. Our old year books show what kinds of high school activities we were in back then. If Gloria and I stayed after school for something Uncle Vinnie would give us rides home. We waited for him at the corner drugstore – now MacLeod's Restaurant – with other outback kids waiting for rides when the 4 o'clock shift got out. It was fun hanging out at Pop Hill's (soda fountain) in town between events, too, playing the jukebox, and going to the movies at the Alamo Saturday afternoon. Out our way we used to skate at the gravel pit in Charlie Cole's field in Jacob Buck Valley. To stay warm the boys built large bonfires. My first work away from home was at a summer inn in Hulls Cove with my neighbor-friend and classmate, Loretta Smith who arranged the jobs for us. In those days, Maine girls came from all over for summer work on Mount Desert Island. After graduation with the class of 1957 I worked in Connecticut, then it was home to Maine. Through the years I have enjoyed hiking, kayaking, camping and sailing. I enjoy visiting, especially with my children and grandchildren, and traveling with family and friends. And I feel lucky to spend a month each year in Florida including a week on a houseboat in the Florida Everglades. I have even hiked on parts of the Appalachian Trail. I enjoy my large flower garden as well as foraging in the wild which I learned growing up in the country. Someone once told me that sometimes they look over expecting to see me climbing Great Pond Mountain!"

Editor's note:
Along this same line, "sunshine baskets" were another custom. Saved boxes were decorated with crepe or tissue paper and might be filled modestly with a book, game, writing or drawing supplies, notions, flowers or pussy-willows, and homemade treats like fudge or jam to cheer someone tending an accident or illness. We made these for friends, schoolmates, and neighbors of all ages and they did lift spirits. The last one I made was for beloved Bucksport elder, Helen Spooner Bennett (Mrs. Stanley) during her final days in 2013.

Roger Powers (1931-2014)
Bucksport

BE CAREFUL IN THERE
OR
THE PRICE WE PAY FOR ONE CARELESS MOMENT

June 27, 1961

Just one more week, I told my family on the morning of June 27, 1961, and we will have the vacation we have waited for and saved for all winter. We had made plans to vacation in Canada at Fundy National Park with friends of ours. After saying goodbye to my two children, a boy 9 and a girl 8 and my wife, I left for work as usual.

We were overhauling No. 1 paper machine at the time and it was a very hot day. The crane operator asked me if I would remove a couple of windows in the top of the paper mill so he could get some fresh air. Yes, I'd be glad to. I removed one with no trouble, but the other one was stuck so I sat astride the window sill of the window I had just removed to loosen the other one and pass it down to a man below me on the roof. *This* was the careless moment, because one foot rested on the crane rail. While I was passing the window down, the crane came back my way. I didn't hear it and the operator could not see me from the control cab. The metal bumper back of the wheel slid over the top of my safety shoe, jamming my foot and preventing me from pulling away. The crane continued traveling back by the window taking me with it. The noisy paper mill room prevented the operator from hearing me holler for him to stop, so when I reached the edge of the window only my leg kept going.

At a point like this you get an instant replay of your life because as you see yourself being pulled apart and feel the pain you're sure you have seen all of life and living for the last time, and God knows that at that time it would be a lot easier if you had.

The crane stopped, started the other way, and knowing that the operator still hadn't seen me, somehow I managed to jump off the window sill onto the walkway of the crane to prevent being jammed on the other side of the window. At this point someone from below had seen me and stopped the crane. My foot still being caught, I could not be removed until someone got a knife and cut my shoe off me. From that point on until I was safely in the hospital still seems it took days. And to this day I know if it had not been for the mill nurse and the comfort she gave me during the twenty-mile trip to the hospital that I would never have pulled through. I spent about three and one-half hours in the operating room that day, but during the night I went into shock.

Being in shock is something I had heard about many times in my life but I never really thought much about it until that time. It's an experience I will never forget. When I awoke I could see the doctor and nurse working over me trying to give me a blood transfusion. When in shock the veins collapse which make it very difficult to get a needle into them. While they were doing this, I had no feeling in my body whatsoever. I could see everything that was being done, but not once did I feel anything. This in itself would scare a person out of his wits. You feel just as though that much of your body must have died already and that it's just a matter of time until it's all over. This all happened in less than twenty-four hours. It's an experience that I wish on no one, but it gives a person a totally different outlook on life. You can see your mistake but it's not like cutting a board too short or forgetting to take the biscuits from the oven before they burn – a mistake like this you just don't have a second try. When you finally wake up to reality and realize what has happened and where you are, there is a lot more to think of beside the pain in your body. You have a wife and two children at home. Where is the money coming from to feed and clothe them? Where is the money coming from to make the car payment? How about gas and oil for my wife to drive to and from the hospital to visit me twice a day? A round trip from our house to the hospital is only forty-six miles. That doesn't sound like much to most people with the modern automobile, but figure out what it means twice a day for eighty days. Yes, a little over 7,000 miles When your insurance check is only $50. a week and you spend $14. or $16. a week for gas and oil it really doesn't leave much to meet all the other essentials.

The average young couple just starting out in life to build a home, buy a car, feed and clothe a family, plus lights, phone and heat pretty much live from week to week. So you don't have much saved for a rainy day. We were young and didn't believe anything like this could happen to us, but it did! This may all sound bad, but just imagine where this would have left me if I had gotten hurt outside my job. At one time I saw the bills from the doctors and hospital and they were in excess of $12,000, the price of a new home at that time. This fact alone has entered my mind many times. Most people work a lifetime to pay for a new home. How would I or anyone ever get a bill like this payed off and still provide a good living for our family? This isn't as far-fetched as it might seem. That is one big reason why we must always be alert and careful at work or at home. Money isn't the only costly part of getting hurt. I spent 80 days that summer in the hospital. 63 of these days my leg was in traction with 15 pounds of weight hanging from it. 6E days I had to lie on my back, not once turning over. Day after day I said to myself, "If only I had been thinking and paying attention I could be home right now or maybe out swimming on these hot days or perhaps working. But it's too late now. Here I am, so just better stop wishing and make plans and promises to work and play safely from now on." After about two weeks I began to get tired of being tied up to that bed so I asked the doctor how long he thought I would be here tied up like this. At this point he pulled up a chair and sat down. Son, he said, it doesn't look good right now. We may have to take your leg off. If he said any more I never heard him. How many people ever thank about what those two legs are doing for them every day? Not many. I do mine every day of my life. I realize what they're doing for me! I had a lot of time to figure this out. How does a man of 30 who has always enjoyed the best of health even start to realize what a doctor is saying at a time like this? By the grace of God this didn't have to be done. The doctor said my good health and youth kept me from getting infection and any more complications. I had the best care that summer, not once did I want for anything. My wife visited me twice a day every day except the last ten days. These ten days she spent in another hospital. The doctor said she was suffering from nervous exhaustion – working too hard caring for two children alone, driving to and from the hospital and trying to manage on so little money. This type of sickness has doctor and hospital bills to be paid later, too.

Seemed as though every day that I was out of work brought new bills that would have to be paid later. These aren't anything unusual, just the normal things we take for granted when all is well, like getting the children ready for school in the fall. It's not really too bad for most people, but try to find that extra when you're trying to live on $50. a week.

During my stay in the hospital that summer I was in the operating room three times. I had to have skin grafts which cover half my leg above the knee. Skin graft is a great thing, it puts new skin where the old was, but let me tell you, it has its disadvantages, too. This skin has no pores in it so it can breathe. When working where it is very hot, which I have to do often, my leg will get hot and feel as though it is burning up and it stays hot like that for some time. The skin has no nerves in it so it has no feeling on the outside whatsoever. I have leaned against a hot steam line and not even realized it until I had burned my leg to a blister, a place about the size of a silver dollar. This took about six months to heal up. During this time you have to be extremely careful not to get infection. So you see, every day I must continually keep this leg in mind so as not to injure it further.

During my stay at the hospital that summer I saw many people come and go. I was very surprised at the number of people who got in the hospital through accidents. I talked with many of these people but very few ever would blame themselves a mite for being careless or not obeying orders or what have you. I suppose that it is the natural thing to blame someone or something for our accident, but I have watched pretty closely since my accident and ther is almost always some small bit of carelessness involved. Not always on the part of the man who gets hurt, but by someone at some time or another. Everybody always says these things happen to other people – not me! I know I felt that way for many years but I learned the hard way. It wouldn't be quite as bad if it only involved onesself, but every person in a family becomes involved in one way or another. It's a hardship on the wife who has to take over completely all the duties that a man has around home, besides her own. Added to that, it takes from five to six hours a day to visit the husband in the hospital. When a woman is this busy the children don't get the love and care they are used to. They become restless and lonely and become much more care than usual. All one's friends try to visit and be of some help, which take a lot of their time and money. So you see, it involves many other people outside the one who suffers the accident.

As I said, I was in the hospital eighty days. This gave me time to think a lot. At a time like this you see things a lot more clearly. You get scared, you get lonely, you wake up in the middle of the night in a cold sweat because you just went through the whole nightmare again. These nightmares kept coming back time after time for almost a whole year. People just don't realize what a mental pressure this puts on a person. Every time you hear an ambulance with the siren howling as it comes into the hospital you break out in a cold sweat. Who is it this time, I would ask myself. On top of all you're going through, things like this steadily pick away at you. There just doesn't ever seem to be any let up. You hope when the day ever comes that you can go home and get a good night's sleep in your own bed these horrors will leave you alone. But it really isn't that easy. These things, just the same as a bad leg, are some you will have to live with the best you can.

Then comes the day when the doctor takes you out of traction. Nine weeks – 63 long days. I thought this day would never get here, but here it is. How long before I can go home, Doc, I asked. Just as soon as you can get around on your crutches. Gosh, I said, two or three days should take care of that. But what a surprise I had in store. A rugged, young man nine weeks ago that weighed 195 pounds couldn't sit up on the edge of the bed five minutes. It was five days before I was able to stay in a wheel chair long enough to even try to walk with the parallel bars, and then a six-foot walk made me feel as though I had run four miles. My one good leg just wouldn't hold me up, even though I had lost sixty pounds while I was there. It was a slow process to me, but in seventeen days from the day I first sat up in bed I made my walk through the hospital, out the door and back to my room to get the OK to go home the next day.

September 15, the summer was all over and my children were back in school. I was finally going home! What a wonderful feeling that was. My leg was stiff, it would not bed more than a couple of inches, but it was all there. The doctor said to walk all I could and bear a little weight on it when I felt like it and it would limber up in time. My wife measured a mile from the house for me and I began my walking. A little further every day until I made the one mile mark and back home. I walked this twice a day until I went back to work in March.

Soon after I got home, friends began to bring in food baskets, which were greatly appreciated. The Couples Club put on a supper for us and gave us $267. It is times like these that make you realize what it means to have friends. When you have good health all your life sometimes you forget how important it is to have friends, but after seeing how hard people will work for you and how much they will put themselves out to help you, it makes you realize how important these things are. So m any times we take so much for granted. It is so easy for us to find fault with the way people live or the things they do that we just don't take the time to look for all the good things in people. When you're down and out you really see people in a different light. You need people more then and you find that they will do just about anything for you and be glad to. Sometimes I believe that having an accident and recovering from it gives a person a completely different outlook on life. For this I am thankful.

The company that I work for – St. Regis Paper Company – does more than their share to help their employees at times like this. I was still using a cane to get around when they asked me to come back to work and learn a new trade until I was able to go on my own job. They wanted me to learn the roll-grinding trade. This was a job where, while learning, I could sit down most of the time. I was paid my regular rate of pay during this time and very little was asked of me. After I was ready to go back on my regular job I was even given a choice –to go back to millwrighting or to stay as a roll-grinder. I went back to my old job because I liked it better and that is where I am today.

I believe that I am much more careful in the way I work now and I hope I set some kind of an example for others who work with me because I know what can happen. I hope when people hear the words "work safely" they realize that this means something very important to them and to everyone they are involved with – at home or at work. I know – I live with it.

Thank you very much for giving me the time to share my true story with you.

Editor's note: **Roger O. Powers** *was born as the mill to which he devoted his life, and which nearly took his, was being born, in 1931. His career there began under St. Regis in 1954 – after Air Force service and marrying Marietta Fanjoy – and ended with his retirement from International Paper Co. 39 years later as Maintenance Superintendent. I knew them as friends of my parents, my dad's co-worker. They would come to the house to play cards and I babysat for their first children when I was in high school in the fifties. I was shocked and touched when I saw them in the audience at one of my first poetry readings where I had been invited to a bookstore down on Mt. Desert Island when my first book was published. And they had come all that way through a blizzard, to boot! I have never gotten over it. To say he had many passions is an understatement. Along with his love of hunting, he had many arts, including woodworking, gardening, carving and stained glass work. One day after my second collection had been published, he knocked at our door with a splendid walking stick he had fashioned of sumac with the titles of my first two books carved among cattails. To this day I lean on it from time* to time in remembrance of my father and mother, Roger and Marietta, and our passing mill-working families and community. On one of his rare visits, Roger brought a hand-typed copy of this story for us, published here with his family's permission. A condensed version had been featured as the center-fold in the St. Regis Bucksport Mill Newsletter, Vol. III, No. 6, Feb. 16, 1984 under the title, "The day Roger Powers didn't lock out and tag out."

Our grandchildren always teased to drive home by Roger's and Marietta's house at night with the unique colored glass and light displays, especially during the holidays. I would exclaim, "What great powers, Roger Powers!" which I envisioned would make a poem someday. What great powers, indeed!

Illustration for September page, 1981 calendar entitled, ST REGIS BUCKSPORT MILL, "SAFELY DONE IN '81". "One's good for your soul the other's good for your health." Signed, "The Saint."

Susan Dugas
Cincinnati, Ohio

PAYCHECK TO PAYCHECK

Editor's note: After I asked through the public "facebook" page entitled, "You knew you grew up in Bucksport, Maine when...", for memories relating to Pay Days at the mill, Dick Bowden of East Orland replied: *Oh yes, my mother used to drive over to the parking lot in front of the brick 'Security' or 'Personnel' building with us kids on Thursdays in summer, sometimes you had to wait to find a spot to get in. Nobody parked in marked 'slots' or in any kind of order. Everybody just pulled in behind the one in front, and they might be 3 or 4 lanes wide! Like a huge McDonald's drive-through. That lot was much bigger back then (1960s). The grocery stores in town would cash mill paychecks. If Dad was working 12 to 8, he'd just pick up the check on his way out in the morning.*

"Anonymous" replied: *Oh, no. Not on your life. Pay Days meant a gallon jug of wine and a bad night for the family and I won't go there.*

Marlene Dillingham posted: *My dad worked from 1945 to retirement in the boiler room and during the wars. He worked long hours. Mom would put up a lunch to last two to three days sometimes. Dad was too young for WWI and too old for WWII.*

John Craig wrote: *Growing up we knew that payday, Thursday, meant at least two or three days of pretty good food. Come Monday or Tuesday, however, the next payday couldn't get there soon enough! We thought actual store-bought bread was quite a treat. I thought of something on the way to work today. Poor food. I've asked many folks if there was a food or a meal that they ate growing up that became a negative in their lives. For me, it was corn chowder - a wonderful meal by all accounts. However, to me it seemed to ALWAYS be on the menu. When we had nothing, we had corn chowder. I avoided corn chowder in my diet for over 50 years before trying it again last year. It was surprisingly good!*

When I picked up on John's food references to ask if there might be Craig family tips on cooking frugally for a large family, obviously mastered at his house, he replied that he would refer the question to his sister, Susan, "our official keeper of the Craig family recipes." Here are the results of that exchange.

* * *

My name is Susan (Craig) Dugas and my brother John informed me that you have been seeking recollections of how we all were kept fed from paycheck to paycheck. Because I was born into the middle section of the Craig Family, with three older kids—John, Christy and Bobby—then the middle four—me, Tim, Paula and Marianne, then three boys – Gerry, Ben and Matt, there are way too many tales to tell everything regarding the food issues around the Craig household as we were growing up. The most notable tale in my mind was during a summer camping trip (we always packed up the tent and traveled to Canada for those vacations, at the end of August each year, simply because children were free for almost everything one could possibly want to do there. They charged for adults to go places, i.e. parks, etc. but it did not matter how many children were included, they were free. I have not heard much about vacations in the 50's, but by the 60's we were a much more mobile family, enjoying a Volkswagon bus with a trailer on back to get everyone and everything from here to there. This memorable trip, the adventure of taking a family of 12 plus 1 in a VW bus and tent setup to Expo '67 in Montreal, resulted in the famous, all day long, corn chowder! (Not one of the kids, so far as I know, recalls being told not to stuff the underneath of the seats with fireworks – the only available space they would fit!)

The particular time I am recalling specifically included corn chowder on a rainy day. My mother made up a big batch of corn chowder to keep us both warm and fed. Here is her recipe, given to me when I was creating the Craig Family Cookbook:

Ma's Corn Chowder
4 potatoes, diced
1 onion, chopped
¼ stick butter

Place into pot with enough water to just cover and boil until done. Add 1 can of cream corn, 1 can of whole kernel corn, 1 can evaporated milk and same amount of regular milk. Heat until hot.

Note – If made when camping, covering the pot might be important, especially if it is raining, however, if company should drop by, just leave the cover off and you will have plenty! The note she added explains what happens when you leave a big pot of chowder uncovered on the campfire on a rainy day. We ate from that pot all day long!

* * *

I graduated Bucksport High in the Class of '73 and the University of Maine Bangor Campus, with a degree in Law Enforcement in 1975. Growing up in a mill family really did not seem like that big a deal to me throughout elementary school, almost everyone else in town was, or some branch of the family was, attached to the mill. I do recall starting to notice other families who were not dependent on the mill throughout my later school years and it seemed a little daunting to me, to not know when the next paycheck would arrive, i.e. scalloping, farming, etc., but I also knew, as a family, that the mill provided some of what we needed in life, but certainly not more than the basics. My father started working in photography when I was very, very young and brought in additional funds for some of the extras, school shoes, notebooks, summer camp, while my mother would take on work here and there, working as a waitress at the Alamoosook Lodge for special events, throughout the year to finance Christmas and making sure we were kept fed. Dad's photography side business was a family affair, since adult hands and fingers were too big to color in the small irises for colored portraits (back when all pictures were black and white, we colored them in by hand/fingers).

From my mother, I gained a great love of family and cooking. She had been an only child and had gone through the Great Depression in early childhood and she vowed that there would always be food and family around to share it and made it happen. From my father, I obtained a love of capturing life's moments in pictures and words, along with embracing the 'next big thing'. He was an early adopter of television, calculators and computers and started his writing efforts after he retired from the mill.

I worked at the mill throughout the summer months and was able to pay my way through school with those earnings (those were the days!). Upon graduation, I took a page from my mother's life and started a family (also mostly dependent on the mill), only returning to work once all the children were in school. I worked at Penobscot County Jail in Bangor, working my way up to acting Sergeant on the midnight shift before I burned out and moved on into the computer field; the same field, oddly enough, that all three of my children moved into. Undoubtedly the influence of a grandfather who embraced technology and change. I am currently living and working in Cincinnati, OH as a Sr. Systems Analyst with Cerner Corporation, an electronic medical records provider. My years in this field have taken me through numerous jobs and travel all over the US. My children; Julie, Jim and Craig, have lived all over the place – Montana, New York, Georgia, Massachusetts, Italy and England. It suits me just fine that they grew up with sufficient confidence and self-esteem to believe that they could 'be' somebody any-where they were and it gives me endless possibilities to travel and enjoy spending time with my four granddaughters.

I have kept searching to find my (and most of the rest of the family's) favorite food to feed a crowd. My Dad, Ben, had spent a few years in the Army during WWll and, mostly because he could not seem to follow someone else's rules, found himself on KP duty a lot. We enjoyed many of his creations made from whatever he happened to find to use to make a meal. The most famous of these was Hot Dog Soup. This recipe was also provided by Ma for the family recipe book, thus the name Meanie's Maca-roni Soup. That is probably due to the invention of forks. See, whenever we would come home from school and there was a big pot of Hot Dog Soup bubbling on the stove top, everyone grabbed a fork and snuck out a few hot dog pieces to eat. Well, you can imagine, with 10 children and assorted friends and neighbors, all sneaking a few pieces of hot dog, why Ma called it macaroni soup! The title "Meanie" is another story: Meanie is the term of well loved and much honored endearment that the grandchildren of Ben Craig were encouraged to use by his "loving" wife, Carolyn. In a family this large, someone had to be the force of control and this role was foisted upon my father after many years of being the enforcer. "Can we open Christmas presents on Christmas Eve? Please, please, please..." was followed with many emphatic "NO"s! He was awarded this moniker after many years of saying no to opening Christmas presents early, though we ALWAYS opened one gift on Christmas Eve, as determined by my mother's overriding vote (since we had to open our new Christmas pajamas for our pictures). Meanie was also responsible for rooting out and eating all the black jelly beans at Easter, being the "heavy" whenever things got too crazy (you kids take it outside, CLOSE THE DOOR, etc.) in the family. With so many children and subsequent grandchildren, maintaining even a semblance of control was beyond human possibilities... thus emerged "Meanie". When things became too chaotic, and the kids were en-couraged to get outside, Nanny (my mother) would send in Meanie to clear the way and then, after relative calm was restored, never failed to have the children lay the blame on that Meanie. Thus his name was created and, since he did the job so well and so often, Meanie became the man, rather than an adjective, to his adoring clan of grandchildren. It appears that my mother's attempt to divert attention and garner the love and adoration of this brood of grandchildren may have backfired. At his funeral, my daughter, Julie, was determined to give a eulogy to "My Meanie", which he would have truly loved! Using such a word and redefining it into one of the greatest expressions of love imaginable. (My Dad was a master at "oppositional debating" and loved taking the other side and defending it fervently.)

Meanie's Hot Dog-Macaroni Soup
1 – 3 lb box macaroni
1 large onion (or two) (or more when Nanny isn't looking)
Large can of tomatoes
Large can of V8 vegetable juice
Lots of salt
As many hot dogs as you can afford, cut up into pennies (should be red ones)
Cook all ingredients together for about ½ hour, then move to back burner and leave until pot is empty, adding as much water as needed to make it soup. It is important to use this pot to toss in ALL the leftover vegetables you can find, especially beans, carrots, etc. More hotdogs may be added, as needed, if available. Meanie claimed this recipe came from his days of cooking in the Army!

As for other ways we managed to get by until the next paycheck, there was a lot of canning of home grown vegetables and, once we moved to Franklin St., home grown protein in the form of chickens, turkeys and pigs. Almost everything was made from scratch, from biscuits and pancakes to bread, cakes and pies. Flour was always purchased in a 25-pound bag and government surplus cheese with a 3-pound box of macaroni was a great time! I do recall begging for store bought, soft, squishy bread like everyone else had... what I wouldn't give to have a slice of the homemade bread I grew up on now. I have tried and tried to recreate it, but I simply cannot get the taste and texture just right.

To go along with just the expense of feeding everyone, there was the workload involved in getting meals together. Eventually everyone came out with their "specialties" that we were responsible for with a given meal. Dad always did the ham for Christmas, Christy did cookies, Paula made biscuits, Marianne and I did salads and sides. As I recall, the boys didn't do anything, but you would have to ask John to confirm that! We all dug clams whenever we could, digging up tons of dandelions over the years, picked seagrass from the shoreline, John went scuba diving for lobsters, we all fished, (mackerel season was great) both at home and on vacation and we spent many a night sitting around the kitchen table picking crabmeat (because it was considered a cheap item that many fishermen threw back) and shelling shrimp bought off the back of a truck on Main St. We only went out to eat once a year, during our annual drive to see the Christmas lights. We had two big chest freezers that ranged from packed full to almost empty, depending on the time of year. Okay, I have a couple more of Ma's recipes to share. If we were ever having company or hosting a group of kids from a band exchange concert, spaghetti was the go to menu item. It was a lot like Hot Dog Soup, lots of leftovers and different every time, but always thick, delicious sauce (except for those few times Ma tried to quit smoking and burned everything from spaghetti sauce to boiled potatoes!).

The "How can I come up with a recipe for spaghetti sauce when every time I make it – it is different" Recipe

4 large cans tomatoes	1 green pepper
4-5 cloves garlic	3 large onions

Blend all these ingredients together in the blender

2 lbs of hamburg – broken up	2 bay leaves

Sneak in a little crushed red pepper (Meanie didn't like it). Cook until done.

Variations: One year we had a big crop of carrots so I blended some of those and put them in. I have cut up zucchini and put that in… maybe some pepperoni, chicken or meatballs. Mushrooms, if we had enough money. One year we raised celery and I put that in. If I used fresh tomatoes, I would add sugar to taste.

Note– most any type of large canned tomato product will do, from whole tomatoes to tomato sauce, tomato paste, etc. The best is a combination of all of them to make it good and thick! Plus cooking Italian Hot Sausage in the pot added the bestest flavor, though, to a child, in those days, the sausage was kinda strange in spaghetti!

Meatballs

1 lb hamburg	1 lb ground pork
Large onion	2 cloves garlic
Salt & pepper	2 eggs
½ cup oatmeal	

Note– Recipe donor suggests the addition of liver or tongue if there is some around that you need to use up. Just grind up meat and add to meatball mixture. Form meatballs, broil and add to sauce.

And, during the summer months, especially when camping, as firewood was around, plenty of kids hanging around needing to be kept busy, to gather it up and there was a darned good beanhole in every single campsite ever. All you needed was a shovel or two to find it. We had a permanent bean hole in the back yard which was a lot less work.

Bean-Hole Beans

10 c. dried soldier beans	1 t. black pepper
1 pound salt pork	4 t. dry hot mustard
2 onions	½ c. butter
2 ½ c. molasses	

1. The bean hole should be 2 ½ to 3 feet deep (or more), depending on your pot. The hole should be big enough around to have a 6-inch space between the pot and the edge of the hole on all sides. To help hold heat, put some old tire chains or stones in the hole before starting the fire.

2. Start the fire and keep it filled with good dry hardwood. Let it burn for about 3 hours. The hole should be at least ¾ full of hot coals. After the fire has been going for about an hour, place the beans in a large pot, on the stove with water to cover. Bring to a boil and cook until skins roll back when you blow on them, about 45 minutes. Watch closely, because they will get mushy if left too long.

3. When the hole is ready, cut the salt pork into 2-inch wide and ¼ thick slices. Place them into the bottom of the bean pot. Peel and cut the onions in half; lay them on top of the pork. Pour the beans and their liquid into the pot, then mix in the molasses, black pepper and dry mustard. Slice butter and place on top. Add enough boiling water to cover the beans by one inch. Cover the top of the pot tightly with aluminum foil so that it goes down over the sides by at least 2 inches. Place lid on bean pot.

4. Before putting the pot into the hole, remove about 1/3 of the coals using a shovel. Remove and discard any burning pieces of wood. Place the bean pot into the hole, and put the coals from the hole back in around the sides and over the top of the bean pot. Now start filling the hole in. You should end up with about 2 feet of dirt covering the pot. Cover the place where the beans are buried with a tarp or piece of metal to keep out rain.

5. Let the beans cook overnight in their bean hole. Carefully dig them out the next day and enjoy!

6. TIPS:
We line the pot with the salt pork slices.
The amounts are only approximate; the ingredients can be varied in any way that makes sense.
Too much water is better than too little.
Do not leave your fire unattended. It is best to have several people around to help with this.
Pull chairs up close to the fire. Make sure the beer cooler is filled with ice and beer and within reach of at least one of the chairs.
Have a garden hose hooked up to a reliable source of water also within reach.
Start the fire around 8 or 9 and burn it until 2 a.m. before putting the beans in. The beans will be done by noon.

And a family pick for sweet treats, the perennial Maine favorite, Whoopie Pies (we did not use box mixes, ever!)

Whoopie Pies

½ cup shortening
1 cup sugar
2 egg yolks
5 heaping TBL cocoa
2 cups flour
½ tsp salt
1 tsp baking soda
1 cup milk

Beat shortening, sugar and egg yolks together, add dry ingredients with milk and beat. Drop on greased cookie sheet in tablespoons-full. Bake at 350° about 15-20 minutes, until toothpick (or broom straw) comes out clean. Cool on newspapers spread on the table while making up the filling.

Filling:
½ cup shortening (Crisco)
2 egg whites
2 cups confectioner's sugar
salt
vanilla

Beat all ingredients together and spread between whoopie pies. Note: If you get too tired making all those little whoopie pies, try making just one big one that you can fill and slice like a regular cake, like Paula might!

Editor's note:
For a taste of Meanie's, that is, Ben Craig's writing, see "Swearing Women, Foreigners, and the Mill."

Susan Craig Dugas:
"Some of our favorite family recipes and memories! Now you know why John sent you on to me! Sorry for being so wordy (is that even a word?), but, as you may have guessed, along with cooking, reading and technology, I dabble in writing, too! Currently I am working on a book with my oldest granddaughter, Bella, about giving a bath to a dirty dragon! We have 7 chapters and are currently editing and spacing the paragraphs into pages to allow her to add illustrations. Since she lives in Georgia, we do this via weekly videochat sessions. Again, technology has allowed me to be a 'present' present day Nana/Grama, as I have a schedule to video chat with them all from Montana to Cambride, UK! Currently we are participating in a virtual Nana/Grama and grandchildren virtual marathon tracking our miles walked or other activities (swimming, gymnastics, etc.) to virtually travel from Cambridge, to Plymouth, England, taking a cruise ship (which virtually sails according to our aggregate of miles moved) across the Atlantic, landing in Bar Harbor, going to GA, OH and ending in MT. We get medals for every goal reached and we are 592 miles into our journey already. Yes, I love technology!"

Theodore Bear Mitchell
Ambassador, Penobscot Nation

PENOBSCOT SKYWALKER:
Theodore Norris Mitchell, Bear Clan

I'm more than willing to give you information regarding my dad's involvement at the Bucksport Mill. He was a superintendent of Ironworkers at that mill in the '60s and worked until all the structural steel was up and then went inside and helped hang the duct work. He was there for two years or more. I hope this helps. He worked for a construction company called Nickerson & O-Day almost exclusively. He was also very aware that that Mill was being built very close to a tribal burial ground and kept an eye out for any disturbance of that area. I don't know what happened after he left.

Yes, he knew a lot of the Mohawk steelworkers, whose courage and pride working on high construction earned them the title "skywalkers," working with them when things were slow.

My brother Dana who was on the tribal Council worked down there in the late seventies and my cousin Francis, who was subsequently Chief, worked there in the early eighties. I guess you could say quite a representation of my family worked on the steel of that factory.

Before the honor of taking his grandfather's name in 2015, **Theodore Bear Mitchell** *served four terms, from 2007, as Penobscot Representative to the Maine State Legislature under the name of his youth, Wayne T. Mitchell. In 2016 the people of the tribe abolished this position and in its place he now serves as the Ambassador for the Penobscot Nation on all matters, Federal, state, and local. As a family elder, he is keeper of the Mitchell history and legacy.*

Editor's note: After Ted Mitchell and his wife, Eleanor Dana Mitchell, raised their 13 children on Indian Island in Old Town, taking all the work they could find, including night shifts at the shoe factory, he went back to school, earning degrees and teaching at the University of Maine in Orono and throughout the region, raising awareness of Maine's indigenous people. As an early childhood educator in Bucksport in the '70s, it was my honor to have him visit our farm school where he sat in circle with us to tell stories and show the children how to act out songs, chants, and the sounds of nature, teaching of the Penobscot People, their history and ways. While the Bucksport Paper Mill came to destruction, as many old Maine buildings do, there is one presence that Ted Mitchell was responsible for creating that shall endure through time--The Wabanaki Center at the University of Maine in Orono which, from his hard-won founding, focuses on Wabanaki Studies of Maine's four federally recognized tribes--Passamaquoddy, Penobscot Nation, Houlton Band of Maliseets, and Aroostook Band of MicMacs. A distinguished tribal elder and scholar, he was the recipient of many awards for his high walking and working, here and beyond.

Eugene Sanborn
Orland

AND THE TOWN SLEPT ON – THE MILL FIRE BRIGADE

One of the biggest fire dangers at the mill was paper dust which, under the right circumstances, could cause a tremendous explosion and subsequent fire. Great pains were taken to keep the dust from collecting by blowing down the areas with compressed air and have frequent cleaning binges. Paper dust will explode in the same way as corn starch, and grain silos do in the Midwest. Wood dust can also be extremely volatile when conditions are right and the dust becomes airborne. Some would think that the bunker C fuel oil burned in the boilers would be an extreme hazard but that was never a problem.

Probably the biggest threat to the mill came in the 1960s when a ship was offloading gasoline at the oil docks and for some reason the ship's crew was for a time absent when a major leak occurred. The river was covered and only by the grace of god it was late at night and there was no open flame near the shore. Should someone have thrown a cigarette into the water from the dock or from the bridge a major conflagration could have occurred. That happened at near high tide when the tide was turning and after a short while the tide started out and with it the gasoline. Then the mill was safe and the town slept on.

Fire protection at the mill was not taken for granted as each day someone would go throughout the mill to check the sprinkler systems to make sure they would operate as designed. Those systems were either classified as dry or wet systems depending on what they serviced. In the earlier years Ed Harding was the person designated to fulfill this duty, and in the years to follow the job fell to Dick Findlay and in his absence one of the other pipe-fitters that were trained in that procedure.

Sprinkler systems was not the only source of fire suppression as the mill had a very active fire brigade or as some would call it fire department. The driving force to get the best possible reaction from the fire brigade was Walter Orey the man behind corporate fire protection. Walter usually visited the mill on an annual basis to train and support the local efforts. Galen Redman was the town fire Chief and the head of the fire brigade at the mill and after him was Paul McCann.

It was normal to have brigade members from different local fire departments such as Orland, Castine, Penobscot, Prospect, Blue Hill, and Bucksport. The towns benefited greatly as the men would receive training that would have been impossible thru their town fire departments. Every section of the mill had people on the brigade and on every shift. That insured that a response was swift and effective.

Fire suppression training was held once a month and consisted of training to extinguish electrical fires, chemical fires, petroleum fires, and hazardous chemical fires and spills. With the monthly training at their respective towns it meant that these people were without a doubt some of the finest call men in the state training on an average of every two weeks when you consider the training from the mill and towns put together.

The men worked with small 5 lb extinguisher to 100 lb. extinguishers mounted on wheels. On occasion the town would send in a fire truck for training with fog and full stream suppression sometimes with a wet water additive. Training with Scott self-contained breathing apparatus was something that was practiced quite often. The mill tried purchasing re-breathers to use but after a trial during a chemical spill it was determined that they were not as good for our purpose as the self-contained air packs.

Ladder training was an important function during these sessions as it was totally different to climb a ladder by yourself and then again with a heavy 1 1/2" hose line filled with water. When pressure is applied by the pumper truck it tends to try to straighten out. Once the nozzle is opened it tends to push the hose and its holder backwards.

An example of excellence in training was when one session consisted of a full day with the Coast Guard, Area Fire Departments, and the crash trucks from Bangor International Air Port all working to subdue a simulated situation on the mill dock. During this time pumper training was set up around the perimeter of the mill and other actions were practiced.

Over the years some of the situations that stand out was the chemical spill at the kraft plant, the switch room fire at the drum barking building, the bark dump fire that took weeks to extinguish by covering the pile with dirt to remove the oxygen and the fire on No. 2 calendar stack which sent flames about 40 feet in the air inside the off machine coater room. That fire was set off by someone using a portable grinder and a spark ignited the paper dust. The fire was spectacular in nature but was quickly extinguished by the sprinkler system.

Author note:
"I have some slides showing training being done at the mill and the waterfront if anyone should be interested. I was deeply involved as I had been trained in industrial fire protection in New Jersey and did my best to pass some of that knowledge on to the Mill Fire Brigade. I also was at one time chair of the Hancock County Fire Training Committee. We at one time held a training session at the mill with participation of all the county fire departments, the Coast Guard, and the Bangor International Airport crash trucks and their people. That training session is what I have the slides of. At the Fire Department I was Captain and Chief Training Officer. I also was sent to the Police Academy for training in arson investigation by the Town of Bucksport. so I did a full review of each incident we attended at the mill and in the town."

Marilyn Jewett
Bucksport

WAY BEFORE ANY COMPUTERS

Just before my children graduated high school and starting college, in the late sixties, I received a call from the Personnel Dept. at the St. Regis mill. A female employee in the Packing Dept. had fallen and broke an ankle and they needed someone to cover for her while recuperating and asked if I, a stay at home mother, could come there for six weeks working as a file clerk and typist. I hadn't worked away from home for 18 years – when the mill was Seaboard Paper Co. I had worked at our church doing weekly bulletins, some correspondence for our minister and taking care of his mail. I ended up staying 25 years at the mill. The Production Department needed a new clerk and worked there for 12 years in interesting work, sort of learning the paper making process, before I was offered a job in the Personnel Department. I had been working some weekends in Production and was anxious to have weekends free so took the job – spending five years there as a Personnel Clerk – a most rewarding job for five years dealing with workers' compensation and health insurance and meeting and assisting the general employees. By this time, St. Regis had been bought by Champion International Corp. This was way before any computers were used. I then took a job in Management splitting my time with the Comptrollers Dept., Plant Engineering and Management.

Twenty-five years in all! In every job I had in the mill there was always a good, fair, working environment, good pay and very good benefits with a savings plan and health insurance for my whole family.

Computers were becoming a big necessary part to staff an office so it was a good time to retire in 1992–an interesting 25 years well spent in so many ways.

Marilyn Marks Jewett *was born in 1930 in Castine and grew up there and in Orland where she attended school in Orland at the Crane's Corner School, then two years of high school in South Portland where her father did defense work. She spent her last two years at Bucksport High, graduating with the class of 1947. She and Ralph met and married after his return from the service. They finished studies at the University of Maine, then three years in Stonington in his first school position. From here they settled in Bucksport where they raised their three children and he served as coach, teacher, assistant principal and principal in the Bucksport system, retiring in 1985. Along with the requirements of being an educator's wife and "stay-at-home mother", she was active in her church and the local garden club. She is an accomplished rug maker, enjoying weekly meetings and exchanges with other master rug hookers, especially in the Castine area.*

Phyllis Daniels
Bucksport

CHANCES

Like many other B.H.S. graduates, I started working at the mill shortly after graduation. My first job was a Clerk position in the Main Office. Part of my duties were "Teletype Operator". Of course, this was way before computers. I believe this Teletype was operated through the phone system and I would type and receive messages from the other St. Regis Mills.

The mill was owned by St. Regis Paper Co. when I started there. It was later owned by Champion Paper Co. from which I retired in 1998. Later it became International Paper and then Verso.

Approximately 1964, I bid a job as secretary to the Plant Engineer and worked there until 1966. I had a few years staying at home but after awhile, wanted to be back to work. My memory is not what it used to be so don't have exact dates, but I went back to work in the construction Office as the #4 Paper Machine project was finishing up.

I had an opportunity to work in the Woodlands Office for a few years. While there, the Unions at the mill went on Strike. I was so thankful I didn't have to cross any picket lines.

There were a few years when I was considered a "spare". Whenever someone went on vacation, I would fill in. So, I got a chance to work in the Purchasing Dept., Power Plant and Production Dept. At that time there were no computers, so purchase orders were typed individually as well as work schedules, letters, etc. Technology certainly made these jobs easier.

When the mill decided to build #5 Paper Machine, I was able to get a job working in that office. I believe that project lasted a couple years. After all that, I went to work in the Technical Dept. as secretary to the Technical Director. My office was quite far back into the mill, past #1 & 2 paper machines. Of course, I knew many of the men who worked there personally, but they always "checked out" any woman walking through. At that time most women worked in the front of the mill so it was a novelty to see a woman walking through. I don't remember exactly when women started working along beside the men everywhere in the mill, but I surely do give them credit for doing tough jobs. Rather than letting the men make me uncomfortable when walking through the mill, I just smiled, said Hello, calling them by name.

My office was adjacent to the Main Laboratory where tests were done on various things to ensure the ingredients in the paper met certain standards Although we were a Lab family, I heard comments that "the Mill was never the same after they let women work there."

During my years as a secretary, the clerical or non-exempt employees became disgruntled and rumors of an Office Union began to fly. It was discovered that of the 39 non-exempt people, 35 all had different salaries. I became involved in this movement and when the Office Union became a reality, I served as the first President. The Office Union remained until the closure of the mill. (Non-exempt meant that if a person worked over their regularly scheduled time, they would be entitled to overtime. I must say, after the Union came into being, the environment was a little uncomfortable with some of the salaried employees including my boss.

When a new leader took charge of the Technical Dept., I was offered a salaried job in the Quality Dept. being in charge of calibrating instruments and keeping records in the Supercalender Lab where paper was tested to make sure it met the standards set for various customers. I also generated monthly and yearly reports of these tests. Champion decided to build a new Supercalender Lab. It was a million dollar project. I chaired a committee of hourly employees to work with the engineers to design the Lab so that paper testing would run smoothly going from non-destructive to destructive tests. This Lab was built at the very back of the mill and turned out to be the pride of the Company with the Governor coming to give accolades.

While I was a supervisor in the Supercalender Lab, I had the opportunity to not only visit sister mills regarding quality reporting, I visited the Corporate Technical Center in West Nyack, NY as well as quite a few press rooms where our paper was printed.

In 1998, the company was offering early retirements to reduce costs and I offered to take advantage of this program. There had been several management changes in the Quality Dept. by that time and I was the only woman in the group. The pressure was on and I recognized it was time to leave. My immediate supervisor told me, even though I was doing the work of a supervisor, I wasn't receiving the pay I should have been receiving and there was nothing I could do about it. I was crushed that he would do that to me. In December, they moved me back to the Main Lab to do a computer project that really had no value.

After 29 years working in the mill, I was mentally exhausted, and except for missing a few people, was glad to be retiring!

Phyllis Stone Daniels was born in Lakeland, Florida. "Mother was there because my birth father was stationed there at the time while in WW II. I attended school in a two-room schoolhouse on Verona (it has since been torn down and the Verona Town Hall now sits in its place). Graduated in 1961. Later on in life I attended Husson College at night and only got as far as 12 credits. Working, children, failed marriages etc., too much. After children grew up, I learned to ski (at 50 yrs old), learned to rollerblade and traveled to Florida for vacations in winter. I worked in the law office of Kee & Nesbitt (later, Fellows, Kee & Nesbitt) for about 4 years. I have traveled to Italy twice, once with John to visit our friends who have a home there. That was probably the most exciting thing that ever happened to me.

Seeing things hundreds of years old like the Vatican, the Colosseum, etc. was fantastic. We have a timeshare in Aruba that we travel to every year. We have 7 friend couples who go at the same time. We have explored the island, eaten different food and enjoyed the sun since 2008 (and we are still friends). I used to play piano for the high school chorus, church, and Theta Rho, the junior order of Rebekahs (auxiliary of Odd Fellows Lodge), family weddings, etc. but when I realized I wasn't playing anymore, I sold my piano." Phyllis was a member of the Office Union while working at the mill and became a member of the Credit Union Board of Directors, serving for eighteen years. "Things I enjoy in my retirement are, visiting with my grand and great-grandchildren, our home in Florida, getting together with friends, playing cards with friends. I've had two knee replacements and have arthritis that requires medicating but will keep going until I get to be at least my mother's age and try to enjoy every minute of it!"

Rick Doyle
Bucksport

NOT MANY DAYS WENT BY

Not many days went by
when you couldn't have seen Alden Weld
out for a drive with his old dog.

Foot on the brake pedal,
middle of the narrow road,
ten miles an hour
down over Condon Hill.

Over the corduroy
past the Grange Hall,
Victory Grange
No. 538.

Foot on the brake,
middle of the road,
ten miles an hour
down Dead River Hill.

German shepherd standing in the back seat
barking in his ear.

Fifteen miles an hour, tops,
that green rusty Nova
rolled like an old locomotive

pulling a train of pulp trucks
all the way to Bucksport.

Originally published in *Puckerbrush Review* (Orono, Maine.)

TOAST

In the summer of 1975 James R. Burgess showed up at 218 Cotton Hill, his son's house, Bubbah Burgess. He had 2 shots of whiskey, a small glass of gas and his 40-year-old dinner basket. We toasted the bucket and put the gas on it. His wife said, "I could use that bucket in Ceramics." Dad said it was his to do what he wanted with after 40 years. It went up in flames and we toasted 40 years.

After, my daughter Cindy Pye said she remembered it because the mess was in her sandbox.

Clayton "Bubbah" Burgess *graduated with the Bucksport High School class of 1958 and went into the Navy the following July. He went to Argentia Newfoundland for two years, applying his BHS varsity basketball skills to the base team. "We won the ServLant Tournament in R.I. I came home in 1959 and bought my first car – a 1951 Caddy. I went from Newfoundland to the USS Wasp – CVS18 and played basketball for the ship's team. We played the University of Keil Germany and beat them. Their high scorer was from Texas. I got out of the Navy in July of '62." Bubbah drilled water wells for a year and then went in the Mill for three years, then into construction. "We built No. 4 and 5 paper machines and the buildings. Before this job was done I became an Iron Worker for twelve years. I worked on a 21-story building in Cambridge, MA, and helped build the engineering building at Maine Maritime Academy in Castine. I went to work at the Bucksport Town Garage as Parts Manager for five years, then went back to the Mill for twenty years, retiring in 2002." "In 1963, after the Navy, I married my wife, Michele Howard. We have been together for fifty-three years and have a son, Clayton Jr. 'Tony', two daughters, Cindy Pye and Leslie Corbin; and ten grandchildren – Clayton III, Caleb, Casey and Cullen Burgess; Amanda Thibodeau and Leamen Allen (deceased); Kyle Burgess and Carson, Carley and Chloe Corbin 'The Triplets'. We also have one great grandson, Brody Thibodeau. We always make a holiday of the Blue Hill Fair!"*

THE STORY BEHIND "THE JIMMY BURGESS DECK"

The late Jimmy Burgess, who spent almost two decades as head decker operator and one decade as stock prep decker, has become the first Bucksport employee to have part of the mill named after him.

The stock prep deck, located behind the wet end of number 1 and 2 paper machines, was named the "Jimmy Burgess Deck" shortly after Jimmy's death, from a heart attack, during halftime on Super-bowl Sunday (Jan. 24, 1993) at his home on Verona Island. He was 81.

Jimmy was hired at the mill in October 1935 as a magazine loader in the Groundwood Mill for 54 cents an hour. He became a deck operator in 1946, head decker in 1947, and stock prep deck operator in 1966. He retired in 1975.

Jimmy's two sons, Arnold and Clayton, are mill employees. Arnold, who has worked at Bucksport for 27 years, is an oiler in the Yard and Drum Barking areas. Clayton worked in the mill for three years in the mid-1960s, left for greener pastures, and returned in 1982. He's now a second helper on the Off Machine Coater.

Maintenance superintended Roger Powers, who suggested naming the deck after Jimmy, recalls him as the type of person "who was very well liked and who wanted to be a friend to everyone."

"Jimmy, he says, was "always pleasant and smiling, and always had something good to say. He had a beautiful disposition – always positive, never negative."

Jimmy also had very good aim, Roger says. If you walked under the deck and didn't wave, you were doomed to a ball of stock on your head," he recalls. "He never missed – he was that accurate."

Arnold said his father had a few tricks up his sleeve when it came to delivering a stock ball. "He'd throw one up in the air, and when you were worrying about that one, he'd get you with a big one right in the chest," he said.

Jimmy was also something of a "streaker," according to Arnold, because he'd take a shower at 3:30 every afternoon and then go get dressed. He had rigged up his own shower in the back of the decker by placing a hose over a pipe, and when quitting time came, he'd just turn the water on (Arnold thinks it was cold water).

Clayton recalls that Jimmy, who worked on the deck "before they had that nice air-conditioned booth," would work bare-chested and go up on the roof "just to cool off." "It didn't seem to bother him," Clayton said.

"He never had any colds."

After Jimmy retired, he played quite a bit of golf, mostly at the Bucksport Golf Club. Arnold said he putted with just one hand – and got pretty good at it.

According to Roger, the deck is the only place in the mill that's ever been known by a person's name," and that, he says, is fitting. "Jimmy was just a special person," he says. "I think anyone who came in contact with him felt the same way."

Editor's note:
From an unidentified Bucksport mill newsletter, author and date unknown, courtesy of Clayton Bur-gess.

Rick Doyle
Bucksport

GREETINGS FROM THE SPARE LABOR POOL:
NOTES OF A FAIR-WEATHER MILL HAND

I worked two summers at St. Regis in the late 70's, when I was a college student attending St. Mary's University in Nova Scotia. They hired a number of college students in those days, and assigned us to the spare labor pool. Not, as it turns out, the kind of pool with a diving board on one end. All of the newly hired millworkers seemed to start there; while the other hires eventually moved on to permanent positions, we students were spares only, called on as necessary to fill in the gaps and let go without ceremony at the end of the summer. Most of the other students were from Orono. Some were classmates and friends of mine from high school. (I also met up with a few classmates who had gone straight into the mill from high school.) At that time Canadian colleges started in October and got done in April, so I was working about a month or so before the UMO students had finished their finals. When they started showing up I had already been called in several times.

The first shift I ever worked was a swing shift in the magazine room. Not, as it turned out, a place where you had time to peruse old copies of *Time* and *Sports Illustrated*. As a magazine loader you were lucky if you had time to grab a bite to eat at the battered picnic table. St. Regis blue, of course.

The magazine room was located in a loft above the main floor of the Groundwood Department. This was the pulp mill, where debarked four-foot sticks of spruce and fir were smashed up to make paper. A conveyer carried cordwood from Drum Barking and dumped it into block bins that ran through the middle of the magazine room. Timbers hanging from the ceiling reached almost to the floor. They held back the mountains of pulpwood by means of steel cables that ran along the bottom of the timber curtain. Along both sides of the bins were the magazines themselves, rectangular steel-sided holes in the floor that fed the grinders below.

The loft smelled like a softwood forest, the scent carried with the steam rising up out of the magazines. The cordwood tumbled and thundered in from above, the grinders turned below and shook the floor. As the great stones turned beneath our feet and ground up the wood, the magazines emptied at a sometimes alarming rate.

The loaders' job was to fish the wood out from under the hanging timbers of the block bins and flip, roll, drag, or otherwise cajole it into the magazines. This was done with a pick pole, a long-handled pike once used by river drivers, and with the occasional assistance of a cantdog. On my very first shift I dropped my pick pole down into the magazine and had to go downstairs to the foreman to ask for a new one.

The magazine room reduced you very quickly to the simple function of feeding the hungry paper mill as it turned out miles of paper each and every shift. New workers soon learned that the best way to keep up was to work together. I teamed up a lot with M., a married guy about twenty years older than I was. He was unflappable, with a wry sense of humor and a tendency to whistle as we worked -- "Yellow Submarine" must have been his favorite song. I also worked with another older guy, stocky and short, very quiet but efficient in his work. He took to the magazine room from the start, and I think he ended up getting a full-time position there.

Finally, there was T., about my age. His father worked in the mill, and I think T. had a young family to take care of. He seemed glad to have been hired by St. Regis after being on a waiting list for some time, enduring a series of dead end jobs while he waited for the call.

Work became steadier as the summer went along and more full-timers took their vacations. My first summer at St. Regis I was in the magazine room a lot. I didn't say no when they called, I think because I was afraid that I wouldn't get called in again if I did. It was brutal work, and let's just say I wasn't well prepared for it after a year of reading the English Metaphysical poets. I can still see the look of disgust on my girlfriend's mother's face as she bandaged the raw blisters on my hands. But I actually came to like working in the magazine room.

One memorable morning the block bins burst open. I had been called in on a midnight shift and had teamed up with T. The steel cable snapped right where we were working – up flew the timbers, out rolled what seemed like a mountain of pulpwood. We backed away and it kept coming. We kept backing away. The wood kept coming. We turned and ran, hard hats and pick poles flying. All of this unfolded in slow motion, the way things do in dreams.

That incident got the attention of the bosses, let me tell you. A small delegation came along pretty soon to look over the damage. They were like generals inspecting a battlefield after the carnage. We were told that the tannic acid in the steam rising out of the magazines had corroded the steel cable to the point where it let go. This happened at the end of a shift, when the daylight was just coming through the tall grimy windows. The next shift came in and saw what had happened. And saw the mess they would have to help clean up. They were horrified. And somewhat annoyed, I'm sure, as T. and I on our way out gave them the "job done" gesture.

In my second summer at the mill I worked more on the paper machines. That summer they were bringing Number Five online. It was supposed to be the fastest paper machine in the world, as I recall, but they were having trouble getting it up to speed. And no wonder, to anyone who's ever seen a paper machine at work and knows what a huge and improbably complex piece of technology it is. Every few minutes, it seemed, there was a wet-end break in the paper. When that happened we'd climb up into the dryer rolls to clean off all the broken bits and pieces of paper, doughy and not yet dried. It was over a hundred degrees in there, and even with ear plugs the noise was terrific.

Tons of paper got ruined on those shifts and had to be peeled off the rolls at the dry end. There was a name for that ruined paper: broke. The broke got slid into the broke hole at the dry end of the machine. Down in the hole huge blades chopped up the paper for repulping. When it came to broke, some of the third and fourth hands were artists. You'd see them making cuts at one end of the roll, giving themselves two tails of paper to grab hold of. Then they'd take those two tails and walk backwards, drawing their hands apart, opening the roll of paper as if with a zipper. When they got to the end of the roll, a layer of broke would slide neatly off the roll and drop into the broke hole. There was so much broke that summer that we got behind, and sometimes most of a shift was spent trying to get all of it into the hole.

I worked at the mill about eight months in all. Not long, really. Nothing compared to the years so many others – family, friends, and neighbors -- put in there. But enough to say that eight months in a paper mill is an educational experience. I learned to appreciate not only the work, but also the artistry that goes into making paper, and the achievement of someone who puts most of an adult life into its making. I drew on my experience at the mill, in later years, and applied the lessons I'd learned there not only in basic training but also in law school. Eight months. Two summers. I could have worked a third summer at the mill but opted instead to take classes so I could finish my degree early. I was in a hurry in those days. What in the world for, I no longer remember.

After earning a degree in English from St. Mary' s University in Halifax, Nova Scotia in1979 **Rick Doyle** *worked at a variety of seasonal jobs in Maine and elsewhere. Among other things, he planted trees in the Deep South for Weyerhauser and in Maine for St. Regis. He served as a Korean linguist in the U.S. Army from 1986-1990. Beginning in 1992 he taught college-level English in which he received a Masters degree from UMO in 1994. He was admitted to the Bar in October 2003 after earning his JD from University of Maine School of Law and since then has been a staff attorney at Next Step Domestic Violence Project. He has served three terms on the Maine Commission on Domestic and Sexual Abuse and currently serves as Vice President of the Hancock County Bar Association and President of the Bucksport Bay Healthy Communities Coalition Board. He lives in Buscksport with his wife Shannon Flood. His poetry has been published in several journals and online. He won a Grady Award for graduate-level writing in 1994 and a SpiritWord Honors Award in 2001.*

STRIKE TALK

Though they remained hushed to avoid false accusations, rumors about strikes – when issues surfaced and anger was high (as it is said) – are still passed among both heads of the mill and the work force. Some reportedly made pacts not to divulge whereabouts of certain people who may have felt threatened. A waitress at the hotel coffee shop might have thought she overheard plans for the possible use of mill trucks left with keys in them for the purpose of crossing the picket line and causing harm, and may have passed it on. The State Police may have been called (since local law enforcers might have been thought to be biased) and may have been waiting at the gate. But it was no rumor that the strike ended "without physical clashes," in strike language. Loyalties to both sides, labor and management, may have influenced the telling. "But remember," one life-long mill man wants it known, "many of the people on both sides were related for generations and the kind of people who would never hurt anyone, especially each other."

Editor's note:
As told by several witnesses choosing to remain anonymous.

Rick Doyle
Bucksport

OYSTER STEW SUPPER TO FOLLOW

Characters
Edgar Dolan, *retired millworker, about 70.*
Raymond Dolan, *his son, about 50.*
Watch, *about 30.*
Sergeant Major, *a millworker, about 60.*

Setting
The anteroom of a fraternal order, the Perceval F. Flynn Regimental Temple, No. 354, of The Sons of Saul. Hand-lettered sign announcing a memorial for Franklin Wallace Ginn, "Oyster stew supper to follow." Also the symbol of the order, reminiscent of the Masonic compass.

Scene One

Enter men in regalia, wearing black crepe armbands. They proceed through the Inner Door. WATCH *and* SERGEANT MAJOR *take up position by the door.*

SERGEANT MAJOR   Worthy Watch, let none pass this Inner Gate but those who count themselves the Friends of Saul.

WATCH   None but Friends shall pass, Sergeant Major.

SERGEANT MAJOR   Have you the challenge?

WATCH   Sergeant Major, I do. *Whispers in Sergeant Major's ear, steps back.*

SERGEANT MAJOR   Right. Password of the day? *Whispers, steps back.*

SERGEANT MAJOR   Right, Faithful Servant. Let those not recognized by this word be barred from entry to the Regimental Temple of Saul, unless they can work their entrance using secret signs or be guided by a Brother in good standing.

WATCH   Right, Worthy Sergeant.

SERGEANT MAJOR   Stand fast. *Sergeant Major goes in,* Watch *closing the Inner Door behind him.*

Enter Latecomer, wearing regalia. Whispers password into ear of Watch, *who lets him enter. Second and Third Latecomers, more or less together, go through the same process.*

Enter EDGAR DOLAN, *wearing regalia and armband.*

EDGAR   Say they haven't started, have they?

WATCH   Not yet, they haven't.

EDGAR   I'd better slip in before they do.

WATCH   Right, Worthy Brother.

EDGAR   High Commander gets touchy about latecomers.

WATCH   Right you are.

EDGAR   Especially when it's the old man! You'd think he'd cut the old man some slack, but not on your life! And the old man a Past Commander four times over, no less!   You'd think that might mean something, but it doesn't.

WATCH   Right, Worthy Brother. Password?

EDGAR   Was that a gavel I heard?

Lights down.

Scene Two

Moments later.

EDGAR   It's right on the tip of my tongue! If you hadn't asked I could have told you!

WATCH   You'll think of it!
EDGAR   I've given every password back to the Great Depression, and you can't let me in that door?

WATCH   Not without the current word.

EDGAR   They're draping the charter for Frank Ginn tonight.

WATCH   That's right.

EDGAR   Do you know who Frank Ginn was?

WATCH   He's come to a few meetings.

EDGAR   Oh, he's come to a few meetings, has he? Is that so?

WATCH   Like I said. Nice old gentleman.

EDGAR   You let me tell you something, young fellow. Frank Ginn was a charter member of this order. He did more than come to a few meetings, now, I'll tell you! Not only that, but Frank Ginn was like a brother to me. We chopped wood together, once upon a time. Hemlock. Dollar a cord – felled, limbed, bucked and barked. Why, Frank boarded with me and my wife May. Great Depression, that was. Later we worked out at St. Regis together. Seaboard, it was, back then. First in the wood yard, unloading cars with a pick pole and a cantdog. Then up in drum barking. Groundwood, up in the block-bins. Finally we ended up on the paper machines. Thirty-five years on those paper machines! Frank retired three months before I did. That's how it was Frank Ginn and me. We were like brothers. And now you're telling me I can't go in there?

WATCH   Of course you can go in. With the password.

EDGAR   Who are you?

WATCH   You know who I am.

EDGAR   Let me in!

WATCH   You're welcome to work your way in, same as anyone else.

EDGAR   I can't remember the damned password!   How am I supposed to remember the Four Secret Knocks?

WATCH   Or you can get a member to verify you, as soon as there's a break in the meeting.

EDGAR   There won't be any break in the meeting, the only thing they're doing tonight is draping the charter for Frank. They'll be hell bent for election, wanting to get Frank out of the way so they can go across the road for oyster stew.

Inner Door opens, and the Sergeant Major leans out. Greets Edgar silently.

SERGEANT MAJOR   How goeth the watch, Brother?

WATCH   All quiet on the Orient Gate, Sergeant Major.

149

EDGAR   See?   They're starting!

SERGEANT MAJOR   *(Reporting to someone inside)* All quiet on the Gate, Worthy Commander.

Response from within.   Edgar tries to slip in, but the Watch prevents it.

SERGEANT MAJOR   Hold fast to your station, Worthy Watchman, and be ever steadfast in the fulfillment of your duties.

WATCH   Right, Worthy Sergeant, steadfast to the final report.

EDGAR   *(At the same time)* Right, Worthy Sergeant, steadfast to the final report.

Sergeant Major goes back in. Watch starts to follow. Edgar grabs his arm. Watch shuts door without going in.

WATCH   There's any number of brothers that would be willing to vouch for you. Or I could ask the High Commander to come out.

EDGAR   No! Don't do that! He's running a meeting in there.

Watch goes in through Inner Door.

EDGAR   Don't interrupt the Commander just because his old fool of a father can't remember the password. I cause him enough trouble as it is.

Edgar notices the Watch has gone in. Makes as if to hammer the door with his fist but stops himself. He turns and looks toward the sign announcing his friend's memorial. Behind his back, the Inner Door opens a crack. Sergeant Major peeks out. Sees Edgar, closes door again. Edgar takes crepe off, puts it in his pocket.

Lights down.

Scene Three

Moments later.

Enter RAYMOND DOLAN from Inner Door.

RAYMOND   What's going on? Dad?

EDGAR   I told him not to send you out here.

150

RAYMOND   Well, I'm not going to leave my own father out here in the anteroom.

EDGAR   As long as you know it wasn't my idea.

RAYMOND   You feeling all right?

EDGAR   I'm fine.

RAYMOND   Take your medicine?

EDGAR   Oh, yes!

RAYMOND   That's good.

EDGAR   I mark it down on the calendar, now, soon as I give myself the shot.

RAYMOND   That's a good way to do it.

EDGAR   Helps me remember.

RAYMOND   So. You coming in?

EDGAR   Not according to the Worthy Watch. *(Putting crepe back on)* Where in the name of God did you find him, anyway?

RAYMOND   He's just doing his job.

EDGAR   By God, Frank Ginn would have let me in.

Sergeant Major sticks his head out into the anteroom.

RAYMOND   Have them do the Elders' Report.

EDGAR   How can they, I'm on the Board of Elders!

RAYMOND   *(Gesturing for Edgar to be quiet)* We'll be right along.

Sergeant Major goes back in, closing door.

RAYMOND   You haven't sat on a Board of Elders meeting for a year. Not since the first time you went to the hospital.

EDGAR   I know how long it's been.

RAYMOND   You said they were a bunch of old fools.

RAYMOND   Are you sure you took your insulin?

EDGAR   Yes, I'm sure. *(He starts to drop his pants)* Do you want to see for yourself?

RAYMOND   Put your pants back on.

EDGAR   I'm sure I took my insulin.

RAYMOND   That's good. I'm glad. *(Pause)* Let me give you the word.

EDGAR   You don't need to give me the word!

RAYMOND   You remember it?

EDGAR   I will.

RAYMOND   You're going to miss Frank's memorial.

EDGAR   I won't be led around by the hand like Frank was at the last of it.

RAYMOND   Big difference between that and being a little absent-minded.

EDGAR   Who are you calling absent-minded?

RAYMOND   Do you have the password, or do you not have the password?

EDGAR   *(Turning to go)* I said I wasn't going to be led in there, and by God I meant it!

RAYMOND   Then let me give you the password.   Come back here!

EDGAR   Don't break any rules on my account.

RAYMOND   Let me give you a hint.

EDGAR   Don't give me no hints.

RAYMOND   Father.

EDGAR   What?
RAYMOND   Your sash is crooked.

EDGAR   Never mind my sash.

RAYMOND   Better fix it. Pretty important... regalia.

Edgar adjusts his sash.

RAYMOND   Yes, a fellow has to look after his... regalia.

Edgar strains to remember, Raymond waits.

EDGAR   Endurance.

RAYMOND No!

Inner Door opens. Sergeant Major looks out, then retreats, closing door.

RAYMOND   Stop this foolishness! I am going to give you the word, and you are going to go into that meeting with me. Just the way you planned to when you came in here tonight.

EDGAR   Don't you raise your voice at me.

RAYMOND   I'm sorry. I'm sorry. You're right. Don't go.

EDGAR   You don't need to raise your voice at me.

RAYMOND   Just let me give you the password!

EDGAR   I know the password!

RAYMOND   What is it?

EDGAR   Ashes.

RAYMOND   No!

EDGAR   Sickle!

RAYMOND   No!

EDGAR   Monument. Winter. Harrow.
RAYMOND   Look at you. Too stubborn to admit you don't know the password, even if it means you can't go in and pay your respects to the best friend you ever had.

153

EDGAR   Oyster stew!

Enter Sergeant Major.
SERGEANT MAJOR   Ray?

EDGAR   Go ahead! You'd better go look after your meeting.

RAYMOND   Be sure and stay so you can get something to eat. Promise?

EDGAR   Go on!

RAYMOND   This won't be long, then we'll all be over for some stew.

EDGAR   Go on, I said! Go on.

Sergeant Major and Raymond go in. Almost as soon as they do, Edgar remembers the password.

EDGAR   Regalia!
                                        Lights down.

Scene Four

*A moment later. Watch enters, takes up position by the door. Then the Inner Door opens.
Sergeant Major sticks his head out.*

SERGEANT MAJOR   Watchman, are the gates fast?

WATCH   They are, Sergeant Major.

SERGEANT MAJOR   Stand by while the charter is draped to mourn the passing of our Brother,
Franklin Wallace Ginn, to the higher realm.

WATCH   Right, Worthy Sergeant.

Sergeant Major goes in.

EDGAR   Password? Password's the least of it. I'm surprised I know my own name, sometimes.
Sometimes I just stand there with the refrigerator door open, wondering what I'm looking for. Quart
of milk. Orange. Plate of mackerel. Insulin. Like things you'd never imagine, not even in your wildest
dreams! It's the damnedest thing! I don't know I'm looking for the butter dish until I happen to notice
the knife in my hand. Or I'll be making a phone call, and right in the middle of dialing the number not
know who I'm calling. Or I'll be talking to somebody and not know who they are. I'll know the voice.
Know the face. But to put them together with a name... I can't remember, to save my soul!

154

Sounds of ceremony from inside: drumbeat, which continues under the following.

EDGAR Do you know what I am? Blackballed. Blackballed by my own memory. Or blackballed by my lack of memory, I should say. Blackballed for life. Just like poor old Willard Francis. You must have known him! The gravedigger. The well-digger. Water witcher. Don't tell me you didn't know him! Willard gets himself nominated somehow. Nobody knows how. Old gravedigger! Well, he's going to get blackballed. Charlie Cole will blackball him. Eddie Fish will. Frank will. Like Charlie says, what's the sense? Why put yourself through the misery? But Willard won't withdraw his name. "I'm as good as any man in the Sons of Saul, by God." So he comes to the Vote on Applications. Waits out here. Right here. First he's got company, you know – four or five other applicants. One by one the others get called in. Then it's just Willard and the Watch. In there, the officers are voting on his nomination. *(Pause)* Why not? Why wouldn't they let him in, same as anyone else? Didn't they let Georgie Colt in? Poor old Georgie! They let him in, just like they give him a job out at the mill. You see him in Groundwood. He cleans up the cordwood they pick out of the magazines. He has a little blue wagon he hauls around. He isn't fit for much else. They let Georgie into the Regiment. *(Pause)* But Willard Francis? Not on your life. And Willard knows what's going to happen. He's sitting right there. Sweat pouring down his face. He's white as a sheet. You can hear the voices from inside, but you can't make out what they're saying. They've been talking for some time. They keep talking. The gavel pounds. Then not a sound. Not a sound. Willard stands up. He turns to the Watch, he's stiff as a pick pole. Puts his hat on. "I am far superior," he says, "to any man that might want to give me the black ball." Turns around, walks out that door.

Slips crepe armband off his arm.

EDGAR But what about you? How's your memory? Oh, I know, I know – you're young, you've studied the bylaws, you've learned the ritual by heart, you know the lore. But how's your memory?

Drumbeat stops.

EDGAR And I'll tell you another thing!

Enter Sergeant Major.

SERGEANT MAJOR Watchman, well done. Thy labors are at an end.

EDGAR I'll tell you another thing –

WATCH Thanks, Worthy Sergeant.

EDGAR *(Dropping crepe at Watch's feet)* Don't think I don't know who you are!

BLACKOUT

155

In addition to poetry, **Rick Doyle** *has written several plays.* Regalia *is a work of fiction about a retired paper-maker, set in the '70s, based loosely on his grandfather, and* Too Good to Be True *deals with a family impacted by the closure of a fictional paper mill.* Oyster Stew Supper to Follow *is a shorter version of* Regalia, *which was selected for reading in the* 2001 Maine Playwrights' Festival *and published in* At Play: an Anthology of Maine Drama, *edited by Laura Emack.* Oyster Stew *was given a staged reading at Bangor Public Library in 1999 and published in* Crosscut, *the literary journal of Husson College.* Other plays by Rick Doyle have been read or performed at the Acorn School of Performing Arts, Stonington Opera House, Penobscot Theatre, and New Surry Theatre, where he was Playwright in Residence *in 2009.*

Patricia Ranzoni
Bucksport

RICH POOR MAN 'S OYSTER STEW

Rich Doyle's play, "Oyster Stew Supper to Follow," brings back memories of my father's way of making it. Because he grew up upriver in a large family with scant resources, fresh oysters were out of the question. Like many working-class people after WWII, canned oysters became the popular ingredient. And because, in addition to his job as a rigger at the mill, he always kept a milch cow, we had an abundance of milk, cream, and our own butter for chowders and seafood stews. Only when the cow went dry prior to calving did we ever buy canned milk. Authentic recipes for oyster stew made with canned oysters are nearly impossible to locate since the method was so simple people didn't write it down. Here's how I remember him doing it and how I still do on rare occasions:

> *Drain canned oysters, reserving liquid.*
> *In large kettle gently cook oysters in butter til edges begin to curl.*
> *Cool a few minutes.*
> *Add oyster liquid to kettle along with favored proportions of fresh*
> *   or canned milk, cream or what have you.*
> *Bring to a simmer being careful not to allow it to boil.*
> *Season to taste.*
> *Serve with oyster crackers – the reason, as far as children are concerned,*
> *for the stew – qualifying it for a Pay Day or special occasion dinner or*
> *supper. Multiply for company or a crowd.*

Patricia Ranzoni
Bucksport

from INVITATIONS/PALAVER/GOODBYES

>   In spite of the fact that as everyone knows,
> the only way to keep the vernacular pure
> is to avoid the corruption of travel, supposin'....
> we'd light out for Lincoln
> with a few six-packs Maine's newest brew
>   to check out moose.
> Or, so's not to have any regrets on that famous score,
> take some less traveled road I'd call outback
> but you, something elegant, soundin' so pretty
> it don't sound queer
> only this time you can't get enough of all I
> have to tell and how I tell it and what have you.
> So we chew the old fat – hook, line, and familiar sinker
> 'til the cows come home to their particular pastures
> and that free-for-all Verona moon
>   all dolled up in a disguise all her own
>   is mine one more papermaking time
> 'til we commence to sober up thinkin' we'd best
> be getting' on home and bein' men
>   nobody thinks a thing of it.

>   *D'ow!*

Author note: "D'ow" or "Daow!", as John Gould explained it in *Maine Lingo*, is an old way of saying an emphatic "No!" or some such opinion that something is beyond belief. Gould illustrates: "Some years ago the federal boys had some Maine lobstermen in court for price fixing, and one of the Washington lawyers asked a witness a sort of foolish question. The answer was, 'Daow!' Court was recessed so the lawyers could find out what this meant, and how to spell it."

The entire poem from which this segment is excerpted was previously published, in two scenes, in the *Puckerbrush Review,* Orono, Maine.

Patricia Ranzoni
Bucksport

INCENDIARY
for my papermill overtime working father

 She took them to be consultants
when they sat beside her
on the Bangor to Boston flight
discussing "the lesson from Bucksport."
You know, "dialoguing the situation,"
as they say. As they said.

"So what!" one said.
"It was only five thousand and
it was extra anyway."
"Only a perceived loss," one said.
You know, "values" they said.

She strained under her seatbelt
against their sickening tone. Them.
She was a child in the frigid dark carrying
finger biting pails from the well
to the cows, trip after slippery
mitten soaking trip; because
a barge was in and had to be loaded and
it was her father's "value" to work
all the overtime he could get
to make ends meet and
the ends didn't. Meet.

"I hesitate to call it sabotage,"
one said, "but we expected morale
to be improved by now."
"Problem is," one said, "they're reminded
of the cut every week on payday."
"The solution to that is to pay them
once a month," one said.
One smiled and said.

She was a teenager being berated
for wanting to accept a party invitation
from friends. Management families.
"Who do you think you are?" her
bitter father instructed.
She hadn't understood.

When the pilot announced
changed landing plans,
(out of his hands he said)
they jostled him through their
textbook talk. Wouldn't want him
working for them, they said.
"Must be a union man," they said.

"_____!" she wanted to answer,
her smoldering anger threatening
to take them down.
And didn't they think it possible
that union people ever travel
twenty miles upriver, or fly anywhere,
or didn't they care how disgusting
their "dialogue" was in a labor
sympathetic state, or didn't they care
or didn't they care or didn't they care?

Should she call the union? Call
the company? Write letters to the *News*?
She wrote and remembered.
(She'd know where. She'd know
when.) And understood her father
a little better, she said.

First published in *CLAIMING, Poems by Patricia Ranzoni* (Puckerbrush Press, 1995).
Author note: In the 1970s when "Incendiary" was written, the possibility of a commercial plane being "taken down" by human anger was not part of our collective consciousness. I remember reaching for words to adequately express how it felt being an invisible papermill worker's daughter hearing this disrespect. For words to "say the unsayable." Were there any? True, my emotions felt "capable of causing fire," figuratively speaking, and these "consultants'" insensitivity and ridicule was "inflamma-tory." Also, I confess, I was left wanting to "agitate," cause trouble, be an incendiary, with the truth of what I had witnessed. But my choice of the image– "...her smoling anger threatening / to take them down"– held another layer of meaning as well – "to dress them down," so to speak. "Put them in their place," and so forth. I trust that given the realities of life for papermill families, as testified to here in

160

Still Mill, readers will grasp the intentions of my words in "Incendiary" and know that I did not mean to suggest any such thing as an act of terror that such language has, in recent years, sadly, come to hint. For these reasons and more, I would not use these words in this hazardous way again. They do, however, continue to serve me well in testifying to my truth in those times.

Rick Doyle
Bucksport

THE PULP CUTTER SPEAKS
After R.S. Thomas

I am the pulp cutter. I am the man
behind the skidder. Twitch by twitch
I fell the limb. Stand and consider,
when the hinge gives way and tree falls true:
half sorrow and flesh, I'm no different from you.

In the kingdom of the bronze borer I let in light.
Will fisher, will budworm forgive my work?

In a well of strong woods I move wreathed in blue.
Listen for distant thunder while my chain saw cools...

I know the widow maker,
I know the glancing bit,
I know the barber chair and the bar jammed tight
when a back cut closes in gust and sun –
you don't know your business, I say get done.
I watch the crown for the turnabout wind,
keep axes ground,
keep wedges to hand.
Flat-file takes the rakers down.

Blue jay and junco my born-again friends,
the baker's daughter eats out of my palm,
I come home in balsam when the day is through,
half hunger and bone, no different from you.

Previously published in a H.O.M.E. (Homemakers Organized for More Employment) Co-op chapbook, Orland, Maine.

Thomas Gaffney
Stockton Springs and Bucksport

SHIFTS: AN OPEN LETTER TO THE PEOPLE OF CHAMPION

Vol. 49 Issue No. 4 – Bucksport Free Press, Bucksport, Maine, Thursday, December 7, 1989

Do you want better health while at the same time reducing the cost for health insurance? Would you favor a more productive, cost-effective mill operation? Would you like to sleep better, and have more quality time with your families? Would you like to be more alert and hove more energy to deal with the stresses and challenges of life today? Are you interested in doing something that will help prevent the abuse of alcohol and drugs in your community, and reduce the number of accidents that result in injury both on and off the job? How about reducing absenteeism and personnel turnover while increasing job satisfaction? It is hard to imagine anyone who would not be in favor of these changes. So, what's the catch?

Would you believe that there is no catch? No hidden costs or agenda, no strings attached, no management or union scheme, just a good, wholesome, everyone-wins change.

Because papermaking is a 24-hour-a-day enterprise, shift work has been an element ingredient in the production recipe. Shift schedules in operation today were designed decades ago, before serious scientific research into the ways humans adjust when they suddenly change the time that they sleep and wake.

If you remember your school prom and the custom of staying up all night, or if you have traveled across time zones and experienced "jet lag," you have sampled a taste of what happens when you tamper with the body's clock. Recent medical research has identified areas in our brains that govern the rhythms of sleeping and waking. The body's clock, which runs on about a 25-hour day, insures we have periods of alertness alternating with periods of rest. Body and mind work better when outside time is in sync with inside body time. When outside time conflicts with the inside time, as when one stays awake when one usually sleeps, or tries to sleep when one is accustomed to being awake, the body and mind to continue on schedule for a while as if nothing has changed. Thus, one has to make oneself stay awake when one feels like sleeping, fighting off drowsiness or using stimulants to force alertness; or one may toss and turn restlessly in bed trying to get to sleep, feeling fatigued but unable to fall asleep. After a few days on a different outside time schedule, the body clock adjusts and coordinates sleep and waking with the new outside time.

Most if not all paper companies in Maine change shift rotation three times every 28 days. Considering that seven on the 28 days are days off, it is common that shift workers have inside/outside time conflicts six times every 28 days. That's about 70 times conflicts a year. Not only that, the direction of the shift rotation practiced by most Maine paper companies is directly opposite to the way the body clock is running. This makes it doubly hard for the body to adjust to time changes when they occur. Suppose you ordinarily go to sleep at 10 p.m. and usually sleep eight hours. Imagine how you would feel if suddenly you tried to make yourself sleep at 2 p.m. and then wake up at 10 p.m. to stay up for the rest of the night. How well would you function, how well would you sleep? Imagine doing this 70 times a year.

Because the present schedule of shifts has been in practice for so long, it appears hardy hardly anyone questions it. Most everyone tried to live with it and accept it as if they have no choice. There is very good news, however, because there are much better options.

Harvard professor Charles Czeisler, a pioneer in sleep research and founder of the Center for Design of Industrial Schedules in Boston has worked with the Philadelphia Police Department, the Great Salt Lake Minerals and Chemicals Company in Utah, Union Carbide and Dupont, among others, in designing shift schedules that take into consideration the workings of the body clock, worker preferences and production requirements. The results of this work are startling.

The police, who had previously worked a shift schedule closely resembling those of papermakers, reported a four-fold decrease in the frequency of poor sleep; twice as many officers reported no problem with daytime fatigue; there was a 25% decline in the number of sleep episodes on the night shift; officers had 40% fewer on-the-job automobile accidents per mile driven; officers used fewer sleeping pills and less alcohol to alleviate the consequences of sleep deprivation; and officers' families reported nearly five-fold increase in satisfaction with the new police work schedule. The result of the shift design changes with other companies were equally dramatic. In general, productivity improved, job satisfaction increased, worker and family stress was reduced, there were fewer accidents, and health improved.

The long-term effects of continuing with the present schedule of shift change has not been established. Laboratory studies have found that mice subjected to sleep-wake cycles similar to the papermakers died 6 to 20 percent sooner than mice kept on a normal schedule. Time will tell if humans fare better or worse.

In these days of spiraling health and insurance costs of ever increasing demands on the time and energy of parents, and of intense market competition in the paper industry, no one can afford to let any stone unturned in the effort to promote health for our workers, families, companies and communities.

I invite managers and union leaders in Maine's paper companies to come together, become informed, examine the alternatives for shift scheduling, and work out a change where everyone will benefit. There is no reason to continue the way of the past, and no one can afford to wait any longer.

Born "a Mainer at heart" near Philadelphia, Dr. Thomas J. Gaffney *came home to Maine in 1979 after completing his education as a Psychologist. "A different sort is he, never looked at what's wrong with people, rather what's in them that wants to blossom." He and his first wife, Gretchen, settled in Fort Kent for three years, where she became an artist, and he directed community mental health and substance abuse services in the St. John Valley. Then they settled in Stockton Springs, and he began serving the people and community of Bucksport, which he has done ever since. Here "the people taught him to listen and care. He kept his eye on doing good for children and families, mill workers and schools. They blessed him by opening their hearts." He and his twin sons, Galen and Christian said a loving goodbye to Gretchen in 1997. Two years later, "loving erupted" with Theresa, and together they raised their five children, tended organic blueberries, while he volunteered for the Bucksport Bay Healthy Communities Coalition, its President for 12 years, winning a* 2 Those Who Care *award in 2012, and the Coalition a* 2 Those Who Care *Agency of Distinction award in 2014. He wrote "the first book of its kind on healthy loving relationships," called* A Prophecy of Love. *He "believes it's possible to do everything in love, and communities striving to love will thrive."*

Patricia Ranzoni
Bucksport

TODAY, TOO

after "Today" by Billy Collins

Billy's *intermittent breeze*
you explain to the boys
because they can figure the rest
even if not how a man contains
a spring day by letting out like this

they love it

especially the part about opening
the canary's cage and freeing
those cottagers from the snowy dome

which means
there's hope for them too

this winter's school photos encased
in whatever that floating sleet is
glittering

when what a boy needs
is to be sifting dirt
for glints of rock to identify

or to rev his 4-engine invention
on the pond to test

and the phoebe pair loops
to the plum tree to wait
while they help air the pillows
and quilts they slept on on the floor
last night before commencing construction
in the chosen location
under the east eaves

and the booted men pull over
in their trucks and neighbor-dear cars
answering the sun's call
with their clods of worms and rods
to wade into the swift brook loud

the way a flooding dictionary is loud

to cast for trout like perfect words
swimming back to their source

and the temperatures are human

and there is that intermittent breeze

if they can just hook the one word one
catch is all they ask the thrill of the hit

the way a rainbow-want tugs
and reels in your mind

one right fish
to show what needs refeeling
to get through another spring

inside that mill.

"Today, Too" was originally published in ONLY HUMAN, Poems From the Atlantic Flyway *by Patricia Ranzoni (Sheltering Pines Press, 2005).*

TESTIMONY AGAINST THE COMING OF THE COAL-FIRED PLANT, AES

Interested Party 19 – A   *9/12/1991*

Chairman Leach, Members of the Bucksport Planning Board:

My name is Dr. Thomas J. Gaffney. I am a licensed Clinical and School psychologist in private practice here in Bucksport. I have served this community since 1983, providing over 10,000 hours of services to children, couples, families, adults of all ages, and schools. I am a citizen and member of the Bucksport Community.

I received a Master of Science in clinical Psychology from Hahnemann Medical College and Hospital in Philadelphia in 1974, and a Doctorate in Clinical Psychology from Hahnemann in 1977. I am entering my twentieth year of scientific exploration of the ways of promoting the health, wellbeing, learning, work and loving of human beings and their communities.

My specialization has been children and families. In a psychosocial sense, the family is the womb of personhood, and community is mother. The learnings and values of life are handed down, for better or worse, from one generation to the next just like the genetic endowment. A respectful, collaborative, caring and cohesive community is the most powerful healing and health promoting force ever seen on this planet.

On numerous occasions I have consulted and provided training on the critical processes of human relating: stress management, problem solving and decision making, communication and conflict resolution, supervision and teamwork, performance appraisal, creativity and play.

I have training and experience in organizational dynamics and performance, and have conducted a variety of community interventions to enhance community wellbeing, for example I am currently involved with a committee looking for ways of increasing the self-esteem of children in our community as part of the Partners in Education project sponsored by Champion Paper Company.

Besides my consulting experience in Bucksport, to prepare my testimony I have talked with business leaders, educators, medical professionals, clergy, social service providers, and community gatekeepers to obtain their views of the current status and qualities of the Bucksport Community. I have studied the

167

history of this community to understand how we came to be, who we are today, as well as to find the learnings from past successes and mistakes. I am confident you will agree it is vital to have this knowledge in mind to decide what will be best for the Bucksport Community.

Before I say anymore I want to thank you for listening to what I will say. I sincerely believe you, members of the Planning Board, deserve the gratitude of our community for the extraordinary job you have done and continue to do, listening to the plans, ideas and concerns of all parties in this matter. Now, you are the only people in town whose listening still matters. You have been entrusted with the responsibility of making a decision for everyone. It is a decision that will alter the town's destiny forever, and affect the lives of our great-grandchildren. Your deliberations have already and shall continue to dominate community relations, citizen-government relations, real estate and commerce, community atmosphere and climate.

You have the responsibility to protect the shores of the town. You have that responsibility for the purpose of protecting the community and way of life in Bucksport. For reasons that are unclear, no one else's choices and values matter any more; the rest of us are helpless. Our way of life, and indeed our lives and our children's lives are in your hands.

You will have to go back 60 years to find a moment of equal importance to what is before you now. Your decision is not unprecedented. This town was at this crossroads before.
The Bucksport Historical Society tells us:

> "At the turn of the century, Bucksport was a place to dream about,
> so lovely it was with the well kept and beautiful old houses on its
> tree-lined streets. The lovely Penobscot River flows through the
> Bucksport area lending its many moods of fog and sunshine, placid
> as a lake and stormy and treacherous as the ocean, but always charm-
> ing and interesting."

In the early 1930s, during the Great Depression, the Waldo–Hancock Bridge was built, and the Seaboard Federal Paper Company began operation. The Town should have been euphoric with the largest and most profitable employer in Hancock County history being added to a community of decent, hard working people along with a new magnificent bridge of commerce and opportunity. What happened?

Town historians, Pooler, Buck, Reed, Hempstead and Wheeler wrote this account in *The 150th Anniversary of Bucksport, Maine*:

> "The town that its citizens had known for half a century or more ended
> when modern industry seized it as a site for the huge mill which dominates
> the landscape and daily life."

The community's attention, energy and human resources shifted from being primarily family, community and nature's caretaker to taking care of huge machines that ran 24 hours a day. The economy of the town came to depend upon the company from away for its very survival. True, greater economic prosperity and opportunity were enjoyed by many, but at what cost to the health and wellbeing of families and the community of Bucksport?

Some say there is no more stressful and dangerous place to work in Maine than in a paper mill. Every sense is under assault. Physical and chemical hazards require alertness and concentration. The body must be made to work when it feels like resting or rest when it is alert. No wonder the life expectancy of paper mill workers is significantly less than the rest of us. Families of mill workers, to a large extent, build their lives around work, it will not adapt to them. It is harder to keep a marriage vital, harder to parent and spend time with children, harder to maintain friendships beyond the mill, and harder to contribute to community. These hardships have weakened family health and the community by generating stress and conflict while simultaneously reducing the power of natural support networks.

Our community and the families within it for the most part learned how to deal with conflict from the generations which preceded. Conflicts which are not resolved well are handed down from one generation to the next. How conflicts are managed has a direct bearing on health and disease. Conflict is the process of managing give and take in relationships. When the process is fair, respectful, voluntary and collaborative, conflict can strengthen relationships and promote health. When the give and take is unbalanced, or forced, distress and disease will result.

Surely on the face of it, generations of mill workers and three paper companies have tried to balance the give and take between them. They could not know, until recently, what was the true scope and accounting in human terms of their negotiations. They simply did not have the science or tools to measure the impact of their agreements. On the face of it, a good wage in exchange for eight hours of work seemed fair. The physical and psychological stresses of shift work, the realignment of give and take in intimate relations, parenting relations, friendships, and community relations were for the most part overlooked in the accounting of give and take between worker and company.

Looking at the leading causes of death in the greater Bucksport community we gain deeper insights about what has happened to our community life. On February 13, 1991, the Bucksport Regional Health Center presented its Annual Report. In it were figures taken from the Primary Care Data Profile for Maine. Prepared by the Maine Department of Human Services in 1989. Heart Disease, Cancer, Cerebral Vascular Disease, Accidents, Cardiopulmonary Disease, Chronic Liver Disease and Cirrhosis, Pneumonia and Influenza, and Suicide were ranked one through eight as the leading causes of death. It is established that environmental contaminants, stress, and addictive lifestyles make substantial contributions to these rates. The weakening of families and community which resulted from the imbalance of give and take between the newcomer industry and the community as a whole is directly related to the way our citizens die.

The Health Center report also indicated that five of the top eleven primary diagnoses for their patients were for respiratory system conditions. If these diagnoses were all lumped together the most common health problems for which people seek treatment in our community by a wide margin would be respiratory problems. Could it be that this is evidence that we already have serious problems with our air? What would happen to the many members of our community with respiratory problems if we gave them more contaminated air?

It took this community fifty years to begin a recovery from the imbalance of give and take begun in 1930. This community cannot afford to do that again, nor can it afford any more environmental contamination.

In 1980 the Bucksport Improvement Group was organized by downtown merchants, and a community wide process of comprehensive planning for revitalizing the town was born. In 1988 a Community Development Block Grant was awarded to Bucksport for rehabilitating affordable housing, rebuilding infrastructure and revitalizing downtown. For the last decade there has been an unprecedented collaboration of citizens, town government, business and community organizations which has followed the plan, producing: The Dr. Thegan Bridge, the Miles Lane School, the Town Office, a sewage treatment system, Main Street, the harbor development, the library addition, a day care and family support center, a Little League ball field, Creative Playground, housing for our vulnerable people, and renovation of the Town Pool. Barriers to the handicapped were removed. Recreational programming was expanding and diversifying. Old businesses were renovating and investing in the future of Bucksport. New business and services were coming because it appeared this was a community with a future. A Chamber of Commerce was organized.

Champion Paper was making a significant contribution to the revival. It developed an Employee Assistance Program for workers and their families, funded for two years a prevention effort to begin addressing the problem of addiction in the community, and like St. Regis before it, contributed to a number of community charities and services, both in dollars and human resources. Most recently, Champion has sponsored the Partners in Education program.

About eighteen months ago a shadow was cast over all the plans and accomplishments. It was a giant newcomer, Applied Energy Services (AES), a coal-fired power plant, creating the illusion it has much to give and little to take. The development of the town has been at a standstill ever since because so much of the time and energies of the community have been absorbed by it.

It has encouraged soul searching, debate and conflict in the community. It has asked us what kind of community are we, and what kind of community do we want to become? It has questioned our values and our power to control our own destiny. It has galvanized the community to rise up and send the newcomer away. The people of the town recognized that it will take far more than it will give.

On the 1979 survey of the community for the current Comprehensive plan 75.9% of those expressing opinion were opposed to the introduction of additional heavy industry. A survey of 56 downtown Bucksport business owners and managers in august or 1990 indicated over 90% were ". . . seriously concerned as to the future of our business should AES be allowed to build their plant in Bucksport. This move would be detrimental to the progress and direction our town has chosen." Petitions of Bucksport voters in November 1990 showed for every citizen in favor of the project there were seven who were opposed. According to Richard Holmes, the President of United Paperworkers International Union

Local 1188 at Champion, "at least 80% expressed opposition to the project, deciding ". . . to put the health of their families and people in the community over money." In March 1991 a survey for the Pending Comprehensive Plan indicated 71.9% of those expressing opinion were still opposed to the introduction of additional heavy industry. As of September 1991 over 1700 Bucksport adults, more than an outright majority of citizens signed a petition asking the Town Council to formally insist AES leave our community. This majority is even more remarkable because only about 75% of the adult community were actually presented with the petition. There probably has never been an issue before the town where the will of the people has been this clear of this strong. To set this aside would be catastrophic to the community of Bucksport. The helplessness and powerlessness that would follow the granting of a permit to AES would discourage community participation and involvement, as well as result in the outright loss of some of the community's finest people. What reason would people have to give to the community after so much would be taken away?

The imbalance of give and take between AES and the Bucksport community is much worse than it looks. Its potential to generate stress, destructive conflict, addictions, and eventually hasten our deaths in the most power-ful of any force in our community during the last 60 years.

Before the first Planning Board meeting on this issue AES had contracts in hand to sell most of the power it would make here to out of state power conglomerates. This deal was hidden from view until recently. Its lawyers have tried to tell you how to conduct these public hearings. It has broken its word, and is staying where it is not wanted. It has deceived you and this community by its conduct in the application process, for example presenting seriously flawed models of risks the plant will pose by neglecting to include such variables as existing levels of environmental contaminants, natural processes which will collect and concentrate plant emisions, the body burden of environmental contaminants already carried by our citizens, and the actual health status of the community. It has overlooked and not bothered to study the real human and natural environment in Bucksport. For these reasons alone most of the testimony from its health consultants should be dismissed as hopelessly biased. Could you trust a doctor who doesn't want to know your health history, or your presenting symptoms and complaints, who has already made up his mind that you are fine, and tell you all you will have to do is make sure you stay indoors 90% of the time?

AES is ignorant of our history, blind to our present needs and wishes, and indifferent to our will. It acts like a Taker.

Considering the health status of the community, the way our citizens are dying, the existing air quality, the volume and kind of pollutants the plant will produce, the way our weather will collect and deliver its pollution to the community, the demoralization of community spirit and weakening of our sense of community, it is prepared to take a great deal. It will certainly create unsafe and unhealthful conditions in Bucksport.

What will AES give to Bucksport? Not much. AES has admitted in its forecasts of socioeconomic effects prepared for the U.S. Environmental Protection Agency that it will be giving relatively little to our community. I quote from the May 1990 report:

"... it is probable that workers will be hired from within a larger regional area that includes the Bangor metropolitan area, and Waldo and Hancock Counties."

"... since the peak construction period is expected to last less than one year, any decrease in regional or local unemployment as a result of the project would be temporary."

"Because Bucksport will only be contributing a fraction of the total construction work force, and laborers living in Bucksport will be providing temporary construction services, no appreciable impact to employment in Bucksport is expected to occur."

"... Since (project construction and operations services) employees will be hired from an existing work force within a large regional area ... indirect employment benefits will be widely distributed. In fact, these new employment opportunities will likely sustain existing employment levels for Maine retail and manufacturing employees."

Richard Rosen, the President of the Bucksport Bay Area Chamber of Commerce does not expect significant indirect economic benefit for area businesses since most of the workers will take the money they earn and spend it in their home communities, just as it occurred during the recent construction at the Champion Mill.

AES also projected there would be "... no appreciable impacts to the human population. . .", and "... no significant growth in demand for resident support services . . .".

The insensitivity and ignorance of AES regarding Bucksport is apparent here. AES will crush and demoralize the fragile sense of community that grew in the 80s at a time when the community is still struggling to address the effects from the trauma of 1930.

If a spouse took as much and gave as little in a marriage as AES will in its relationship to the community of Bucksport, there would be a divorce. If a parent took as much from a child and gave as little, the parent would be prosecuted for abuse. If a person took as much and gave as little to others there would be condemnation, and rejection for the sake of self-preservation.

The people of Bucksport do not want AES here because the people care about their community. They know a taker when they see one. They have learned from the past. They have a vision of the community they want. They have come together, and they are prepared to do whatever it takes to send AES back where it came from.

The twenty years of my professional training and experience have taught me one overriding and powerful lesson. The most important, and essential ingredient for the health and growth of human beings is a healthy community of people who share fairly of their time, energy, knowledge, skill and support. If this sense of community is lost, all is lost. To permit this thing into our community will amount to giving our community to this thing. Surely you understand as human beings the kind of hurt, stress and conflict takers have brought to your lives. The community of Bucksport is asking you for protection. Don't let AES in.

Our community has dared to imagine. It has begun a recovery from a profoundly disorganizing trauma to its spirit. Our community has come together to plan its future. The first stage of that plan has been successfully completed. It is not time to abandon what has been accomplished or betray the healthy recovery of spirit that has been so long in coming. It is time our community got back to its business. It's time to channel the talents, energy, caring and commitment this crisis has brought out in our community to build on the accomplishments of the 80s. Economically, let's follow the course set by the Town's Comprehensive Plan. Let's strengthen the business already here with our patronage. Let's use local skills and resources to create cottage and home-based industries for local and tourist markets, as well as for national and international markets by way of established mail order companies. Let's add to the harbor development and bring back the successes from the past. Let's be progressive and think about the future, for example by learning how to manufacture products on a small scale from materials collected by our Town recycling center. Let's develop service industries for local and state needs such as a Maine travel service that could plan and arrange hunting, fishing, naturalist, recreational, and cultural excursions for consumers during each of our beautiful seasons. Let's consider a non-profit economic development corporation to stimulate businesses that will enhance and enrich our community. I am one voice, one source of ideas, I know in concert with the many remarkable people of our town we will not lack for good ideas, if anything we will have more than we can use.

Let's create a future for our children. Let's support our schools to prepare our children to participate and enrich the sense of community through cooperative learning, learning to learn, and conflict resolution curricula. Let's enrich our relations with our surrounding communities for mutual prosperity.

Champion, you will benefit more by investing in our community than by supporting AES. If the sense of community is lost you will significantly complicate the already stressful lives of your workers, and risk losing the trust of this community. Support the community and let us join your workforce to enhance your productivity and competitiveness.

Town Government, listen to the voices of your constituents. Let us create and build together the community we really want for ourselves and our beloved children and grandchildren not yet born.

Editor's note: An account of the outcome of AES's effort to locate their coal-fired plant in Bucksport can be found at *https//archive.bangordailynews.com/1992/02/01/bucksport-appeals-board-ends-aes-hearings*. *"*To me it seemed AES was surprised by the determination and passion of the Bucksport Bay communities, so after failing to win Planning Board approval, and failing the appeal, they knew they would not prevail, and so gave up," recalls Tom Gaffney. "I believe this event challenged the community of Bucksport to determine its identity with the result that people discovered what they could do together to decide their future. Just three years later, the Bucksport Bay Healthy Communities Coalition was founded, another grass roots collaboration that has accomplished much. People with remarkable hearts settled here." Among those dedicated people who are remembered for powering the opposition to the location of a coal-burning plant here are Carolyn Brennan-Alley, Kathleen Jenkins, Paul Liebow, Bill O'Neill and Don White. As Don recounts, "While we were the core organizers, the group we formed for opposing AES – *State Taxpayers Opposed to Pollution (STOP)* – had a mailing list of several thousand from our bio-region and beyond. Following permit application, rejection, refiling, acceptance, appeal, and unanimous overturning up through the Bucksport Planning Board and Appeals Board, with their sets of hearings, resulting in AES filing in Hancock County Court, they finally pulled out because of the overwhelming area opposition. When it became undeniably clear that the people here, Bucksport, itself, didn't want them, they announced that they were 'moving on.'" Those committed to this successful effort count the outcome as a major accomplishment of their lives, continuing to devote themselves to non-polluting industry and development.

Author note:
"For the 200th Anniversary of the Harbor Church in Searsport, I became Captain Benjamin Franklin Pendleton to tell the story of faith, family and community that produced over 400 sea Captains in the 19th century. What wonderful stories with brilliant light to shine upon us today!" Tom Gaffney

Ralph Burgess
Orland

"IN BED WITH MANAGEMENT?" IF SO, IT WORKED FOR WORKERS

Union local president at Champion International heard the charges, but he calls it teamwork, and says it has paid off.

A former machine operator, Ralph Burgess, is a union local president and a self-taught expert on Total Quality Management as it applies to union workers and paper mills.

A couple of years ago, Burgess saw that the future held unemployment if management and labor didn't improve production at Champion International's Bucksport mill.

He was willing to forsake traditional contract negotiations for problem-solving teams. He then proposed management-labor teams to deal with customers and the quality of Champion's product.

Burgess has managed to win the confidence of both labor and management in the application of quality management. He spoke with Doug Ford, *Press Herald* staff writer, on how to make a quality management process work with unionized labor. Here are excerpts from their conversation:

Q. How did you persuade your membership to go along with a quality management approach, particular when that can mean cutting jobs?
A. I said to members, 'Look, about the only industry that hasn't been touched by the competition, by the Japanese, is the paper industry.'

I've seen what happened in the steel industry and in the auto industry. A friend of mine in management, who I'd grown up with, said, 'Come with me, I want you to see some things.' And we saw a huge rusting steel plant that must have employed 18,000 people and now employed 1,700. We also saw the 'greenfield' technology, the new plants being constructed to work with a lot less people.

The biggest thing with a union is job security, but if you don't have a product you don't have a job. I told the guys, 'We've got to serve our customers here or we're not going to have a product.'

So management made up a black book of where they wanted to cut. I took it to the workforce and they were real upset. I said, 'This is what we're going to try to do.' So I told management, 'If you want our people to sit in on the redesign of the plant and look for ways to cut jobs, then we have to have job security.' We got it.

Q. How can everybody get job security if you are going to make job cuts?
A. Well, we take care of the job cuts through attrition. And workers' pay rates were red-circled. So if their job got cut and they went back to the gate to start another type of job at the plant, they would get that pay rate for a new job.

Q. What were the toughest things to overcome to make the process work?
A. People being skeptical, members seeing it as another company program. We'd seen lots of those, like the flavor of the month.

Q. So what did the company have to bring to the process to make it work?

A. The company has to bring money. A lot of money goes into training in something like this. And Champion has done this. For example, they have to provide the resources for a team to visit another plant for two to three days. And that also means getting people to take their place on the line during that time.

Q. So it costs the company a lot up front. How long does it take to recover the investment?

A. I'll put it this way. Three months after we signed our '90 contract (that called for quality teams), we set a production record. Since then we've won paper quality awards from Sears and Avon.

Q. What were the risks for those involved?

A. The union has to get involved with the company but maintain its own identity. This is important. Our union labels go on the product wrappers. We're a business partner. This place has got to make money. We're now looking at gain-sharing (profit-sharing) agreements where not only the bargaining unit but management gets a share too.

I had to take the risk of the guys saying, 'Ralph's in bed with management.' The line manager had to take the risk of empowering the operators, which was putting his job on the line. He told the guys if they think a roll of paper is 'beatered' (sub-standard), you take it out of the manufacturing process and if somebody says not to, you call me at any time even if it's 2 in the morning.

Q. And what were the risks to the machine operator?

A. Now he had the risk involved with making those decisions and making the right decisions.

Q. How did the customer teams get started?

A. One of our customers, *Time Magazine*, was very dissatisfied with us. Management asked me to sit in on the meeting. They basically said that we'll give you six months to improve the quality of your paper. We're going from five suppliers to two and you're number five on the quality scale.

After that, I approached the line manager and said we've got this problem with *Time*. I asked him if he had ever heard of quality customer partnership teams. He said, 'I don't know anything about it.' I said I didn't know anything either, so we've got common ground here. We still supply *Time* with paper.

The teams have reduced product defects from a ratio of five defects per 100 to five 1,000. Recently one customer was going to bring up a quality issue in our regular meeting and the team already had solved the problem.

Q. How did you get involved with quality management?

A. It was an idea being thrown around out there. The company never came to us with a comprehensive plan. They started with the team concept in the '87 contract. But it was driven on us, because it was in the contract.

But the '87 contract was a poor one. It was a take-away contract, and plant profits showed it during those years. People didn't like each other; people didn't talk to each other. We were supposed to be the Jay, Maine, Standoff. (In 1987, union workers struck International Paper's Jay plant and were replaced by non-union workers in one of the state's most bitter labor disputes.)

I did some reading on Deming. I read several books. And I kind of went along with some of the things. I always believe in working in teams. I had been an assistant football coach at Bucksport High for seven years and I thought we could use teamwork at the plant.

In '90 we were all geared up for traditional negotiations – I give you an offer, you give me an offer, that kind of thing – and management was too.

But the day before they said, 'Will you try this non-traditional negation, where you get in a room with a facilitator and put the problems on the table. And it has to be a problem, not just a want.'

We said we'll consider it if you take a couple of issues real dear to us off the table. They did. We signed a five-year contract.   — With Doug Ford, *Portland Press Herald*, 6/29/1993

*After graduating from Bucksport High School in the class of 1958, **Ralph Burgess** worked the summer hauling asphalt for a new runway at Bangor International Airport. That September he joined the U.S. Army under the "Buddy System" with class and sports team mates Frank Dunbar and Eddie Lowell. "We were to be kept together and we did stay together for the bus ride to Fort Dix, NJ where Eddie stayed for basic training and Frank and I went on to Fort Knox, KY, for our basic training. So much for the 'buddy system'!!!!" After basic training Ralph went to Aberdeen Proving Grounds for schooling in mechanics, then did tours of duty in Korea on the 38th parallel, in Ft. Lewis, WA, Ft. Devens, MA, two years in Germany, "and finally back to Washington, D.C. to finish my six-year re-enlistment with an Intelligence Group." He was discharged in December of 1966. In the community Ralph was involved with the Bucksport Little League both as a coach and officer for ten years during the late '60's and '70's. From '70 to '77 he was an unpaid volunteer assistant football coach, becoming offensive coordinator at Bucksport High School; and in the late '80's and into the '90's was a member and chair-person of the Orland School Committee. He and Leila Marks, class of 1959, married in '61 and she finished her education at UM while he was in the service, teaching in Bucksport when he got out. Their son, David, was born in '63. "Along the way we've built a camp on Lake Alamoosook, bought a home in Orland, and enjoyed watching our son grow into a wonderful adult. Also along the way I have gained and lost 80-100 pounds three times-the final loss coming in 1998 when I was diagnosed with Type II diabetes. I decided if I was going to be around for long that a total change in lifestyle had to take place. With the support of my family my diet was changed (no more Snickers bars!) and a regular exercise regimen was started. It took a few years to finally get comfortable with the whole process but after a year I had lost 90 pounds by eating sensibly and walking daily. After 10 years it had become a way of life." Through the years Ralph's hobbies have been fishing, duck hunting, snowmobiling, golfing and being a 'spectator sportsman' of just about any sport going." He and Leila have also enjoyed traveling and have been on a tour of the Alpine Region of Europe, made trips to Disney in Florida, and trips to Las Vegas and the Grand Canyon. "After retirement, we enjoyed spending the months of March and April in Daytona Beach Shores, Florida, having a great time just enjoying the good weather with friends from Bucksport and our family. Our son, David, who worked at the paper mill, now Verso, married Linda Munson in 1985 and our favorite grandson Justin was born in 1998. They have been able to spend a week or two with us in Florida each year, making our stays even more fun. These days life revolves mostly around my 6 am coffee group and family activities. We have had a lot of fun keeping up with our grandson's activities at school, in sports and Scouts, in which both he and his Dad have been deeply involved. Camp life became a lot more active with a grandson and his friends enjoying the lake with us."*

Dave Davis
Orland

OPENING THE DOOR TO MEMORIES TUCKED AWAY

SETTLING IN

Push open slightly
ajar bedroom door, toss
tired travel bag on the bed.
Room seems stuffy so Ginny
throws open the window to
a welcome breeze which
caresses our tired bodies.
We hold each other close
and hear the clank
of the sea buoy bell
hung on low branch of
Jane's pine.
Know we are home.

September 3, 2015: How some 66 years ago now, when Ginny and I got married, in those days the mill used to shut down and start fresh each Monday. So we took advantage of that, taking an extra day off to go with Labor Day for a honeymoon at Toddy Pond.

Tricks guys played on each other in the parking lot, like lifting up a car and putting bricks under, just skimming the ground so the guy gets in the car and sits there spinning his wheels. Then there were the lunch box poles....One of the jobs of the 6th hand on the paper machine was, at the appointed time, to go collect hot dinners from the Town Site which they carried on poles through the basket or pail handles, delivering them to the workers.

One remembrance is walking off shift all of us with our lunch baskets on our arms glad to be going home–the joke being bandied about re lunch baskets? It's not what you bring in for lunch but what you might take out. One guy was taking one brick at a time, he was building a chimney? Another had a basket full of nails. Seems these baskets got tired and worn out from time to time and when their bottoms dropped out, no one stopped or missed a step. So it wasn't what you brought in for din din, it's what you might be able to lug out. Or one guy had a new wheelbarrow full of dirt which was looked over thoroughly? Nothing there. The wheelbarrow was the object of theft. Had enough?

Peace & Love.

"Settling In" was first published in Narramissic Notebook #10, *2009.*

David Llewellyn Davis *has lived on the banks of the Narramissic River in Orland with his wife, Virginia Soper, since their marriage in 1949, her ancestral ground. He knew it was where he wanted to settle, too, with her family, among earliest settlers of the area, after visiting his own relatives here following WWII. He worked in the Bucksport paper mill from 1949 to 1972, beginning in the woodroom and ending as an oiler; then for the University of Maine Cooperative Extension doing community development for close to a dozen years. After retiring, he started and enjoyed a successful greenhouse business for the better part of a decade. He and Ginny, an historian, have always been active in town affairs and community organizations. A Quaker, Dave was instrumental in starting a Friends meeting in Orland. When the shooting tragedy at Columbine High School occurred in April, 1999, "I was so moved that words just came tumbling out as fast as I could write." And that was the beginning of his writing every day for years, from life along the river and beyond. His poetry has been published in the* Bucksport Enterprise *where the editor called him Orland's poet laureate;* Narramissic Notebook; ECHOES The Northern Maine Journal; *and in the anthologies,* SENSE OF PLACE, Collected Maine Poems (Bay River Press, 2002); H.O.M.E. Words (St. Francis Press); *and the bicentennial history,* Best Remembered: Orland, Maine 1800-2000. *In 2004 his poetry collection,* Ready to Be Surprised, *was published by the Narramissic Notebook Project. He has read with other Maine poets including on the community radio station* WERU's Writers Forum *where his and their voices are archived. Also archived, at* Northeast Historic Film in *Bucksport, amateur division, are films and notes documenting the annual fun Orland Raft Race and Dave's role as founder, with his brother Dr. William F. Davis, who conceived of the race together for Orland's celebration of the Bicentennial of the United States in 1976. According to the story, the race was originally called the Clement-Herod Memorial Raft Race in memory of Timothy and Mary Clement and Jonathan Herod who drowned January 16, 1795 on the Narramissic when rafting from their place on the Upper Falls Road to a funeral at the "burying place," near where the Davises would, years to come, build their home. In 2016, Ginny and Dave celebrated their 90th birthdays there on the Narramissic with their two children, Frank and Jane and their families, and community of well-wishers at the Orland Community Center, adding all the more grateful echoes out over the river.*

Anonymous

HARD HEARTED MEN

There was Yippy and Woodbridge
Lally and Keene.
Grant making the fifth
On this bloodthirsty team.

They stalked the green forests
Solemn and grim,
In an old hunters crouch
Where shadows grow dim.

When the old law of average
And a stroke of pure luck,
One for the record,
They shot a small buck.

Their joys there were boundless
And their prayers were true blue,
To all gods of the hunt
And a stray bullet too.

Said Keene, "It's my job
I'll do it up fine,
I'll cut out his gizzard
In less than no time."

But Yippy yelled, "Wait!"
Let's not make a mess,
Now I'll do the job
With the Nickless finesse."

Lally grabbed up a knife
While they talked it over,
And he started to cut
Like a scythe in deep clover.

And as the knife entered
The stink it came out
The stinkinest stink
Well aged and stout.

The talking all stopped
Not a word did they speak,
But turned as a group
As their stomachs did leak.

And the gurgling sounds
Filled the woods far and wide,
While the poor little buck
Still had his stomach inside.
But they tell me, this year
They've a cure for their ills,
For, now they take hunting
"Anti-seasickness" pills.

"Got a little note in my lunch basket asking me to print this.
I'm going to attempt it. It refers to last year but I think it
is good enough to print for this year. It is a poem so here goes!"

> – Richard O. Chase, Editor
> SEABOARD BULLETIN Vol. 15
> November 1953

Editor's note:
While all of these names will be recognized by their community, Keene was Russell, father of Bucksport's present mayor, David Keene, who remembers his dad was a swiper at the mill. Writing about her father Don's work as a swiper, Sandra Bowden Dillon notes that "the Swiper Crew did very dangerous and hot work – cleaning the paper machines – very hot and steamy. All the men of that crew had burns."

from THE PEOPLE & THE PLACE – ST. REGIS OF MAINE

Maine boasts of many fine waterways. One of these is the Penobscot, and it is a river which knows a very special heritage. Fed by a network of lakes and streams, the several branches of this powerful river system merge and flow through vast stretches of Maine timberland to her meeting with the sea at Bucksport.

St. Regis came to this river several years ago with the purchase of the Bucksport mill, built in 1930, and with that acquisition became in integral link to the magic that makes the Penobscot River all that she is. A river which has seen the explorers, Verazzano and Champlain; the English harvesting mast pine in the 1600's; the beginnings of American shipbuilding in the 1700's; and the birth of America's logging industry in the 1800's.

The Penobscot is a river that welcomes those willing to sustain all that she is. St. Regis stands firm in just such a commitment. People who are willing to challenge the odds so easily mounted by the Maine outdoors. People who take pride in their great heritage and who possess the skills and the initiative to do a job right. People who know the merit of an honest day's work and the pleasures of enjoying the crisp, clean environment which St. Regis strives so diligently to maintain.

Yes, it is these hardworking, dedicated, enthusiastic people and this place together that gave St. Regis Paper Company the mettle to stake $85 million on an expansion program which will see an increase of 65% in daily capacity to produce the paper which was projected several years ago to be required by the publishing industry today. Mettle born of the intense interest and determination of St. Regis to continue in its leadership position as the largest producer in the United States of coated papers for the magazine industry.

St. Regis indeed has every reason to be proud . . . of the People, the Place, and the Product .
> *--From a St. Regis booklet, author and date unknown,*
> *probably for the mill's 75ᵗʰ Anniversary observance in 2005*

Editor's note: *Historians will recognize that this account is incomplete, as if there were no inhabitants in the Penobscot River Valley before Europeans arrived. To the contrary, as the Penobscot Nation's history timeline at www.penobscotculture.com shows, their ancestral presence along the Penobscot River dates from the Paleo-Indian Period – 12,000 to 9,500 Before Present.*

WORKING FOR ST. REGIS MY GOOD OL' DAYS

"I don't know anyone who wasn't well pleased working there."

"Forty years and a half I worked there. Starting in the early '50s and retiring the last day of 1991. At first I traveled three years down from Bangor to work at the mill starting in the woodroom. I also worked summers some, worked mixing bleach "liquor" as a bleach plant helper and in the woodroom winters. Then upstairs to groundwood before going to work for Wally Thomas up in the clay building."

"Earl Bailey told me there was an opening in the Oilers which the Lubrication Department was called, so I became an Oiler Specialist, sometimes filling in as foreman on the oiling crew, until transferring to become a Vibration Analysis Technician monitoring pumps, electrical motors, and bearings on the paper machines and super calendars. Once David Baker retired I ran that department."

"We struck only once that I know of, around the year we went from St. Regis to Champion. Over the wages we were to get paid, I think."

"What should be remembered about the mill? Hard to say. It was good for the Town of Bucksport. There were as good pay as there was to be made in the State of Maine. People talk about "the good ol' days. Well our "good ol' days" were when we worked for St. Regis and Champion. I don't know anyone who wasn't well pleased working there. Otherwise we would have been out digging ditches."

Jesse Richard Rollins was born at the Eastern Maine Hospital in Bangor in 1932. He grew up in Bangor, attending Bangor schools and lettering in football, basketball, baseball and track at Bangor High. "I've enjoyed all sports my whole life. Softball and bowling, along with stamp collecting, have been my favorite hobbies." Jesse served in the Air Force, "getting out somewhere in the early '50s. I started working at the mill in 1952, traveling back and forth for three years. Somewhere in there, about '54, we moved down to Mechanic Street. We moved out to Bucksmills in the '60s. I have remained active in the Masonic Lodge and my wife, Joanne and I enjoyed everything together. We traveled from Prince Edward Island to Hawaii and from PEI to Florida. She died in 2009." Jesse and Joanne's family includes daughters Terry Rollins Egilka and Barbie Rollins Grindle; three grandchildren – Randy Grindle, Josh Egilka and Shelby Kirk; and two great grandchildren – Sidney and Wesley Kirk.

Stan Marshall
Veazie, ME, and Lakeville, MN

PULP AND PEOPLE:
BUCKSPORT'S CRITICAL PAPERMAKING INGREDIENTS

Papermaking requires three principal ingredients: wood, water and power. Shipping is needed to move products to market. Bucksport offered all the critical materials and transportation with ocean shipping directly from the mill to areas where the paper was used. It was located near Silver Lake which was a good fresh water water supply, initially wood moved down the Penobscot River and in 1930 Central Maine Power Company built Wyman dam on the Kennebec River to supply electric power to drive the grindstones which converted softwood trees, harvested locally, into a pulp of acceptable whiteness using grind stones powered by huge electric motors.

The pulp was relatively inexpensive as by grinding the wood the process used the entire tree trunk which initially was delivered as four foot logs and later in tree length. A more recent process, but probably 30 years ago, another type of grinder, this time two disks rotating in opposite directions with carefully controlled clearance between them, converted chips delivered by truck, into a stronger and brighter wood pulp.

An advantage of northern softwoods is that because the growing season here is short the fibers that make up the wood have thin walls which make thinner paper than pulp made from southern softwoods which have thick walls because the trees are protecting the water in the wood from evaporation during the longer, hot, growing season. Because the fibers from ground up wood are short, the paper is not sufficiently strong to process through the papermaking machine or a printing press. By adding long softwood fibers produced, typically in Canada, by cooking to eliminate the non-fibrous part of the tree the overall product from Bucksport was much stronger and consequently could be printed with high quality. *Time* magazine was the initial customer for Bucksport paper with Seaboard Paper Company as the owner.

When coated with paint, made at the mill from imported minerals and adhesive, the resulting paper was both light weight and smooth. Since magazines and catalogs, and similar printed matter, is commonly distributed by US Mail where freight is shipped by the pound, it was advantageous to use Bucksport paper which was thin and had more area (pages) per pound than most competitors.

Bucksport had a good labor supply as the result of offering relatively high wages and, for the most part, steady work. It was common, as you know, for young people to leave school and spend their entire careers working at the mill. As ownership of the mill changed over the years generally the workers continued to work at the mill so some may have had paychecks from three companies.

I believe that in the end the changing demands for the kinds of light weight paper made at Bucksport reduced profitability even with some modest efforts to produce types of paper not made at the mill in the beginning. It is my impression that non-U.S. producers have made significant inroads to supply U.S. paper needs and more modern machines in areas with lower energy costs allowed products to be made less expensively. There is no doubt that the emergence of the Internet and e-readers reduced the demand for print advertising and distribution of news using paper and for paperback books which were the mainstay of the Bucksport mill.

February 23, 2017

It is with a heavy heart that I pass along the news that Stan Marshall, Jr. passed away this morning at his home in Minneapolis with his wife and stepdaughter at his side. Stan sat in my seat at the helm of the Pulp and Paper Foundation longer than any other individual, and he was truly the heart and soul of this organization. He built the framework for all of us to follow; initiating the co-op program, starting the Consider Engineering residential summer program for high school juniors, and tirelessly encouraging the alumni and corporate members to give back. Stan's dedication to this group was unmatched. After retiring as Executive Director, he served as a member of the Investment Committee right up until his cancer diagnosis last fall. As recently as just a month ago, he requested that I send him more Consider Engineering brochures to pass out to potential students. There are numerous scholarships at the Foundation that we can attribute to Stan, including the Stanley N. Marshall, Jr. USA Scholars Fund and the Stanley N. Marshall, Jr. First Year Scholarship Fund. For me, he was a mentor not only because he sat in my parents' living room when I was a junior in high school and explained to them the reasons why I should pursue Chemical Engineering and a Pulp and Paper Scholarship, but also because of the interest he took in me personally as a student here at UMaine. He made me feel that this office was a sanctuary, and we have tried to continue that sense of community and belonging for our students today.

Carrie Enos, President
University of Maine Pulp and Paper Foundation

Editor's note:
Unbeknownst to me, my request for a contributor's note from **Stanley Marshall** would arrive during his last days, his death coinciding with our mill's. As this goes to press, he is being remembered for the remarkable, involved, exceedingly generous man he was, as evidenced by these selections from his resume': Stan earned his B.S. In Chemical Engineering at UMO in 1961, his M.S. In Pulp and Paper Technology in 1964, and was a candidate for Ph.D. there in 1973. Concurrently he earned 9-12 Maine teacher certification followed by graduate studies in education and business administration, and became computer literate. He taught advanced math and science at Machias Memorial High School (1961-62), was a Research Engineer for Texon Inc., So. Hadley Falls, MA, developing process and product improvements using paper to substitute for leather (1962-1963); followed by five years as Technical Writer/Teacher for Process Licensing, S.D. Warren Co., Westbrook, ME as liaison for papermaking process technology transfer to companies located in Europe and Japan. From 1969-1974 he was Lecturer in Chemical Engineering Technology, University of Maine, Orono where he taught and developed curriculum including modifying and coordinating an associate degree in Chemical Engineering Technology, designing and successfully implementing a self-paced chemistry class for underachievers, implementing UMaine's first cooperative education program with curriculum changes,

designing and implementing summer residence program for gifted math/science high school juniors, conceiving and writing the first home study course, "Introduction to Papermaking Technology, offered by the Technical Association of the Pulp and Paper Industry (TAPPI). From 1974-2001 and 2006-interim, Stan served for 27 years as Executive Director, University of Maine Pulp and Paper Foundation; and for five years (2002-2006, 2008-2009-interim) as part-time Executive Director, in affiliation with Penobscot Valley Senior College, Bangor, establishing a new organization from steering committee of 20 to membership of 350 seniors, including incorporation, curriculum development, and instructor liaison, financial planning, administration, and reporting, fund raising, and coordinating logistics with 14 courses per fall and spring semester and six special events annually. His civic activities were more than impressive, many to live into the future, like these, among others: National and regional volunteer coordinator and tax aide for AARP (American Association of Retired Persons) Foundation; Director, President, Freeman Forest Housing Corp., Orono; Director, Treasurer, Chair (10 years), Maine Legal Services for the Elderly; Founder, Bangor Area Single Again (for widowed and divorced persons; Chair/Director Bangor Regional Speech and Hearing Center; Chair/Director Hersey Retreat Corporation (in affiliation with Unitarian Universalist Society of Bangor; Council President, Independent Congregational Society (Unitarian) of Bangor; Chair/Trustee, Finance Committee, Maine School of Science and Mathematics; President/Director Maine School of Science and Mathematics; Director for 30 years of the Penobscot Theatre Company including numerous administrative positions; Founding President, first Executive Director and volunteer teacher, Penobscot Valley Senior College; Church Council Chair/Moderator and Endowment Trustee, Unitarian Universalist Society of Bangor; and Founding President of the Unitarian Universalist Fellowship of Greater Portland, Maine. Considering the depth of Stan's devotion to all in which he believed – family, friends and collaborators do not think of his life as ended. His own awards and honors include the 1981 1st Annual Maine Science and Technology Commission's Science and Engineering Award; and the 1992 Distinguished Service Award from the University of Maine Pulp and Paper Foundation. In 1996 he was honored by the establishment of a $50,000. scholarship in his name from 200+ contributors; and in 2001 by the Vision 300 Award from the Paper Industry Management Association for improving the paper industry image. In 2002 he received the University of Maine Pulp and Paper Foundation Honor Award for improving the reputation of Umaine; and in 2006 the Stanley N. Marshall Jr. Conference Room at U Maine Jenness Hall (chemical engineering) was dedicated. In his elder years he has been featured in numerous magazine and newspaper articles documenting his many volunteer awards. In 2013 he was named the Maine Philanthropy Council/Colby College Philanthropist of the Year for Community Service. Considering the depth of Stan's devotion to all in which he believed, family, friends and collaborators do not think of his life as ended. Before he died, Stan dedicated himself to endowing as many Maine causes as he could with his earnings, especially through the University of Maine Foundation. His sons, Lee and Andy, are known to be his most meaningful legacy.

Stan Marshall's note from a November 15, 2016 e-mail to STILL MILL editor:
"It is hard to be sad or mad as I am able to reflect on lots of satisfying activities over my 76 years."

Patricia Ranzoni
Bucksport

from RETURN

A jay floats up over night's black treeline and turns into day.
Becomes first light at quarter after four.
All the birds in the whole north woods turn into their very songs.

The animals have long been about, their breaths risen into clouds.
Clouds turning the white pink of this moon's forest flowers.
Clouds the pinkwhite promises of this season's wild fruit.

Trucks. Trucks. Just trucks on the road.
Trucks with trees.Trucks with trees. And trucks with tree business
and what tree business can do. The road is a river of tree business.
The road is a log drive the way the rivers used to be.

Author note:
*These lines are excerpted from my longer poem, "Returns," which was inspired by
attendance at the May 22, 2002 ceremony returning Bear Island in Washington County,
Maine to the Passamaquoddy Tribe by Montreal-based Domtar Industries, Inc., pulp and
paper mill. The story of the island's historic loss, spiritual meaning, and voluntary return
introduces the poem in the words of Donald Soctomah, then Passamaquoddy Preservation
Officer, and published with his permission in* ONLY HUMAN, Poems from the Atlantic
Flyway *by Patricia Ranzoni (Sheltering Pines Press, 2005).*

Patricia Ranzoni
Bucksport

TAGLIABOSCHI / WOODSMAN, WOODCUTTER

– for young Joe studying forestry

Let there be no doubt
from whence this cellular drive sparks.
Along with your maternal and paternal
Canadian, Yankee and Indian sides, be hereby advised
that the occupation your great-great-grand-
father Pasquale gave on his marriage certificate
with Rosalinda before leaving for America
in 1905 to plant your family here
was *tagliaboschi*. Woodsman!

And that that alpine mountain
where he cut and hauled by mule
has been waiting for your return,
the pocket village, Monteviasco, calling
your family's name everywhere, music
to our ears. You need only look
on the internet to find how they did it
and still do, their saws and rigs on slants
out over the steep foothill and valley sides.
You, a descendant of these skills
with every crosscut and chop. Every cord
hauled to the mill. Look them up –
tagliaboschi, Monteviasco – and grow!

Bucksport native and STILL MILL editor, **Pat Smith Ranzoni**, *met and married Ed Ranzoni from Chatham, N.Y. at the University of Maine in Orono where he came in 1958 playing baseball and working his way part-time at the Penobscot Chemical Fiber paper company in Old Town. In their youth, his grandfather, father, and uncles had been charcoal makers in the Berkshire forests, skills recruited in northern Italy by the American pig iron industry in which they cut and built 10 ft. wide X 15 ft. high* *circular hardwood mounds, camping in the woods to tend the smoldering wood against flames. Ed and Pat returned to Bucksport in 1970 purchasing the Smith subsistence homestead in Bucksmills where they raised Gina, Joseph and Daniel and founded New Alderbrook farm school, the first state approved early childhood program in the region. He went on in education as guidance counselor and varsity baseball coach at Bucksport High School, continuing, with their sons and grandsons, to cut and haul pulpwood to sell at the mill to supplement income from other work. In the 1980s, while attending UM, Joe senior was on the mill's summer spare list, filling in for workers who were sick or on vacation. Three generations of Ranzoni men still take their family's winter supply of wood from their place.*

NO DEAD WOOD NO DEAD WOOD NO DEAD WOOD
BUCKSPORT MILL
Spruce and Fir Pulpwood Specifications
Jan 2013

Species: Spruce/Balsam fir
Scale: Weight Scale Only

Diameter: No less than 3.5" or more than 21" D.I.B.

Length: Four Foot 47" – 49" inches
          Cut to Length   12' – 6" or less and 24' feet
          Tree Length   12' feet or longer

Rot: 4 – 9 inch minimal Rot Allowed
          10" inch and greater: 50% (of butt diameter) solid rot allowed for tree length.

Red Heart: Sound red heart is acceptable as long as the growth rings are visible.
          No Soft Rot

Age: Live trees only – Wood must peel cleanly with a knife, have no excessive
          discoloration (gray)

NO DEAD WOOD   NO DEAD WOOD   NO DEAD WOOD   NO DEAD WOOD

Load Preparation   All wood trimmed flush and no brush. Free from
                        excessive crook. No forked tops or dog legs No burnt
                        wood

Tree Length Load Preparation   All Butts in one direction – Use of a riser is mandatory
                        when changing directions

Four Foot Wood   All four foot wood must be delivered on trucks that can
                        unload them self (self unloaders) 10 ton minimum size
                        load

| Unacceptable Wood | Out of spec wood will be placed back on the truck |
| | Off species wood will be placed back on truck |

Woodyard Policy
Hard hat, safety glasses, steel toe shoes, must be worn when outside the cab.
No riders beyond Scale house. Driver must remain in cab during unloading.
No firearms or alcoholic beverages allowed inside the gates.
Load straps must be removed from the ground. Anyone requiring to get on top of their load must be trained and use the fall protection located at North Gate.

VERSO PAPER CORP.

Specifications for kraft pulpwood and aspen ground wood

I. GENERAL
The supplier is responsible for adhering to the following specifications and all laws pertaining to wood sales, insect and disease quarantines and wood movement in the State of Maine and New Hampshire to be acepted for payment. The supplier is responsible for the proper loading of a woods trailer so it can be unloaded safely, as detailed in the Woodyard Operating Procedures. Otherwise the load will be rejected. Authorization to deliver wood must occur through the Purchase Order and Wood Order process.

II. ROUND WOOD SPECIFICATIONS – 8' ASPEN GROUND WOOD, ASPEN GROUND WOOD LOGS, ASPECN TREE–LENGTH PULP

8" Aspen Ground wood
Acceptable species:	Aspen, poplar (popple) and Balm–Gilead
Length:	90 to 96 inches
Diameter outside bark:	Top diameter 5" minimum, maximum of 21" Butt
Form:	Knots trimmed flush to bole of stem
	Gradual crook or sweep that is less than 2" in 8' of length
	Butt flare not to exceed 1" (the diameter measurement one foot back from the butt, plus 1" per side)
Rot:	50% of the butt diameter measured on the flat surface of hole or rot; No dead Wood or burnt wood or foreign materials, including metal or plastic

Wood Freshness:	Live trees only – cut less than 30 days prior to delivery, have no excessive discoloration (gray or black) and no excessive end checking

ASPEN LONG PULP – WHOLE TREE STEMS (No High–grading. The intent is to receive the entire stem. If the scaler determins that the load is substantially all tops, or that the butts have been high–graded from the load, the load may be rejected.)

Acceptable species:	Aspen, poplar (popple) and Balm–of–Gilead
Length:	Tractor Trailers–tree-length, minimum length of 16' (wheelers–first cut 23'6", then the top cut random as long as it's a minimum length of 16"
Form:	Whole-tree no logs removed, limbed flush to meet kraft specifications
Loading:	All long wood should be loaded so that it can be unloaded safely and efficiently. Butts and tops should be aligned; pieces of wood should not be intertwined
Rot:	50% of the butt diameter measured on the flat surface of hole or rot; No dead wood or burnt wood or foreign materials, including metal or plastic
Wood Freshness:	Live trees only – cut less than 30 days prior to delivery, have no excessive discoloration (gray or black) and no excessive end checking

III. ROUND WOOD SPECIFICATiONS – KRAFT Species Groups Hemlock–Tamarack, Pine, Spruce-fir, Mixed Softwood, and Mixed Hardwood

<u>Species mixes:</u>   All softwood species separated by load or tiers or mixed softwood (defined as 8 off species sticks per load) or hardwood loads

<u>Length:</u>   8' wood: Between 48 and 100 inches long. Pure loads of 4' wood are not accepted.

Limited amounts of short (4'-7-) wood an be mixed in the tiers of 8' wood, if the wood can be safely unloaded.

Tree-length (long length): Andro Mill: 12 foot minimum length for long wood is 16'.

Tree-length kraft is accepted at the Andro Mill only with approval of the buyer. Wood cut by processors should be in 8' increments. Long-length wood should be loaded so that it can be unloaded safely and efficiently. Butts and tops should be aligned as much as possible, pieces of wood should not be intertwined in the load.

Diameter inside bark: 3 to 26 inches. Loads with oversized sticks will be refused. The driver may go to an area designated by the scaler to remove the sticks from the load, and then return for scaling. Wood must be able to pass through a 26" diameter cylinder.

Form: Knots or burls must be trimmed flush; crooks, sweep and forks are not acceptable

Quality: Rot–up to 50% of the butt diameter; No cedar, hickory, dead wood or burnt wood, or foreign
        materials, including plastic or metal

Freshness of wood: Live trees only – cut less than 30 days prior to delivery, have no excessive coloration (gray or black) and no excessive end checking

CULLWOOD POLICY:
    1. All sticks not meeting the above standards will be refused
    2. All cull sticks will be removed by the seller
    3. The company will request that the contractor remove all refused material from the yard
    4. For the purposes of this contract, it is agreed that the truck driver may act as an agent of the seller in reviewing wood identified as cull, deciding what action to take for disposition
    5. Wood that does not meet ground wood specifications will be downgraded to Kraft if the kraft specifications are met

    Verso Paper Corp. has the right to reject any portion or all of a load not meeting these specifications. The scaler will have the final decision as to accept or reject individual stems, sticks or the entire load not meeting specifications.

    IV. INSECT AND DISEASE QUARANTINES (Contact your procurement representative for the latest information.)
1. The Androscoggin mill may not accept larch (tamarack, hackmatack) cut in designated towns in the USDA European Larch Canker Quarantine area in Lincoln, Knox, Hancock, Waldo and Washington Counties, and New Brunswick.
2. Deliveries of hemlock cut in designated towns in the USDA Hemlock Wooly Adelgid Quarantine area in Southern York County, Maine and points south are subject to restrictions.

    V. CHANGES IN PULPWOOD SPECIFICATIONS
Verso Paper Corp. reserves the right to unilaterally make changes to the above specifications upon written notice to the Seller.
Revision Date 1/17/201

As told by Jackie Dunbar
Bucksport

JACKIE THE TRUCKER & JOKESTER

"You were a good worker," the doctor said.
No one had ever told me that before."

"Rosie the Riveter" comes to mind. That sweetheart of American industry during World War Two. One favorite poster of her, still findable on the internet, shows her in the knotted bandana women wore those days to cover pincurls or do housework, in her iconic pose, sleeves rolled up, flexing her muscles, proclaiming, "We Can Do It." Well, they could and they did, stepping up to American industry to keep things going while so many men were gone to war.

Although the times and reasons were different, women being given equal opportunities in traditionally male-dominated jobs more and more, the story of Jackie Dunbar's work at the Bucksport mill is reminiscent of how strong women have always "held their own" in good as well as hard times.

It isn't easy tracking Jackie down for her story, she's so busy on their farm in Millvale, especially during whelping seasons. But a couple of full conversations over time yield an account worth working for.

"I applied on kind of a lark when Frank got called it. He had talked with them a year or so before and when he put his name in they called right away when there was an opening. He was very grateful but had decided to stick with barbering. I was surprised when the Personnel Manager, Phyllis Gross, called suddenly saying, 'I want you to come in at midnight'.

"My introduction had to do with a broken conveyor and the grinders. I had to keep it cleaned off, taking bark away. Wilbur Wilson was my first foreman."

"Eventually I trained on everything in the mill, all as a spare when they needed me. It was quite a shock for a 40-year-old grandmother coming from the kitchen." But Jackie knew about some aspects of mill work from her father, Raymond Willett, who had worked there long enough to earn a Rolex watch upon retirement. (Frank keeps it in his sock drawer.) An educator, they had lived all over the state following his jobs. She was twelve when he went in the mill and they moved to Bucksport to stay. "He had taught hard courses in chemistry and advanced math that prepared him to work in the Coating Department. It was hard on him because of the dust containing the coating material as well as wood and he had allergies as I did. He eventually returned to teaching but with mill work he was able to pay back what he had had to borrow from his teaching retirement fund."

"I worked just about everywhere. You had to put in "bids" to get certain jobs. I would do anything to avoid being around the paper machines. Too hot and noisy and some places got up to 120 degrees. I unloaded wood from flatbed railroad cars, picking up by hand any that spilled. The wood in those mountainous piles had to be used up frequently to keep the supply fresh. I also worked in the Train Shed, rolling, wrapping, and loading trains with a forklift. Some were stacked very high and had to be wrapped and strapped them tight on the train to keep them from moving. The lab was boring and I couldn't be around that steamy pulp. The dust from Supercalenders??? bothered me very much. I liked being in the riggers crew, driving truck and working outside most, being an outdoor girl. Working with the riggers often meant good walks outside."

From time to time I would be assigned to clean out those huge big vats on 'wash ups' during shut downs around the Fourth of July and Christmas. We'd have to clean everything in the place, everything in the mill – the wet stuff and the dry stuff. Of course they dangled overtime pay which, according to the 'code,' people kept private.

"Ron Potter trained me on driving truck. Some of the men teased him for having to train a woman. I got my Class II license after taking my test in a storm. That qualified me to drive 13-speed, 12-yard dump trucks. I trucked whatever before conveyors. Had to back in around a sharp corner and down a narrow opening with just a couple inches clearance each side to be loaded. Sometimes in ice I couldn't get out til some-one came to sand. And I had to truck the bark and de-watered sludge to the bark dump up across Rt. 15 before they started burning it in the boiler house, that last big chimney stack. You had to make sure the trucks, on any job, weren't overloaded. I also drove bulldozer and payloader. There would be two drivers taking turns driving up around the clock, 3 shifts."

"The bark dumps were slippery, like Crisco, all the time but especially treacherous when it was snowing. You couldn't see. There was danger of tipping over on the tiers, three at least, and you couldn't see. One snowy dark night I got in trouble down the tiers and there was no way to contact anyone for help. No radio. No flashlight. So I had to do double duty and pull myself out. Hooked up a dozer to my truck and pulled it out."

The Wardwells loved to have me drive their trucks because I took good care of them. Some guys didn't care, would crash right through a gate."

"A funny story – some of the guys were apt to leave 'adult material' on the seat of the truck. I would spread them out on the ground and bury them with whatever I was hauling. No one ever said anything and after a while no one left any more 'reading material' on the truck seats. I would tease them. Being full of yourself and snotty would just make it worse. People had special ways of teasing each other – some mean, some fun – and worked better when they could."

One such story had to do with their life-long friend, Barry Murchie. Everyone who knows Jackie's husband, Frank, knows that along with being a scrapbooker and historian from childhood, he was a prankster. With photographs to prove it! His schoolmates, especially, knew how Frank loved to capture evidence of their times in and out of school and never knew when Frank might share it for fun. So it was not a mystery, still it was, when copies of one of his pictures showed up around the mill, with affection, of course, of a best friend. Seems some of the boys from those devilish days in the '50s had attended a gathering of pals and teammates at the old Dunbar homestead in Penobscot. Through one of their country antics, their clothes got wet and they hung them out on the clothesline to dry. Unbeknownst to Barry, Frank snapped a shot of him back to, hanging up his clothes with just his tee shirt on. Frank captioned it 'the bear is bare.' Decades later, no one knew who made copies of that picture to post throughout the mill, or no one told. Until Jackie confessed to Barry on his death bed. He and Regina were both tickled, the story goes. Clearly, the mischief made working in the mill bearable.

"Eventually I had to stand up for myself and plead for some day shifts. Must I have all midnights? I did learn that maintenance is the hardest work for the least pay but you could select your own hours. Growing up here, taking a break or going easy wasn't part of our work ethic. 'She hasn't changed,' chimes in Frank. Eventually they cut back on the spare list and you lacked seniority but worked in maintenance, ending up being harder."

"Over time, the physical labor got to be too much and took its toll on my body. I suffered from fibromyalgia and could feel myself wearing down. Once I broke a finger and didn't say anything, feeling like I needed to tough it out and be a man. By September of 1980 I didn't feel well and knew something must be wrong. I underwent 25 radiation treatments in October and November. I had three days off without treatments over the holidays and I had surgery in January of '81. Thank God it was successful and I returned to the mill after six weeks off. Before this I had put in to go into the Woodroom Dept. where wood goes into the mill in 4' logs. So six weeks after surgery I was doing a real old-fashioned job, lifting and throwing 4' logs and keeping them from jamming like the old-time log jams. I had to fill and shut these massive antiquated wooden doors and use these big pick poles for 40 jams on one shift. I got through in 1998. I had to. I could feel myself failing. My doctor told me that I had been a good worker. No one had ever said that to me before."

"Working for St. Regis and Champion helped us through a lot. It was hard and fun. I was fortunate not to work for Verso. I never knew til I got in there how many other jobs were so necessary to making paper."

— With Pat Ranzoni

Jacqueline Willett Dunbar was born in Newport in 1940. At the time, her father, an educator, was working at schools around the state, including three stints in Bucksport, before moving here for good when she was 12, enabling her to continue growing up here and graduate with the Class of 1958. "No time has been as wonderful as those '50s! By the fall of '58 I had landed my first 'real' job in a new law office (Fellows, Browne & Gray) on Main St. above the Alamo. I was the only secretary so got to do many interesting duties. My high school sweetheart, Frankie D. had joined the Army that fall and at Christmas when he came home from basic (with pneumonia) he gave me an engagement ring. He went back to Ft. Knox, KY and then to CA until Aug. '59. When he came back we told everyone – 'We are getting married!' We were 19 and 20 years old and had 10 days to plan a wedding at the Franklin St. Methodist Church on Sept. 1, 1959. Then he was off to CA again. In a month he sent for me and I had my first plane ride, all alone across the whole United States. I took off in a lightning storm and was pretty scared, and managed to lose my travelers checks. I guess love will make you do crazy things. Today I hate to even drive to Bangor. We stayed in Pasadena until April (saw the Rose Parade). I worked for Bank of America while Frank attended Nike Missiles. We found out that the West Coast loves Maine people because we know how to work. When he was eventually transferred to Warner Robins, GA, we were thrilled because it was closer to Maine. By then we were homesick and had had our fill of adventure. We soon learned it was only a stepping stone to the devastating news that the Army was rewarding him with a 'wonderful' trip to Thule, Greenland – 500 miles from the North Pole! Just 2 weeks from our first anniversary, for a year's tour and spouses couldn't go! This was such a low point but only served to mold our relationship even stronger and kept us together for 50 plus years. I worked at the Merrill Trust Bank while he was gone. Our first daughter, Diana, was born in '61 and Frank started Barber College that fall after his 3-year Army hitch. After he finished we moved to the Olde House in Penobscot with no electricity, no running water, no bathroom, no heat, and no phone – marvelous! Again, love certainly fills in the rough spots! While there we endured the blizzard of the century, snowed in for over four days and I was pregnant with our second daughter, Molly, born that coming April. We finally moved to town for a year and then bought our first home in July of '65 on the Silver Lake Road that we called 'Sunnyside Farm'. We lived, loved, and laughed there for 39 years, raising our daughters, Quarter horses, Labrador Retrievers, plus farm animals and various wild animals. We all loved deer hunting as a family there and had a farm pond for swimming and skating and raising trout. We have NEVER been bored!" While the girls were growing up I worked at the Bucksport Police Station and after they graduated, I worked in the mill for 19 years. After my parents died we decided to move a mile over to their farmstead on top of the Millvale Road on the hillside down into the valley". In addition to her work in the paper mill from 1979 to 1998, Jackie and Frank have raised world-class Labrador Retrievers for 42 years. "Our dogs have gone to California, Alaska, Switzerland, and two Chocolates to Israel. We have donated dogs to Seeing–Eye, Guiding–Eye and Service Dog programs for people with disabilities, and Reader Dogs that sit with children to help their interest in reading. In addition to breeding and showing our dogs and horses we have been active in our Church of the Nazarene in Belfast since 1969. We toured the state with the 'Evangelaires' singing group. It was our Christian faith that helped us through the dark months of my cancer bout in 1981. We took up line dancing in the '80s and '90s and at the tender age of 60 I decided to take up running. I really loved it and surprisingly did very well in the Sub 5 Track Club. I didn't have a clue what I was doing but came within 1 point of winning my age group for the whole year after 16 races! Unfortunately, my knees gave out and I had a total replacement in 2006 and can't run anymore. Now I just run errands, run to the doctor and run in circles! The birthdays of our 5 grandchildren and 3 great grandchildren keep us on track as to what day or month it is!"

Frank Dunbar
Bucksport

WHAT THE BARBER KNOWS AND LOVES TO TELL

Frank Dunbar is one of the region's, indeed Maine's, most informed sources of history here and relating to here. That applies to the mill, being from a mill family, and all things before, during and after the mill, having been born to descendants of the earliest European settlers to Penobscot Bay, just nine years after the mill started making paper. If he doesn't know it, he is devoted to finding out, collecting and exchanging local lore. No one likes to tell stories and "chew the fat" more than Frank. Sometimes when he has a few other story keepers in his shop, like Richard Tennant, Cuddy Gross, and Bubbah Burgess, knowing what he's witnessing, and so as not to miss a thing, he closes up, pulls the shades, and they carry on for hours. One of the stories that may come up involves the 4' logs that would "escape," from 2-mast schooners that would list in the wind, or float over from the mill log pond while being unloaded. This would be in the 1930s. And the locals would retrieve and stack them on shore to sell back to the mill.

Frank knows what he knows not only from growing up the son of a mill man, Don Dunbar, but from being schoolmate and neighbors to mill workers his whole life. And because of all the natural ways mill town culture gets passed along and preserved. But even more–because of what he has witnessed in his barber shop and how that good luck and his devotion to it, has made him one of the most interviewed and sought-after sources about life here. For the same reasons, because every topic takes the discussion down any number of roads one wants to follow, it is a challenge to get it recorded in an organized way. Years ago I wrote a poem inspired by Frank entitled, "What the Barber Knows" (*SETTLING, Poems by Patricia Ranzoni*, Puckerbrush Press, 2000) having to do with sons growing up. It is in this spirit that I respectfully approach this offering of his memories and elder perspectives, working to do it justice.

"Being barber to the mill for a half a century was like working there myself. Everything was geared to pay days, of course, when family business would be conducted in town. The men coming for haircuts talked a lot about their jobs and promotions, labor and management issues, and so forth. I loved it. We knew pretty much what was going on in town including what the young people were up to and pranks the workers played on each other."

"I also liked to recall tales from my childhood so the old-timers would join in and the young ones, too. So local history would get passed on. My first memory was of when I was three-ish and I put our pet dog in the rabbit pen. There was just a little ball of fur left. This is what life was like for small town boys in those years."

"I used to hang around the Western Auto where there was a small unit of army people as there were all up and down the coast those war years. That's where I bought my first Sears 20-gauge pump shot gun, thanks to Lionel Veilleux who let me pay on time. Those were the days when Alton Grindle over to the IGA would let you get groceries and put it on your bill to square up on pay day. Sometimes he'd just scribble your purchases on a brown paper bag with a pencil and figure it up faster than an adding machine."

Frank did put his name in at the mill with Phyllis Gross of Personnel in 1977. "She said it might be months before I'd hear but she called the next day. I decided to stay with barbering."

Long-time Bucksport residents remember when Frank rented shop space from Ivan Braun's long building near the present location of the Veteran's Memorial, which he did for 18 years. From his childhood, he remembers when Braun opened and years later, when he closed his enterprises in that location. And all the lore from that part of town, like how where the Ming's parking lot is now, there was a garage where a team of work horses was once shot in one bay while they were fixing a car in the other.

During WWII, Frank's father went to Searsport to load ammunition boats with other men, who'd come back and wait outside the gate hoping for jobs. Both my mother and father had to go to work. I was seven. That was the year I lost my childhood. My older sister, Betty (Thurston) became like a mother to me. I could be a devil. Once I peed out the window when Betty had her girlfriends over who were going to Katahdin Girl Scout Camp. I sprayed and she didn't know who it was. When she found out, she said 'I'm going to kill him!' She was the first employee of the Alamo Theater, working the concession stand." Frank lost his beloved sister during the time we were losing the mill.

"I was 12 when my father went into the mill. He was a rigger. We had moved to Orland, then back to Bucksport for work there. But right on top of the depression there was nothing to be had in Penobscot and Castine. Everyone's fear was of losing their job. My mother would take one look at my father's face when he got home from work and if he looked the least bit down or upset she'd immediately go to, "What's the matter—have you lost your job?" They were so grateful for that job". "Work was everything. My father's father died when Dad was 16, murdered at sea. So he had to support his mother and four sisters. He did anything he could—worked in the woods, in the Penobscot Bay brickyard, went to sea, for example, all as a young man. No wonder the good-paying jobs there were so prized when the mill came along."

Frank tells how Mill Manager, George Bearce, had a beautiful garden and how "on my way by, I would grab a bunch of flowers and run down to give them to an old lady who had a lot of cats." When Mr. Bearce would call to complain, Frank's mother would tell his father, "You've got to do something with that boy." So Mr. Dunbar would take him to the shed and hit his own leg to sound like he was spanking Frank. "That's the closest I ever came to getting a licking from my father. Another Bearce story involves the time there were non-union workers loading potatoes at the dock and he called my father to get some union men there to break them up. So my father had to round some up fast, even hiring on the spot. That's how 'one-eyed Sam Sheehan' got into the mill."

"Another time when I was a kid playing on the mudflats along the waterfront, I came across a mound of coins someone had robbed from Grindle's Market. When I lugged the pail of them home, Dad knew who'd done it. I was never allowed to take a reward, but was given a Whoopie Pie every day right through high school. I always said, 'Put it on our bill,' but they never charged us for them. My father wouldn't take so much as a bolt out of that mill."

"I was aware of the class thing but it didn't bother me. I earned my way the hard way. My father bought me a bike for my birthday when I was twelve and I couldn't stop crying. I had a paper route when papers cost 7 cents apiece. My father hated me having to. Once a neighbor boy stole my money. And I had a garbage route. I used to take a short cut through the Jewett School field. One of my father's good friends got killed on the railroad tracks from a car stuck across the tracks, so I dreaded every railroad track."

"Summers I struggled to load chunks of limestone at the mill that I could barely lift. I didn't make my quota and when I defended myself against a reprimand my father gave me a talking to-- "You don't talk back to your bosses!"

Many of the stories that get passed down have to do with people getting hurt. Like Carroll Lanpher of Verona telling how his father, Malcolm, lost an arm on a cable crane in 1945 and how they had no workers comp back then and how he went back to work in a few months with one arm, operating a bulldozer in a woodyard the mill had up behind the Oblate Seminary. And how in the late forties Bob Thurston's father was working with a jack hammer up on some staging and fell, into a trench below. He broke his neck up high and died 6 months later. And how John Kennedy of Orland drove a wood hook into himself and called in, in pain, "If I can't come in to work I'll get someone else." "Another thing--men who worked the chippers didn't have ear protectors in those days. The horrific whining of the machines made them go deaf." These stories contain the work ethics of the mill people.

"One of the hardest times for our family was when my father got hurt at the mill. He was carrying blocks to put under the crane he was working on because it had no brakes. He was walking under the boom when Wayne Bridges yelled, "Watch out Don!" My father stopped to look and when he did he got hurt so bad he begged Wayne to hit him and knock him out. I remember George Jewett coming to the house to tell us about Dad and how they didn't know if he'd live or not. He had a head injury and many broken bones. George took me to a father-son banquet and gave me jobs in his filling stations. In those days there was no workers comp. It was a long haul. I helped Dad learn to walk all over again. I remember lawyers calling, wanting Dad to sue but he was loyal to the mill for giving jobs to his friends in Penobscot and wouldn't. He got back to his rigging work after more than two years of recovery but got hurt again a couple of months later, working on a flatbed, when a 1,000-pound motor slipped off its pallet onto his foot. More recovery. I worried through the years about his smoking because he got emphysema. He promised me he'd stop but when he came home for lunch he'd light up. We were estranged for a time over it." With a twinkle in his eye, Frank adds, "And he was a horrible card cheat. People loved to watch a new guy play polka with my father! And another thing – he used to joke about having his liver raw in milk."

"Eventually, Bubbah Burgess and I drove oil truck for Jewett's. Our junior and senior years, 1957 and '58, Bubbah and I worked in the core room at the mill making pipes for the size of paper to be rolled.

He worked there again in '63 and during the '80s. Bubbah was a steel worker so he helped build the Bucksport buildings for paper machines #4 and #5 while working all over the state for Atlantic Roofing." Bubbah (Clayton) Burgess installed the *St. Regis Blue* exterior sheeting the mill is remembered for.

"My father was instrumental in organizing his union and there was never a time all the years he worked at the mill that he wasn't an officer. My sister, Donna Hoffman, [an expert historian herself] has the original hand-written charter." A call to Donna yielded these details: "It was the Local Chapter #1357 of the International Longshoreman's Association, organized August 27, 1892. The Bucksport charter was dated the 12th of September, 1934, with the note "This charter was a new birth of freedom to labor in this district." Dated 1935 the first officers, as listed, were: President Bob Bridges, Vice President Don Dunbar, Recording Secretary Dick Gott, Finance Secretary Kermit Gray, Treasurer Bill White. Our father, Don, was president from 1937 to 1942. On the back it was noted that after the death of the holder, the charter was to go to a living member and since our father was the last one of the organizers to pass, it came to him. I remember them being at our house all the time, working around the card table."

"And both my father and mother were active in reinvigorating the Democratic Party here after decades of Republican dominance, helping to get Edmund Muskie elected Governor of Maine. In fact, there were so few Democrats in Bucksport that when Ed and Jane visited town, my mother had to take them around to the businesses to introduce them because none of the Republicans were supportive of them, saying they were wasting their time to even ask. There were only 52 registered Democrats in Bucksport at that time." Muskie went on to become a U.S. Senator and the U.S. Secretary of State. He held the highest political office by a Polish American in U.S. History and was the only Polish American ever nominated by a major party for Vice President.

From his various barbershop locations along Main St., Frank had a front row seat to the changes in town through the years. He can recite which businesses were where, when, and how they were threatened by the changes at the mill, throughout the prosperous and not so prosperous years. An example is his downtown neighbor Tozier's Market. "When the mill ran on the old regular shifts, the workers would often stop on their way in to get sandwiches for their lunch baskets. When they went to 12 hour shifts that stopped." Clearly, as long as Frank Dunbar tends shop on Main St., there will be a story-keeping place. And long after, in memory.

"My father was a man of integrity. I want to think he was proud of me, too, but he had trouble letting me know if he was."

— With Pat Ranzoni

Editor's note:
For a poem based on Don Dunbar's disabling accident at the mill, please see "He Worked at the Mill All His Life" by Frank's cousin, Anne Walls Smallidge of Blue Hill.

Frank Manley Dunbar *was born in 1939 on Pine St. in Bucksport, across from the future location of* his first barber shop. "It cost $35. worth of rolled dimes," my father always said. "We lived in Orland village for a few years in half of a three-story house. When I was three I ran across the road to the fish shack with the dirt floor to get some alewives!" But he grew up and attended school in Bucksport during a time he calls "truly the 'Happy Days'! (Remembering that t.v. show.) "We knew everyone in our whole school, not just our class. Jackie and I married Sept. 1, 1959 after graduating with the Class of 1958. I did three years in the Army and after my hitch I went to Hanson's Barber School in Lewiston, Maine and our first daughter Dee Dee was born while I was in training. And our second girl, Molly, followed 18 months later when we lived at the Olde House in Penobscot. Back in Bucksport I got involved in town government in the 1970's for 7 years, during which time we changed from selectman to a council form of government. In 1968 I went to Auctioneer School in Kansas City, MO, and was very active for over 12 years on a part-time basis doing all types of auctions statewide while still maintaining my barber shop. Our oldest daughter eventually helped me 3 days a week and our youngest also has a Master Barbers license and filled in when she was able. I have been active in my Church of the Nazarene for more than 50 years. They even had me teaching Adult Sunday School and singing in the worship band occasionally – imagine! I became a Notary Public in 1989 to offer that service to my customers, never realizing it would develop into performing wedding ceremonies! I am now known as the 'Marrying Barber'! Plus I have the distinction of moving my barber shop more than any other barber in Maine – a total of 7 times in a 1 mile length of Main Street! I became the second oldest continuous business owned by the same family in our town after Rosen's Dept. Store. I had the privilege of raising my oldest grandson for the first 3 years of his life. I had the pleasure of uniting him and his wife in marriage in 2000. Last summer I also performed the marriage of his sister and her husband. I was honored in that sacred responsibility." The arrival of their grandchildren and great grandchildren, and other aspects of their life together, are noted above in 'Jackie The Trucker and Jokester'. "I have a new job in my 'old age' with the State of Maine Inland Fisheries & Wildlife Commission. I even had to submit a resume, something I had never done before as I have been self-employed for over 54 years. Some of my interests have been: Advisor to the Inland Fish & Wildlife Commissioner, Historical Society, American Legion, Chamber of Commerce, Town Councilman 1970 to 1977 plus finishing out Jeff Robinson's term when he died, Bucksmills Rod & Gun (32 years), Notary Public (60 plus weddings), Maine Antler and Skull Trophy Club. (Antler & skull scoring – 20 years), Barber Shop (54 years). Jackie and I used to do a lot of hiking and whitewater rafting in the '80's and '90's. Jackie and I also love to hunt deer, moose and turkeys. We enjoy boating and fishing as well as snowmobiling and 4 wheeling. I love history and it all started with the Civil War diaries of my ancestor Ed Dunbar. I knew 3 World War I veterans and over 100 W.W.II vets, "The Greatest Generation," but sadly none are left. In March 2005 my pursuit of historical interests landed me on top of Mt. Suribachi (Iwo Jima) for 8 days with about 80 men who fought with the ground forces in 1945. What an awesome trip! It was a great joy to help with the planning for the new Veteran's Memorial on the waterfront in Bucksport. The waterfront has had my personal interest since I was in the J.C.'s in 1973 and even more so after serving on the Town Council during the early development of the project. I thought when I became of retirement age I'd do this and that. Ha! The mind is willing but the body isn't. Health issues, medical appointments and trying to adjust to my limits is very frustrating. I look forward to all our class reunions and town celebrations, taking lots of pictures, as usual. My old scrap book needs a face lift and so do I!

Sharon Bray
Orland

meanwhile, across the Penobscot River

BUCKSPORT, MAINE

two sisters hold up traffic
at the credit union entrance
windows down, not raining yet,
as Robin hands across another sister's
May basket and the words
I love you

MAY BASKETS FOR MY BELOVEDS

Imagine, if you might, a basket of words
I-love-yous round and round
names of ones we love and stories
in and out, up and down
handle twists of favorite songs
ribbons of remembered laughter
and my few new poems bundled lightly
as if an after thought

From the "Shared Souls" section of *PUTTING POEMS BY* by Sharon Bray, 2014.

Editor's note:
Sharon's sister, Robin Bray (1955 – 2013), was an esteemed teacher at Orland Consolidated School who enriched her students' learning opportunities by extending their experiences beyond the school walls. In her honor, her family, friends, colleagues and students established the Robin Bray Museum – Based Learning Award. The stipend is given annually to a fifth through eighth grade teacher from a Blue Hill, Brooksville, Bucksport (including Orland, Prospect, Verona Island), Penobscot, Sedgwick or Surry school to develop a project working the resources of the Wilson Museum in Castine into their curriculum.

Sharon Bray
Orland

GRADUATION GIFTS

There's always some rich kid in the class whose father buys her a car for high school graduation, but most of us in the Bucksport High School class of 1964 were very happy with smaller gifts that might help shape our futures.

My grandparents gave me a typewriter – Olympia portable. It still works. It was a really good tool for going off to college.

A number of boys in our class received their first lunch baskets, essential for going off to work at the paper mill. Remember when graduating from high school would assure most young men of a future at St. Regis? A job at the mill meant good pay, decent health insurance, accumulating vacation time. My classmates who went to work at the mill made a lot more money in 40 years than I could ever dream of.

Their lunch baskets were symbols of responsibility and manhood. I was surprised in later years to learn that most men working in mills across the country would think those two-handled, woven baskets with sturdy lids were kind of strange to take to work. At steel mills, shoe factories and even other paper mills, most men carried a lunch basket or pail of metal. Today, various plastic, insulated carriers (such as one might take a 6-pack to the beach in) are the trend.

At the Bucksport paper mill, real men carry a basket. And many of them still wear red or green plaid jackets. Once upon a time, large and larger baskets were useful to carry home discarded (or misplaced) mill surplus after carrying in very substantial lunches.

My dad often ate homemade frozen dinners for his noon meal at the mill. Mom got those aluminum divided plates from people who bought enough tv dinners to have dishes to throw away. After supper she would pile in meat, potatoes, gravy and vegetables, wrap it in foil and freeze it. Dad heated up those leftovers by putting them in an oven used to dry out motors in his shop in the electrical department.

But back to the lunch basket that is still first choice for many Bucksport mill workers. I saw a great one the other day. Its bottom third was completely covered with duct tape (unheard of in the old days, but wouldn't those old guys have loved the stuff?) That basket belonged to no sissy. Its owner carried it to his motorcycle and put on his helmet before roaring off in a quiet sort of way, basket secured on its paper rack.

I guess anyone in the BHS class of 2006 who receives a handmade ash basket with handles and lid will be more likely to use it for picnics. Since paper making now demands more technical education than most high schools provide, graduates who carry their lunch baskets off to college or technical school stand half a chance of taking them to work at the mill someday.

Previously published in *ECHOES, The Northern Maine Journal*, 2006.

Rick Doyle
Bucksport

POEM BEGINNING WITH A LINE OVERHEARD AT A FUNERAL
FRANKLIN STREET UNITED METHODIST CHURCH, BUCKSPORT, MAINE

"This one really brought out the Orland boys…"

Out of the woodwork,
out of the woods…

They came from the woods,
shut down their skidders.
Came off the back roads, set their brakes.
They came off the boats, their traps all hauled.
They came from the pulp and paper mill
clothes smelling of clay from the coating machines.
They came from the weir and the shining alewives.
Left off work, their chores half-done.

They came up from Hardscrabble right as rain,
up from the mudflats lugging clam hods,
out of the barrens, down off the mountains:
Great Pond, Flag, Flying Moose, Oak.
Emerged from the ponds, their faces streaming:
Craig, First Toddy, Alamoosook.
From the floating islands, the rocky narrows --
they came from Fish Point and the Eastern Channel
where bald eagles watch from great white pine.
They came from the Village and came from North Orland
(the pastor he came from North Orland too
ironically raised on a sheep farm out there).

This one really did bring out the boys,
who came from the shore where the osprey are,
who gathered their clothes when they'd finished swimming,
whose dogs came running whenever they whistled,

205

who walked out the door when their mothers keened,
who looked away, brothers crumpled in grief.
Oh, this one really brought them out!

Out of the beech wood, out of the cedar swamp,
out of the ash grove golden and green.
They came from Dark Mountain and Upper Falls,
they came from all over Plantation Two
by way of the Boy Scouts, the Masons, the Grange,
by way of the barracks, the psych ward, the jail,
by way of Chicago and Denver and farther:
Fallujah, Khe Sanh, Chosin, Saipan.

Up from the cellar and down from the roof,
they take off their caps, necks burnt by the sun,
to take in these words of consolation --
this acorn, its white meat, bitter, meager --
to refind, such as it is, their faith,
an oak, its bronze head coiling with doubt.

Oh, this one really brought them out
to pay their respects to one of their own.

Author note: *"The funeral was for a classmate. It's a 2011 poem where the past is everything. But what drove the poem was the experience of being there and feeling that there were generations present together in the church. As Faulker said, "The past isn't dead, it isn't even past." Generations here and gone all there, present, in the moment. That's why there's a sort of crowded-present feeling to it, for me."*

Sharon Bray
Orland

AFTER CHURCHES

". . . 'tis only the splendor of light hideth thee."
– from "Immortal, Invisible, God Only Wise"
  by Walter C. Smith, New Century Hymnal

My pagan self has risen up
to search again the dark for god
along edges of my father's fields
where trees lean in and shade the hay,
and sidewalks in town my mother walked,
her mother, too, and hers and I
back when questions sounded clear
as church bells over shingled roofs.

The dark, I write, because I long
for nights without infernal lights
the neighbors burn, the mill sends up,
for dark where angel arms once held
safety from the mind of my own youth.
For surely god and mother god
the goddess of our minds
can hide as well in dark as light
inside as out.

So far, I've found the edge of the field,
tide risen over river rocks
and friends along sidewalks in town —
measures of godness enough
for dark or light among our days.

From "Gratitude, Always Gratitude" section of Putting Poems By *by Sharon Bray,
Narramissic Notebook Project , 2014.*

Minnie Bowden (1915 – 2000)
Orland

BEAUTY... INTENSIFYING TIES TO ORLAND
May 15, 2000

As the oar extends the arm
so the Orland person
seeks to extend the self
by making do, doing without,
seeing possibilities.
The forest becomes
a woodlot, pasture, garden.
Clay becomes brick;
granite becomes
cobblestones, cornerstones.
Rivers, lakes, brooks
provide power
for sawmills, gristmills,
machine shop, and woolen mill;
provide protein for strength
funds to build a school
path and peace for tankers, vacationers.

Beauty, enduring or fleeting
surrounds the Orland resident or visitor,
comforts those returning from the heat
of the Bucksport paper mill,
eases the trials of retirement,
infiltrates mind and heart
intensifying ties to Orland.

Originally published under title, "Orland," in BEST REMEMBERED: ORLAND MAINE 1800 – 2000: History and Recollected Stories to Celebrate Our Bicentennial. *Used with permission of Minnie's daughter, Sandra Bowden Dillon, and courtesy of Connie Brown, Orland Town Clerk.*

Patricia Ranzoni
Bucksport

WELCOME TO BUCKSPORT, HERE IN THE NORTH,
PAJARO JAI / ENCHANTED BIRD

For the Chocoe Indian crew of the Panamanian ketch Pajaro Jai, August 4, 2004

Today's rains honor you, we swear, 3,000 miles afar, drumming on all our skins
the same way the sun shows us we are all kin, however far from homeforests
we ride the water and wind.

News of you reached us outback where we left our summer work to greet you.
Left our wood piles we can't afford to leave in the few weeks remaining before frost.
Left our gardens we can't afford to leave to save what can be saved before the freeze
due to arrive not long after you.

> *Wish you could see it! See these shores snow white!*
> *See what we of the north see of earth's death again and again*
> *followed by each undeserved resurrection come spring.*

And Johnny has helped make this cake to bring to town to catch you before
you sail upriver where our Native neighbors and friends are waiting with ancient rites.
This bay is theirs. We, crumbs of their history.

Here -- flour, oats, seasalt, gingerroot, blackstrap, a bit of fat. Cinnamon,
clabber with soda, today's eggs Ed just brought in for it, just-picked wild fruit
from the ledge. A little lemon. Old fashioned downeast Maine (because
sails go down over the horizon) blueberry gingerbread still hot from the oven
to say *welcome*.

To say *thank you* for resting here, showing us the deep maps of your tattooed faces
and limbs bared in trust and what we've lost. Stirring our currents with your tongues
and songs. We know foreign sounds from vessels joining our people's work
at the paper mill you slept near but can you see our ears straining for the spice of yours?
That the very trees of our shores are this moment leaning to your wings,
dreaming you nestling here?

Take this -- the best we have to give, to show you how life here tastes.
And in this way we give praise for your presence and go with you,
wishing to know what you would have us know before lifting off.

As published in the Blue Ocean Institute's 2007 *Sea Stories*, online journal
of international ocean writing and art, and read at the Darien Rainforest Conference.

Frank Berry
Bucksport

NIGHT SHIFT / MY LITTLE KOAN

as told to me by Chris Berry
allegedly from Doug McDunnah

You sit for awhile and watch the roll grow, then walk over to the bathroom.
Then you walk over and re-reread the bulletin board, go into the canteen
and drop money for a lousy cup of coffee. Then you sit for awhile and go
get a drink of water out of the fountain. Then you look at the clock and
it's been 10 minutes.

I used to think about this story every shift I worked in the Mill
during my time as a Summer Spare.

Editor's note:
*koan: A riddle in the form of a paradox used in Zen Buddhism as an aid
to meditation and a means of gaining intuitive knowledge.*

[Japanese: ko, public + an, matter.]

*Frank Berry, "a proud member of the Bucksport High School class of 1987," worked summers at the
Mill while attending college. It was, he recalls: "hot, terrifying, intensely dull and hilarious;
sometimes all at the same time. My Dad, Tom, worked for thirty or more years in the Mill. His title
was 'production assistant' or some such banal descriptor. What he really did was ensure that each
little space on the big job chart that hung in the Supercalender department foreman's office had a
name in it. There were many little spaces and each name was a person with their own life and their
own agenda. Spread that over three shifts, four teams and 365 days a year and it was a job that would
still be difficult – even in the digital age. What does a computer know about November hunting camp?
At one point 'they' decided that my dad needed to be Management. It was not a good fit. His family in
Livermore Falls were mill people. He'd been an Army NCO and being "a Boss" chafed. He much*

211

preferred to be the man behind the scenes, doing his part in keeping the place going. (And able to work for overtime.) And it was overtime that was my dad's thing. At one point during my childhood, he went from one day off per week (Friday) to no days off per week: No Days Off. He wouldn't always go in for the whole day, but he did go to work every single day. As a grown man I marvel at this. As a parent I am amazed that despite this insane schedule, he still showed up at every game, meet or show for three very active kids. Heroic in his quiet, behind the scenes, way. When my siblings and I were working summers (and school breaks) my dad made sure that our names were always on a big job chart somewhere in that mill. He would joke that he didn't have 'a lot of pull' but that he did have 'a little tug'. Between the three of us I wager we worked in every area of every department doing everything imaginable. But we started adult life with a perspective and a work experience that cannot be duplicated. We also finished college without student loan debt. A little tug indeed."

Editor's note: Frank's, Chris's and Jane's mother, Patricia Fellows Berry (1942 – 2014), was a champion BHS cheerleader, devoted mill wife and mother and booster of Bucksport and Maine whether through her support of teams, historic embroidered quilts, heirloom recipes, or famous family 4th of July parades with pots and pans and costumes of famous people from history for guessing.

Eddie Lowell
Bucksport

WHY ALL THE OVERTIME

He excelled in all sports. Such a good shot and ball handler. Such a big, strong man.

– Frank Dunbar

Representing a life on one page is hard enough, but doing it in the last season of a good man's life when he can no longer speak for himself, let alone reach memories stored in his heart and head and must rely on his loving wife and classmates for communication, is a privilege. Living in our home town all these years we take for granted that we'll be seeing one another at the market, barber shop, games, parades, and observances where our circles over-lap everywhere. We've been missing Eddie around town these days else he'd be in on this reunion. Very much in our thoughts each meeting, Linda asked if we might do a Q-A type interview to gather Ed's story, and generously invited us to visit, the sad but grateful day of this exchange.

* * *

Ed and Linda began dating when she was a junior at BHS and he was home on leave. Eddie, Frank Dunbar and Ralph Burgess had gone into the service together under "the buddy system," Frank recalls, but went their separate ways after Fort Dix. Married in 1962, the Lowells are approaching their 46th anniversary. Frank, their best man, toasted their 25th by numbering the thousands of days they had shared, looking forward to counting the thousands more days of his friends' time together at their golden. But it is not to be. In 2006, Eddie was diagnosed with an inoperable brain tumor. Radiation and chemo-therapy provide no help and he has begun the passage away.

* * *

Not feeling worthy of this opportunity, but having known the medical loss of speech, I have, with deepest respect, done my utmost to enter what Linda and others think should go into the record on Ed's behalf, concentrating on conveying, with and without words, our affection, admiration, and the unspeakable. (*In a braver world.../ Poets / and orators would seek / those whose muscles / and nerves speak or write / an uncommon repertoire / to learn the holy heart / of language. / Why not / to lie, or how to, for truth / or art. How to pass, / get across what words alone / cannot. Ways to show / what we know or don't / without speech. / How hope / in any world depends... / on harking to those who can't / talk on not wasting chances / with voice. Come sit by me I'll show you what I mean.* (Patricia Ranzoni, from *SETTLING* (*Puckerbrush Press, 2000*)

* * *

While Ed says, "Hi, Pat" when he sees us come in, when Linda asks if he knows who I am, he shakes his head, "no," in the same way he replies to each question from any of us. So Linda fills in. How Eddie had worked summers through high school at the mill, returning to work part time after the

Army, working his way all over the mill until becoming Quality Control Coordinator. How they've lived in Bucksport, raising two boys, Edwin Jr. (Lee) and Anthony. How Lee died in 2002 and Anthony is up against melanoma. How they have five grandchildren, one of which, Dakota, they have raised since age 10 when his father died. The Lowells are known for keeping a warm, open, home to those needing them, and the kids and grandkids have provided their greatest satisfactions, Linda says. "But it sure has been work, work, work!"

Eddie's favorite pastime and most fun has always been watching the kids play ball and supporting them in their sports. He has enjoyed candlepin bowling, winning individual and team trophies. And he's been an avid golfer, especially after retirement, and especially at Senior Golf at Rocky Knoll in Orrington. But also with friends and his brother, Philip, who have met, years past, at Myrtle Beach to play.

Linda and Ed's most fun together has been going on vacations after the kids were grown to places like Florida and the Caribbean. For a couple of weeks and once for a month. By themselves and with friends. On this journey, Linda tends him tenderly from his hospital bed in their living room. "What can I say," she offers with her whole adoring self, "He's still loving Eddie."

With brimming eyes, I tease his toes mischievously through his blanket and tell him we love him, his class, and that he'll always be with us. And kiss his big strong hand goodbye.

Linda thanks us, his class, but it's we who, wholeheartedly, thank her.

He lived for school. What meant most in his life was his school.
His football and stuff. And being a good father. Making sure
his kids had what they wanted. That was why all the overtime.

– Linda Lowell

Eddie was a big, rugged football player. He did a lot of blocking
and made the holes for us. He was a big factor on all our teams
in all the sports he played and we were over-average teams in all sports.
Once, our senior year, we went to Belfast and played in the armory.
Coach Don Rice had benched most of us starters. It was the end of the
first quarter. Finally, Rice called Eddie to go in and "bust this game
wide open." Well, Eddie went the entire length of the court, firing a shot
that never touched the backboard or rim, just swished. After that, we'd
always joke with Eddie to "get in there and bust this game wide open."

– Bubbah Burgess

— By Pat Ranzoni

Author note:
Remembering with Eddie and Linda Lowell on Silver Lake Road for BHS Class of 1958 50th Reunion, July 2008.

Sharon Bray
Orland

AND, SO FAR, OUR MILL STILL MAKES PAPER

St. Regis, 2012

Coming home through Bucksport
in the warm, spring night,
the smell and thrum of the mill
put me on my knees at Nana's
bedroom window, 1962,
looking over school roofs to the rest of town –
Penobscot River Narrows and Waldo-Hancock
historic Bridge beside Maine's Fort Knox.
Lighted steam and smoke
rise from our mill with no foul
kraft like rotten egg smell
from other paper mills.

Fifty years later
our mill still smells of ground up pulpwood,
spruce and fir sap mixed with not-quite-vinegar.
And, so far, our mill still makes paper.

Editor's note:
The writings of well-known local historian, Sharon Bray, can be found in libraries and book stores throughout Maine. Please see her author notes accompanying other poetry and prose throughout this collection.

Sharon Bray
Orland

HANDMADE BOOKS

Consider the book of poems
handmade, indeed, on
paper made by hands of neighbors
who labor in the woods
and bring wood out to market,
bark the wood, grind or chip it,
cook and mix and test
until wood is paper
rolled and wrapped
by working men and women.

Some self- designated intellectuals
belittle papermakers.
And find foul names
for towns around the mills,
boast of personal book collections,
subscriptions to glossy magazines
that print obtuse poems
on Maine mill paper.

Editor's note:
In 2006, Sharon Bray was presented the **Betty Billings (1922-2003)** *Rising to the Challenge Award* *"in recognition of more than a quarter century of contributions to inform, educate, and advocate to improve the health of people in her communities. Her determination and dedication helped to found the Bucksport Bay Healthy Communities Coalition." In giving the award, Chair of the Coalition, Thomas J. Gaffney, said Sharon "exemplifies Betty's tenacity to move the unmovable for the benefit and welfare of those at a disadvantage," recalling that "through-out her lifetime Betty worked to overcome any challenge to ensure that children, elders, families, and neighbors received what they needed. Her characteristic remark, 'Let me think on it,' produced many a miracle that made our communities a better place to live." Sharon reports that she keeps the framed award, with its picture of Betty rocking on a porch, hung on her kitchen wall.*

Patricia Smith Ranzoni
Bucksport

BUCKSPORT ~ WHAT CAN BE SEEN ABIDING

first Poet Laureate poem for our town
presented May 27, 2014

A wooded village at the salt mouth of Maine's greatest watershed.
5,000 souls more or less any given day according to who arrives
or leaves, in all the ways humans come and go, cheering and crying.

Four modest, compass mountains, a drinkable lake, ponds and brooks
running to a riverway between sovereigns almost becoming
the Canadian border when presidents arguing it signed in at our hotel.
But after the treaties, dams, mills, and log drives the Penobscot People
still prevail. We do not exist without our neighbors, all directions.

Echoes of shipping circle the bay off mighty bridges we depend on,
and off the fort across the water sculpted royally against crowns *in case*,
reminding, lest any forget, how we grew up playing on stones stacked
against empires so never stop believing what we can make of rock.
And our native drive to protect and endure, giving our best for peace
or, *God forbid*, war.

We keep hardy shops, book and movie places, and public hearths in
and out of town. Woodsmen and women, farmers, fishers. Makers
and fixers. Traders and commerce doers. Seekers and teachers.
Our children grow up learning how to work.

We stage all manner of races, ball games, and shows between shifts.
Music drifts over the paper machines tended by families of masters,
over our tears and prayers. Not one of us whose heart hasn't been broken.
Not one who won't again, someday, laugh. Listen, and with the other
creatures, you will hear us sing and dance when we celebrate. And debate.
We lift each other up. Our newspaper proves it.

Where the council we choose to do our business meets,
the incoming tides bring knowledge of the world, and, going out,
carry word that we are here,
　　　and striving,
　　　　　and all our long welcomes.

V. GRIEFS, ANGERS, & RESPECTS PAID

Milissa and John Paul LaLonde
Bucksport

OBITUARY

BUCKSPORT – Verso Paper Mill
went to the Great Beyond in
December of 2014, after a
long, courageous battle with the
economy. It was born in 1930
and lived many wonderful years
along the Bucksport waterfront.

It provided 1200 people jobs
during its heyday and guided 4
generations through good times and
bad. The mill enjoyed success
under many names and owners
for most of its life, but it
began to fail in more recent years.

The mill is survived by thousands
of past and present employees, a
whole community of citizens who
benefitted from its taxes, contributions,
and many buildings, parking lots
and smoke stacks.

May our mill rest in peace!

Milissa and John Paul LaLonde moved to Bucksport in 1983 where they, with their four children, became keepers of Doc Thegen's house and active community contributors. He worked for the mill (or various companies which ran it) for 36 years in the Timberland and Operations departments, and she taught in Bucksport, touching and being touched by mill families for 25 years, being nominated for Hancock County Teacher of the Year in 2015. She recalls using the paper machine felt for birthing 3 litters of lab puppies years ago at the suggestion of Jackie and Frank Dunbar, reporting that "it worked so perfectly as a comfortable bedding for mother and babies that I think I would have used it had I given birth at home." With others, the LaLondes were instrumental in bringing Matthew Foster's "Before the Wind" Schoodic International Sculpture to the waterfront and have been active in various groups devoted to Bucksport's future. John Paul will be remembered for reading his favorite poem, "The Cremation of Sam McGee", in the gazebo on the waterfront with the mill still in the background for a 2014 community observance of National Poetry Month hosted by Bucksport's poet laureate and Mrs. LaLonde's 4th Grade. John Paul and his extended family continue a maple syrup operation on family land in Wisconsin each spring. "My parents bought the property in 1946 and raised some of the family there. They then sold the house but kept the woodlot. We built a cabin on the land in 1974 and rebought the farm house around 2000. The property is now owned by my siblings and I. Four generations of LaLondes have made maple syrup on the property yielding up to 26 gallons a season with some relatives at the cabin from as far away as London, England! Lots of fun and fond memories." In addition to church activities, Milissa volunteers, even in retirement, at the Miles Lane School Garden which she started and which now bears a sign of dedication to her. She also participates with John Paul in the Bucksport Heart & Soul program and Blue Hill Window Dressers. John Paul is also involved with Main Street Bucksport, Bucksport Wood Bank, Gardner Commons Board, CARE (Community Action Resource Exchange) and the Maine Community Foundation.

Gregory Orr
Virginia

THIS IS WHAT WAS BEQUEATHED US

This is what was bequeathed us:
This earth the beloved left
And, leaving,
Left to us.

No other world
But this one:
Willows and the river
And the factory
With its black smokestacks.

No other shore, only this bank
On which the living gather.

No meaning but what we find here.
No purpose but what we make.

That, and the beloved's clear instructions:
Turn me into song; sing me awake.

*Award-winning American poet, **Gregory Orr**, has authored more than 11 collections. Considered a master of the short, personal lyric, his work has been widely anthologized and translated into at least ten languages. In a National Public Radio story on his craft, Orr stated, "I believe in poetry as a way of surviving the emotional, chaos, spiritual confusions, and traumatic events that come with being alive." He is professor of English at the University of Virginia where he founded the Master of Fine Arts program in 1975 and was poetry editor of the* Virginia Quarterly Review *from 1978 to 2003. A grandchild of Penobscot Bay, Orr recalls summers spent with his grandfather in midcoast Maine. His poem, "This is What Was Bequeathed by The Beloved," from his book,* How Beautiful the Beloved *(Copper Canyon Press, 2009) is used in* Still Mill *with his blessing to Bucksport.*

Chris Soper
Orland

SMALL TOWN AMERICA
Maine folk song

I grew up way too fast   on this old riverbed
Hear that whistle blowing   you knew it was time for bed
Generations before me have walked down the line
Now it's just a memory   it's a piece of time

Chorus:
Small town America   where'd you go
So much money   nothing left to show
Just like a candle that's burned to the floor
Small Town America   NO MORE

We all have freedoms   but we can't speak our mind
In a world of deceit   honesty so hard to find
Just like this mill town   everything will sell
Rich getting richer on their way to hell

Chorus:
Small town America   where'd you go
So much money   nothing left to show
Just like a candle that's burned to the floor
Small town America   NO MORE

Rip out your heart   and they'll take your soul
Get what they want   then they'll take some more
You're not a person and you're not supposed to feel
You're just a number on this   Corporate wheel

Chorus:
Small town America   where'd you go
So much money   nothing left to show
Just like a candle that's burned to the floor
Small town America   NO MORE

"This original song by Chris Soper is about the mill in Bucksport, Maine, but could just as easily be about any small town with the rug pulled out. It tells a story of sadness and anger that is becoming all too common these days. Hear it. Sing it from the rooftops until it shakes the walls. Feel it and share it so others can feel it too. 'In a world of deceit, honesty is so hard to find.' Well, here's a little of that honesty you were looking for."

– As posted on *YouTube*, December 11, 2014

"It was 4 A.M. Wednesday morning when Chris Soper put pen to paper writing the lyrics to *Small Town America* in a matter of 15 minutes. The closure of the Bucksport mill, the emotion behind his words. 'You know the words just started flowing because I feel their pain,' said Soper. 'My dad worked there, all my uncles worked there, both my grandfather and my great grandfather worked there.'

Hoping to show his fellow residents his support, he posted the song on "facebook" online, not assuming the video would get almost 10,000 clicks. 'I'm not sure what to think about this. I just never expected to get a response like this. But it has been generating a buzz with the media and so many more.' Soper says 'the chorus reflects the ripple effect that the October 1 announcement has taken on the community. It's like our entire heart has been ripped out right now and everybody is scared.'

'You're not a person and you are not supposed to feel!' Soper singing those vocals, speaking to how he feels the almighty dollar can instantly make sweeping changes. 'There's no humanity anymore,' explained Soper as he sat on his couch Thursday afternoon. 'It's all about the dollar bill and not about people's lives.' Yet Soper believes even the Canadian scrap metal company that is purchasing the Verso mill doesn't know the resilience of the coastal town. 'I just want them to understand that just because we are the small guy and the underdog we can still overcome.'

So he'll continue strumming until that day comes."

–FOX22 WFVX Bangor ABC 7
December 11, 2014
Printed with persmission of the station.

Editor's note:
This song was one of the first local artistic expressions inspired by the closing of our paper mill, so it introduced our preview exhibit of *STILL MILL* writings in our Bucksport Area Poetry Route on the waterfront, summer through fall of 2015. Chris can be heard and seen singing *Small Town America* on the internet by searching his name. In comments with his October 2, 2014 posting, he said his original song lyrics were composed "to support my 570 fellow family and friends who lost their collective job at our Bucksport Paper Mill due to corporate greed and mismanagement! Due to the overwhelming support from the original posting online on *facebook*, I had many people who were in favor of helping turn 20 minutes of writing into a powerful statement! *Small Town America* is a rally cry against what

big business is doing to the working class. My special thanks go out to all the musicians and production people who did their collective parts in producing the video: Husson University's New England School of Communications (NESCOM); musicians Josh Small, Becky Bowden, Ryan Curless, Joline Drew, Brad Radley; and Ozgur Akgun and Berkay Tok of Innovative Media, Research and Commercialization Center at the University of Maine."

Author note:
"I wanted to keep it local, featuring mill families. It's for all the former mill workers who have 'kept their heads up' through the rough process. I just wanted to throw something out there for everyone that's been dealing with this. I wrote this for these guys. I'm always writing songs and plan to really dive into my music after lobster season. 'It's kind of unbelievable that I wrote something that has meant something.'"

– As told by Chris Soper
to Charlie Eichacker for the *Ellsworth American*
October 2, 2015

Chris Soper "*grew up in downtown Orland USA and have never ventured too far from the area until after graduating from Bucksport in 1997. After, I went to Husson for sports management/ business administration, but mostly to play baseball for Dr. John Winkin which took me as far as Japan to play. I hurt my shoulder and then decided college was not what I wanted to do, so I went into the work force doing many various jobs from construction, landscaping, harvesting wood, to installing leather interiors in vehicles, working with kids in crisis, teaching, and commercial fishing to name a few, always trying to find the best opportunity for myself and my son Cameron. I now commercially fish out of Stonington Maine with my friend Joe Trundy on the* Fishing Vessel (F/V) Guess Work. *I always entertained the thought that I might be a mill worker, but as I got out of school and the years after, the jobs were few and far between. Pretty much my entire family were all mill workers. My great grandfather was a part of building the mill originally, but a lot of my uncles, my dad, both grandfathers, great grandfather and many friends were all career papermakers. I was very fortunate to have the mill to grow up with. It provided very well for my family! Now I have been concentrating on my kiddos. My family consists of m*y fiancee Joline Drew (who is one tough lobsterbabe) and she has Sam who is a freshman at Thomas College and is going to be a history teacher, and her second kid Solomon is a senior in Bucksport and does the Hancock County Technical College (HCTC) welding program, and is the furthest advanced certified welder that the program has seen since it started 20 years ago. He is entertaining job offers from very prestigious businesses and has already surpassed what college can offer him as far as certifications. My son Cameron is a freshman at Bucksport High School, and is a fantastic athlete and a fluent musician on the guitar and piano. I don't play music too much anymore as both Joline's and my schedules are pretty grueling. We hit the road daily by 3 am, and have a 80 mile commute to work 6+days a week, and then chase our boys around with sports and other events they have. I do try to play when I can with friends especially on*

Sunday mornings when we go to Stonington to play music at "The Church of the Morning After," lol [laugh out loud]. they are a great group of fishermen from Stonington, Vinalhaven, Damariscotta, and surrounding areas. Musically I try to follow the blues. Joline's Uncle Tommy Castro is one of my favorites. We just went to NY at Daryl Hall's place to see him on his new tour. He is the 2-time BB King Blues Entertainer of the Year, and rumor has it may be up for a Grammy this year with his last album.

Small Town America *was a great project. I was feeling very strong about the mill closing, and wrote the song in a few minutes of passion/ frustration for all my family and friends. It was the first time I ever did a video of just me and the guitar and post it online. 40,000 hits in 3 days was crazy. I never expected it to be anything but a show of solidarity for my friends and family. Then next we went into the studio at NESCOM (thankful I have friends who teach there) and we did a studio version of the song with a lot of my musical friends from Gilpin Railroad Incident, my Bangor musicians, to even Dick Curless's grandson was on it. After the recording was done, I had been contacted by a couple Turkish fellows who are producers and working at University of Maine. They loved the story behind the song and they donated their time, and UMO donated the equipment to shoot a music video. Can you imagine all this coming from a facebook post! It was a great time doing this song for so many reasons. The biggest reason is knowing that I created something that meant so much to our community and feel like it was my way of giving the proverbial salute to Verso, AIM, Apollo, and all the other money sucking corporate pigs who could care less about the 570 employees that will suffer.*

Emery Deabay
Bucksport

LIFE-CHANGING NEWS / NOTHING WORSE

TAXPAYERS HAVE SUBSIDIZED VERSO, WHERE'S THE RETURN?

On Oct. 1, I was called to a meeting to hear an announcement from the company that runs the mill where I work. Verso Paper announced that day that it would permanently close most of the Bucksport mill on Dec. 1; the power plant in the mill would keep running.

Because I am one of the union presidents, I now had an obligation to inform my members of the life-changing news. There is nothing worse than telling workers they are going to lose their jobs.

The company closed this mill because it was unprofitable for a number of years, according to Verso. It was unprofitable in spite of years of the Bucksport mill workers doing all they could to make this company successful like it was before International Paper bought us in 2000.

Verso's mill was unprofitable in spite of the state of Maine and the town of Bucksport giving all they could in the form of tax breaks through the state Business Equipment Tax Exemption and Business Equipment Tax Reimbursement programs and through local Tax Increment Financing arrangements. This company took all it could and promised that these tax breaks would secure jobs and the mill's future. Yet four years later, Verso is shutting down most of its operation.

Verso is shutting us down without even listening to the workers and letting us work with them to keep it running or maybe letting us search for a buyer. When asked if the company had any intention of selling this mill so, maybe, someone else could come in and run it, company officials said they would, but not to a competitor and not until they sold the power plant.

It's just plain wrong that companies can take from us – the state and municipalities – and not be held accountable. This has happened time and time again across Maine. From the Jay mill the Wausau Corporation shuttered to consolidate its market share to when Georgia Pacific destroyed machinery in Old Town so it could not be used again, companies take our money, run away with the profits, then put us all out of work.

This is one of the reasons I decided to run for the Legislature in State House District 130, which includes Bucksport and Orrington. If elected I will offer legislation to make it law that if a company takes tax breaks or taxpayer incentives and then decides it no longer wants to run an operation, it cannot refuse to sell that asset to somebody that has a chance of running it successfully. Many times, mills are closed that are profitable just so the company can control the market.

It is time that we stop letting these companies come in and take from area residents, then close-up shop and leave the education, public safety, infrastructure and all other services that a town provides in jeopardy. This closure not only affects the mill workers but also the municipal workers and the business owners of Bucksport and the surrounding towns and cities. Companies should be accountable to the people who give them money to help them keep running.

Our grandparents built these mills across Maine. We have poured our sweat and blood into making them successful and making profits for these companies who come and go. Our communities have subsidized their success.

If a company is not interested in running a mill anymore, we deserve a fair shot at keeping these jobs in our communities. Companies that took tax dollars should have to make a good-faith offer of sale at fair-market value to another company, to the state, or to the worker who may want to buy it and operate it.

This is just one example of what we can do in Augusta to help manufacturing workers like us in Bucksport and across Maine.

Originally published as a *Letter to the Editor* and guest column in area newspapers.

Emery Deabay was born in Presque Isle, Maine and lived in the Ashland, Sheridan area for the next 11 years. "This was an area where most people worked in the woods in one occupation or another including my father who worked for Great Northern Paper Company. In 1966 he applied for and got a job working for St. Regis Paper Company in Bucksport, Maine. We moved to Bucksport and I have lived in this area ever since. I started my work history by mowing lawns and delivering papers in my youth. When I got to be 15 I went to work at Millett's restaurant on Verona Island after school and weekends. I started as a busboy and moved up to working as a waiter. My last two years at the restaurant I worked in the back of the house as a cook. The July after I graduated I got a job at St. Regis and have been there ever since. The company I work for now, Bucksport Generation is the power plant that was part of the mill but is now a stand-alone operation. My education was the first 5 years at Ashland Community Elementary School and when we came to Bucksport I went to the Jewett School and Bucksport Junior High. My first two years of high school were at St Joseph Oblate Seminary in Bucksport. I finished my education by graduating from Bucksport High School with the Class of 1973. I still have a camp up around Ashland so I enjoy going there and doing a little hunting and fishing and a whole lot of relaxation. It gives me a chance to spend time with people and relatives I grew up with. Outside of camp and my job, my other time is spent working on issues that affect all workers. I serve on the Maine AFL-CIO Executive Board and the Maine Workers Compensation Board. I also serve on the Bucksport Board of Appeals.

Patricia Smith Ranzoni
Bucksport

STONE ONES

only in the company
of what's gone soft
do we feel hard

among our own
it's called *strong*

dishonor us
lie to or about us
deny our tenderness

we'll be the rocks
we've had to be

Previously published in the author's second collection, *SETTLING* (Puckerbrush Press, 2000).

Wesley C. Stubbs
Bucksport

SHUTTING DOWN #5 PAPER MACHINE "THE BIG DOG"

Some Thoughts of a Displaced Machine Tender

"I knew my machine."
– Chip Stubbs

October 1st 2014, my wife, Marie, called me from Fort Kent and asked what the big mill announcement was. I didn't know, so I called the machine tenders booth and was told that the whole mill was shutting permanently. If not for her call, I have no idea when or how I would have found out. I am now beyond just the planning stage of leaving the mill, my coworkers, my career.

Now that the final months of my paper making career have been defined, I've decided to work all the overtime that is available. Another machine tender elected to have his knee replaced so that allowed me much overtime--mind you I like getting paid time and one half better than straight time. Coming into the final days, I was told that No. 5 Paper Machine (#5PM) was to be shut down the morning of Tuesday, December 2nd. The machine tender who went out for knee replacement was on that crew. They wouldn't let any overtime in December. So, the junior most trained man was going to shut the machine down--a lot of good-natured jostling about that went on. The last thing I said to him Sunday night when I left was you are the man who shut #5PM down Ha Ha Ha, shook hands and parted.

Sunday, I was walking out with my work mate that was my alter ego machine tender on #4PM D crew when he said to me Stubby it's kind of sad that we will never make paper again. I looked at him and agreed and added but I can't get the smile off my face. We both laughed, an insight of just how bad it had got to be working for Verso and its band of many henchmen. The last three years of working there had become unbearable. Their goal was to find out what you did wrong.

Paper making is a process that needs to be tweaked at times--sometimes a tiny tweak--sometimes a major move-- to find out what direction moves need to be made. A little tweak may cause a hole or a break or just some subtle flaw--a wrinkle, weight bump, or profile change. They then come down, call you into your booth and want to know why you did what you did, not listening to the fact that things done the same way don't always give the same effect. Conditions warrant different results. By many years of experience, you see the effects of your moves, and it lets you know where to go from there--

rather than wasting run ability time trying to make sure what you do is perfect, your odds are still at best fifty-fifty.

So, what a big surprise I got when I looked up at the mill Tuesday. When I pulled into the parking lot, #5PM was still making paper--you can tell by where the vapor is belching from vents. When I reached the machine tenders booth, I was now on the receiving end of the still good-natured jostling about me now being the man who shuts down #5PM. We had a good run, for the most part, on the early part of the shift, but about 10:39 p.m. The Big Dog (#5PM) had had enough of what was the declining quality of furnish or as we called the groceries. She decided to puke and broke back to the wet end at about 10:39 p.m. After looking at what I had for vacuums, I decided to take stock off for the last time. Checked time--it was 10:42 p.m. (I made an announcement that stock off at 10:42, the Big Dog went down on her terms). Make it known that the Big Dog was shut down in an orderly fashion flushed and cleaned so it could have been started up in the future. Even then, I truly felt it was over. During the night, the crew washed the Machine with the pride and dedication that we felt was our duty. The rest of the week, we worked nights cleaning. Day crew did the same.

Monday December 8th was a different story. We were called into a meeting and dispersed throughout the mill to do other cleaning (crap). Looking back on that crap, and the way the mill is now being scrapped, could easily destroy good work ethics. Also noticed during that day the Information Technology people were removing all computers and the information they held.

Tuesday night, my scheduler called me and told me we have been given the rest of the week off with pay—told the scheduler I loved her. At a later date was let known that my last day would be from 7 a.m.-3 p.m. December 17, 2014. I went to work on that day to find out that we were to clean out the booths. I had already cleaned my file drawers and lockers of my personal stuff but while we were out, someone had gone in and cleaned out every scrap that was in notebooks, posted on walls, bulletin boards, drawers--every scrap that had anything to do with making paper, training manuals, start-up procedures—everything. It was mind boggling--went through our personal stuff. As I said, I had already taken care of my stuff, as I think most people had.

Upon the announcement the mill was being shut down, if I remember correctly, Avon wanted every scrap of paper that was made on #5PM. We had a real decent run 'til the shutdown. Verso was trying to use up all the furnish, chemicals, etc. What a novel idea--put the best you can in your product to make the greatest product.

In the process of paper making things happen, whether sometimes by accident or by design--whichever way the sheet flows. Sometimes an accidental break opens the way for an unseen need--for cleaning or contamination in the sheet, missed flaw--and sometimes you take the sheet back for a need to find an issue and nothing can be found.

A smart person, when asked a question, finds a way to make sure you will remember the answer. Once I asked a production manager why they just didn't use bigger bolts and less of them to speed up the process of the repair. Just when I figured I had asked enough questions and was going to fade into the background, he said "Stubby, if you wanted a tight seam would you use big thread and long stitches or small thread and many short stitches for a tight seam?" That was over forty years ago.

I was in machine tender's booth talking with 2nd in command of the mill about the SKF–the machine monitoring software program and how it should be "operator driven" not "corporate driven." When I said we're on a wet-end break, she said "What?" About that time, the alarms and whistles started to go off and the sheet disappeared. She said, "Wow, you really know this machine."-- *EXPERIENCE*.

I took great pride in learning my machine, its components, its ins, and its outs. I asked questions about everything from what's that vibration, bearing failures, checking bolts, and watching build ups and how they effect the machine. I tried to pay attention to everything--noted mentally what happens--became part of #5PM. In talking with maintenance about issues they would come to me and say Stubby, tell me what you hear or feel; describe the difference--the whine, screech, vibration. The more you learn and know about your machine and job, the easier it is. You can anticipate what is going to (or may) happen, knowing what's building up and where and how to clean it, clear it, and hopefully not break it.

Some of the most satisfying times were feedback about the way I trained them to do the job safely and right. Knowing that I had given them the tools to advance their careers and not just limited them to being a paper maker but the other support fields as well. One other thing that I had always conveyed to people was when you are doing your job sometimes things happen, and it's best for everyone to let other people know what's been done. If you're a constant screw-up, hide, but when you're trying to be part of the solution and create more issues (as holes, breaks, defects) by finding and correcting a problem, hey great. I know what happened to cause that, so I don't have to look in that direction to solve that issue with the machine. You don't have to broadcast it to the masses, just let the right people know--the ones that can and will use discretion depending on the case.

One time we had a green 5th hand (new worker) who later became a superintendent. He messed up a splice for the third time. The third hand (who lived on Central Street) called this green man over, handed him some money and told him to run down to Tozier's Market and get him some change. What a look of shock came over the 5th hands face when he saw that he was handed a penny.

Then there was the time when my foreman came around the Rereeler, and it was shut down. A pained look came over his face; he says what's wrong? I said it's lunch time; he says Oh OK. We all had a hot lunch waiting, and we were caught up—except had a hole in the paper that needed to be spliced. I told my crew we can take five and finish our lunch.

I've been called (tongue and cheek) and not in such polite terms, a "pain in the butt," but in the next breath that I was a "necessary pain in the butt."

Sitting here tonight (writing this) a thought jumped into my mind about changes that were made to what the machine tenders will do on wash up. The trust that has been there in the past is no longer felt (wonder if it's because management knows they're not trustworthy so they can't trust). So, when they see a machine tender sitting in his booth they feel he is goofing off when actually they are contemplating or discussing what the next move will be or perhaps explaining how to do a job to a coworker, discussing maintenance issues with mechanic or electrician etc., or taking a deserved break. In other words, they don't trust us to work but feel we should be able to jump at their beckon call.

When the machine is down and clean, it's the best time to take close checks of bolts, welds, connections, air leaks, cracks--all the stuff that can't be looked at when the machine is up and running with its steam, water, slime buildup and moving equipment. What I do on wash-up days when working days (after becoming a machine tender): I direct wash-up crew, clean and check places that can't be accessed while machine is running and covered with stock, water and slime, and work with maintenance to guide them as needed (this is not right, or that equipment is right over there, or this is where that goes or is positioned, or that needs to be longer or shorter, this is how this needs to work, etc.).

When working nights, I had been given permission to come in at my leisure to look a machine over before a startup, because it is known that I find things that have prevented minor to major failures of equipment. If I have a chance to look the machine over, I do that. By that I mean I scrutinize every inch of the wet end. A roll falling may destroy the fourdrinier or press at some point. Looking back, it makes me wonder. What if I had just waited for them to tell me what my job is or just what to do, how much would I have missed--some of the broken loose bolts, leaks (water, air, grease, etc.) that control everything from guiding to lubrication cooling, etc.? If some of this stuff had been missed and #5PM had a major machine crash, would this mill have shut down sooner as happened to the Sartell mill. I did what I thought was right, as I was taught by my parents, that ethics matter. When you have a job to do, do it to the best of your ability. A job well done is a job done right; and when I know how to do it, I am going to do it right. I butted heads over that a lot in my years at the mill; the last 3-4 years, they came close to breaking my will but they didn't succeed. I left that place with my head held high, and tell you I know that I was in the right.

I had bad times too, shut my eyes for a few seconds and my superintendent opened the door to my booth and decided that this was my time to be the next example of the new wave of "neglect of duty."

I had to meet about an hour later with Human Resources. From that meeting, I was led to believe that I would have a discipline meeting at the start of my next shift. So, when I came to work the next day, I was waiting for the meeting. It didn't happen, so I finally started to do my rounds. We had a wet end break, cleaned the machine up, started to thread machine and heard a clink, clink--and then the start of a bad rumble that I knew wasn't good--ran to shut presses down--too late. The clink, clink, that led to the rumble was a 1-1/2" x 8" long bolt that fell out of the machine that holds the stone roll in place. I still wonder that if I had done my rounds sooner if I would have seen this bolt coming loose. It was in a conspicuous place and I have found these bolts loose before. I once asked a maintenance foreman--Hey, there are 8 bolts that hold that stone roll in place. How many of them are supposed to be working? He said to me, you're trying to tell me something aren't you. All 8 should be working--called a crew and they slug tightened them up (hitting a short wrench with a sledge hammer). I came to work the next night and found one about ready to fall out, so I took it out by hand, about a turn and a half to remove (received a letter of commendation signed by area, line, and department managers), pushed to get new replacement bolts ordered, and did--but still failed to get them to drill and wire them so they couldn't vibrate out. After this failure, they were wired together. Another interesting note about this is when a machine failure like this happens there is an investigation launched. I, as the machine tender on duty, was not involved in this investigation. I do feel they knew what I would have had to say because if they had listened to me this wouldn't have happened because the bolts would have been wired. Also it was brought to my attention that because of the bull crap about having my eyes closed (and the accusation of neglect of duty) that the Paper Gods were smiling down on me is why the machine crashed. (Working in a Paper Mill with machines droning along, dozing off is very common any time of day.)

Black Sunday, January 1, 1989, we lost our double time Sunday pay. History of Sunday pay, the mill used to shut down on Sunday so double time was offered to production workers; they voted it down. Then, it was offered to the whole work force and was voted in. Black Sunday, January 1, 1989 we lost our Sunday pay, workers only gave work effort of a 100%, instead of our previous of 110%. So, the next contract those who lost 3 out of 4 Sundays got a dollar an hour raise extra to make up for it; work effort went back to 110%. We are at a new passage, much bleaker than Black Sunday. IT SHOULD BE KNOWN AS *BLACK VERSO DAY, Wednesday, December 17, 2014.*

I've been all over the mill in the years that I've worked there starting as a spare--working, then being involved in training, on safety committees, etc. A bit of history--the chip loft area of the mill. I had forgot about that area 'til I was up there cleaning in my last days in the mill. Those parts of the mill were riveted together, old style construction, as were many other parts--sad to see this history disappear.

Sitting here at 11:00 p.m. looked at the mill's "face book" page got to thinking . . .Thanks to all of you who held office in the forty plus years that I worked at the mill, and the ones who started the union, and all who kept it strong and viable--the officers, the shop stewards, and everyone. Thanks to all my fellow union members, past and present, who made our mill the number one mill in the world. To all the people who taught me my job or helped me to make the right decisions about what to do (maybe laughing at my reaction but making sure I learned something and I did), thank you. To you who taught me by screwing me over I thank you, but I especially want to thank the people who guided me and also made sure I didn't get screwed over. I hold you all with the respect that none of you would have let me get in harm's way. I tried my best to train people right and one reminded me of it—Lance Raymond I will always remember what you told me about the way I trained you--I had a responsibility and I took it seriously, and you respected that and understood, and I have tried to do it for everyone that I trained.

Let it be known that some of the best people in the world walked through the gate into the Bucksport Paper Mill to make the best of the best, did so even in times of adversity. They were not only great to work with they were like family; their hearts were in the right places. When it came time to help in the community, they not only lifted their hands to help but opened their wallets to those in need. -- Cleaned out my locker today, found these Bucksport All Sports Booster Club 50/50 Split Ticket templates that I used to print out for March 1993 thru June 1994. I personally want to thank each and everyone who supported this and all of the donations that you have given over the years. Just to name a few that I have personally been involved with, SADD, St. Jude's, Cystic Fibrosis, Snowmobile Club, Meadow-Muffin (For All Sports Booster Club), MS, Jaycees, Little League, Pop Warner Football, Bucksport Fire Auxiliary, the needs of local families, the United Way, Bucksport Community Concerns, Christmas for Kids and others. This is stuff that I want to thank you for that I've been part of. I know there are many others who have sold tickets here because I won a lamp once and $50 on another. On behalf of the Kids and Adults who have spent countless hours at the main gate of OUR MILL selling cookies, cakes, candy, flowers, tickets and more, I again commend and thank you all for your support, especially for our Veterans.

Wesley C. Stubbs (Chip).

Resume of a displaced Machine Tender

HIGHLIGHT OF QUALIFICATIONS
Dedicated skilled production worker
Machine Tending independently with little or no supervision needed while operating machinery, proven troubleshooting and decision-making abilities to ensure proper and efficient production
Directing and leading a crew
Keen attention to machine components, detailed observational skills to find potential for machine failure due to loose or broken bolts, shafts, frame cracks, bearing heat or noise, etc.

Received many compliments and commendations for preventing catastrophic failures
Monitored guiding, flows, levels, profiles, weights and investigated errors to adjust
Safely operated numerous types of high speed industrial equipment
Communicating with company representatives to resolve problems, prevent damage to equipment,
        and to reduce downtime

RELATED TRAINING & LICENSES
Safety Trained in chemical, electrical, fire, hazardous waste, industrial work,
Lock Out/Tag Out
Powered Industrial Truck License

PROFESSIONAL EXPERIENCE
Verso Paper Formerly International Paper, Champion, St. Regis
Machine Tender (1974-2014)
Dedicated skilled production worker started as an entry level worker ended as a Machine Tender
Served on the mill-wide Safety Committee for many years, served a term as Chairperson
Wrote machine training manuals with attention prime to safety, the details of what happens in
        different situations, including interlocks and how they work
Created the routes to monitor all equipment on #5 Line

LIFE EXPERIENCES
Born at Eastern Maine Hospital in Bangor in 1953
Grew up in Bucksport, graduating in the Class of 1972
Built two houses and a camp
Proficient with hand and power tools
Operated a private saw mill
Private woods operation
Gardening
Family man--with wife, raising 2 Children and watching Grandchildren

Just want to express again respect for all who have ever been a caring part of the work force.

Opinion: Why Shut the Bucksport Mill.

Bucksport Mill and Bucksport Paper was the number one mill and paper in the world when it was St. Regis Paper. Then, it became Champion Paper Company. Champion soon realized that Bucksport's paper was truly a special product and had the ultimate respect and the demands of printers and advertisers, so they kept Bucksport's level of performance and perfection at the forefront, even though they had suffered the aggravation of previous expectations that their paper should be able to match

Bucksport's quality and performance. Then, along comes International Paper (IP) who has suffered the same or worse aggravation. Tired of hearing about Bucksport Paper--its quality and performance in terms of print and breaks per hundred rolls--quite a stick in IP's craw. Upon acquiring Champion including the Bucksport Mill, International Paper planned on extending their profits by leaps and bounds and could have and more, but printers wanted Bucksport Paper and when asked, International said there is no more Bucksport Paper. To prove it, the standards of Bucksport Paper were brought down to International Paper's standards of quality, but the standards of Bucksport would not be forgotten. Verso was created. Why? I don't have a clue, why it is managed the way it's been managed less of a clue, why is Bucksport being shut down?--perhaps to get rid of union but mainly to try to make Bucksport Paper forgotten. It will be missed and perhaps someday forgotten, but forgotten only by those who have never experienced the opportunity to work with, print on, and view what jumps off the pages . . . Bottom Line, Bucksport Paper was the best and could still be so, so get rid of it completely!

Author note:
Final log and crew of #5 Paper Machine and supercalendar crew, stock off at 10:42 p.m, December 2, 2014:

Giau Ngo, Hugh Clark, Bob Berry, Dave Silver, Wesley Stubbs, Steve Bowden, Mike Allen, Ed Arey, Mike Carrier, Jeff Ashey.

Photo by Steve Moser, Mill Project Manager, and Wesley Stubbs, Machine Tender #5 PM / "The Big Dog." Used with their permission.

Eric W. Stover
Orland and Verona

NOW COME ON! MY THOUGHTS ON THE MILL CLOSING

*. . . as an old mill worker who spent more time with my fellow workers
than I did with my own family. 39 years. Retired 2003.*

Even after retiring from the mill I figured the mill had at least
twenty or so years more to make paper who would think no.

On October 2nd 2014 just outside of Conway, N.H. at a gas
station hearing on their news cast that the Bucksport mill will cease
to make some of the best paper in the country and sell it to a junk
dealer. . . . now come on !!

I was blown away and thought this is a mistake in the media
then remembered back when Verso bought it from IP hearing that they
were just an investment firm and have no idea how to make paper.

The more I heard from the workers still in there not all
was well in Kansas.

When I first joined St Regis Paper Co. there were around 1500
men employed there and was in a big hiring with a new wood room, new
paper machine #4, new calendars and winders being installed. I was hired
right off the streets with no experience in this work at all. I started off as
an on-call worker all over in the mill with by the seat of my pants training.

Just before I married my first wife I was called to go to school
on #4 P.M. We started this machine in June of 1966.

When I retired I was the last of the original charter crew
which fired her up way back when.

In learning of this shutdown so many memories of work
flooded through my mind and more sorrow of the fellows still trying
to support their families in our community.

When I went to the mill support day for the men and women

coming out the door for their last day I had to hold my emotions in
check as for the feelings I had for these people.

The Mill was a great support to my family and children and
I wish it was for the rest of these great workers who always did their
top best to make our mill what it is today. I have no reason not to believe
that we made some of the best paper in the USA.

I have met many good friends and pals and worked with the
greatest bunch of workers ever. I am sure our area will bounce back
and we will persevere.

LIVE LONG AND PROSPER.

Eric W. Stover: *"My life in few words. I was born in Portland, Maine at Portland General Hospital which was off the Marginal Way on a ridge where now is a big condo. My Dad worked in South Portland at the ship yard as a tinknocker. He built World War Two 'liberty ships'. We lived in Red Bank which was located in So. Portland. When I was two years old we moved to my mother's parents' house in Maxfield, Maine and Dad worked at the mill in Howland for a while. We then moved in with my Great Grandfather John F. Holden on Elm St. in Bangor. I went to school at Longfellow school on Center St. where now located is the St. Joseph's Hospital. Next I did second grade at Mary Snow then we moved to the air base housing when the end of World War Two was done. We then moved to Brewer. In 1957 we bought our 1st and only home on Essex St. and I graduated from Bangor High down town on Harlow St. which is now an assisted living center. After graduation I went active in the Navy which years before I had joined through the reserves located on Essex St. Coming back from my 1st Mediterranean cruise we were immediately sent to the Cuban Blockade to keep the Russians' missiles away from 90 miles off the coast of the USA. It was very scary for a 19-year-old standing on the deck of a Russian ship full of missiles and holding them on deck with a 30 caliber machine gun while a boarding party checked out the ship. I did enjoy the travel though. I was out in July 1964. I went to work at Brake Service in Bangor for a couple years then one day Dad and I went to go to the old farm where I have lived on the Castine Rd. for over 40 years to cut brush and we stopped at the St. Regis mill to see if they were hiring. I got hired on the spot. I worked spare for one year then was sent to school for a new paper machine being built #4. I worked there on # 4 from 1966 to 2002. I retired with a buy-out at 59. It was a great living. I have 3 wonderful children – 2 boys and a beautiful daughter. Wes, our oldest, is 49 and is married with wife Carla whom he met in college and two daughters Charlotte and Madeleine. They live in Florida. Daughter Destiny is married to Daniel Cook and they have 2 sons, Seth and Jake and they live in Gorham, Maine. And our youngest son Jaison who lives in Houston, Texas has two children, Dylan and daughter Harley. My wife Terry and I have been together for 39 years and would not have it any other way. Now our lives have changed again. My wife has retired and we have a new home on Verona Island. I guess I have bored you enough but my life at the mill will always be a big part of my whole life."*

Don Houghton
Bucksport

MOVING AHEAD!

We don't – and won't – diminish the sorrow and outright pain caused within so many families by the planned
closing of the Verso Paper mill here on Dec. 1. Verso and
the company that controls it, Apollo Management, in
effect, have elected to shut down the lifeblood of this community since 1931, saying it no longer is financially viable
— at least not for them. But reality requires the time to
mourn be brief for the future of this community lies in
moving ahead with what we continue to have to offer, not
lose momentum sobbing over our collective loss on the
River Road.

Initially though, our leaders should seize the election
season moment, a time when our politicians are so obviously swept up in their sudden zeal for paper and unbounded
compassion for those who have made it through the years.
Let our local leaders put our Congressional and gubernatorial
candidates to the test, asking each to go on the public record
to identify by name the chief liason each will name on Nov. 4
or shortly thereafter to work with each of the several Maine
communities so recently devastated by the realities of the
paper industry.

They should tell us who they'll appoint to work with
us as we seek to return our mills to working assets. It's highly
unlikely the sometimes tattered baskets that for decades so
many paperworkers have used to transport their lunches
from their trucks to and from the local mill ever will see similar service, but the people of the Bucksport-Orland-Verona
Island-Prospect area are too gritty, too resilient, too tough not
to continue to tote their load in life. We don't expect the
liaisons we seek in Washington and Augusta to bring us government checks, but we do seek all the expertise and support
they can muster as some communities move on as others battle to just keep their identities.

Our leaders there must work with our leaders here,
and we should demand they speak clearly on exactly what
they can – and cannot – accomplish on our behalf. And,

please, include all of us in the conversations, for we don't
think any leader or group of leaders has a single slam –
dunk solution. And one solution won't embrace us all! Still,
if we are to support big projects we've got to be included
in the formulating and then promoting those ideas.

Don't squander our rainy day reserves, money
Bucksport at least is so fortunate to have amassed for just
this sort of financial hit. And don't squander your and our
time with too much talk and no action. Time, too, is precious.

Published by Editor, Don Houghton, in *The Bucksport Enterprise*, October 9, 2014. Used with his permission.

Donald M. Houghton *has been "the 'journalistic stern man' on the good ship* Bucksport Enterprise *since 2001, and has handled all of the reporting on the final years of the paper mill from the uncertain times at the beginning of this century to the ultimate tear-down of more than 80 years of Bucksport history. Sandy Holmes and I ARE the staff of* The Bucksport Enterprise, *and our goal is to keep a public voice alive in the four communities we serve. The paper also has become a treasured link to former residents of the area who now reside in more than 30 states." Don's "favorite reminder of what the newspaper seeks to be was a time when a youngster at the middle school shot his first buck and couldn't wait to tell his friends at school what he'd accomplished. His friends denied his claim, saying,: 'no you didn't, your name wasn't in the* Enterprise.' *When his dad told me what happened, and assured me his son's deer was tagged at a station far from Bucksport, I immediately added the youth's name to the next list of successful hunters. The boy's friends then congratulated him. I've been 'a newspaper man' since graduating from college, and fell into the business only because I didn't have a job and needed one ASAP. I didn't know what I was doing five decades ago, and sometimes I still don't!"*

Editor's note:

Presiding over and marking his time here as editor and publisher of the *Bucksport Enterprise* weekly, under the banner, "It's a Wicked Good Read," is a stately black and gold Verdin pedestal street clock Don Houghton had installed on the bank in front of their building at 105 Main Street. The clock has joined the town's new Veterans Memorial Monument, Maine sculptor Matthew Foster's granite "Before the Wind" at Flag Point, Jonathan Buck's maligned gravestone, the millstones at Buck Memorial Library, the stone watering trough in front of the former Jed Prouty Tavern, the new historic interpretive panels at Compass waterfront Park –where the mill will always be pictured – and other features off Main St. highlighting our town.

Sharon Bray
Orland

SHUTTING DOWN PAPER MACHINES

mill still hums but we all know
next week 500 families
will tighten their trousers,
put guns, camps, 4-wheelers
up for sale
cancel winter vacation plans

the work of Bucksport paper machines
used to show up on
every page of *Life* magazine
made from trees cut with chain saws
hauled in from Road 9 on the airline
put through drum barkers
clanked along overhead conveyors
into steam and noise of the wood room
where shifts of union men
wore ear protectors

workers jostled for places
on the Sunday list
double time
better than church

train cars brought in chemicals
carried out white clay-coated
rolls of paper

silence and darkness come on
they sold our mill for scrap metal

Sharon Bray has been a frequent reader of her poetry and prose on WERU *Community Radio Station in Orland where her voice, archived, can be heard. "My writing career has ranged from Harvard Medical School to local* newspapers and literary journals." *She established* The Enterprise *newspaper in Bucksport in 1992 which she published and edited for 9 years before selling it in 2001, and is known for her* Narramissic Notebook *publications. "I support myself with freelance writing, mostly for Penobscot Bay Press, which I fit, with my own writing, around farm chores, community commitments, and responding as best I can whenever anyone asks for help or needs a jar of homemade soup."*

Richard Campbell
Orrington

MOVING FORWARD IN BUCKSPORT AFTER VERSO

Last week, the employees and residents of Bucksport and the lower Penobscot Valley were dealt a tremendous blow. The Verso Paper mill will be permanently shut down.

"Permanently" is a powerful word.

Bucksport has been a leader in papermaking for over 80 years. Eighty years of well-paying jobs, 80 years of world-class paper, and 80 years of a strong economic base for our region and Maine.

We are faced with a decision. Do we look at this as a doomsday event or an opportunity to become the next leader in the next generation of the next product or service?

The streets of Bucksport have been teeming with reporters and television cameras since Verso made the closure announcement last week. Politicians have been playing the blame game. Employees have been, rightfully, very concerned about their future.

State and federal government departments are already providing the employees and their families the assistance to ease the pain and help them recover as quickly as possible.

In the last 50 years, Maine has gone from a leader in papermaking to scrambling to save the few remaining jobs left. It's time for a reality check.

The single most influential element in this debate is public policy. Unbalanced policies for the last 50 years have devastated an industry where once we led because of our outstanding wood fiber, Yankee ingenuity and work ethic.

Public policy swings like a pendulum. I remember an environment so polluted that you could almost walk across the Penobscot River. I remember the smell from the mills would burn the inside of your nose when driving through mill towns. Maine people were dedicated to changing that, and we have.

But the public policy pendulum has swung so far that it is time to mitigate the negatives of over-regulation.

Lawmakers over-regulated the woodlands operations to a point that paper companies had to sell their forests to specialized companies to manage them. Paper companies lost control, and that increased the cost of their raw materials.

Lawmakers over-regulated the production side of papermaking so the industry spent more time and money to satisfy regulation that it wasn't feasible to invest in upgrading technology for competitive and cost-effective production.

Then there is the business environment. Maine's energy costs are among the highest in the nation. Taxes paid in Maine are among the highest. The cost to do business also is one of the highest. Incentives for businesses to stay in Maine and invest to create more jobs are under the constant threat of elimination.

Why would anyone invest in Maine with that kind of public policy environment? We need to change the policy and build on our assets.

I have always maintained Bucksport and Orrington are blessed with good local leadership and

244

great economic assets. Our location in the center of Maine, on the Penobscot River, at the intersection of the east/west and north/south highways, with major rail service, the latest upgraded power line grid in the northeast, two power generators, and accessible industrial sites is ripe for becoming the driving force for Maine's economic recovery.

We have another asset – the Verso mill property. While it is devastating that this part of our history is ending and jobs are lost, residents and lawmakers have to work together to create a prosperous, though different, future.

The site has great potential. It has a major natural gas line and a deep-water dock. Bucksport's waterfront is world class.

It is time to think outside the box. It is time to seize the opportunities and capitalize on the assets right here in Bucksport.

Suggestions are as whimsical as the world's largest indoor year-round water park the size of Disney's Blizzard Beach beside a casino to the most innovative wellness retirement village. Or we can look up the river 15 miles to the accomplishments of the Cianbro Corporation, which has transformed a former paper mill site into a world-class industrial facility. Together, we can do this.

The employees of Verso and the residents of Bucksport and the Penobscot Valley are counting on leaders who will work together with them on innovative solutions.

I pledge to set aside politics as usual, remain open-minded, continue the search for viable economic business models and support public policy that creates a strong job market and vibrant economy. Maine people deserve a prosperous future.

Originally published
 as a *Letter to the Editor* and guest column in area newspapers.

*A familiar figure in the Bucksport mill area, lifelong Maine resident, **Dick Campbell** is the 7th generation of his family to live in Orrington where he grew up. He attended Brewer High School, Eastern Maine Technical College in Building Construction and Technology, and the University of Maine in Political Science. He works with his sons in the passive solar/green design construction and development company, Dick Campbell LLC, which he has owned for 43 years. Dick has served as a member of the Maine National Guard and in the Maine House of Representatives from Bucksport and Orrington from 1992 – 2000 and 2012 – 2016, being Assistant House Minority Leader from 1996 – 2000. In 2000 and 2002 he was a candidate for the United States Congress. Dick was named the* American Legion 2016 Legislator of the Year. *Devoted to the lower Penobscot River basin and community, he is known for his work on Orrington's Old Home Week, the Save the Bucksport Wilson Hall effort, Chamberlain Freedom Park in Brewer which he designed, and the Wreaths Across America convoy. Dick has served as trustee of the Bangor–Brewer YMCA, John Bapst Memorial High School, All Souls Congregational Church, and the Maine Technical College. For hobbies he has enjoyed landscaping, rock walls, cycling, and alpine skiing as well as activities associated with past times, and designing and building arts and crafts from old, recycled and natural wood materials, especially birch bark, branches and logs.*

Don Houghton
Bucksport

MOVING ON!

"We don't have time to hang our hat on the mill reopening."
                                    –Town Manager Derik Goodine

Last week, the town manager told the Town Council it's time to get real. That marked a change in direction and attitude from the days immediately after the Oct. 1 announcement the Verso Paper Co. would close its mill here before the end of the year.

While this week brought word of a proposed sale next month to a non-papermaking enterprise, 570 people – many veterans of decades of making paper here – still will be without jobs as the new year dawns.

And Town Manager Derik Goodine's words from last week still seem to ring true this week for the proposed sale does not hold much promise or hope for those who know so much about how to make paper. Some may be heartened by Gov. Paul R. LePage's efforts to intervene and by his preference to keep the paper mill alive for the purpose for which it was built so long ago.

On Oct. 1, local officials were somewhat upbeat, knowing the town has roughly $8 million in reserves for just this sort of dilemma the town and the region now faces. But that was then, and this is now: this area's economic future will not be decided in Washington or Augusta or at Verso's distant headquarters in Tennessee. More than likely, the pattern will be set here, and we all must get on with encouraging new purposes for a vital piece of property.

If we are proved wrong, and the papermaking machines get to clank away once again, great. But let's not count on that. The time for positive, upbeat actions remains now, not later.

Bucksport Enterprise *Editorial, December 11, 2014*

Patricia Claus
Orrington

THE TWO FORTS

My two stoic grandfathers, back when the mills began,
Not complaining about the noise, the danger
Not complaining when they lost fingers to the machines
Proud to work and to provide.

Stark smokestacks pierced the sky – ugly but
Reassuring too – assuring the future of a town and
The future of families.
The self-respect of work.

No more stopping for workers crossing the street
After a long, hard shift at the mill.
A small courtesy which bound us together
As a community.

The view, like twin forts
Across the cold mirror of the winter river
Across the shimmering mirror of the summer river.

Can we imagine our town otherwise?
What can we make now?
Not just memories for summer people.

Patricia Claus is *"an almost lifelong resident of Orrington (born here but went away for college). And I have always felt a great kinship with the town of Bucksport. I grew up going to Wahl's Dairy Port and Fort Knox, and still do those things, and now my husband and I go to MacLeod's and attend the Alamo as often as we can as well. We love the small town atmosphere of Bucksport, with its well-kept shops, its beautiful waterfront and its obvious strong sense of community. Both of my grandfathers worked at Eastern Fine Paper in Brewer all their lives and of course I know many people who have worked at St. Regis/Champion/Verso Paper as well. I was very upset about the closing of the mill for all these reasons, and I felt I had to express my feelings about it in a poem. I wrote it for all those, like my grandfathers, who spent their lives in mills of New England and for my neighbors who are suffering today with the loss of this mill. Thanks so much!"*

John "Bubbah" Campbell
Dedham

MAINE REAL

Plumb the depth of time
Sitting by shore of moving water
Deep in the crowded forest of memories
Dredging up the glorious past
That's now soggy and devoid of life
Like the drowned beaver pulled from trap
Dead animal sell the pelt
Waste the meat, pocket the money
Honor the totem animal?
They snicker and laugh
Grandfather worked the wood camps
Other grandfather worked the mill
Three generations cut wood
Families worked the mills
The mills were our families
Always beside the rivers
Small towns surrounded by forest
Part Mic-Mac we're born to water and trees
Worked twenty four hours sometimes
Keep the machines running, they got a sound
Then a sound came from New York and Boston
From Men wearing gray suits
Heard them snicker and laugh
It echoed up the eastern seaboard
Way up the rivers in Maine
Close the mills, Smokestacks crashed
Like trees we used to fell
Defaulted scam loans fill gray suits with cash
Broken contracts shattered lives
Bulls of Wall Street in the china shop called Maine
Hundred million dollar paper machines, sold for scrap
Politicians say service economy, tourism, retraining
They snicker and laugh
Send us to hamburger school, can't wait
In season serve a hamburger to tourists, smile, Minimum Wage

Funny thing happened on the way to poverty
They increased our taxes
Saw some suicides too
Gray suits, fancy dresses at parties
Dancing to the wisdom of greed, didn't save one mill
What got saved?
We live in the woods, cut firewood
Can't afford to burn oil, heat with wood
Neighbors and friends buy the extra that's cut
Sometime I see hard times in their eyes
Read between unspoken lines give them an extra half cord
They helped me plenty when I needed
Forty five year old tractor breaks down, Henry fixes it
We give him raspberries when they come in season
Bill visited gave me five fresh caught trout
When I raised pigs we shared the meat
Snowstorm, not even light yet
Kenney's plowing my lower driveway
Must be five people give us deer meat, moose, turkey
Years ago I cut meat up for them, they remember
Let a neighbor graze his sheep my field
My bush hog broke down can't afford to fix it
He bush hogs my other field, I'm thankful every gift
My wife sews beautiful quilts, gives them away, family
We make our own Christmas cards, send them
Give them away, she worked the mill once
Don't have much money
All this giving made us all rich in the soul
We're sewn together like my wife's quilts
Not a writer but I know what's real
It ain't torn down mills or greed

Previously published in Dana Wilde's *A Parallel Uni-Verse, Poetry from Maine and worlds elsewhere*, *www.danawildepress.net/universe/*.

John Campbell, *"part Mic-Mac of Canadian heritage," was born in Dedham in 1947. His wife, Linda, "100% French, was born in Old Town, also of Canadian heritage." He grew up in Dedham attending "mostly" Dedham Elementary. He earned an Associate degree at Eastern Maine*

Community College as a millwright, "courtesy of Eastern Fine Paper," and is a certified welder and licensed stationary engineer, "all courtesy of Eastern Fine Paper sending me to classes." Linda grew up and attended schools in Old Town. "As a teenager, I went to Washington, D.C. then lived in ten different states before moving back to Maine. We have lived in Bangor and Dedham longest and between us have four sons." Linda worked at the Bucksport mill under Champion Paper Co. for twelve years, in the yard for the super calenders and from 1984 to 1986 in the Lab. She is a potter and sculptor, and makes quilts and original greeting cards. John has cut wood for the mills with family and worked as a millwright at Eastern Fine Paper for twenty-five years until the mill closed. His artistic interests include drawing, poetry, painting and sculpture. He is a member of the Maine Stoneworkers Guild, and she, the Quilters Guild. "We ex-mill workers truly appreciate the effort put into such a huge body of work as this. People need to hear the voices about and of the working people. This may be all that is left of Maine's many mills – writings and pictures. Strange that much of this will be put on paper, what our mills used to produce."

Author note:
"Your neighbors, the Greg and Leslie Wilson family, hayed one of our fields and bush-hogged another. We knew Greg's father, Wilbur, and cut up some beef critters for him years ago. Things are going full circle and this is nice."

Hazel Smith Hutchinson
Manhattan, Kansas and Bucksport

THIS WOODSMAN

most days he
tromps through his
woods
his woods
where he's

trekked
cut wood
hunted and
gathered for some
forty years

his woods
his sanctuary
his university
of the highest
education

shsssssh . . .
can you hear it?
ahhhhhh . . . that still
silent wisdom of
maple   spruce   pine

shsssssh . . .
can you hear it?
the crunch and
snap underfoot of
thicket and cone

the seasonal squish and
suck of mud all
cautionary notes on the
musical score of *this*
woodsman's soul

251

shsssssh . . .
can you hear it?
that powerful life-giving breath
of spirit   whispering
through trees

intimately
connected
to creature breath to
his *own*
breath

shsssssh . . .
can you sense them?
The sensitives   the bear
moose   coyote   deer
tutors of stillness and silence

and the roots
the infinite forest roots
growing deep
shsssssh . . .
can you hear them?

echoing his own infinite depth
his strength and stamina
his deep connection
to earth
to you and to me

beckoned back by
sometimes blustery
sometimes calm
always wondrous
sky

he forever
treks home
to hearth
to love
to tend fire

can you hear it?

the crackle . . . shsssssh . . .
the smolder and blaze as
fanned flames serve up ash
and haze bridging wood and sky

and this woodsman
this hearth-keeper
summons us back
you and I
to heart's hearth

shsssssh . . . to a soul-
tending fire

Author note:
In honor of Ed Ranzoni, family since I was 8 years old.

Patricia Smith Ranzoni
Bucksport

HOW HEART GETS HAULED TO THE PAPER MAKING MILL

Spruce/Fir Short Groundwood   ticket # 20252959

How it comes to them between jobs, hard times, the way sun
occurs through clouds. How the calls get made – what new regs apply,
how much per cord these days? How it gets figured by weight now,
still @ about a hundred a cord minus Pelkey's trucking cut per load.
How the calendar is checked, days counted, plan set. How their old
tractor is joined by another old one dickered for from *Craig's List*
to shore up the operation, Stutzman's '43 Farmall ready to retire from
his crops but still with life in 'er. How saws are sharpened, oiled, fueled.
Tractors oiled, greased, gassed up, and tires checked. Trailer. Foresters
consulted. Maine *Intent to Harvest* plan approved. #471831. Filed.
   How the grandfather and son drop, limb, measure and saw trees
to length as they go, grandsons following, lifting, grunting, carrying,
heaving the 4 footers into stacks to be loaded on the trailer. Whatever
needs to be done when. How three weeks into the cut, coming down
to cross the brook, the trailer-hitch breaks, fetching up the load. How
some of the wood tumbles into the water, the rest needing to be off-
loaded, lightened enough to allow a scabbed chain hitch for limping
home for a weld. How the family will haul this last harvest for the mill
up to their roadside for Tom to grab with his grapple rig, lift and set
down, neat, squared off, secured. Scaled at the mill: 25.46 tons.
12.12 cords. 969 dollars and 60 cents. One Fall.
   How the women take pictures for after the mill is gone. Soon.
How their last pitchy load to sell there creeps out of their yard, waits
for speeders down Cotton Hill, then turns, swaying and groaning
onto the road to town and the end. How the men, spent and proud,
watch their one heart strain out of sight, never to disappear, knowing
wherever this paper is headed, they are going, too.

Author note:
*Dedicated to our grandson, Joshua Nylund, pro welder, and all the youngsters who've grown up
learning the way to do this work, keeping things going. And all the oldsters who've taught them how.*

Ernie Smith/Angus E.S. MacLellan
Bucksport

WHEN THE FOUR O'CLOCK WHISTLE BLOWS

Downtown, Mill town paper boat in harbor
Call in from the spare list double shift is harder
Long night harder day and everybody knows
We're ready to go home when the Four O'clock

whistle blows. So many years ago they started cutting back
First with the pay and then the bennies sacked
No more Sunday double time and don'tcha just know
It's time to go home when the Four O'clock whistle blows

Papermaking a way of life what will we do now
Don't want something else we don't know how
Don't want another job paper's what we know
And it's time to go home when the Four O'clock whistle blows

News paper, magazine, was our claim to fame
Mill's going down it's such a damned shame
Just before Christmas our town and families now know
It's the last time they'll go home when the Four O'Clock whistle blows.

Ernie Smith *(aka **Acadia Piper**), born at Castine Hospital in 1949, grew up in "the Bucksport Mill Town atmosphere." He attributes "everything good" in him "to the influences in his life, starting with Sunday School at the East Bucksport Methodist Church with teachers like Ruth Wardwell, Joyce Johnson, Betty Mann and yes, his Mom, Dorothy "Jean" Smith, all wives of Millworkers. I remember my Dad, Percy "PD" Smith, worked 6 days a week as a team leader in the riggers crew being called in many, many times in the middle of the night. A good many of these Mill workers were also Masons. I recall more than once when my dad was out of work for an operation/injury that a group of Masons and other co-workers showed up with groceries and one time a box of moose meat to help us through* *a rough time." A 1967 graduate of Bucksport High School, Ernie was "one of very few young men in Bucksport who would never work in the Mill. My father would advise against it. Being a long time employee of the Mill, he knew that it wasn't for everyone given the trials of things like the 'spare list' and shift work. I found my own way and worked at Brawn's Red &White, Sampsons and IGA, before starting my long career at General Electric." After "some wandering and technical schooling I settled down, in Bangor, where I met and married my wife Paula in 1971, and worked at General Electric where I held multiple machining positions, as well as Product Inspector in all departments. Focusing on PD's well-placed advice – "If you have something to show, someone will see it and you will do well"– hard work and good personal ethics paid off as I then moved on to supervisory positions in Rotors/Airfoils, and later became a certified Six Sigma / Green Belt for the Quality Group (a Jack Welch initiative) where I spent the last 15 years of my GE career." Ernie retired from GE in 2007 with 38 years of service. During his last years there he began working on more personal interests such as relief carving, gold leaf signs, stained glass and the "Great Highland Bagpipe" which "proved to be my niche." Ernie and his wife Paula, former Food Service Manager at Reeds Brook Middle School in Hampden School system, and Manager of his piping work, have retired to Bucksport near Jacob Buck Pond. They have one son Anthony (Tony) Dow Smith, a Computer Aided Dimensioning Designer for Ntension Corporation in Hermon and drummer with Anah Highlanders Shrine Pipeband of Bangor; a granddaughter Lorryn who is a registered nurse working in Augusta; a grandson Hunter Smith, 14, and granddaughter Madelyn Smith, 12, both of Bangor; and a great grandson Carson Pinkham, 4.*

Marie Duplessis
Bucksport

THE MILL WHISTLE:

Blew at 7 a.m. And again at 8.

Blew at 12 noon for the beginning of the lunch hour and then again at 1 for its end.

Blew at 4 for the end of the day shift.

Used to be a courtesy whistle blow at 9 p.m. As a "curfew" reminder to kids
to get home and get to bed!

The whistle used to blow when there was a fire in town and there were specific codes
depending on where the fire was. Apparently, this practice was stopped when too many
spectators would go to the location of the fire and would interfere with the firefighters.
Don't know when it stopped, though. I'm trying to get a definite date.

We think the whistles stopped blowing for the mill shifts when the #8 boiler was installed
@ 1984, 1985.

No word yet if the button to make it whistle is still hooked up and operational.
I'll follow up with the fellow who was going to check.

Editor's note:
While the Bucksport mill whistle stopped being blown in the 1980's, to those who grew up with it it
never stopped being expected, heard, and wished for. Ask the people of Millinocket, like esteemed
elder LaVerne Ennis, how it was after their mill signal was halted. They protested in parades through
town long after their mill was closed, proposing it be brought back even if the mill wouldn't be. A
Bangor radio talk show mocked them unmercifully for "stupidly clinging to the past," taunting their
aspirations disrespectfully with "Great—the graduating class can look forward to a horn." But those
of us in other mill towns knew what was going on. We knew that like other messages sent 'round the
world by drums, horns, shells, gongs, guns, whistles, bells and chimes, sirens, and other signals of
cultures calling people to work, worship, gather or run, celebrate or mourn, this was ours, we
papermakers, so we stood in solidarity with them. To this day, however far we travel, many work
toward getting supper ready on time when we know that whistle will be blowing, letting the hungry
day shifts out. Home.

Marie Roy Duplessis was born in Rumford, Maine in 1959. Her father worked on construction jobs all over the state and New Hampshire, drilling and blasting, "so we moved around, all in Maine, living in Rumford, Mexico, Medway, Houlton, Sherman Mills, Sherman Station, and Kenduskeag, until I was in 4th grade when we grew roots in Charleston." She graduated in 1977 from Foxcroft Academy, part of School Administration District 68 with Dover-Foxcroft, Monson, and Sebec. As an adult she has lived in Bangor, Bucksport, and Orrington. "I advanced through the ranks from a clerk in the typing pool to the Center Director's executive secretary at Penobscot Job Corps in Bangor from 1979 to 1986. Wanting to work closer to home (Bucksport), I worked at the Champion paper mill in Bucksport part time through a temporary employment agency until I was hired as a spare in the secretarial union in May of 1988. I have been at the same location ever since under each new owner and in positions such as accounting clerk, personnel services assistant, administrative assistant, and now office manager for Bucksport Generation, the operating power plant at the former Verso paper mill. How lucky is that? My first husband's parents, Laurence and Barbara Bridgham, gave us land in Bucksport where we built a home and raised two sons who graduated from Bucksport High School. My mother-in-law was a long-time employee of Rosen's Department Store until it closed. With my mother's passing from pancreatic cancer, I participate in activities to increase cancer awareness sponsored by The Purple Iris Foundation out of Brewer. And Smile.Amazon.com does a thoughtful and wonderful thing by donating a small percentage of each of my purchases to The Purple Iris Foundation, so I try to do a lot of my online buying through that website. I also donate to Foxcroft Academy's annual giving campaign". Over the course of about 9 years while working a day job, Marie took night courses at Eastern Maine Community College to receive her Associates Degree in Business Management with concentration in Office Administration. She graduated in 2007 - the same year her oldest son graduated from high school. And for the last 10 years has taken up the art of making quilts and quilting "and more". "I enjoy sewing and creating things from my fabric stash including bed quilts, lap quilts, wall hangings, table runners, baskets, tote bags, purses, fabric boxes and leaves, doilies, you name it!" Each of Marie's family members has a homemade quilt and she has quilted a large number of quilts for customers through her now closed business, "Quilt Sandwiching" for which her son, Casey, designed her logo. She has 13 blue ribbons for quilts or quilted entries at the Blue Hill State Fair and one of her quilts appeared in McCall's Quilting magazine. "I don't sew as much as I used to, but I usually have a project or two going. I just want to say that both of my sons live out of the state of Maine and even though they are grown men with lives of their own, they are always happy when I call them and apologize that if it's been awhile, that they didn't call me. I love them very much and they know it and they love me right back. I love my sons, miss my Mom, and am closer than ever to my siblings. Family is everything."

Sandra Bowden Dillon
Philadelphia and Orland

A LOT OF PRIDE IN ALL THAT HARD WORK, PART II

From stories my father, Don Bowden, told me, if anything went wrong in the mill in its early years, someone had to be blamed so they were either suspended without pay or fired. Many times the problems weren't due to the workmen who were blamed, but to the lack of poor mill maintenance (the bosses didn't want to spend the money or have any "downtime" in the mill), or poor administrative decisions. In order for the workmen to be better able to protect themselves from this kind of mill abuse, my father felt that men who worked on the paper machines needed a union to protect them and their jobs. "If you don't like it quit! There are plenty of other men who would be glad to have your job." He felt this was a stupid philosophy, especially on the paper machines. Each man was part of a team on each machine that had to work quickly and efficiently together – 3 shifts a day, seven days a week. It took a lot of time, effort, and danger by everyone before a new member had developed the skills necessary to be a safe, effective team member. Time was money! He kept repeating, "We need to form a union for our protection." "Everything is good. We don't need one," came the reply each time. "That's the time to form one so it is in place in case something happens," my father would reply. He had been taking law correspondence courses on the side. Eventually he got his degree (in the mail) but never took the Maine Bar Exam. On his own, he did some legal research. Just to see what it would look like, penciled out a proposed union charter and contract and kept it in his lunch box. Once in a while, if someone was disgruntled about something the mill had done, he told me how he would take his proposals out of his lunch box, but no one was interested in getting this union started. They thought that Don had done a good job but a union wasn't really needed.

My father told me how once there was a major part on a machine that was starting to badly wear. At each shift someone would report the problem to a boss who theoretically reported it to his boss – on up the administrative chain. Nothing was done. He was very worried, saying to everyone, "When that goes, there will be hell to pay!" It finally burst, spewing parts and bits of metal all over the paper machine room. Other than cuts and bruises, it was a miracle that no one was seriously hurt and no other equipment damaged. Men were fired on the spot "for negligence." Everyone was furious! "If the machine had been fixed when the problem was first recognized, the mill would have lost only a few hours of "down time" while it was being repaired. Now the machine would be down for weeks – no work and no paychecks. Those men did not deserve to be fired! The mill's administration was the problem."

My father said the men immediately went to him, "We want a union now!" He replied, "It doesn't work that way. You have to have a meeting with everyone in a neutral place to see if they want a union to speak for them. They have to draw up a charter and vote on it – then elect officers who will draw up a contract and present the union charter and proposed union contract to the mill's administration. A place was found and the next day everyone came, approached my father's penciled union charter and contract, signed it, and then elected officers. The meeting between the union officers and the mill's officials was the next day. Needless to say, the manager was shocked to be confronted by a papermaker's union. He said that it needed to be typed, copies made, and sent to Corporate and their lawyers before he could do anything – with their approval. In a few weeks Corporate had approved the contract, allowing the union to represent the papermakers in the mill. The manager distributed beautifully typed copies of everything to all the members. He also said that Corporate would be at the mill in a week for the "official signing" of the contract. After the official signing of the contract by all parties, Corporate announced that this new contract was the fairest they had ever seen, as it had exact procedures for the workmen, mill employees, and the mill administration to be able to address any problem. One of the first Papermakers Unions in the country was formed at St. Regis Paper Company in Bucksport, Maine and that contract was widely replicated elsewhere. When my father, Don Bowden, retired after 34 years in the mill, the company gave him a party at the Jed Prouty Hotel. One of the gifts they gave him was the original hand written penciled copy of the proposed contract between the Papermakers and St. Regis Paper Mill – with much wear and tear.

* * *

The men started asking my father about other legal issues. He was very clear when it would be in their best interests to see and pay for an attorney's advice. They had a lot of income tax questions so he started carrying forms, pencils and pens in his lunch box during tax season. He soon had too many men with too many questions that he couldn't do at the mill. He then decided to invite them to his house. The problem was when the wife came, too, if she wanted to visit with Don's wife who needed to be doing her teacher's school work. So he rented part-time office space, hired a secretary and his income tax business was born, the first income tax business in the area. It grew so big that he brought in another person, Ralph Gonzales, and he is continuing that business today.

While doing taxes for the elderly, especially the women, they would tell Don their problems. Their biggest trouble, especially if they had lost their husband, was trying to find someone to do the maintenance on their property before it became a major problem; someone who was qualified but was also fair in the cost and wouldn't cheat them. Don went to the Human Resource Office of the now Champion Paper Mill in Bucksport. Since the mill had a lot of retired men and women who were well trained in a variety of skills, could the mill sponsor an organization of those people who would be happy to help those who required their services, with the client paying for the materials for any project? The mill agreed, and REAP (Retired Employees Aiding People) was born. Through fundraising events, eventually there was money available for people who couldn't pay for the materials. It was a great community service and it turned out to be a lot of fun for those who participated.

Since the workers enjoyed the socialization, they asked if someone could organize social outings for the retired people and their spouses. My father and mother, Don and Minnie Bowden, volunteered to organize monthly trips to various places in the area and the state. There were no trips in the winter. The bus trips were filled with singing, games, stories, and jokes so there was never a dull moment. Eventually, a summer "lobster feed" was born, sponsored by the mill, which evolved into the "Family

Fun Day" for employees and families. Unfortunately, it eventually got out of hand so the mill stopped the great event. Don and Minnie had to give it up due to poor health, and it died. Thank goodness for the Senior Citizens' Center that has done a wonderful job fulfilling many of the seniors' needs in the area.

My father left the paper machines to join the Swiper Crew for more money – very dangerous and hot work, cleaning the paper machines – very hot and steamy. All the men of that crew had burns. He was having major physical problems so he was able to join the office as a Dispatcher.

CODA:

Last summer when Verso gave the mill tours during the Bay Festival (Remember they changed it to "Woods Festival" because Verso helped to sponsor it? Mistake! I told the new mill Manager that when a mill suddenly opened its doors for tours, it eventually closed. He laughed and said, "That's not going to happen!" I then said, "You've been here for a while, long enough to look for a house in the area especially with so many houses up for sale. When are you going to move your family to the area?" "Oh, we're working on it." I replied, "With school starting in a month, I don't think that's going to happen. This has been a mill town for many years; I hope you are not leading your company to stab it in the back by closing the mill." He walked away.

I loved the mill tour. It was wonderful to see the mill of the '50s transformed into a much brighter, cleaner, less dangerous, and MUCH cooler space. However, there were a lot less people working the paper machines – all computerized. That was not good! I resent the fact that for most of fifty years when the Bucksport Paper Mill was running, the people in the area suffered but tolerated the air, water, and noise pollution coming from the mill so that people who wanted to be employed by the mill could have a steady paycheck and benefits. Those who earned their living by cutting wood would have a convenient place to sell it. Now conditions have greatly improved! Why would anyone close a mill that out–produced its other Maine paper mills, has its own power plant (with enough power left to sell "on the grid"), sewer system, direct rail, and deep water port, as well as a Canadian fuel line close by – resources that no other Maine mill has? Verso didn't want to sell the mill to another paper company (as others were interested in purchasing it) because they didn't want additional competition. To make sure that didn't happen, it was quickly sold in weeks at bargain prices to a scrap metal company to demolish it. To add insult to injury, they gave their hard working, loyal employees 3-weeks notice and would not allow the town officials into the plant for the final tax evaluation. Doesn't this sound like a few company officials received some huge "dividends" in making this executive decision at the terrible psychological and financial expense of the Bucksport area at Christmas time?

* * *

Thank you to all the paper companies who saw the great potential of the workforce of the Bucksport area and were very generous with support in a variety of places and ways. The companies, making a lot of money with their great product, recognized that it was being accomplished with a good, efficient, hardworking, dedicated, proud people. Verso – you didn't deserve to have such a good workforce with such a great history!

261

Now residing in Philadelphia, PA, summering in Orland, ME where she grew up, **Sandra Bowden Dillon** *was born in her grandmother's front living room in Waterville, Maine. She attended schools in Orland, Castine, Milo and Bucksport, graduating (Class of 1958) from Bucksport High School and going on to earn undergraduate and graduate degrees in Music Education from Boston University and Temple University. She taught elementary, middle and high school instrumental and vocal music in Menadnock Regional School District, N.H., Lisbon and Belfast, ME, and the School District of Philadelphia for 43 years. She conducted and hosted many music festivals in Maine and Pennsylvania, plus served on three evaluation committees for New England and Middle States Accreditation before retiring in 2005. "Just for your information, I consulted to the Philadelphia School District for three years after my retirement. Two of my main projects were distributing 20,000 CDs to the schools and producing two films that the School District made, all very interesting work!" When Sandra's father came home from serving in the Army Air Corps in WWII, he wanted to help his father on his farm. "He soon discovered that he needed a regular paycheck and benefits to support his family, so he 'joined the mill' doing whatever they needed at first, at any hour. Thanks to the mill, we got our first telephone as my father was 'on call' – on an 8-party line!" "Get off the line, Gert! Don may work tonight." Eventually he was a 'regular' with shift work on the machines." My mother decided that when I was 10 years old, I needed to play an instrument. I chose a clarinet. At that time, St. Regis paper mill had discount catalogues of many items from which employees could choose to purchase. My father chose a metal clarinet and then four years later, a wooden clarinet from those catalogues. Thanks to the steady mill paycheck and the purchased clarinets, I was able to have clarinet lessons at the Northern Conservatory of Music in Bangor, be in the Maine All State Band for three years, attend music camps in the summer, play in the Bangor Symphony two years and win a music scholarship to Boston University. I feel very lucky to have been a daughter of a papermaker who not only brought home enough paper in his lunch box to motivate a young girl's creative fantasies but also bring home a secure paycheck to help her achieve her musical goals. Thank you, St. Regis Paper Company!"*

Rhea Côté Robbins
Brewer

CHAMPION PAPER VISIT

                to see the ancestry
                of paper making
                            at work
                after   lifetimes
of soldiering
                machine tenders
                maintenance
                "maintainance"
                            word coinage
to deeply describe
                the tendering.
make an appointment to go
                and then he asked
                to go again
he said can I bring
                a friend.
Mostly harrowed
                hall
                hollowed-eyed
feeder of logs
                ghosts
                at the machine
                I look into
                the eyes of
                the machine man
feeding three foot
                chops
                into the chipper refiners grinder
                conveyor belt to digester
                fires of hell.

Cerebus, his mouth
                open, ready to devour
the trees of knowledge.

The tour moves on
to the rings of hell
as glossy stock
emits the outside
fashion magazines
plentiful measures
of success.

Trains come and go
trucks deliver
woods
wood lots emptied
to create knowledge
pressed on paper
truths of the decades
lives emboldened
embedded in
print.

Metric tonnes of paper
delivered world-wide
until the end.
Mill shutdown.
Closed. not just for
"maintainance"
shuttered.
All the industrial
magic castle in reverse
for the
tear-down
generation.
Electronic news fashions
overtaken
by the represented
greed of the vacant
owners gone
bust.

Empty of trust
the years
of slaving to the
gates of hell

eyes gone vacant
skin paler than the
morning mist
            change of shift
ghostwalkers.
            To fade.

Rhea Côté Robbins was brought up bilingually in a Franco-American neighborhood in Waterville known as the South End. She currently lives in South Brewer. Côté Robbins is the author of creative nonfiction, memoirs titled, *'down the Plains,'* and *Wednesday's Child*, winner of the Maine Writers and Publishers Alliance Chapbook Award. She is editor of *Canuck and Other Stories*, an anthology of translations of early 20th century Franco-American women writers who wrote about their immigration experience. Côté Robbins writes, among many aspects of her life, of the mill experiences from the stories told in her family and community about the generations of those who worked in the paper and textile *moulins*. Côté Robbins is the founder and director of the Franco-American Women's Institute, FAWI, which disseminates information about the contributions of the French heritage women's lives. FAWI celebrated its 20th Anniversary in 2016. She edited an award-winning collection of one-hundred and thirty women's works to celebrate FAWI's 20th Anniversary, titled, *Heliotrope—French Heritage Women Create!* This book project was crowd-funded by the Franco- American community and its many supporters. Côté Robbins' writing and research has appeared in many publications. She is currently working on research in expanding the definition of the French heritage women and their "hidden contributions." In 2004 she was awarded an Honorary Doctorate from the University of Farmington, Maine.

Beverly Robshaw
Bucksport

YES, THE MILL NEEDED A MEDICAL DEPARTMENT

I have written on information from my long time at the mill. Hope this little note will help you have many good memories of my years working there. As you know, I was the nurse there for a long time. My husband, Ralph, worked there for 39 years!

Yes, the paper mill did need a Medical Department. Dr. Edward Thegen, M.D., was hired as the mill physician. Ann McMahon, R.N. was nurse there for many years. When she retired, Lilla Chiavelli, R.N. became the nurse in charge. She asked me to work with her as needed so during her tenure, in the '60s, I worked part time, filling in for vacations etc. when needed, later becoming full time. In time an on-call system was set up. After daytime office hours, employees would go to a temporary First Aid Station at the Switch Room. The employee on duty would evaluate and call in one of the nurses if needed. Virginia Shirley and myself did this for many years.

In 1976, when I was hired for full time, Ellen Hersey, R.N. Came to work. She and Virginia Shirley continued to be on call and for extra hours as needed.

The Emergency Rescue Team was formed by already hired employees with the guidance of Ellen Hersey who later on became the mill full time nurse.

The Medical Dept. was a very busy place, and everything had to be recorded. So a lot of paper work and record keeping. Most of the injuries were minor, but needed treatment and follow ups.

The mill had a good Safety Program for its employees.

The mill's title changed with ownership, from St. Regis to Champion to International Paper which it was when I retired in 1983. All those years I knew all of the employees and their families, and had a good relation-ship with them.

I really have a lot of good memories of the years I worked there. It was a nice place to work and I'm sorry to see it go. It's nice to see the workers outside the mill environment.

It upsets me now to see the mill being dismantled. I'm glad you are doing this book.

Beverly Perkins Robshaw was born in Boston in 1924. "My parents, who were originally from Maine, moved back to Penobscot, Maine during the depression. So I grew up in Penobscot, graduating from the Clark High School in 1941. Soon after, I moved back to Massachusetts. Went into nursing school during World War II under the Cadet Nursing Program at the Cambridge Mt. Auburn Hospital School of Nursing graduating in 1947. I returned to Maine when Castine Community

Hospital was advertising for a nurse and Dr. Babcock wrote to me about the position. Then marriage to Ralph Robshaw, and we were blessed with three lovely daughters. Was a busy time with family, but limited nursing time. I now keep very busy enjoying our family camp on Toddy with my children, grandchildren, and "almost" twelve great grandchildren, the eldest on his way to Maine Maritime Academy." Beverly misses her gardening and oil painting, knitting and crocheting as much as she used to, but still uses her sewing machine. "I love to sew." She just this day finished a set of blueberry print pot holders for her eighty-six-year-old niece in California because of how she misses the berries here. "And I love to read."

Anne Smallidge
Blue Hill

HE WORKED AT THE MILL ALL HIS LIFE

I remember my Uncle Don Dunbar
Now gone so long ago
He worked at the mill all his life
He was the baby of the family
My mother, his sister, loved him dearly
Although their politics did not blend
They argued when we met in Penobscot
At my grandmother's house
Labor Unions? Communism?
No difference says my mom
Ah but we must fight for our rights
Uncle Don says in a quiet voice
Their voices always respectful and low
I remember once a crane landed on top of
My Uncle Don
And he spent weeks in a
Hospital bed at home, and his
Daughter, Betty, a nurse who traveled
Came home to care for him
I remember going to visit
It must have been in the 50s
So long ago. He had broken bones
And bangs and lacerations and such
Uncle Don fought for the rights of the workers
He had a huge influence in establishing the union
At the mill
When I was a little girl
When I was a young woman
When I was a middle-aged woman
I would never have believed anyone if they
Said *Bucksport Mill will close*
Life goes on and sometimes it is very scary
But, I truly see a town halfway into its next phase

The beautiful new bridge
The righteous, ancient fort
The winding, graceful walkway along
Our Penobscot River
The old lovely captains' homes
The historic Alamo
It's youth who will stay and make it even better.

Born in 1929 in Mount Desert, Maine, **Anne Dunbar Walls Smallidge** *attended Seal Harbor Elementary and graduated in the Class of 1948 from Gilman High School in Northeast Harbor, Maine. She completed Ring School of Attendant Nurses in Arlington Heights, MA in 1950, and "I earned my BA at Goddard College in Burlington, VT in 1978. From 1970-1980 I devoted myself toward deinstitutionalization of Mental Health and Mental Retardation institutions in the State of Maine, working at Pineland Hospital, Pownal, Maine during that transition, then at the Levinson Center in Bangor, Maine, a new facility serving severely disabled children." From 1980 to '81 Anne served as a Volunteer Health Educator for the Peace Corps in The Gambia, West Africa, earning a Masters in Community Economic Development from N.H. College in 1984. From 1982-1985 Anne was Director of the Therapeutic Foster Home Program at Community Health & Counseling Services, Bangor. For the next ten years she worked for the American Association Retired Persons (AARP), Washington, D.C. and Boston, MA, covering twenty states as the manager for local volunteers in Health Advocacy Services. "Since retirement in 1995 I have returned to The Gambia about twelve times, each time living in the village of Jambanjelly with the families I became attached to while serving in the Peace Corps. My projects there have included helping to get a water system established after the government confiscated the solar panel which provided the pump with energy to pull water from a bore hole. Once the second panel was installed by several good folks from Mount Desert Island who raised funds, shipped the panels, traveled there on their own dime, and installed it, sadly, it too was stolen. The second and more successful project is the building of a community library and filling it with books. A local librarian is paid by fundraising here in the states. I also worked with Acadia National Park as a volunteer with the Peregrine Falcon reintroduction project." Anne has authored three books*: Up North, A Piece of the Core, *and* Adama's First Love. *Her family consists of three children, eight grandchildren and six great grandchildren. In recent years she has enjoyed making beaded jewelry.*

Editor's note:
For stories of her Uncle Don Dunbar's life please see "What the Barber Knows and Loves to Tell" with her cousin, Frank Dunbar.

Minnie Bowden (1915 – 2000)
Orland

HALF WAY

When ebbing tide
leaves Half Tide Rock
halfway out of water,
I ready gear and boat to catch
the outward rush of tide
that helps me down the river
and round the point.
I empty traps and bait them
finishing in time to catch
the tide's incoming rush
that helps me home again.
This half tide sign,
this midway sign,
has eased my work for years.
How much we need a sign
to mark the line between
too late and too soon!

Editor's note:
According to Minnie's daughter, Sandra Bowden Dillon, who gave permission for the inclusion of
"Halfway" in Still Mill, *this poem was published in her last book,* Hardscrabble. *Maybe her 2nd,*
People Poems 2, *but I really think it was her 3rd.*

Lynne Findlay
Verona

LANDSCAPE OF OUR LIVES

Ever changing, day by day
Unseen happenings we have no say.
Conglomerates play out their show
Behind the scenes, before we know.
What heavy load is sure to fall
Changing the landscape overall.
Regardless a town's life depends
On a paper business soon to end.
Now a need to tighten our belts
With job security no longer felt.
Empty pockets must be filled
Taxes will rise and sewerage bills.
Gone are the jobs of men who strive
To keep this landscape in their lives.
Decisions made by heartless men
Could not be swayed, they win again.
The mill that soared for all to see
Is now to be scrapped, left to memory.
Corporate greed, the worst downfall
Of another town that once stood tall.

Author note:
"I have never shared anything I have written with those I don't feel I know....I am not a writer, nor claim to be....I am not a college graduate or have studied. If the truth be known, English was my least liked subject in school. So: what you see, is what you get. I like to keep what I call my Poetic Diary mainly for my family and close friends. Good memories or a laugh or two. I had no intention of even thinking of writing a poem about the mill. Funny thing with me, I sleep, wake up with a thought that inspires me. That is what happened for me to write this. Most people do not rhyme but that is the only way I seem to think as I scribble. I feel honored that you even considered one of my poems. So thank you."

Marilyn "Lynne" Findlay, *was born in 1933 in Lawrence, MA where she lived until moving to Maine in 1978, living in Brooksville and Verona. On Verona Island, Lynne owns and operates Island Trader Antiques, the business her husband Fin started in 1965 and they ran together from 1996 until Fin's death in 2008. She is the author of* Grieving My Way *(White Barn Press, 2011), "my way to let out the hurt . . . .to continue the healing process. I have written poetry since I was in grammar school. It has always been a release for my emotions. I guess you would say it was a way to keep my life in order, so I wouldn't forget the good or the bad" In her author note at the back of her poetry collection, Lynne has written, "The heart has to be open to let out the pain and allow friendships to bring much needed solace," in the way she and her friend and customer, Evelyn Beede, helped one another in their time of mutual grief, "kindred souls, walking the same path." As for other interests, "I do everything from woodworking to baking, like an 'energizer bunny.' Every Thursday I bake and give it away to the trash man, mail lady, or the guy at the garage. And I make pillow cases and aprons for the penny sale at the Franklin Baptist Church where my son is Pastor. I used to make all my own clothes. You can just say, 'I've lived!' My favorite hobby right now is fishing. When my son found out I'd like to start a 'Fishermans' Mingle' in Verona, he said, 'At your age, if you had any bites you'd have to help them into the boat!' The greatest part of life for me is right here on the Island."*

Gary Lawless
Nobleboro

PROSPECT

My grandfather Lester
walked down, down
to his store
at the crossroads of town,
now buried with Hannah,
across the road low
on the hillside,
my mother's first school.
My uncle walked down,
down to the marsh and
Bucksport beyond,
to the mill, making paper,
the mill now
closed down,
soon to be gone –
From Prospect the land
falls down to the river,
Verona, to Bucksport, beyond
and the whole world,
somewhere, below us now.

(*for Lester, Hannah, Ruth and Earl Dow*)

Author note:
"My mother's brother worked in this paper mill for much of his life. Another mill closing, and the poets and artists trying to honor its history, and the people who worked there – wonderful."

Gary Lawless *was born in Belfast, Maine where he grew up the son of the Chief of Police. After a disabling automobile injury his senior year, both limiting and widening his perspectives, he graduated with the Belfast High School Class of 1969. Following Colby, he hitchhiked to California* *to learn from the emerging poet and environmental activist, Gary Snyder, becoming the same for the rest of his life back home in Maine. His great grandfather was a stonecutter at Mt. Waldo, and his grandparents, Hannah and Lester Dow, lived in Prospect where Lester also worked at the Mt. Waldo quarry and then had a store at the crossroads in Prospect that had a fondly remembered dance hall on the second floor. Their son, Gary's uncle Lester, worked at St. Regis Paper in Bucksport and built the Rocky Ridge Motel in Sandy Point.*

Editor's note:
The dance hall over the Prospect Store was one of the few reasons we went over there as young people. Saying "across the river" was like talking about another country. The wonderful country dances always had local musicians and ended with the waltz, "Irene Goodnight."

Gary Lawless
Nobleboro

DRIVING HOME FROM BELFAST, INTO THE CRESCENT MOON

I hear the granite singing
and it is alive.
I want to tell you
that granite is
a migratory species
(think plate tectonics, continental
drift, glacial erratic)
but you can read the flow lines
from when granite was
liquid, and moving, quickly -
I want to tell you
that lichen is a language of granite,
that granite speaks
with air and
water and light -
we might never know
what stories it holds
deep within the rock

(*for Dudley Zoop*)

Originally published at *Mygrations.blogspot.com,* Gary Lawless's internet blog.

Gary Lawless *has published 16 collections of poems in the United States and 5 in Italy. He has read poetry in 9 countries, and has worked with refugee communities, adult artists with disabilities, the homeless and prison population here in Maine. Gary and his wife Beth Leonard own the Gulf of Maine Bookstore in Brunswick and since 1986 have been caretakers and interpreters of Chimney Farm, Maine home of the esteemed American writers, Henry Beston and Elizabeth Coatsworth Beston, then their daughter, Kate Barnes, Maine's first poet laureate. He also, as editor and publisher,* *established Blackberry Books Press. In all these ways, and more, he has been a prime benefactor of Maine literature. The University of Southern Maine has honored Gary with an honorary Doctorate of Humane Letters, and recently Gary was honored with the Contance H. Carlson award from the Maine Humanities Council. In the fall of 2017 he will be resident artist for the Emily Harvey Foundation of Venice, Italy. "Right now I am working as artist in residence at Spindleworks art center for adults with disabilities, and in the spring will be teaching 'Canterbury Tales and the Literature of Pilgrimage' at MidCoast Senior College – busy busy –"*

Stuart Kestenbaum
Deer Isle

from ROCKY COAST

First there was the pink granite
molten and buried for 350 million years,

then there was the ice encountering the ledge
dragging rocks and trees over the land

and then the lichen working in the cold, ceaseless wind,
cleaving to the stone, resurrecting the soil by eating away

at the mica and quartz to make a thin layer of earth
that the coast rests on. And then there was the Dunkin' Donuts

built on the ledge in 1989 in Bucksport, Maine, the town where
the paper mill makes clouds and sends them billowing

out into the landscape, the Dunkin' Donuts where
the coffee is always fresh and when you inhale its aroma

it's as if you are starting the day again or starting
your life over. One more chance. . . .

. . . .

Stuart Kestenbaum *is the author of four collections of poems,* Pilgrimage *(Coyote Love Press),*
House of Thanksgiving *(Deerbrook Editions),* Prayers and Run-on Sentences *(Deerbrook Editions),*
and Only Now *(Deerbrook Editions) and a collection of essays,* The View From Here *(Brynmorgen
Press). He has written and spoken widely on craft making and creativity, and his poems and writing
have appeared in numerous small press publications and magazines including* Tikkun, *the* Sun, *the
Beloit Poetry Journal, Northeast Corridor, and others and on Garrison Keillor's* Writer's Almanac *on
National Public Radio. He was appointed Poet Laureate of Maine in 2016. Former US Poet
Laureate Ted Kooser has written "Stuart Kestenbaum writes the kind of poems I love to read,
heartfelt responses to the privilege of having been given a life. No hidden agendas here, no theories to
espouse, nothing but life, pure life, set down with craft and love." He was the director of the Haystack*

Mountain School of Crafts in Deer Isle, Maine for 27 years, where he established innovative programs combining craft and writing and craft and new technologies. He is an honorary fellow of the American Craft Council and a recipient of the Distinguished Educator's Award from the James Renwick Alliance.

Editor's note:
Please note that Stuart Kestenbaum's "*from* Rocky Coast," excerpted with the author's permission, is the opening portion of his longer poem, "Rocky Coast," which can be located and appreciated in its entirety in his fourth book, *Only Now*, (Deerbrook Editions), available through Maine libraries and bookstores.

Thomas J. Gaffney, Psy.D.
Buksport and Stockton Springs

PULLING TOGETHER

Letters to the Editor   **The Bucksport Enterprise**   *October 22, 2014*

Verso [Paper Co.] has made its choice. It has shown an appalling indifference to its workforce and their families; the surrounding communities, as every single person will be affected by Verso's choice; and to the State of Maine and the town of Bucksport, whose citizens gave generous tax breaks, and will now bear greater tax burdens with potential loss of services.

Verso remains aloof and secretive. It could have planned with state and local government, and with the workforce to tap resources beyond its own means to continue some form of production or prepare for a less costly end, but apparently self-interest won out.

It is humbling to admit we don't have control over events or what anyone else will choose, but it can be empowering to know each of us has control over how we will react, and inspiring to consider what we can do together.

There will be family, friends and neighbors who will have no choice. They must look for livable wage jobs where they can be found. They will need our help to get through the winter, and get back on their feet.

Sadly, some will have to leave the place that has been their home.

For everyone this is a defining moment. Once a mill town, now . . . a prosperous . . . creative . . . achieving . . . caring . . . resourceful . . . healthy . . . (fill in your vision for the town's identity) community known for the character and resiliency of its people!

The future begins with a vision that organizes people of character to make it happen, and discover along the way nothing is impossible when hearts and minds work together as one.

Surely there are regional resources to tap in the state and county. It will be important for the leaders and citizens of neighboring communities to explore how they might support each other, now and long-term.

The Eastern Maine Development Corporation has the mission of connecting communities, business leaders, state and federal officials to boost economic development. Any and all help and experience is welcome.

Wisely, the Bucksport Town Council has asked everyone to contribute to "an idea pot."

But don't forget, you, me and we are the most-valuable resources. No one will fix this for us. This is not a time to watch and wait. It is a time to act!

We all have gifts and passions to contribute. Building upon what's here, together we can become child and elder friendly communities; have the best schools in the region; the most dynamic chamber of commerce that welcomes and supports business growth; a thriving arts community engaging people of all ages; grow farmers to bring local food to local communities, food pantries, schools, and food processors for value added products and year round jobs; and while we're at it, let's make healthy lifestyle changes, expanding recreational opportunities, and promoting safe, caring communities, free of addictions and abuse. Just think how attractive such communities would be for people to live and business to invest.

Each of us has a choice to make now. Everyone is more important now than ever. What kind of town will you call home?

Editor's note:
Tom is President and Chair of the Bucksport Bay Healthy Communities Coalition.

Dan MacLeod
Syracuse, New York

MY DAD FOUND A WAY

AND BUCKSPORT CAN FIND A WAY TO THRIVE, TOO

When my father opened a restaurant on the corner of Main and Central streets in downtown Bucksport in 1980, the paper mill down the road was doing well — which meant he was, too. For 20 years, St. Regis and Champion paper mills were his biggest customers. He catered events and delivered meals to workers nearly every day. They filled his dining rooms and drank at his bar. At lunch, a line of managers and their clients would snake out the front door, while the dishwasher loaded the truck out the back door with hundreds of mill-bound deliveries. He even set up a dedicated phone line for taking orders from Champion. MacLeod's served 1,200 turkey dinners around the clock at the mill one Thanksgiving.

As a child growing up in the area, it felt like our mill had always been there. Its loss was always a possibility, but it was hard to imagine what it would look like. Then earlier this month, Verso Paper brass announced they were halting paper making on Dec. 1. The mill just wasn't profitable, they said.

For as long as I could see over the dashboard of my family's car, watching the mill rise from the trees on River Road meant we were home. The sawdust smell, billowing steam and workers crossing the road at shift changes were as much a part of Bucksport as the view of the dark fort across the river.

Generations of my schoolmates' relatives worked at the mill. My best friend's father was its manager for a time in the 1990s. The company sponsored local sports teams and hung Christmas lights along Main Street on the holidays. It once provided three-quarters of the tax revenue. The high school where my mother works is funded in part by those taxes, which now total a more modest 44 percent of Bucksport's municipal budget.

From a very young age, it was clear to me that the town needed the mill. But it was never clear whether the mill needed the town.

The shuttering of the town's largest employer means immediate pain and unspeakable heartbreak for dozens of Bucksport families, an economic impact that will likely take years to fully realize, and a harsh confrontation with the question of what happens to a mill town when the mill goes away.

From the outside, it would be easy to write off Bucksport as a failure, to say that it can't recover from the loss of the mill.

But that's just not true.

Bucksport is a beautiful — if underutilized — town that sits across the Penobscot River from two popular tourist attractions. It's on the way to Acadia. It has the infrastructure of the mill as well as railroad tracks and a river. It has skilled workers. You can't deny all that potential.

The mill closing hurts. But it also is an opportunity.

In the days after the news of the mill's impending shutdown, gubernatorial candidates jumped on each other to assign blame. There have been calls to keep the mill open, to bring in new investors and keep making paper. It's always easier in the short run to keep things as they are. But what's the next step? Where will the paper industry be in 10 years? Where will be Bucksport be? What about Maine?

The town needs leaders to offer a new vision — one that keeps all those workers employed in a sustainable, growing industry. One that can truly help Bucksport thrive, not just survive a few more years by doing what it's always done.

When International Paper bought out Champion in 2000, the new bosses starting cutting costs. That's when the mill phone at MacLeod's stopped ringing. There was less catering work. Management didn't go out for lunch meetings. Business slowed.

Dad eventually had to stop serving lunch altogether to cut costs.

That was 14 years ago, and he's still in business. Four years ago, he resumed serving lunch.

He found a way to keep going. So can Bucksport.

First published as Special to the *Bangor Daily News, October 17, 2014. Used with permission of the author.*

Dan MacLeod *is a musician and writer living in Syracuse, New York. He is an Orland native, and he can be reached at dansmacleod@gmail.com.*

Used with permission of the artist, George Danby/*Bangor Daily News*

Linda Marie Smith
Bucksport

SHUT DOWN OF VERSO PAPER MILL

> *Friday, December 5ᵗʰ, 2014*
> *Bucksport, Maine*

White sky, sanded icy roads and streets.
My son, Edward Percy Arey, works his last day,
on the night shift.

The paper mill is closing.
The mill where both of the grandfathers
he was named for worked when it was St. Regis.
> Edward K. Arey
> Percy D. Smith

Bangor Daily News says: The third machine
is expected to be shut down at midnight
or which side, Thursday or Friday, it is when
the last quantity of paper rolls off the machine.

From my apartment I can see there is still smoke
coming out of the great big smoke stack.
Just a few lights can be seen at the Verso mill.

A little bit of steam rises from Verso mill's roof tops.

Closing. . . . little by little.

Linda Marie (Arey) Smith was born in Castine in 1947. She grew up in Bucksport where she participated in 4-H and East Bucksport Methodist Youth Fellowship, and was known for her musicianship as a trumpeter, receiving the John Philip Sousa Award in high school where she graduated with the Class of 1966. She started working in her neighbor Ernest Cole's hayfields for 50 cents a day as a youngster, then at the age of 14, taking care of her sister's children in Arlington, Virginia one summer, and she worked for Harborview, waitressing, while in high school, and the Iron

284

Kettle as cook, cashier, waitress and dishwasher. She also worked summers for Ivan Braun's and Sampson's supermarkets. Linda has lived in Orono, Emporia, Kansas and back to Bucksport, working in a range of occupations through the years, including at the mill, in security, briefly. She did secretarial work for Roland Grindle's Insurance and Haffenreffa Brewery companies in Brewer. She worked at Bangor International Airport as an airplane cleaner on call "24 – 7" for international flights, then at Wells Commons at the University of Maine in janitorial services, advancing to apprentice cook. Back in Bucksport, she worked at Doug's Shop 'n' Save, now Hannaford's, as cashier. She also enjoyed participating in the East Bucksport Methodist Church Couple's Club and choir, in Pamona Grange, and McCobb's Company re-enact-ments of Benedict Arnold's march to Quebec. Linda is proud of serving in the Gould's Landing Volunteer Fire Department Auxiliary, learning advanced first aid and to drive a tanker truck and ambulance. She worked for Maine Information Systems as a reconciler, and before retiring home in Maine, worked "out West" researching cemetery records to be computerized and selling vaults on commission, then at the Emporia Country Club as line cook and whatever was needed, and as cook for the three-kitchen Emporia American Legion. "I have seen a lot of changes in the hiring of women, in terms of multi-racial and national security checks." At her home in Knoxview Apartments, Linda is known for being a good friend and helping neighbor. She loves playing her electric keyboard and dreams of a new trumpet someday that she can play at camp and family places in the country. She is an artist with black ink abstract drawings and says she "dabbles" and colors with gel pens in adult coloring books. She is known for being a Scrabble, Canasta, and other word and number games champ, and for writing poems and stories and keeping journals. She is admired and appreciated for the extensive greeting card list she tends faithfully. Her two sons, Edward Percy and Sean Patrick Arey and her grand and great grandchildren were the lucky recipients of her crocheted, knitted, and sewn creations before arthritis interfered. Ed, who had worked at the mill for 14 ½ years, was working as 4th hand on #5 papermachine at the time of its closing, witnessing the tearing down of the room where he worked. His Grandfather Arey retired from the mill in the 1980s and his Uncle Dick Arey, a calendar operator, retired around 2013. His Grandfather Smith had worked there as a rigger in the 1940s, 50s and 60s. As for her memories of working there herself, she will tell you, "I had to get out of there. There were certain places I could only stand for a short time. I wondered how people could work there. But my first impression was walking through the wood chips and the very refreshing smell of wood. The mill was awesome, amazing to see where paper for newspapers and magazines was coming from, our little town. It was interesting with all kinds of people being there for all kinds of reasons and I had to log them in and out. I carried a key on my hip for various checkpoints. I was amazed at the work that went on there with all the machines and men. It was overwhelming! People should appreciate paper! I can't and don't want to believe talk of going to a paperless society."

Brian MacQuarrie
Brookline, MA

CLOSING THE BOOK ON A MILL, AND ITS TOWN

Maine papermaker provided way of life for generations

Boston Globe, December 20, 2014

BUCKSPORT, Maine – Dan Wentworth left behind more than a job when he finished the final shift on the final day at the Verso paper mill Wednesday afternoon.

Wentworth left behind a way of life.

It is a life that transcended the smoke and grime of a belching, monster mill. Where visitors saw a gritty blot on the landscape, four generations of Wentworth's saw good incomes, small-town camaraderie, and the comfort of neighbors who shared values.

The 84-year-old Bucksport plant is the latest paper mill in Maine to fall victim to increased energy costs, global competition, and a decline in demand, which have upended the industry. Verso is the second paper mill, both on the Penobscot River, to have closed in Maine this year with a combined loss of 700 jobs.

Now, Wentworth and hundreds of others in this small, stunned, waterfront community are wondering what the future holds. When the last millworkers trudged out of the plant at 3 p.m., greeted by a throng of townspeople, about 500 jobs and 44 percent of Bucksport's tax based went with them.

"You're wondering if this is just a dream, but it's not," Wentworth, 53, said a few days before the end.

Wentworth now finds himself on the outside, reimagining a life that suddenly changed when he received a text message from a supervisor while driving home from the Fryeburg Fair in October.

Verso planned to close the mill, the message said.

Wentworth was stunned. "we're done. It's over!" he said, throwing the cellphone against the dashboard.

That news signaled the end of 80 years of family employment at the mill, beginning with Wentworth's grandfather, who landed a job there after emigrating with 11 children from New Brunswick. Wentworth's father and mother went on to work at the mill, too, as did two uncles, a younger brother, and a son.

Even after Verso's announcement, townspeople hoped the mill would be sold to another papermaker. But those lingering hopes were dealt a body blow last week when Verso announced that the mill had been sold to a subsidiary of American Iron & Metal, a metal-recycling company.

"They've made clear they're not going to operate it as a mill," Town Manager Derik Goodine said, adding that he doesn't know what the buyer plans to do with the paper-producing facility.

An attached power plant will continue to operate with about 50 employees.

The mill once produced paper for magazine giants such as Time and Newsweek and nourished generations of Bucksport families – and not only those who worked in papermaking. The mill benefited suppliers who trucked wood to the plant, the small businesses in this riverfront town, and hundreds of ancillary services.

"I looked at it as money, not a mill," said Don Houghton, editor and publisher of the weekly Bucksport Enterprise newspaper.

The sprawling factory can be seen from nearly every vantage point in Bucksport, a strategically placed town that the British burned to the ground in the War of 1812. Its smokestacks tower over the pine trees, and the view down Main Street ends with its big, boxy profile.

The mill has been a generous giant. Particularly during its halcyon days more than two decades ago, the mill donated heavily to local charities, sponsored banquets, helped the Little League, and even catered meals for employees who worked overtime.

"I grew up here, I'm from the town, and my dad lived it every day," Wentworth said. "I loved it."

Now he's making plans to commute 80 miles each way for a new job, at half the pay, at the Bath Iron Works.

Workers have realized for some time that the industry is under pressure, but most believed they had five, maybe ten years left at the mill. Then, on Oct. 1, the ax fell. Many employees heard of the closing from reporters, who waited outside the gates as the workers left to ask them for reactions.

"It had been kind of like we were dying a slow death. Then, all of a sudden, we had cardiac arrest," said Alden Blodgett of Penobscot, who started at the mill in 1981.

Bill Cohen, a spokesman for Verso, said the Memphis-based company tried to make all workers aware of the shutdown at the same time. But Emery Deabay, president of the United Steel Workers local that represented 200 workers at the mill, scoffed at that.

"I feel that the disrespect was terrible. It was low-brow," Deabay said.

Daniel Milan, the town's economic development director, said the sale seems like a strategic decision linked to Verso's efforts to acquire NewPage, another manufacturer of coated paper used in magazines and catalogs.

The proposed acquisition which would make the combined company the dominant US player in the market, is being scrutinized by the Department of Justice. Without the Bucksport mill, the merger is believed to have better chance of approval.

To most people in Bucksport, however, talk of sales price, strategy, mergers, and federal approvals is only extraneous noise in the discussion about where the town goes from here. To optimists, the sudden availability of 400 prime acres is a once-in-a-century opportunity. But to pessimists, Bucksport will become a ghost town.

"The feedback I'm getting is the town is going to die without the mill," said Donna Brickett, manager at Gold Star Cleaners and Laundry, which sits on a ridge beside the plant.

"I see people moving out."

One of those moving out is John Bakeman, a 60-year-old millworker who put his house on the market the day after the shutdown announcement.

"A way of life is coming to an end to another small town in Maine," said Bakeman, who worked at the mill for 38 years. "I'm looking for employment in the Bangor area, but I know I'll never make the money I was making here."

Goodine, the town manager, predicted that budget cuts and tax increases are on the way, but that

Bucksport will diversify and be transformed.

The community is located near busy highways, has a deep-water port, and is an appealing place to live, Goodine said. "We survived the British burning us down," Goodine added, "and we'll survive this."

The road to rebirth, however, could be a difficult one. For Glenn Baker, a 60-year-old from nearby Searsport, the loss is personal.

"You know what it's like? You've got a 93-year-old grandmother, and you know some year she's going to die. But you go to wake her up one day, and she's dead," Baker said.

"No matter how much you prepare mentally, it's still a shock, and the grief is painful."

Raised in Norwood, Mass., outside of Boston, **Brian MacQuarrie** *has been working for the* Boston Globe *since 1987 "after stints at various newspapers up and down the East Coast, including the* Philadelphia Inquirer, Fort Lauderdale Sun-Sentinel, Providence Journal, *and* Middlesex News *in Framingham, Mass. At the moment, I roam New England for the* Globe, *looking for stories that capture a bit of the heartbeat of the region, an area that is richly unique in our country. That's what led me to Bucksport. I've had the privilege to cover many fascinating and important stories for the* Globe, *including the invasion of Iraq in 2003, when I was embedded with front-line troops for the entire campaign from Kuwait to Baghdad. I've been back to Iraq three other times for the paper, as well as two trips to Afghanistan as I followed the turmoil and trouble in the long and continuing wake of the 9/11 attacks on New York, where I was one of the first reporters from outside NYC to arrive in Manhattan that night." Brian also covered President Obama's reelection campaign in 2012, has been "the paper's national roving reporter, and covered Hurricane Katrina's devastating impact on New Orleans, as well as the earthquake in Haiti." He attended Colby College, "where I was introduced to the great state of Maine," as well as a year at the University of Edinburgh in Scotland and the University of Missouri where he earned a graduate degree in journalism. "My professional ambition had always been to work as a reporter, which gives me a rare opportunity to speak to people of all types, in all kinds of situations, about the issues that affect them the most. It's an honor. Outside that, I'm a runner -- competed in cross-country and track at Colby, and have run 26 marathons, including 18 at Boston. I have also authored a book, "The Ride," published in 2009, about the surprising aftermath of a horrific abduction and murder of a child in Cambridge, Mass., in 1997. I'm currently working on another book, about the collateral effects of the opioid epidemic sweeping our region and country. I can't get enough of Celtic music. That's a bit of a long-winded summary of my career and interests." Brian lives in Brookline, Mass. "and can walk to Fenway Park to watch the Red Sox, which I do many times a year."*

288

Angus E.S. MacLellan
Bucksport

PAPERMAKERS LAMENT

lyrics to slow air composition
for the Great Highland Bagpipes

The mill has closed its doors
        Jobs forever gone
                Ever gone
The mill has closed its doors
    Our jobs forever gone

What will we do now
The mill was our life
            Our life
The mill has been our life
    And now it is gone

We will move on now
We'll find other jobs
        Other jobs
We will find other jobs
    And we'll carry on

Now we are strong folk
We'll start a new life
        New life
We'll start a new life
And we'll carry on

*Angus E.S. MacLellan is the pen and performance name of **Ernie Smith**, taken from his paternal great grand- father, Angus McLellan of Parkers Ridge, New Brunswick Canada. During his high school years Ernie Smith tried a few sports, track & football but focused mostly on music. From piano in 3rd grade, "not to be stifled to one instrument, through the years I played any instrument I could get my hands on, ending up with a brand new, school purchased, white fiberglass, double B flat*

Sousaphone which I played proudly through my senior year. More than one instructor would ask me why I couldn't stick to just one instrument, my response always being 'why'?" Ernie started to learn the bagpipe in 1996 "which opened up a whole new world of music, travel and excitement from Maxville, Ontario to Glasgow, Scotland! I performed with the West Eden Highlanders Pipes & Drums of Bar Harbor for about 6 years, after which I joined the Masons working my way through the chairs to 2009 Master of Hampden's Mystic Lodge #65 and The Anah Shriners in Bangor and the Highlander Pipe Band Unit." The Highlanders' motto is "We March so Others May Walk." Ernie continues to perform as Pipe Corporal, with Anah Highlanders, raising money to support the Shriners Childrens Hospitals. As a solo bagpiper he travels the state performing at weddings, parties, celebrations of life etc. "I have tried to write music for several years but most always way too busy! However, 2011 was a very special year for composing with one 6/8 March, written for the incoming 2011 Potentate of Anah Shrine, in memory of Robert MacLeod who passed before he could fill the position of Potentate. Also, one of the founders of the Anah Highlanders, in 1976 Past Potentate Herschel MacIntosh, passed away and I composed a Lament in his honor. These tunes are appropriately named: "Robert Macleod's Divan" and "Lament for Herschel MacIntosh." I intend to get them copyrighted soon along with a couple others with a goal of creating a CD of personal compositions. I am currently working on another tune composed for a fellow Shriner, Marvin Tarbox, who met an untimely death while supporting the Shriners Children's Hospitals. The name of this tune is 'Tarbox GoKart' and simulates the revving of his go-cart engine. Although this tune still needs technical tweaking, I was able to perform it at the Shrine Winter ceremonial where the Highlanders also performed "Robert Macleod's Divan" and "Lament for Herschel MacIntosh." I can't tell you what an honor it is to have your tunes performed so majestically at such an event!" Ernie's most recent composition, "Papermakers Lament," was written as part of this STILL MILL *project to honor all the paper mills that have closed. His goals – "spending time with Grands, more piping, more composing and a little more piping!" Ernie's personal website is: www.acadiapiper.us and the Anah Highlanders' website is: www.anahhighlanders.com*

Michael Shaw II
Bucksport

MY SLEEPING STREET

A silent road leading
to a silent Mill.
The roads were alive
helping me in my
slumber. The loud roars
shouting through the
streets. Loud trucks up
til dusk til dawn.
A natural sound it felt
during the night. The
Mill has closed leaving
the truckers in Eternal
Sleep.

First published at the request of Maine writer, editor and poetry critic, Dana Wilde, in his electronic journal, *A Parallel Uni-Verse, Poetry from Maine, and worlds elsewhere.* (www.dwildepress.net/universe/)

Michael W. Shaw II, *17, knew he wanted to be a writer in third grade. These are his first published poems, written as a student assistant to the* STILL MILL *anthology project under the mentorship of Pat Ranzoni, Poet-in-Residence at the Bucksport Recreation Dept. "My Sleeping Road" was shown at the "Good Tern Cafe' Gallery" in Rockland, Maine with entries from all over New England as well as California, Florida, Illinois, Ontario, Quebec and Washington DC. during their 2016 Poetry Month* Post Card Poems *exhibit,* Poet & Art V. *Both this poem and his "I Am a Paper-Maker" will be exhibited with Michael's handmade paper at the* STILL MILL *book launch. Michael's great grandfather was a papermaker in the East Millinocket paper mill through its closings, as was his father, Michael W. Shaw I, who then worked multiple jobs in the Bucksport mill until its closing in 2014.*

Leslie Linder
Penobscot

WHO WILL BEAR OUR ANCIENT MARKS?

"Fill your paper with the breathings of your heart."
                    --William Wordsworth

Trees have long been our kind collaborators as our human aspirations carve revisions on their skin. Perhaps they never minded, since trees also know what it is to spend one's life stuck in the mud, yet tirelessly reach out toward the sun.

Does the cut tree forgive the woodsman, as the cut worm forgives the plow? Perhaps the tree really yearns, somehow, to play a part in a great epic novel, a sappy sonnet, or a recipe for champion chowder.

Perhaps some sentimental trees would like to deliver a long love letter that leads to a marriage and a family. A family spreading under this tree's roots, like leggy saplings, so that one day great and greater Grand Children will caress her ancient, golden flesh with reverent hands in cotton gloves.

Do the ghosts of trees hope to be honored, just once, before ending up as toilet paper or ashes at the dump? Or, once their earthly time is concluded, do they cease to care, or to watch as the ephemera of the human race is transferred to some web's cold, silicone embrace?

In our fifteen minutes of information (and technological fixation), we forget the lesson the forests taught our forebears, long ago. A web is only as strong as the stem off of which it grows.

So who will bear our ancient marks when our network crashes, like a fallen birch, disappearing in the white noise of the snow? And if no one is there to hear it fall (as the old question goes) did it ever happen at all?

*Growing up in Blue Hill and Penobscot, the Bucksport mill was "always a reality for the community" around **Leslie Linder**. Leslie has worked at the local Domestic Violence Project (www.nextstepdvproject.org) since 2001. "For victims of domestic violence, lack of financial resources (including the job opportunities the mill always provided) is always an increased risk." As a writer, Leslie contributes a regular column to* SageWoman, *a women's spirituality magazine. Her poetry has appeared in* Maine WordShed *(http://www.thewordshed.com/),* Stanza *(the newsletter of the Maine Poets Society) and the* Project Intersect *journal (http://cargocollective.com/projectintersect).*

Don Houghton
Bucksport

STARTING OVER
Bucksport Enterprise Editorial
April 9, 2015

With the sudden departure of hundreds of paper makers toting their well-used lunch baskets, the myriad of aspects of the closing at Verso continue to surface.

The immediate toll was financial. Hundreds of families were forced to make the many unsettling changes in order to cope with their lives after Verso.

On the municipal front, officials continue to scramble to cover the up to 40 percent of Bucksport's taxes. Real estate taxes are going to rise dramatically and those who use the sewers are now finding higher utility bills lie ahead.

It's too soon to judge what those property taxes and utility rates will do to the area's long-term prospects for economic development.

In the meantime, we find that some of our neighbors are no longer residing in our communities and their children are no longer in our schools.

Decades of daily camaraderie, thousands of acts of community support – from blood blanks to gifts for the Little League from the paper mill are no longer available.

And the list of losses, big and small, goes on and on.

Milissa LaLonde, Marissa Brown, Hannah Mantsch, Hannah Varnum,
Elsa Theobald, Kelsea Gaff, Meg Morrison
Bucksport, Orland, Prospect, Verona

A TEACHER SHOWS THE WAY

The more I am exposed to poetry, the more joy I receive from it so this became the foundation for my work with RSU 25 4th graders from Bucksport, Orland, Prospect and Verona Island. We played with language and read many poems by varied authors. We wrote free verse and acrostics and invited our poet laureate, Pat Ranzoni, to visit and share her work with us, and ours with her, at a special tea party. We made a booklet of our writings and drawings to thank her. The culmination of our study came when we joined Pat to share favorite verses with the public along Bucksport's water front, passing out "poems for their pockets" and reading at the gazebo with passersby during National Poetry Month 2015. These are a few of the poems written by my students in response to the mill closing.

Marissa Brown has a depth of feeling which comes through in her poetry
which she makes all the more expressive with original designs.

Hannah Mantsch loves to work with her hands to create crafts from yarn
and other materials. Her poetry is also her craft.

Hannah Varnum grows plants in her garden and poems in her journal.

Elsa Theobald loves horses and is a natural leader in many ways, as
well as being a strong writer.

Kelsea Gaff's writing is full of voice and is fun to read. She has many
interests and has attended a summer writing workshop at the University
of Maine at Orono.

Meg Morrisson is a girl of few words with an uncanny ability to write
her thoughts and feelings so that they come alive for the reader.

Author note:
"I was at the Academy of the Sacred Heart in Grosse Pointe, Michigan for my own 4th grade, knowing I wanted to be a teacher when I was about 10. From there I moved to St. Clair, MI where I finished elementary school at St. Mary's. I then went to Holy Cross High school graduating with the Class of 1973, followed by the University of Dayton, Ohio for college. (16 years of Catholic education!!). I got a Masters Degree in Literacy Education at the University of Maine. I began

teaching special ed. in Michigan in 1977 then 5th grade in Pittsburg, New Hampshire. We moved to Maine in 1982 and I established a tutoring business for 5 or 6 years. In 1991 I became a Migrant Ed. Teacher until 1999, when I went back to classroom teaching in 4th grade, continuing this until June of 2016 when I retired. I had a particular nun in high school who was determined to help me get organized and would meet me at my locker each morning. She would insist that I clean my locker, show her my homework and organize my books for the day. It was painful at the time but so valuable for my life thereafter."

Editor's note:
Mrs. LaLonde's nomination for 2015 Hancock County Teacher of the Year stressed how it is one thing for a teacher to excel under ordinary circumstances but quite another to demonstrate extraordinary skill in the face of the kind of cultural emergency that the closing of the local mill has been for her students, their families, and communities.

THE BUCKSPORT MILL WAS

Terrific
Helping
Epic

Best Mill ever
Utterly amazing
Cool
Keeping up
Standing tall
Paper Mill
Open
Rad
Taking it all in

Magnificent
Incredible
Likeable
Liked by everyone

Wow
Awesome
Super

       – Marissa Brown

PAPER MILL

Perfect
Amazing
People's Jobs
Enormous
Rough Life

Marvelous
Incredible
Lovely but old
Large

— Hannah Mantsch

MILL

Loud, Loud, Loud is the mill
Slow, Slow, Slow are the trains
Happy, Happy, Happy are the workers
Sad, Sad, Sad are the trees
Quiet, Quiet, Quiet is the mill
Gone, Gone, Gone are the trains
Sad, Sad, Sad are the workers
Happy, Happy, Happy are the trees

— Hannah Mantsch

THE MILL; DENNIS

My uncle named Dennis
lost his job at the mill.
But when the mill closed
my uncle was out of work
because he hurt his back.
Now he can't return to work
because the mill is closed.
I am very sad for him
and everyone else who lost
their job at the mill.

– Hannah Varnum

HOW IT FEELS

answering the t.v. reporter about the mill closing

My friend
       may have
             to move

                away.

– Elsa Theobald

Editor's note:
This powerful truth, "saying more than it says," expressed by Elsa on the television news, is an example of "a found poem," poems that can be found all around us, every day, if we pay attention. And sometimes we speak in poetry without realizing it, for others to find, as here.

MILL TOWN

Magical Mill

Incredible Mill

Loud Mill

Lovely Mill

Terrific Mill

Official Mill

Wonderful Mill

Now can't be found Mill

– Kelsea Gaff

GOOD–BYE MILL

For 80 years Bucksport's been a mill town,
but now you're gone and I want to frown.
I will get better, from my love wrapped up
in this little letter. Good–bye mill.

– Meg Morrison

Participants in National Poetry Month reading at the gazebo on the waterfront in April, 2015

Mrs. LaLonde's 2015 4th grade class:
Cody Monreal, Silas Moore, Drew Gaudreau, Haley Gomm, Kelsea Gaff, James Kennard, Garrett Carrier, Talia Robbins, Marissa Brown, Mackenzie Bridges, Hannah Varnum, Carlos Herrerra, Meg Morrisson, Elsa Theobald, Hannah Mantsch, Tristen Gomm, Emily Morrisson (mom), Hope Melton, Evan Trojano. Bagpiper, Ernie Smith and sister Linda in back and teacher Milissa LaLonde with Bucksport poet laureate, Pat Ranzoni, on right. Photo by Paula Smith.

Tom Gaffney
Stockton Springs and Bucksport

GIGANTIC MILL

Out of the darkness came hope.
The last ships had sailed away,
leaving the river empty with fears.
From the heavens a bridge was suspended
to tie North and South together.
A giant laid down there on the riverbank,
where life had always flowed beneath the sky
from mountains to the sea and back.

With one hand the giant loved,
giving common people a place and time.
Light fell upon their gardens,
warmth and songs could fill their homes.
Children's laughter was in the air,
wives and mothers tended hearts,
and men set their strength to good work.
But the people and the giant became lost
in the illusion of belonging.

With the other hand the giant hated,
demanding souls to enter its body,
suffer its heat and noise to care for it
more than anything, surrendering all.
No more day or night, songbirds silenced,
miseries growing, neglected and dulled.
No end in sight, no turning back,
counting over and over the cost
of hearts and spirits resisting.

Then, one day the giant weary, stood up,
walked away, leaving its ghost behind
with the setting sun and ebbing tide.
That night the common people embraced,
saving each other's tears as dreams arose
from long ago both wise and dear.

The sun came for them in the morning,
glistening in the river flowing beneath the sky
from mountains to the sea and back.

(*For the common people of Bucksport Bay.*)

Editor's note:
For the 2015 200th Anniversary of the Harbor Church in Searsport Tom "became Captain Benjamin Franklin Pendleton to tell the story of faith, family and community that produced over 400 sea Captains in the 19th century."

Knowing Who We, Still, Are

Gene Sanborn
Orland

THE MILL AS I KNEW IT

"Until we all pass on."

My first recollection of actually focusing on the mill was when young Fred Sprague and I decided to build a camp. We were about 10 or 11 years old at the time. Fred suggested we go to the mill to get some lumber. In those days, some 65 years ago, you could see the scrap lumber pile by the back of the mill from the Town Site where we lived. We got our red flier wagon and headed down to the mill to the gate. When we got there we were greeted by the watchman, who later I learned was a Mr. Jay Clement. I think he was Millard Clements' father. Millard came to work in the mill later as well as his son in the years thereafter. Well anyhow, after we told him what we wanted he told us to help ourselves and to watch out for trucks. We then rounded up our wagon and headed for our building site on the pipeline.

I believe all the people living in the Town Site were all employees of the mill. A good many I remember as Preston Robinson (engineer), Earl Johnson (electrician), Lester Gray, Gus Swenson (maintenance superintendent), Gus Gregorys (supervisor), Steve Barry (plant engineer), Arthur "Buster" Grunwald (millwright), Harold Salisbury (lab), Levi Chase (millwright foreman), Dick Bray (electrician), my dad Levi Sanborn (millwright), the Bourgoins SP..., Bobby Oliver (supervisor), George D. Bearce (mill manager), and many others that I can see in my mind but don't remember their names. It was a great place to spend my early years. In the evening all the kids would be out playing hide and seek or kick the can until the 9 o'clock whistle sounded from the mill to signal curfew time and we all had to go in. At that time there were several whistles either starting or ending the work shift. It was common in those days to see a group of men walking up the hill towards home after the 4 o'clock whistle signaled the end of their work shift. It was a closeknit little village where our childhood friends remain friends today, at least those of us who are left.

My grandfather came to the mill in the 1930s to work on building the mill and after him my father followed to the mill. In the early '40s the machine shop was turning out cannon barrels for the war

302

effort. Those same lathes were still being used when I went to work in the mill in the late 1950s and were still in service when I left in 2002. I can still remember standing on the porch of our apartment hearing all the church bells, sirens, and horns as the announcement had come over the radio that World War Two had come to an end.

When dad began work in the mill he started out in the power plan, then moved to the mechanical dept. as a mill-wright, then to the yard as yard mechanical foreman, and his last position was wood yard superintendent. I went into the mill several times in those early days with dad when he got called in for a quick repair job. Of course I couldn't go in the building with him so I had to wait in the car. I got to know a lot of the people in the mill before I ever went to work there as I delivered the *Bangor Daily News* on one end of town in the morning, and delivered the *Evening Commercial* on the other end of town in the late afternoons. I would meet them with their lunch basket or dinner pail either going to work or coming home.

When I reached the age of 18, I started to work in the mill summers. My first initiation was unloading lime rock from an open rail car called a gondola. The lime rock was thrown from the car into a little mine cart on rails. The same thing you see in movies when they are in a mine hauling ore. It was hard work, but from the top of the car you could watch the men loading paper onto a ship bound for France or Chicago. The pin boys were putting pins into the paper cores that were attached to straps. The man on deck would signal the man operating the steam driven winch which would raise the boom and lift the roll of paper. The signal man would direct the paper into the hold of the ship and it was lowered into position to the men working in the hold. I was told this later on as I had no idea what happened in the belly of the ship, because you couldn't see them from the top of the rail car.

While watching the loading operation you could also see barges loaded with wood laying idle in the mill pond waiting to be unloaded. The next day the big ship had gone back to sea and the men were now unloading the wood barges. There were two men standing by the end of the conveyer steering wood onto the chain with long handled pick poles. The wood went by conveyor to the wood yard.

After many shifts with the lime rock I got a chance to throw pulpwood. I don't remember it being as enjoyable as the lime rock job. I reported to Ted Gross in the wood yard. While waiting for my instructions I got to m eet some of the guys I was going to work with. One of the people was Gordon Clement, another was one of the Bridges boys from Verona. Thank the good Lord I was paired up with I believe his name was Oscar or Ivan, one of them because I would still be there lugging wood one stick at a time out of that rail car today. Once the wood was clear of the car door he piled wood so that it worked like a chute. When you threw the wood it slid along the floor and around the corner and out the door onto the conveyor. No lugging.

From then on that summer I went to the charging floor to again throw pulp wood but this time it was easier. The grinding room was directly underneath the charging room floor. All you had to do was slide the wood across the floor from the wood bins and into the hole above the grinders. I also got an initiation to the wood room working at that time for Oscar Briggs. There we had to pick the wood off the chain and direct it towards the splitter if it was too big to go down the mouth of the chipper. Willey Waterman, or Bed Johnson usually had the splitter job. Wood with defects was also directed to the chipper mouth, the remainder stayed on the chain to be carried on up to the charging floor bins. That finished my education for that summer and I went back to school.

The next summer the Company had decided they could no longer bring wood to the mill by barge and were going to take the conveyor system that led from the log pond down. I started working in the riggers with Tom Stubbs, a childhood friend. We were assigned to drive trucks from the pond wood yard. Tom and I were to haul the big timbers that held up the conveyor to a pile in the yard. The ladies of the Garden Club were going to have a meeting at one of the cottages on Lake Alamoosook. I was assigned to grade the camp road to the cottage where they were going to meet. The Company often was doing things to help out the town's people when it made sense to do so. I started working as a six hand on No. 1 paper machine mid-way through the summer. That consisted of tearing down the outer slabs of paper and feeding the slabs that had been torn off the roll into the beater which was mulched up and then reused in the paper making process. I felt good working on the machine as there were a lot of people I knew there such as George Adams, Arthur Adams and occasionally their young brother Tickey. Their father Guy had worked in the mill prior to my working there. I knew the Adams family well as I used to deliver the *Bangor Daily News* to their house. I looked forward to Saturday as Mrs. Adams (Edna) made the best doughnuts in town and always had a hot doughnut ready when I came to the door.

Another family well represented in the mill were the McAllians. Charlie, Jimmy, John, Fred, Harold, and Arthur as well as some of their children could be seen in the mill. Their sister Ruth worked just beyond the end of number 1 paper machine in the wrapper section as well as Bertha Lord, and other ladies. In the wrapper area they used a paper cutter called a layboy that cut the paper into small blocks for the ladies to wrap. Loyd Bridges and Lawrence Robbins also worked in that area. They also had a mechanical wrapper that wrapped the big rolls of paper. They manually put a large sheet of wrapper paper with glue on the ends in front of the roll as it turned to completely cover the rolls and then they inserted round pieces of paper on the ends and then the machine applied pressure to complete the wrap. On my shift, Lawrence was usually operating the wrapper machine and I think Loyd was running the layboy. Then fall had come and it was time to go back to school again.

When I returned the following year I got a chance to work in the pipe fitters crew and stayed there with Tinker Arnold, Don Mann, Bob Harper, Horace Sukeforth, Joe Gallant, Ed Harding, Dick Soper and Don Eldridge. At this time the company had decided that we would no longer ship paper by water, and Ed and I were sent down to the wharf to dismantle the steam winches. Later on that summer Dick Findlay joined the crew as temporary help. Further on into the fall, Dick and I were offered an apprenticeship which put us permanently into the crew for the next 40 years.

Those first few years were great working in a relaxed atmosphere that had been instilled by the Seaboard Paper Co. and except for one bad morning. I had been working with Bob Harper up on Jimmie Burgess Decker during the big snow storm of 1962. Bob had gone home with Aron Labree, Don Soper and others. Don was riding on the front fender directing the driver to where he thought the road might be. It was snowing and drifting so much that the driver could not see the road on his own. Bob got out and decided to cut across the field on his own to get home. The next morning his wife called the shop and wanted to talk to Bob as he hadn't made it home. Tinker, our foreman, advised her that we hadn't seen him that morning. We got a call a short time later that they had found Bob sitting beside the dog house, just a hundred feet or so from the house. He couldn't make it the rest of the way. We all felt very bad in the death of Bob as he had been a key member of our crew.

Over time the rules instilled in the men during the time that Seaboard Paper had owned the mill gradually became more rigid, but still it was a great place to work. I was often sent to the steam plant which was headed up by Bill Walsh. He was a great guy to work for, he knew the plant inside and out. He never asked you to do anything that was in the least bit risky. When he wanted something done it wasn't that maybe it should be done but that it had to be done and made it plain to you when you came to work. His shop mechanic Harold (Rooster) Door was also the same way. Bob Terrill was working as his helper at that time. Bill thought I might make a good person in his ranks so offered to teach me and others about the workings of a power plant. Through his tutelage I was able to sit for the steam engineer's exam in Augusta and as a result was given a first class Engineers License. I never did get the opportunity to stay in the power plant but I will always remember Bill Walsh as the man he was.

The mill was full of real good people. Steve Barry, the plant engineer, was rather a stern guy but he showed a lot of concern to the people around him and the town, even if some didn't think so. The mill was very generous to the town doing such projects as building the athletic field next to the Town Site. They also sponsored the triple A baseball team that was popular in those days and hired the premier baseball players such as Whinny Weston, Gib Snowman, Eddy Dorian and others from around the state in order to have the best team possible. They built the Boy Scout cabin that has since been torn down, the bleachers for the high school field, the annual manger scene and other projects in the area for the benefit of the people. All these projects had the support of and were under the direction of Steve Barry.

Another person that appeared gruff on the outside but had a heart of gold, especially when it came to people who were less fortunate was Gayland Redman. I have seen tears come to his eyes when he didn't think others were looking because someone else was struggling. Gayland was the mill fire chief as well as the town fire chief. Many times Gayland would call me to go out with him on the ambulance to either an auto accident or to someone's home who was seriously ill. I remember one time when the fire department was called to Willie Waterman's home to a chimney fire. After putting out the fire an inspection was made of the chimney in the attic. It was then that a case of dynamite was found next to the chimney. Gayland asked Willie why he hadn't told him of the dynamite. Willie stated as a matter of fact, that if he had told them of the dynamite they wouldn't have put the fire out. He was right, of course. We wouldn't have been anywhere near that neighborhood. Gayland was always available to the town day or night. He was instrumental to having the mill pay to send me to the Burgon County Fire Academy in Mahwa, New Jersey.

In the years to come I worked as an area mechanic in the acid plant with Jim Stone, Whoopee Atwood, Basil Leeman and others. The plant made acid which was used to cook down the wood chips in the digesters. Every so often they would shut the plant down for clean up. They then would clean as much of the mercury and sulfur residue out of the equipment as they could salvage. They then would rake the remainder into a wheelbarrow to be taken to the bark dump. Sometimes the plant area had an odor that would burn your nose and make it hard to breath. I didn't stay in that position for more than a few months before I asked to go back to the central crew as a pipe fitter. There I stayed until Champion Paper Co. bought the mill and brought in more changes both to the working crews as well as upgrading a lot of the equipment.

Over the years I had worked as a lobster man besides my mill job. The company took notice of my boat and asked me if I would be willing to take on the job of using it as a diving platform for a commercial diver so that the pipes under the river could be inspected. I accepted the job and the following week a truck showed up at the mill carrying what appeared to be a large air compressor, and all the equipment for a hard hat diver. After moving into the river and anchoring from both the bow and the stern, the diver, a Mr. Pooler, lowered a ladder into the water and after donning his diving suit and checking his air, moved down the ladder to the bed of the river. After what seemed an eternity he returned back up to the boat and announced that all the pipes were clear and in fine condition. That, for me, was an experience for the books. After I stopped lobster fishing I would fill in for the police dept. working for Chiefs Charles Hunt, Guy Snow, and Toar Gross. I would work when others had the weekend off, for unexpected vacancies or when others were on vacation. I usually could work it around my shift at the mill.

During the Champion years the mill gradually relied more and more on hydraulic equipment. Not that they didn't have hydraulics before but it had become much more technical. At that time a few of us were sent to Detroit, Michigan, for training at the Vickers Hydraulic School. Then under the new leadership we were divided into area crews. At that time Charlie Downs was the foreman in the area that served the Off Machine Coater and the Super Calendars. I knew Charlie as a good man with untold mechanical abilities. I elected to move down there with him as the area pipe fitter. By this time they had put in a totally computer driven roll wrapper that was fully hydraulic and governed by computer. John Daniels was assigned to the computer equipment to maintain its functions. That was my specialty and I enjoyed the people and the work.

I was elected to become the President of the machinists local union after serving many years as the vice president. I then was selected to be a directing business agent for the northeast territory of the International Association of Machinists. I took a leave of absence from the mill that lasted for seven years. During that span of time I also sat on the board of directors for the AFLCIO of Maine and the Workers Compensation Commission in Augusta. The Workers Compensation Commission was a result of industry attempting to shed themselves of any liability and costs when an employee got injured on the job. I took a leave of absence from the mill that lasted seven years. I hope through these efforts some people at the mill found living a lot easier than it would have been without us.

I have to think of Barry Murchie who spent nights sleeping in his car getting up frequently to sample or to test a chemical that it seemed no one understood. It is my opinion as well as others who believed that was the primary cause of Barry's injuries and the thing that finally caused his demise.

While I was on leave a new culture had taken place in the maintenance department. Those people who elected to could cross train into another trade thereby supposedly be able to perform two trades on the

306

same job. Mill-wrights could now be pipers or pipers could cross train as welders, welders could be tin smiths, carpenters could be millwrights or pipers. The tin smiths turned into blacksmiths. Riggers turned into pipers, etc. and everyone would now do their own rigging. Now anyone in the mill could paint without the training to understand the chemicals they were applying or the danger of the fumes they were inhaling and getting on their skin. Most people were trained to operate fork trucks and some learned to operate back hoes and excavators. Everyone could cross train in what they wanted within reason.

When I went back to the mill I applied for the job of Maintenance Training Coordinator. The best part of that was teaching and interacting with all the people involved in different phases of training. I'm not sure it went as well as they thought it might as supervisors were then telling the men how to do a job they themselves hadn't been trained in doing. This in turn created short cuts that created dangers and down times that shouldn't have occurred. I guess it stands to reason that a few months of training is hollow without many years of experience that turns that training to a fine skill.

I stayed with training until the management thought it could be done on a part time basis. Not believing that I wanted to be part of that, I again transferred back to the area that I came from where Jerry Leach had been the foreman. Eventually that area was to include the truck shop and coating plant. The coating plant was like a giant kitchen full of stainless steel cookers in which the clay, silicone, starch, and water were cooked to make the coating slurry that was applied to the outside of the paper to improve brightness and print quality. Skip Taylor was the department mechanic in that area.

During all these changes, attempts were made to modernize the process with many changes to an old technology. New high-speed paper machines were installed and new super calendars and On Machine Coating had come of age to take the place of the Off Machine Coaters and they were shut down one by one. Thermal Mechanical Pulping was installed to augment the old pulp grinders that were part of the original mill back in the 1930s. It's my opinion that it just wasn't enough and the time had come when Champion Paper realized what was happening and decided to sell the mill in an attempt to recoup at least some of its investment. Through this and through each year less and less people from Bucksport were given employment at the mill. Some from modernization and finally from not modernizing enough.

But when you look down at what remains of a once flourishing work place you can't help but think of the generations of people who toiled there day and night 365 days a year. Good people, great people. Some of those families – the Smiths, Adams, Sopers, Eldridges, Wentworths, Sanborns, Grosses, Stubbs, Manns, Burgesses, Grunwalds, and many more too numerous to name will stay in our minds as one family until we all pass on.

A lot of these families helped build the mill and stayed on sometimes with three generations working at the same time until the bitter end. As I think back I don't miss the mill structure as it was, but the people, who to me were family that you had coffee with every morning and lunch with every noon and during those times discussing the issues of the day. I miss them a lot.

Ruth McAllian McKay
Hollis

PLACES OF HONOR AND SWEETNESS

<u>Still Mill.</u> How much that title says. We have been so saddened by the Mill closing and all that means to the people of our town. We have prayed often for these families with their livelihood cut off, several in our own family.

We very seldom get to Bucksport but have so many happy memories from younger days. I am not sure what I can remember. We have a family wedding in August. I told Mary and Chuck I was going to pick their brains to jog my memory.

One thing I remember about Daddy working at the Mill was how much it meant to him. He was a Millwright (as was Chuck). The men in his group meant so much to him, how they cared for each other and the loyalty was high. As a Millwright, he had access to many areas and people willingly helped each other.

When he retired the men made him a beautiful chest which he treasured. It still has a place of honor at camp. At the retirement ceremony, people spoke of his loyalty and work ethic in appreciation. He was very moved. He always hid his emotions well but that night they showed, he was so moved.

Before we had our camp we often came out to the dam to swim. We were all so thrilled when the family was able to buy a piece of land on Alamoosook. The 3 of them shared it, Ruth, Arthur and Dad. Building just a small basic camp was such an adventure. Many family and friends helped. We had a party on the foundation the weekend it was capped. We had music and dancing, Aunt Lillian's accordion, I think. Were you there?

The camp has evolved a great deal. First when Dad retired, with expansion and winterization and then when my sister Mary and Jim took over and Mom and Dad passed on. Mom was so happy to have room for her horse and Dad a garage for his truck. We had so much fun with the boat and swimming and fishing. The children grew up enjoying the lake and the grandparents. This was all supported by the Mill and hard work.

Remember when it was such a treat to go to Crosby's for an ice cream? When I worked there a small cone cost 5 cents. We had lines at both places that were very long. Those lines were almost fun as we chatted and caught up with friends. Small Town advantage.

The Mill was a mainstay for my family all my life. The majority of my uncles, some aunts, many many cousins, my brother and my sister in-law worked their careers there. Such a long history. We have seen changes in so many ways in our lifetime, some good, some not.

I will talk to my family and see what we can come up with. Looking forward to reading <u>Still Mill</u>.

P.S.
I have searched my memory of so long ago to give you additional information. So many years have passed, so much life has happened, so many moves have made things fade. As far as recipes that are associated with camp, they were mostly basics like beans or cookies and cakes. We had lots of family and children. Mom always wanted to give hungry children a treat. We also had homemade bread and rolls. We often picked strawberries and blueberries up back. I will send a couple of Mom's old standbys.

We were always grateful for the Mill. Dad loved his work and the men. From his 12 siblings many worked at the Mill. Of course Chuck, my brother, worked there also. Garrett, Chuck's son also. Dad's brothers' John, Jim, Arthur, Fred and Sister Ruth worked their whole lives there.

I think I mentioned in my last letter that we were very grateful for the Mill's support of the college students. Our first son Charles (Chip) worked there one summer. They gave him long shifts and paid him well. He paid for college that year and some of the next.

The Mill was like "life blood" to the Town and those who lived there or even in surrounding areas. (Our vet paid for college with summer work and he was from Blue Hill.)

After we moved away we would often bring friends back to visit. We were proud to take them on Mill Tours so they could get a feel of the paper making process.

This is a huge project you have taken on. I would love to sit and chat. We have precious memories.

P.S. My Aunt Ruth, Ruth Bowden (Melvin's wife) is 97 and a sharp minded treasure trove of information. She is in Florida now but will return in April. She wouldn't write, but she would talk. She is fun and funny and worked at the Mill a long while.

<u>Swedish Molasses Cookies</u> (Gertrude McAllian)

2 cups sugar	Sift:
1 ½ cups shortening	4 cups flour
2 eggs	3 Tsp. ginger
½ cup molasses	3 Tsp. cinnamon
1 Tsp. vanilla	4 Tsp. soda
	1 Tsp. salt

Mix soda in molasses, set aside. Cream sugar and shortening together. Add eggs, vanilla and molasses mixture. Combine wet and dry. Roll into walnut sized balls. Roll balls into sugar. Place on ungreased cookie sheet. Bake at 375 for 10 to 12 minutes.

Soft Molasses Cookies (Gertrude McAllian)

1 cup sugar	4 cups flour – add more if necessary
1 cup molasses	1 Teas salt
3 Teas soda in molasses	1 Teas ginger
1 cup shortening	1 Teas cinnamon
1 cup warm water	½ Teas nutmeg

Chill mixture at least an hour. Roll – cut out circles. Bake at 375 for 10 – 12 minutes.

Congo Squares (Gertrude McAllian & Ella Leach)

Melt ¾ cups shortening in saucepan.
Add 1 pound brown sugar – mix well – cool.
Add 3 eggs – one at a time – mix well.
Sift – 2 ¾ cups flour
      2 ½ Tsp baking powder
      1 Tsp salt
Gradually add to batter – mix well.
Add 1 Tsp vanilla – 1 pkg choc chips – 1 cup broken nuts – stir – spread in greased pan.
Bake at 350 for 25 – 30 min

Ruth Arlene McAllian McKay *was born in the house next to the Dairy Port on Main St. in Bucksport in 1940 and grew up in Bucksport, graduating with the Class of 1958. "I married Jim and graduated from the University of Maine in Education in 1962. We moved to Delaware for Jim to work for DuPont but moved back to Maine – YEA! —in 1969 where he worked for Maine Savings Bank, Coastal Saving and York County Federal Credit Union. From 1968, our three sons, Charles 'Chip', Brendan and Christopher grew up with us in Hollis, Maine – very rural – horses – dogs (Collies and Shelties). Both Jim and I have been very active over the years at the Hollis Center Baptist Church. We have been Youth Leaders, coaching basketball and cheerleading. Also, leading a ladies' and men's weekly Bible Study (over thirty years), Food Pantry Ministry (20 years), Fellowship Committee (35 years). I am in the Choir and Jim an Elder and Treasurer. I taught pre-school many years and worked as a volunteer several days a week at Greater Portland Christian School, 11 years while children attended. Raised and showed Collies and Shelties in obedience and breed. Our three grown sons – very grown – are all 6 ft. 6! Grandchildren, we have 8, from 24 to 4, but they are spread all over the world. Chip is a teacher,* *his wife, Mariko, a graphic designer. They live in Japan with their children, Nikki and Kota. Brendan is the manager of a storage company. He and Sherri, a music minister, live in Maryland with Jessica, Jonathan and Jackson. Christopher and wife Nicole live in New Sharon and he manages the Poland Spring Plant in Kingfield. Their children are Kayla, Kyle and Morgan who've been here a lot so we have spent many hours at basketball and baseball games, school events, music, dance, plays and lovely grandchildren events. I have loved volunteering often at their school. Dear ones. Although they give us the opportunity to travel often to see them, (5 trips to Japan and several times a year to Maryland) we don't get to spend as much time with some of them as we'd like so that is why we are on Facebook. They are very good about talking and sending pictures. No one writes letters in the younger generations. Our grandson Kota is coming from Japan to stay with us for a semester while he attends college. Looking forward to getting to know him more. His sister Nikki stayed with us 8 years ago when she was in 8th grade. Jim is on the school's board and I do a lot of busy work there which I love. Jim has been on the board of Bonny Eagle's ice hockey association for ten years. Our grandson Kyle has played on the school teams and many other teams for all those years. We do every job for the team that is needed. We are big fans and very proud! We are cozy in our little log cabin, our second, smaller and more efficient, retirement log home in the woods. We love burning wood from our own lot and growing vegetables and flowers. Our beloved blue merle Sheltie has passed on and we now have a Tri-color Sheltie named Skye – both came from Bucksport – instead of the 5 or 6 usual dogs we once had. Once, 22 dogs! We work many hours on local projects. Though we have had trials and hard times like each of you, we are grateful for all our blessings including reasonably good health, thanks to God, and appreciate each day. Many of our dreams and goals have been realized and some that haven't, those we didn't need after all. We cherish friendships, old and new. We love visiting Bucksport when we can. Though Mom and Dad are gone, many Aunts, Uncles, sister Mary and brother Chuck are still here and the camp at Alamoosook is popular with the grandkids. I sure would love to chat and catch up. Can you believe how old we are and how much life we have seen. So many changes."*

Ruth McAllian Bowden
Bucksport and Lake Wales, FL

CABOOSE RIDES TO BANGOR, JOB FOR YOUR DAUGHTER & OTHER FAVORS

"Ruth will remember," so many say while recalling the mill's history in Bucksport, and for good reason.

At 97, her mill memories go back to 1939 when she was just 18 and wanting work. Her father, William McAllian, was the Railroad Agent in Bucksport, "used to doing favors to accommodate the mill. For example, if the mill didn't have a shipment of paper quite ready on time, he would agree to hold up. Every so often the mill would call to ask for these important favors so my father decided to ask for one in return – for a job for me. It was hard to get in there so I was lucky they agreed. Our family had a good relationship with the railroad. We were a large family, you know, and there were no cars in those days. We were very lucky because the conductor would take us to Bangor in the caboose when we were only kids."

BUCKSPORT RAILROAD STATION
BUCKSPORT HISTORICAL SOCIETY
CIRCA 1874

"As for my job, I worked in the Finishing Department wrapping reams of paper. In those years, #4 paper machine made school paper. That was before they went to magazine and news paper. Some people today don't know that the mill once made all kinds of school paper." I (Editor) knew because that's what we used in school and had all we wanted. The mill also provided kits for us to learn to make paper in elementary school. "Some blocks of drawing paper were so big that the men had to move them from the machine, turn, and place them by the cutting machine to be cut to size, also for tablets. They had to

312

feed the cardboard backings, 2 or 3 from the same block. We women sealed and wrapped the blocks. Every so often we had to count the blocks to make sure there were 500 sheets in each ream."

"The area where we worked was a compartment by itself. About ten women and ten men. The paper machines were located in a layer below us. What I disliked most was that it was so, so hot and we couldn't have a window open because a breeze might bother the drying process. It wasn't a bad place to work. I didn't really like working in the mill but it was a big wage then, the best money around at the time. The part I enjoyed most was that there were a lot of different people and everyone was like a family, very interesting with good relationships. We looked out for each other. It was hard work, though, and some women just couldn't do it. Our department was known to wrap 500 or more packages a day."

"I worked there around a dozen years. In the second half of my life, as I call it, I worked for Head Start in Bucksport as cook and 'mother to all' and I recall that experience with great fondness.

"After about eleven years, I went on to explore other options. I always had a great drive to learn, so took all the lessons that H.O.M.E. Co-op (Homemakers Organized for More Employment) in Orland offered, plus basket weaving from a lady on the River Road, then one in Winterport a day a week. All kinds of sizes and materials. Once I made one almost as big as a laundry basket and filled it with flowers to give to my daughter for a house warming gift."

"I've done everything. After seventy I took painting lessons, oils, and became quite a good artist. My last best one I did at 91, and second last best one at 92, saved for grandchildren. It takes three or four months to make a good one."

"We go to Florida every winter, this one our 25th. We go to the same place, a small house trailor, very livable, and are very lucky to have a lot of close friends down there. It's a trailer park with a community building where there is something going on for the residents every day."

By the time we had neared the conclusion of our long-distance phone visit, Ruth and I realized we not only knew each other, but were long-time friends from our years pioneering in early childhood education in the Bucksport area. While she was working in the first Head Start program in the area, my husband and I were establishing New Alderbrook farm nursery school. I had wondered why, having known the McAllian family most of my life. I had missed this one, and it dawned on me that I hadn't! One of my best school pals, Ruth, had been named for this Ruth, her father's sister. We knew one another all along. What it means to be home.

– As told by Ruth Bowden
in conversation with Pat Ranzoni

Ruth Irene McAllian Bowden was born in 1920 to Elsie and William McAllian. She grew up and attended schools in Brewer and Kent's Hill before returning to Bucksport in 1938.

Charlotte M. White
Bucksport

FROM THE TOWN FARM ROAD: A DAUGHTER LOOKS BACK & FORWARD

I have glimpses of how my dad, Howard Bridges, might tell his story of working the Bucksport paper mill. He said things like: "It allows me to do the other things I like to do...." "I work with a great bunch of guys...." "It ain't all bad." After he'd been retired about twenty years, he'd grin and say, "I guess I beat those bastards!" But did he realize that it cost to work there year-after-year? I think so. He never got enough sleep and it eventually affected his health. Not being able to have a natural rhythm of family and social life also bothered him.

Part of his exhaustion was his choice as he hung tight to his homesteading way of life: cutting wood, growing our food, carpentry, and raising animals, particularly his beloved herd of purebred Herefords. He was always busy, tired, and mostly unavailable. I was very proud of him, and he was still nice to me; but with his rare free time he went fishing, hunting, and camping with his buddies or hung around in his workshop, often with the guys, where they would share a sip from time to time and it wasn't tea. Girls were not part of that life back then, although I thought being a tomboy might change that. I missed him!

It was not always so. I was born during World War II, and after Dad's service ended, he tried to farm and eke-out a living cutting wood and Christmas trees and hiring-out for carpentry and odd jobs. But he also took time for fun – swimming, horseback riding, playing ball, ice-fishing and skating, visiting friends and family, etc. He loved to tell stories, and we had a constant flow of visitors over for supper. Because he was not rushed and tired, I could tag along and help with tasks as he took time to teach me. Of course I did not realize how hard those years were financially. My sister Stevie, younger by four years, does not share the same early memories, as when Dad finally decided to go work at the mill, he was just too busy trying to get things done.

So, financially stable, our lives revolved around shift-work. The finishing department had an odd schedule of two shifts instead of three: 7 am to 3 pm and 7 pm to 3 am. We loved the day shift and hated the night shift. One shift changeover was brutal. Dad got home around 3:20 am, tried to sleep a couple of hours, fed the animals, grabbed a hasty breakfast and his lunch basket, and left at 6:40 am. He would be dead-tired for several days, then things would settle for a few days until shift change. The evenings seemed long and lonely on the night shift and the next morning we'd tiptoe and try to remember to be quiet so he could sleep.

The men who worked the same shift a long time really bonded, like extended family, and they helped each other outside of work when needed. Occasionally the families came for supper, and Dad would relax and tell stories. Mostly the women weren't included. Dad treasured those friendships, some of which continued for his 23 years of retirement.

We had a likable neighbor, Ralph Libby, who worked in management, only days, and got off at 5 pm. I was able to catch rides home with him by walking from the schools to the mill gate. I remember wishing Dad had his schedule until he was transferred to New York, I thought without a choice. We missed that family a lot. But at least our family wasn't uprooted. We could still live across the road from our homesteading grandparents.

I was proud to have the job of making Dad's lunches but hated having to iron his work clothes which seemed to wrinkle badly no matter how they were laundered. I tried putting his pants on stretchers to dry, but that was a worse job. When Dad worked days, I would make his lunch the night before, putting left-overs in jars and a thermos and adding fruit and dessert. When possible I put in more than he could eat. Mom was a great cook and he enjoyed sharing his lunch with others. They were "in it together." On rare occasions I would find a treat in his lunch basket as he'd bring home a little drawing on construction paper. I assume it was okay as he said sometimes the guard checked their lunch baskets as they left.

As Dad got older he developed diabetes and other health problems. There was a system changeover that involved computerizing that he found stressful. His hair started falling-out, but the gray remained and it appeared like he turned white overnight. He never seemed to want to go to work after that, but he plodded along. Finally, our family urged him to take an early retirement at 62, arguing that he could supplement the reduced pension from the farm. It was hard to convince him, but the decision probably saved his life. And he truly enjoyed his retirement, while we got back our Dad. Some of the other men were not so lucky, having heart attacks – etc. before they retired, or soon after.

I am thankful for one direct benefit from the mill. We married young, and my husband Brent Keene got a construction job there. He worked with a jack-hammer and the excellent money helped us both attend the University of Maine. Brent continued to work summers at the paper mill enabling us both to graduate. Some of the young men intended to go for higher education, but stayed at the mill because of the money. A paycheck was sometimes a trap but more often it was a way young people could remain in their hometown.

Although grateful, I also have mixed feelings, especially about the mill's environmental impact. But that's a whole other story. When Dad died at 85, we found an 8x10" glossy aerial view of the St. Regis paper mill in his desk drawer. In his workshop, his well-worn lunch basket hung from a spike. He hadn't burnt it so he must have worked through any conflicted feelings, and mulling this over and writing it down, has done so for me.

Thank you for collecting some of the history of the mill, for it is important to remember what it was like, so we can now go forward with Bucksport's future. Dad took a job he didn't really want and made the best life he could around it. The details vary, but it is the story of many!

Charlotte Bridges White grew up on Town Farm Road and attended Bucksport Schools for K-12, Class of 1961. She attended the University of Maine at Orono to obtain undergraduate and graduate degrees in teaching and counseling. She worked in those fields for forty years: 3 in New Hampshire, 3 in Alaska, 16 in various Maine settings, and retired from the Bucksport School System after 18 years at the elementary school level. Charlotte and her husband Donald White built a post-and-beam house in her Dad's low pasture, planted an orchard and several large gardens, and later built a greenhouse. She has a daughter (Denise Keene) a step-son (Joshua White), four grandchildren, and one great-grand-child, and says "I am very devoted to my black lab, Ollie. My special interests include cooking and preserving, sewing, drawing and painting, reading hiking and camping." Charlotte is a devoted envi-ronmentalist and "spends much time in nature." She especially enjoys Great Cranberry Island, Schoodic, Mount Desert Island, and Baxter State Park, "but would not choose to live anywhere but Bucksport." Recently, she has focused on Bucksport's economic recovery, joining the Orson Family Foundation's 'Heart-and-Soul' program "as one way to find creative solutions for moving ahead."

Photograph by Benjamin Magro, date unclear (1967 or '87?), from the desk drawer of Howard Bridges, courtesy of his daughter, Charlotte M. White.

George Skala
Bucksport

THIS OLD PLACE

a Maine folk song

This old place, calls me back again
Even though the walls are caving in
This old place, is where it all began
I'll have that memory with me until the end
Life in a mill town, getting sold out, and run down
Because they're sending jobs away
Closing lines, cutting time, to save a dime
Despite them folks who gave their days
I belong to this old place
It's hard to make, a living on the land
That their father's father passed down hand in hand
And the kids these days – they don't understand
There'll be nothing left, if they turn their backs
Life in a farm town, getting sold out, and run down
Can't live on what they used to raise
Hard working people, staring down a repo, praying in the steeple
That their life ain't going to change
 I belong to this old place
Another day, another miracle - What can I say? I guess I'm getting old - Just like this old place
Life in a farm town, or a mill town, or any small town - I feel it slipping away
Red, white, and blue pride standing on a hillside underneath them lights of a 4th of July
At a hometown baseball game
You know it all ain't quite the same, But I belong to this old place, And I'll be strong for this old place
This old place calls me back again even though the walls are caving in

George E. Skala:
"I have done a lot in my lifetime and I have a beautiful life, for which I am grateful. I am the first in my family to get a college education. I am most proud of that. I earned a bachelor of arts in English from the University of Maine in Machias. There I met my wife, Jennifer, while an undergrad and she encouraged me to pursue a doctorate in Chiropractic. Both of our professions have led us to the town of Bucksport; she is a teacher at RSU 25 and have my little practice, Maine Coast Chiropractic, here

317

on Main Street. We have a son, George Clifford, who we love with all our heart. Music has always been a calling of my soul. I am a self-taught guitarist and songwriter writing hundreds of songs, many of which have been recorded. I have enjoyed many great musical experiences that include: singing our nation's National Anthem at Shea Stadium, performing summer weekends on the four-masted schooner, Margaret Todd, in Bar Harbor, and working with many, many talented people through the years. 'This Old Place' is a song about the decline of American industry, inspired by the events that occurred here in Bucksport.

George Skala and his band, THE GREAT AMERICANS, *produced a fund-raising CD of "This Old Place" for the Bucksport Mill Crisis Fund. Participating sponsors were* BookStacks *(Bucksport),* Community Pharmacy *(Bucksport),* MacLeod's Restaurant *(Bucksport),* Maine Coast Chiropractic *(Bucksport),* Tozier's Market *(Bucksport and Searsport),* Dino's Pizza *(Searsport),* Red's Automotive *(Stockton Springs),* The First Bank *(Bangor, Blue Hill and Ellsworth), and* Eastern Area Agency on Aging *(Bangor), with interviews by* WABI TV 5. *Through the* Washington Hancock Community Agency, *they raised over $3,000. for the Mill Crisis Fund. The music was performed by George Skala (lead vocals, A. guitar, and banjo) with guest musicians: Louis Dugal (drums); John Kumnick (bass); Jake Sturtevant (keys); Dave Stone (keyboards); Jeff Haskell (bass); Dave Ames (B. vocals, E. guitar); Bill Thibedeau (mandolin); Mike Martell (drums); Willy Kelley (guitar, harmonica); Kevin Carver (pedal steel); Joe Allard (B. vocals); and Jonathan Wyman (melatron). Produced by George Skala and Jonathan Wyman, the C.D. was recorded by Jonathan Wyman at* Halo Studios *in Windham, Maine; mastered by Adam Ayan at* Gateway Studios *in Portland, Maine; and produced by Crooked Cove in Eliot, Maine.*

HE WOULD HAVE BEEN VERY SAD TO HAVE KNOWN

Charles K. Wight grew up in Bucksport at Wight's Dairy and graduated from Bucksport High School in 1957. Shortly after that he began to work for St. Regis Paper Co. in the wood room. Then "Uncle Sam" called him into the service – Army. After his duty was over he went back to the mill and worked in the Power Plant and stayed there until he had to retire at age 41 due to disability. He liked his coworkers and had a good time with them throughout his 20 ½ years of employment. Anyone working in the Power Plant had to aware that they didn't turn a wrong knob, or whatever, because it could have shut the mill down. Charlie was very talented in whatever he did. He also had his own welding/automotive shop on Route 46 where he repaired automobiles and trucks, and made steel stoves for people to burn wood in in their basements. He could fix about everything that any one brought to him. He built our home on Route 46 which he enjoyed with his wife Elizabeth and three sons (Chuck, Mike and David). Charlie was an avid welder and was always ready to help anyone who needed something done. He was a quiet man who worked hard and kept himself busy most of the time. He hated to leave the mill, but had to because of his disability. He had a lot of stories to tell about his buddies "raising Cain" and laughing during shift work but said they always had their eyes on their jobs. Charlie always respected the mill and the Town of Bucksport. He knew that the employees could make a decent living by working there. Of course, he passed away in April off 2012 and would have been very sad to have known that "The Mill" would close.

Elizabeth Wardwell Wight, the daughter of H. Robert and Una Hutchins Wardwell, was born in the Castine Hospital on May 21, 1926, "taking turns with the Soper twins, Dianne and Joanne, for time in the incubator." She grew up and attended school in Orland and graduated from Bucksport High School in the Class of 1964 and Beal College in 1993. She and Charlie raised their three sons on the edge of Wight's Dairy Farm over-looking Hancock Pond in Bucksport in the home he built for them. She has been a devoted organist and pianist for area churches, Off-Broadway Chorus at the Senior Citizen Center here in Bucksport, and at Order of Eastern Star Chapters (OES) in Maine, "working my way up" to Worthy Matron of the OES in Orland, Riverside Chapter #123. She was Grand Organist in 2009-2010 for the Grand Chapter of Maine OES. I survived a life-changing automobile accident in 1977, cancer in 1998, and a stroke in 1999, bringing a wheelchair into our family," but she carried on as Charlie's mainstay, supporting him with his disability. She has been known for her crafting and gifts made for family, friends and causes to which she has been devoted, and taken great pleasure in travel-ing as able, especially a trip to England, and maintaining friendships from those journeys. "I also have enjoyed collecting dolls and building a miniature Christmas village, arranging and adding to it each year." She is famous for her sense of humor and old-fashioned biscuits, "having made thousands through the years. I make them for church suppers in Orland." "I love time with my family as they don't live close by. My sons help when they come up, especially mowing the lawns and doing odd jobs for me. Family means everything!"

LIZ WIGHT'S BISCUITS

4 C flour	1 tsp. salt
4 tsp. Bakewell Cream	½ C shortening
2 tsp. baking soda	1 ½ to 2 C cold milk

Mix and sift dry ingredients, add shortening and mix with a pastry blender. Add milk all at once stirring quickly with fork or big spoon. Turn on a floured board, knead several times, roll out ½ to ¾" thick, cut out and bake at 480 degrees for 8 minutes. Just be careful as ovens do vary and may take a shorter or longer time. I also rub a tiny bit of Crisco oil on top of the biscuits after they come out of the oven to bring out the brown and brush off excess flour if any.

Editor's note: *Bakewell Cream* is a baking powder developed by Bangor chemist, Byron H. Smith in response to a shortage of cream of tartar during WWII. Sold throughout the U.S., it is most popular in Maine. Still containing his unique ingredient, *sodium pyrophosphate*, Smith's company was succeeded by its current manufacturer, New England Cupboard. (*Wikipedia*)

Richard (Dick) Findlay
Bucksport

WHAT WAS UNDER THE KILT!

I and many family members worked at the paper mill under its various names. I retired from International Paper after 43 years.

The mill was our livelihood and gave us a good life. Benefits from the mill gave families the opportunity to experience a comfortable and happy life. Always proud of our "Mill Town." Everyone knew their friends and neighbors and would lend a hand.

Once retired the men missed their comradeship and would meet at local town locations to reminisce about the good old days in the mill.

I played the Bagpipes in the ANAH TEMPLE pipe band. Endless comments as to what was under the kilt! Pictures posted online!

The closing of the Mill changed our town. We look forward to a new and positive future.

Life goes on.

Richard Findlay *was a member of the Bucksport High School Class of 1956. Says wife Dianne: "As a member of the* Anah Temple Highlander Band, *he played all over Maine and Canada and New England for charitable and celebratory events. He will tell you he wasn`t the greatest bagpipe player but was very dedicated. He couldn`t read a note of music when he started but never gave up. He played his pipes for twenty-five years. He proudly wore his kilt with the Highlanders and played his bagpipes."*

321

Dick Gaudet
Douglas, Alabama

TO GROW THEIR LIVES

My first job at St Regis was cleaning boilers. Not a good job if you are afraid of small, dirty hot places! Eddie Rankin and l worked together, scraping and grinding several big tubes that had to have air pumped in so we could work. This took several weeks to complete. After that, work was scarce and l was laid off.

I came back to work around 1964 as a spare and started in, I guess, the debarking room picking logs off the belt that were not fully debarked for the magazine room. I worked the magazine room a few times feeding 4ft. Logs into 4 ft. Magazines, dangerous work. I also worked unloading train cars of frozen pulp wood, with wood hooks. It was cold work, and occasionally, would get stuck in the leg from the hook slopping off the frozen wood. It was ruff times trying to support a wife and 3 kids on 1 or 2 days a week work.

Then l finally got on full time as a Swiper. The job consisted of cleaning the paper machines of greasy paper scraps around the driers, motors and all under the paper machines (2), not a bad job, hot and messy. Then l got blessed with a job making paper! Money was good and l was able to build my first home!

As far as the work was concerned, it was a dangerous place to work, Hot, Noisy and your stomach didn't know if it was night or day. It was, for me, a boring, slow paced job at most times, but when things were not running right, chaos! Constantly cleaning up paper, tearing up paper to feed the paper machines. From there the paper went on to the re-winder, to be cut from one huge roll into 4 smaller rolls. When this was being done we had to check the paper for defects. When we found them they were cut out and sent on to the re-winders for another process.

I was very pleased to have had the work for helping my family to have the things they needed to grow their lives.

Richard Philip Gaudet *was born in 1939 in Brewer, Maine, "and raised on a vegetable farm in Bangor. I attended all of my school years in Bangor and in the summer of my junior year I went to Lackland Air Force Base in San Antonio, Texas for basic training. When I returned home thirteen weeks later, my family had moved to Bucksport, so in 1958 I graduated from Bucksport High School. Needless to* *say, it was hard for me as I didn't know any of the kids in the school. But many of my classmates tried to make me feel at home and for that I was thankful. The year after I graduated, I married Anita Varnum, my first and only love of my life. We celebrated our 50th anniversary in 2008. We have four children (two boys and two girls), 10 grandchildren and 6 great grandchildren. Boy, where have all those years gone. In addition to the work I did at the Bucksport paper mill, I was employed by R.J. Reynolds Tobacco Company for 26 years as an area sales representative and retired at the age of 55. I had met many personalities in my travels as I covered as much as two thirds of the State of Maine. I really enjoyed the art of selling and, I may say, I was pretty good at it. In 1997 my wife and I bought a new fifth wheel R.V. and diesel truck. We set out to see this beautiful country. We did finally make one complete trip around the United States covering all but five states. One winter was spent in Florida and four winters in South Texas. We regret not seeing the Grand Canyon, but found Utah, Western Montana, Wyoming, New Mexico and Maine to be the most beautiful of all the states. We really never met any unfriendly people but the people in Texas were the friendliest. Anita's health began to fail so we needed to settle down somewhere as she needed a lot of medical care. We chose the Gulf Shores area of Alabama and later on we sold the R.V. and truck and bought a place in Summerdale. Then Ivan and Katrina blew in. Those two years were spent running up north in order to avoid them. When we returned, we had repairs to make on the house, etc. We got tired of battling the hurricanes so we sold that place and moved north east to Douglas, Alabama. By that time, Anita needed specialized doctors and hospitals because she was diagnosed with A.L.S. (Lou Gehrig's disease) along with many other problems. Time became more precious than ever. We had a nice new home in the country where we stayed for the rest of our lives together until she finally passed away at home March 18, 2010 with my two daughters and I, from ALS. Life in Alabama is not for me, too hot and humid. Nothing like good ole Maine. Wish I had made better decisions years ago! I'm still here in Alabama until my home sells, then back home."*

Carol and Dick Lally
Bucksport

LIFE & TIMES OF PAPERMAKING, FOR THE MACDONALD/LALLY FAMILY

Joseph MacDonald – Father of Colon; Grandfather to Carol; Great Grandfather to Scott, Dennis, Jana
Colon MacDonald – Father of Carol; Grandfather to Scott, Dennis, Jana
Carol (MacDonald) Lally – Mother of Scott, Dennis, Jana
Richard Lally – Husband of Carol; Father of Scott, Dennis, Jana
Scott Lally – Son of Carol and Richard
Dennis Lally – Son of Carol and Richard
Jana (Lally) Hanscom – Daughter of Carol and Richard

Joseph MacDonald, my Grandfather, was very proud of his position as security guard, hired by the mill personnel department. He retired with a pension from St. Regis.

Colon MacDonald, my father, worked at the mill as a welder. He took early retirement from St. Regis after 25 years to start a new career, as a Square Dancer Caller. You see, after an 8-hour day job at the mill he, with the help of my mother, Hazel Rich MacDonald, were teaching Square Dancing every evening to young and old in Bucksport and the surrounding communities. Square Dancing became "all the rage." Eventually, they moved to St. Petersburg, Florida where he become a full time Square Dance Caller and was very successful!

Carol (MacDonald) Lally was hired at the St. Regis paper mill in 1979. I worked in many departments through advancements: Human Resources, Payroll, Accounting, IBM, Engineering, and Maintenance. I fully enjoyed every job, some more challenging than others, but I loved going to work each day knowing my job was part of making paper and retired after 24 years.

Richard Lally, Carol's husband, was hired by St. Regis in 1961 as a laborer in the wood yard. He advanced to the Labor Department as a "paper tester," then to the Super Calendar Department. All these jobs were night shifts. The next job was a day position as a Painter in the Maintenance Department, then a few years before retiring, he worked in the Stores/Receiving Department. He retired with 39 ½ years of service.

Dick and Carol's three children each were chosen to work summers after graduation. *WOW!* This really helped with college costs.

Son – Scott Lally worked one summer, went to college for three years, received a degree, then was hired at Champion in a permanent position in 1986. He lost his job when Verso sold the mill and is now employed at Acadia National Park.

Son – Dennis Lally also worked summers there while going to college. He decided he did not like shift work (mostly nights 11 pm to 7 am). Today he's very happy with an early retirement from Bangor Police Department after 24 years of service and now is employed in the Federal Court system.

Daughter – Jana (Lally) Hanscom – was employed, too, at the mill summers while attending college. Her first day at the mill she was given a ***Heavy Weed Wacker*** that she carried around all day. Boy was she hurting, arms, legs, back, and all over! She did weed wacking most of the summer. Sometimes she drove a truck while working in the Riggers Department. Jana also received a $1,000. Champion Int'l Corp. Scholarship.

Remembering Back:

The "Swedish Wool" we used for ear protection – did not work! Most people who worked in noisy areas are "paying the price" of hearing loss!

We made a good living and had fun every day.

We had good bosses that didn't bother us as long as we did our job. We even could share a short story or joke now and then triggering smiles and laughter.

I'm sure most retirees will agree that we had "the best of the best" – but most of us didn't realize it at the time.

Our whole family has been so blessed and privileged to have so many memories of the Bucksport Mill.

Proud to have been employees,

Richard and Carol MacDonald Lally *were both members of the Bucksport High School Class of 1960. Their son, Scott, was a member of the Class of 1982; Dennis, 1984; and Jana, 1988. They were all outstanding athletes and athletics boosters, among other community contributions.*

As told by Beulah Richards
Ft. Meade, Florida

L. RICHARDS & SON

"He loved being a papermaker."

"38 years, starting out with St. Regis, through all the changes in mill ownership through the years, Laurel went from 4th hand on the paper machines working himself up to foreman and day superintendent on #1 and 2 until retirement in 2001 when we moved to Florida. He was a hard, hard worker. And he loved being a papermaker. He got hurt a lot in the mill as many did but it provided us with a good living. Laurel loved flying, for example. He had two planes, one he kept at Swett's Pond in Orrington and one at Doug Smith's small airstrip in Millvale. When St. Regis left, things changed drastically. Let's face it, St. Regis was top notch. We don't like to drag up the hardest parts. Some things you love remembering. Others you wish you could forget. We are very happy with our friends and life down here. Laurel has loved the golfing, especially, and we enjoy the sunshine and warmer weather. We come home to visit when we can but are feeling too old to do as much traveling as we used to."

"Our son Wayne –and wife Michelle (Flannery), both Bucksport High School alumni, as were their daughters, went on to graduate from Washington Academy and went into the mill at 21, working his way from foreman to superintendent over 35 years. He left Verso shortly before it closed. Now he works at Bath Iron Works where he is Government Property Administration Manager. He was defensive coach for Bucksport High School Football for about 15 years and is now coaching in the same position at Bath-Morse High. They hired him on the spot. Though he and Michelle, who found work down there as a medical secretary, and we, have had a lot of sorrow and missing from the loss of their daughter Jill Landers, Mrs. Scott T., at 29, they are very happy where they've moved. Wayne built themselves a new house and they now live close to their family so can watch the little ones grow up. Their daughter Jana's and husband Jason Grant's children are Eli and Finn. I think it was one of the best things Wayne ever did, moving down there. He was so dedicated, I worried he was overworked in Bucksport and he loves it where he is now."

"Including our daughter Zina, who is still in nursing, her husband Kevin Black, who works for Bangor Hydro –also Bucksport High School grads – and their family, Casey and Jake, of course we feel blessed. And we love to laugh!"

"Well, there..." we say to each other in the old Maine way.

— With Pat Ranzoni

Beulah Smith Richards *was born in Enfield, Maine in 1941. She grew up in Lincoln and Bucksport, graduating with the Class of 1960. After attending D Lors Beauty School in Brewer, she dressed hair for five years. "Then I went to Bucksport High School as a 'gofer' – office worker, substitute, and cheering coach for nine years. We won five years of State Championships." Beulah was awarded "Coach of the Year" by the Maine Principals Association and in 2011 she was inducted into the Bucksport Hall of Fame. "After retiring from coaching in 1997 I went back to hair dressing and ran my own business for close to ten years until Laurel retired from the mill and we moved to Ft. Meade, Florida where we still live."*

Jane Berry Donnell
Bucksport

TOO PAINFUL AND NOT SCABBED ENOUGH

I just wanted you to know. I wanted it to be organized and pretty. The way life isn't after the Mill. But I blew it. I wasn't ready. It is too painful and not scabbed enough.

This new life for my family is so different. So much harder. I wanted to contribute to this beautiful project. I wanted to help the collective memory. I have stewed endlessly over my feelings and memories of the Mill. I have scraps of paper in my purse with scribbles. The language in there (the Mill), was so specialized or was it the same in all of the mills? The hand gestures that symbolized nearing the end of a long shift, the clever quips at the college spares, "Summer help, some are not." I Need to remember all of these things. The things my brothers and I share when we walk the Townsite and reminisce about our summers in there. In that insulated world where you could stay for 24 hours and never see the light of day.

I'm sorry that I couldn't get it out as anything beautiful and concrete. Stephan says that the most profound thing he heard after the Mill closed was from me. When I said with tears in a quiet heart baring whisper, "Everything I have I owe to that mill."

Jane Berry Donnell: *"This is such an important thing. I go and check the progress on the dismembering and dismantling of the Mill almost every day. It was easier once Dad's office went down. I cried right there on the waterfront for the little girl whose very first phone call was to that office. 'Extension 290 please.' I have thought about so many things that I hope found its/their way to you. Just the language, spoken and signed, that happened in there. My mother watching us build horse shelter after horse shelter out of mill felt and asking, 'What do people without mills do?' I was born in 1970. My dad immediately applied for a job in the Mill, expecting me to be expensive! Plus he returned from Vietnam after missing the birth of Frank, bound and determined to have a baby girl named 'Jane.' I grew up in the Horace Buck House on Hinks Street. Technically I only lived there until I was 9 but I consider it my childhood home. I still dream about it. I still have a terrible longing to tour it. We*

328

moved to what started as Mast Hill Road but is now Duck Cove Road. After a brief exile in Orono and Orland and a seven -year horse farming stint on the River Road, we built a house back at the Berry Compound behind my parents, and between my brothers that is now Pasture Pine Road and the only home my sons remember. Luman Warren, G. Herbert Jewett, Bucksport Jr. High, Bucksport High School (Class of 1988) and the University of Maine. Out of college I was a retail data collector, a Vermont Coffee Roasters merchandiser, a horse farmer, a mill worker in the summers during college and then on a special assignment after gaduation. When the mills up river got shaky, it was too dangerous to have both mine and Stephan's income from the same place so when the greatest, out-of-the-blue job offer came from Northeast Historic Film, I took it. In my 21st year now. I spoke at BHS graduation June 11, 2010 https://www.youtube.com/watch *I love to walk and hike and swim. I love every minute of the rat race that is my life with two brilliant and talented sons. My husband created and has administrated Bucksport Area Youth Basketball for the past eight years. We have scholar-shipped and driven and housed and fed and loved countless children in the program. Stephan and I met in the Mill my first year as a summer spare. He was on the Roll Wrapper and I was on Number 4 Winder... He started working in the Mill when I was 11 years old! He had a huge role in keeping the Bucksport Mill running for as long as it did. I am very proud of that. Now he commutes back and forth to Baileyville every day and has hired dozens of mill workers who lost their mills. Very rewarding."*

Kimberly Goon
Baltimore, MD

ELEGY TO BUCKSPORT'S MILL

Silently, we stand at your perimeter
The overcast sky soon to swallow you into memory

Your might, once reflected in the Penobscot
Washed away with the tide

Smoke stacks alive with breath
Will not exhale again

Once vibrant, you fed, clothed, sustained
All who called you The Giver

Our hopes placed upon your shoulders
Blown on a gust of Bay wind

What will become of your people
Who coursed like blood through your veins

You, now old and worn, will be cast aside
Metal scraps traded for paper currency

Silently, we stand at your perimeter
The only sound, your flesh ripped from your bone

Kimberly Goon *has visited and vacationed in the town of Bucksport "several times over the last twenty-seven years. The small town friendliness and slow pace allowed me to leave the bustle of Baltimore behind. Close friends, long time Bucksport residents, kept me up-to-date on the town's news and the fate of the Mill. On a recent visit to the waterfront, I stood beneath a thick, overcast sky. In the eerie quietness, I heard only the sounds of the metal façade being stripped from the structures—a reminder of all that was stripped from the town and its people."*

Johanna Dorr
Orland

THE SOUND OF ORCAS CRYING

Those of us who grew up here know how it has always been true that our town has had a sound as well as shape, like the living presence it remains. And how this sound has varied according to how near or far we've lived from the mill once it got blasted into and built on Indian Point. Those at certain distances could identify the sounds of pulp being dumped from the trucks arriving daily and nightly and knocking along a conveyor from the woodyard to its drop inside, for example. The whistle heralding shift changes and other community signals those years always come to mind. And there would be sudden crashes and bangs from time to time which we simply attributed to the business of the mill.

Those who've lived adjacent to the mill up and down the River Road, the Town Site, and streets connecting to Main, and areas across the river in Prospect and Winterport, heard the clearest sounds and we in the outback distances, variations of that industrial noise (or music, depending on one's opinion). So it has been, that those living next door to the mill have been witnesses to the sound as well as the shape of making as well as ceasing to make paper in Bucksport.

One of the closest groups of neighbors, both in proximity and relationships, has been the Seaboard Federal Credit Union (SFCU), born, nurtured and sheltered by the mill, itself, for 77 years. To hear first hand how it was for these folks in the dying days of Bucksport's paper mill, I visited Johanna Dorr, Loan Officer and Marketing Coordinator, in her office directly overlooking the deconstruction of the mill. Having worked at the Credit Union for 25 years, she is a source of both knowledge and feelings about what has happened there.

Thanks to Joanna, who provided a copy of a March 29, 1990 *Ellsworth American* feature, "After a Half Century, It's Still Growing," celebrating the grand opening of their new building, my vague awareness of the mill-credit union connection was clarified for history's sake. Close connection, all right!

The story goes that the idea for a credit union was first suggested at a union meeting in the fall of 1940. (Being the year of my birth, I can relate to the times.) According to the article, mill workers at this meeting told how difficult, if not impossible, it was for employees of the then Seaboard Paper Co. to get bank loans in those days. An October 1940 meeting provided a sounding board for the "nightmare" they had experienced "trying to get credit in the Town of Bucksport" and how they were treated by bankers. A representative of the Maine Credit Union League was invited to speak at the next meeting and an organizing meeting was held on October 31. Twenty-one mill employees were present. According to the record, a "Mr. H.E. Ingells of the Credit Union section in Washington was present to explain a few details and the following directors were elected: Leo Ashey, president; Arthur Kimball, treasurer; Charles Stewart, vice president; John Harvey, clerk; and Harold Sullivan as chairman of the Educational Committee." Minutes show that the first meeting of the board was held immediately following the organization meeting with the following actions recorded: The Credit Committee: Edward Harpe, Charles Tyler, and John England. Supervisory Committee: James Bedell, Matthew Rosebush, and Edward Nickless. "VOTED: Treasurer's bond to be placed at $1,000. Bucksport branch of the Merrill

Trust Co. to serve as depository. Maximum shares in any one account not to exceed $250. Maximum secured loan not to exceed $100. Interest rate on loans one percent per month on unpaid balance. Maximum repayment period on all loans not to exceed one year. To pay an outstanding bill for supplies in the amount of $15.10 as soon as funds are available. That the SFCU be affiliated with the Maine Credit Union League. All borrowers will be required to pay at least 25 cents towards a share with every loan payment."

The article goes on to say that "the credit union has come a long way since then," quoting Sally Drake, manager from 1977 to 1987. "Our sponsors, Maine Seaboard Paper Co., St. Regis Paper Co., and presently Champion International have always given our credit union a great deal of assistance. In the early years of our existence, they provided our office space, supplies, equipment, and 'help' to operate our business. As our enterprise grew, it became apparent that separate quarters would have to be found, and once again, the mill came to our aid by providing the lot where our former credit union was located." The credit union moved into its first new building early in 1964 and Philip Luce became its first full-time manager. Continuing to grow through the availability of payroll deduction and other "modern services" as a result of affiliation with the Maine Credit Union League. Under the management of Drake after his death, "assets were increasing by more than a million dollars each year" reaching more than $32 million. Marilyn Pierce took over following Drake's retirement until the "staggering blow" of her death.

In her write-up, "Steeped in History, Poised for the Future" (*2015 Business Resource Guide of Bucksport Maine*), Melanie Brooks quotes Joanna Dorr, "We are about family, friends, and people helping people. We are one big family." And so it has been that the 77-year-old credit union family has grieved the death of the mill as deeply and honestly as any profound loss. During the 25 years that Joanna has worked there, she became well aware of the generations–birth to death–of "her family, the mill family" suffering with them as they began to move away. "When we meet in the store we embrace. Cashing their checks every week, we knew them and their wives and kids. It was like seeing relatives. Can you imagine how heartbreaking that last day was? I just couldn't go out but stood by the window crying, seeing the men and women leave for the last time."

"Not all loans are happy," confides Johanna. "I've had to keep my tissue box handy." "What am I going to do?" they would ask. All I could say was, "We're here for you."

"The worst days were the sounds of the mill being torn down. Being right next to it we could hear the buildings' distress like the sound of orcas crying."

"I get passionate."

–With Pat Ranzoni

__Johanna Dorr__ grew up in Matawan, New Jersey, moving to Orland, her husband's ancestral ground, in 1988. She started working at the Credit Union on December 27, 1989. "I feel drawn here as much as I feel drawn to Ireland, who knows why." She is accomplished in horsemanship, is "an avid gardener," and is known for her cooking. "Italian, but any kind of dish you can throw at me. I've been cooking since the age of nine, my first accomplishment being a leg of lamb!" Neopolitans are one of her specialties and she is "a self-taught cake decorator."

Don Houghton
Bucksport

OFTEN IN PICK-UPS

ENTERPRISE PHOTOS BY DON HOUGHTON

ON TUESDAY, the entire Verso Paper Co. took the inevitable step, filing for federal bankruptcy protection as it attempts to eliminate $2.4 billion in debts - and still stay in business. The Tennessee-based firm's stock had been listed at a penny-a-share, assuming someone could be found to buy it.

Up close & personal

They arrive in ones and twos, usually sitting there for just a few minutes, often in pick-up trucks. Some bring cameras; one even had a small pair of binoculars, the better to see the details of what the salvagers call "deconstruction." It does not matter that the weary paper makers tend to view the process as one of destruction, not just removing steel and corrugated metal but lives and careers that most accept never will be the same again. Over the next year-and-a-half, the remains of a workplace hundreds came to call home will be done. There;ll be a new opportunity, the first in over eight decades to do something new with prime Penobscot River frontage. Like the tannery that preceded it, the paper mill now is but part of Bucksport's long history. Still, sitting in those pick-up trucks, those who watch the process of change, a process they may not be a part of, can be afforded a few more quiet moments in which to sit silently and reflect.

Sharon Bray
Orland

LETTER TO OUR NEWEST NEIGHBORHOOD

You live in the house of our childhood
working to make your own home
and restore the farmland.
Your new house is full of ghosts only we can see,
five noisy, strong-willed children teasing,
laughing, crying, driving our mother
to raise her voice and small, strong hand
among us; sometimes landing one swift blow,
sometimes not.
A teenager, a baby, three more between,
share secrets, learn to roller skate around the cellar floor,
feed chickens, crawl through their little door;
coax BaaBaa the goat to roll her oil barrel house
around the muddy dooryard;
build snow forts, yes, even into March,
while our Dad works at the mill
and Mom bakes in the clean, warm kitchen.

We have a few ghosts newer –
our grown-up selves in grief and celebration
at family turning points.
We see our ghosts at the maple table
talking over and eating together,
singing and listening to Dad's violin.

From the "Selling the Homeplace" section of Putting Poems By
by Sharon Bray, a Narramissic Notebook Project, 2014.

334

Sara Berkeley Tolchin
Ireland and California

WHAT JUST HAPPENED?

'What just happened,
and where does it leave us?'
'Same place,' he said, but that's not true.
We are in a different place now,
this place is new, we've never been here
before, the air's a different shape,
no colours I've ever seen, the view
has shifted, and the ground
is shifting, too, not so easy
to walk around without a fall.
Still, what is there to risk
in this endeavour if not all?

Miners are trained when things go wrong
to lie on the ground, breathe slow
and shallow, wait until the light breaks at last
through a chink and they are found.
Sometimes behind their self–made barricades
they lie there breathing low
until their lives rise up and float around
above them, no colours they've ever seen,
memories shedding light in the coal–dust gloom,
making room for what's to come.

We've been lying here for quite some time.
I'm wondering when we'll be done
with all the shallow breathing
and the oxygen conservation.

From What Just Happened (The Gallery Press, 2015), *used with permission of the author.*

Sara Berkeley Tolchin *was born in Dublin, Ireland in 1967 and educated at Trinity College, Dublin, and the University of California, Berkeley. Her first collection of poems,* Penn, *was published to unprecedented critical acclaim when she was just 19, and was shortlisted for the* Irish Book Awards *and the* Sunday Tribune Arts Awards. *Since then she has published* Home Movie Nights (*poems, 1989*), The Swimmer in the Deep Blue Dream (*stories, 1992*), Facts About Water (*poems, 1994*), Shadowing Hannah (*a novel, 1999*), Strawberry Thief (*poems, 2005*), The View from Here (*poems, 2011*), *and* What Just Happened (poems, 2015). *She was nominated for a Pushcart Prize and was among five finalists, along with Pulitzer Prize winner Paul Muldoon, for 2011's prestigious* Irish Times Poetry Now *award, won by Nobel Prize laureate Seamus Heaney. Her work has appeared in 25 anthologies, as well as numerous magazines, journals, and newspapers. Sara lives in a rural community just north of San Francisco with her husband and daughter. All her previous books were published using her maiden name, Sara Berkeley. "I was moved by* What Just Happened *by Sara Berkeley Tolchin. She works as a hospice nurse in America and the everyday realities of death pervade poems that reflect on nursing and explore the relationships between mothers and daughters, written in the shadow of her mother's final illness in Ireland. She refuses to seek comfort in platitudes so that while these poems are heart-breaking, they never lose their poise or sharply minted clarity." — Dermot Bolger*, Books of 2015, The Irish Independent. *"Sara Berkeley Tolchin's* What Just Happened *contains poems that explore 'The heart without compass/The journey without a map' in an Irish and Californian setting. These wise, sensory poems achieve 'a benediction of some sort'."* — Niall MacMonagle, Books of 2015, The Irish Independent

Leo Grunwald
Orland

GOOD MONEY, GOOD FRIENDS, GOOD LIFE
36 Years Without a Sick Day

A.R. Grunwald, Sr.

My grandfather was brought to Bucksport from Corner Brook, Newfoundland, in 1929. He was brought here to start the mill, Maine Seaboard Co. He was the superintendent of the Sulphate Dept. which took in the acid plant, lime rock and other chemicals to make paper. He was one of the first people to move into the Townsite which the mill built for the executives coming in.

A.R. Grunwald Jr.

My dad went to work in the mill around 1932 and worked for 44 years as a millwright. He left before he could retire as he had cancer and could no longer work. He moved into the Townsite in 1938, the first hourly person to have a Townsite home.

Ruth Grunwald Coombs

My Aunt Ruth worked as a secretary before she married. She and Lillian Rosen became very good friends as they worked together at secretarial jobs and stayed friends till death.

Wm. A. Grunwald

My older brother, Billy, came back from the Navy and went into the mill. Worked for 44 years. Also, as he worked after school, he got 4 years while he was in the Navy. Bill worked on # 1 and 2 paper machine.

Billy Grunwald, Jr. also worked in the mill, in the train shed.

Leo W. Grunwald

I went into the mill in June of 1961 also after returning from the Navy. I got 38 ½ years before retiring, working on #4 paper machine.

Leo W. Grunwald II

My son, Leo II, worked there for 30 years as a maintenance worker.

Many mornings we left work to go up north or down east to fish or hunt a day, then come home to get a couple hours' sleep before going back to work. There always was someone wanting to go.

After retirement we formed the Young Retiree Group to have coffee at the waterfront. We like to think we solved a lot of problems and good ideas for the town.

We had our good buddy Dick Stubbs, known as "Stubby," to pass on information in case you were late or sick.

We had people join us from all different walks of life, not only mill workers—from boats pulling in, buses and cars traveling to Bar Harbor or visiting our little town, having dinner at MacLeod's or getting a ice cream at Wahl's.

I always stop at McDonald's to get my coffee and talk or say hi to the "Senior" Seniors, as they like to stay warm (winter) or cool (summer). They miss the beauty of the waterfront and talking to the walkers. We also sadly watch them tearing down our beloved mill but hopefully something of beauty will replace it?

I've had a good job with the mill and can't complain but I feel sad to see it go.

My dad passed in 1974. His clock # was 3500. When Leo II went to work he was given Dad's clock # 3500 after all those years!

I had many friends I worked with and a lot have passed, but I see people I worked with in all different places – bank– shopping – Dr.'s office. The problem is I can't always remember their names so I go home and hours later I finally remember.

I made good money and we were able to go and do things with our family as we had a lot of time off with shift work. But we also missed a lot because of shift work. I went 36 years without taking time off for sickness!

I've lost several good buddies due to age, cancer, stroke, heart and other illnesses! One of my good friends just passed due to cancer, Cleve Kennedy. Right to the very last week we still talked about the good days hunting, fishing, drinking Boone Farm Wine because we couldn't afford anything else and what good times we all had, our children and wives getting together over cook-outs, cards, etc. When our shift was right we relaxed with other families that worked our shift. Our children talk about how much fun they had swimming, cook-outs, etc.

Most of the workers at that time seemed to be towns nearer so we all attended everyone's sports, music and plays in school. We tried to be there for support as a lot of times the Dads would be working so the Moms filled in.

We took pride in our jobs. I ended up on the #4 paper machine. I started in the wood room and worked in about every department, then Albert (Red) Ridell got me a job on #1 and 2 papermachine in 1966. I stayed there til I retired Dec. 31, 1999. (Machine Tender)

I remember being asked to show a young man what he was to do. So I showed him and then said if you have time sweep the broke (scraps) down into the beaters. He told me that "they don't pay me enough to sweep." (He was there a few weeks.) So I picked up the broom and did it (I was there probably 30 years). The boss (Larry Johnson) came and asked how we made out with him. I told him to put him in the wood yard. I never saw him again. They always rewarded good workers but always remember don't mess with hard workers.

Leo W. Grunwald *was born in 1938 in Belfast, Maine. He grew up and attended school in Bucksport where he played baseball and basketball, graduating in the Class of 1956. He has enjoyed fishing and hunting, 4-wheeling, boating, going to camp, and in addition to "renovating our house to our taste," is well-known for his creative woodworking projects which he generously gifts to family and friends. "Leo is always helping out people that need an extra hand," admires wife Joanne.*

Editor's note:
Lucky those invited through the years to play on his custom-made table-sized game board. We prize our LWG-crafted moose wall rack, a double-decker pie carrier, a folding wooden trivet set and, especially, a masterfully finished cane in the shape of a hand saw which I lean on for special, always bringing admiration.

ALL THE WAY BACK

Billy Stubbs is home. To visit his and Nancy's place in Bucksmills valley is to tread the ancestral grounds of his people on the banks of the brook – Stubbs Brook – bearing their name. Monuments to their love for this history abound. Rust-beautiful mowing machines and a plow once hauled by horses. A replica outhouse tribute to times past. And Nancy's high summer wildflower hedgerow up the knoll displaying the wild roses, buttercups and daisies of the season. Haying season. And there's neighbor Floyd Clement tedding their back field just beyond.

Billy's garage is the break place for the men of the neighborhood, equivalent to a coffee shop in town where the talk is as refreshing as the drink. With luck, you might be there with Dick Tennant Jr., greatest treasure of local history and folk knowledge in the area.

From the road going by we have admired the license plates and tin signs outlining the doorway and bay, knowing that they were entrances to a classic workshop variously called "man cave" or "sulk house" and such around here. And there they are – signs announcing "Warning! Yankees Fan Man Cave" and "Access by Permission Only" and today I have permission. I write fast: "Beauty is in the Eye of the Beerholder." "Historical Vehicle OLD FART." Clearly, he gets a chuckle from these. Signs and historical memorabilia outline the walls displaying his collections making it a museum. He points out one he is especially proud of from one of the papermachines– "SIDEWINDER by Appleton Machine Company."

For this meeting, Billy and Nancy have set up a table inside their open garage space inviting us to sit with them to talk (like notables in a military campaign I imagine) so that, this time, we are, no doubt, the envy of those driving by.

"I'm gonna go all the way back to my family's history with the mill the best I can," he begins. "My grandparents Harry and Sarah Mercer moved here. Their kids, George and Clara Stubbs. Grandfather's brother, Ed (not the Eddie Mercer's store Ed). Originally from Newfoundland. Wound up in Massachusetts, coming here for work helping to construct the mill in 1929, being carpenters by trade. Even the old pipeline bringing water in from the lakes, was made of wood. After the mill was built, they put in for jobs and were hired. Their roots are still here. Grandfather Stubbs hauled dairy and wood to town by horse and buggy."

"My mother graduated Eastern Maine Seminary for high school in 1933 or 4. My father was a native of Bucksport through the Gross family. He worked several jobs in town, ending up in the mill in several positions, finishing up in the carpenter shop. This would have been in the '40s. Dad took over as foreman after my grandfather died."

"There were seven of us. Marlene, Joanne, Richard, Tommy, Judy, myself and Bonnie. Richard, called Dickie, died not too long ago, retired from the mill after working as an oiler, on the paper machines and with the swipers. Oilers had to put gloves on, it was so hot working on some of the machines – up to 160 degrees. He was known for his red Chevy pick-up. Everybody knew him. He was one of the boys that met routinely on the dock mornings to 'chew the fat.' And he used to drive up to Millinocket or Cherryfield just for the ride and might come upon someone needing help. Tommy worked there til his death at 41. We always questioned whether the chemicals caused his leukemia."

"I started in 1964 and retired in 2002. At what jobs? Every one of them. One of my first was in the magazine room. When I heard that, I thought we were going to be making magazines! They handed me a pick pole and I had blisters everywhere." "Jobs? Every one of them. As a spare, pulp thrower, swiper, on the paper machines, unloading clay cars. Sometimes you needed to be ready to run if a whole load fell. It's a wonder somebody didn't get killed. Old wood room, new wood room, for carpenters and electricians as a gopher, mowed lawns, janitorial. You'd take what you could get when working off the spare list. I never refused. In the early days I sat by the guard gate hoping to be called. I worked on the off-machine coater, put up splicers on all roll wrappers, at first by hand, working with my uncle wrapping. Rigging. You name it. I've probably been involved in all of it. I retired from the stores department working with supplies."

"Way back, over the years, people got together to help each other build their houses, cellars, etc. They were always knitted together, got along. But each time managers changed or we (the mill) changed hands, we thought 'here we go.' Things really changed. The atmosphere. They didn't even want people to talk. Back along, most people never got fired, then more people got fired in one year than in olden days. A hundred went out on a buy out but the ones with a lot of knowledge they wanted out."

"Back to the paper machines – one of the first jobs I had was on #3, 'Little Oscar.' It made colored construction paper sold world wide. There was a fire once and it was eventually replaced. The tallest man in the mill, Walter Leighton, 7' 2, worked there rolling up broke (scraps) back into the beater. The wool felts on the machines, from Knox Woolen Mill in Camden, had to be changed every month or so. That worked good but they eventually went to synthetic felts."

"I worked shift work, 'southern swings' [a slow rotation plan that uses 4 teams and three 8-hr shifts to provide 24/7 coverage], eventually all days. With the swipers, the clothing crew, we dressed the paper machines with felts and wires and ropes. We also cleaned up around and did different other jobs that needed to be done. Vacations were hard to get. One week after one year. Second and third years you worked up to getting two weeks. To get more you had to work ten years, then you dropped down til you could earn only six weeks. Base wage when I started was $1.90 an hour. Women might have gotten $1.60. Quite a few women worked in the Converting Dept. That's where they started at union wages, according to the union book listing wages for various jobs back in 1964. Women were as hard workers as anyone else but they still got paid less. It was the times."

"Lots of practical jokes. Once a man on his job at #2 coater, sitting in a chair on the midnight shift, was sleeping about 2 a.m. and a guy tied a rope around him. Another guy below blows the whistle to alert that the coater operator needs to break the sheet down. When it woke the guy and he tried to get to get to it to fix it, he soon discovered he'd been had and was not going anywhere. But there was danger, too. Like 'The Yellow Line.' One misstep, crossing that line and you could be gone."

"Lots of memories. In my father's day, cars would be lined up at the gate at change of shifts when the men would be passed their lunch baskets. He'd always look to see what he had and we kids would always check for anything brought home. Our boys, Mark and Robbie, worked as summer help in the mill. Mark went into education and Robbie went on to work on papermachines and supercalendars, working his way up. When the mill closed he went to Walgren's in Belfast."

Nancy goes looking for one of the early tin lunch pails from the first generation of mill workers in their family, to show us. With it she brings 2 jars of her strawberry and raspberry jam which we consider blessings on this storytelling, on these, our people, and their, our history.

"I'd like to see a statue of a man with his dinner pail on the waterfront dedicated to the people who worked making paper here through the decades," Billy concludes. Clearly, his stories have no end.

— With Pat Ranzoni

William Bruce Stubbs was born in Castine in 1943. He grew up in Bucksport, graduating with the Class of 1961. He recalls scrimmaging with the respectful Oblate priests-in-training on their small basketball court and how clean linens would be folded and waiting for them. He also remembers Coach Norris starting a dancing class in gym and how he'd "otherwise never be able to dance with a girl." When he and wife, Nancy (Phillips) and boys lived in town, they enjoyed the pool and sports. Vacations were spent hunting and camping. They moved to the house they built in Bucksmills in 1988. He has been active in the Rod & Gun Club, the Masonic Lodge, and as a missile field Vietnam veteran, the American Legion. As a volunteer with the Bucksport Fire Department, he worked under chiefs Gayland Redman, Paul McCann and Gene Weston. He and Nancy enjoy a team approach to gardening. He grows the vegetables and she freezes or cans them.

Mark Stubbs
Auburn

THE ONES THAT DESERVE THAT VICTORY PARADE

The mill meant many things; often it encompassed every part of my school-aged life. Wherever I went, be it Shop n' Save, Western Auto, the Little League field, high school basketball games, or Wight's dairy the mill was a constant source of conversation with adults. As a child the conversations were half listened to and created a vision of the inner workings, albeit a bit distorted from reality. The wash ups, changing a wire, the magazine room, and the stores sounded like glorious and special events and places. It was a common language that bound the community that worked in the mill. The large circular signs that dotted the telephone poles on route to the Bangor Auditorium tournaments each year were supplied by the mill. When we came back into town via a parade of firetrucks and a police escort, it started at the mill parking lot. Bucksport did not begin until you could see the conveyor belts and woodpiles.

Even a strike or two, there did not seem to be a worry that things would not get resolved, it was the mill after all and it would always be there. The daily whistles kept us on track for meals as kids. When there was a fire, my brother and I raced to the kitchen to decipher the whistle codes and where in town the fire was. When there were occasional fires at the mill and dad was working, it made for an uneasy summer afternoon until he came home again. The mill was safety, the mill was constant, and the mill was larger than life.

After my senior year ended, I accepted my fate working summers during college. It was not what I had imagined. The people I saw outside in the community were different inside the mill and shadows on their faces cast a different affect. The magazine room was dangerous, exhausting, and an endless task as I had to pull logs into a hole in the floor to be ground up for pulp. The supercalender area was where I worked the most the first two years, watching the final product get rewound into smaller rolls. The droning of the machines, the dangers of moving parts, and making a mistake where coworkers would tell you quickly how you screwed up and loud enough to get through any ear protection.

My dad would come around from time to time to check in on me, fewer times than I think he really wanted to. As much as a college student enjoys hearing their dad give them advice, I secretly cherished his and it was often quite helpful. The hours were long, erratic, and exhausting but the money was exceptional. Within a month, I had appreciation renewed for my dad, uncles, grandfather and anyone else that worked in the mill and understood. I understood how the mill provided, how the mill exhausted, and how the mill created heroes in households all across town. They are the ones that deserve that victory parade.

Author note:

This was hard to write, but when you write with your heart and not your brain, I suppose that is the result. It hung in my head for weeks. This is probably not unique with others' experiences. I am grateful for the opportunity to heal through writing.

> *'The thought of writing hangs over our mind like an ugly cloud, making us apprehensive and depressed, as before a summer storm, so that we begin the day by subsiding after breakfast, or by going away, often to seedy and inconclusive destinations: the nearest zoo, or a branch post office to buy a few stamped envelopes.' E.B. White*

Writing this may have given me some impetus to review the first draft of a picture book that I hope to finish one day. Not surprisingly, it is based on a brook...similar to our Stubbs Brook in Bucksmills and Mill Stream in Blue Hill where I spent many summer days with my grandmother fishing, bottle hunting, catching fireflies, and making rock dams.

Mark Stubbs was born in Blue Hill in 1968 and grew up in Bucksport "until graduating from Thomas College with a BS degree in Marketing/Management in 1990 and MBA in 1993 as well as playing basketball there for four years. I spent the next 16 years working at LL Bean at various positions including retail manager for nine years. Always wanting to teach, I went back to school and earned my BS degree in early elementary education and have been teaching the past five years at Spurwink, which is a special purpose school helping severely at risk students. It was my formative years at New Alderbrook school and the close knit community in Bucksport that helped shape my beliefs and sense of giving back in a quality way. Making my home in Auburn, Maine, with my wife and now three children, my main focus has been contributing to community sports through the various programs as well as finding the nearest stream to fish and explore. Streams and rivers have been the time markers of my life, from Mill Stream in Blue Hill, to Stubbs Brook in Bucksport, the mighty Kennebec in Waterville, and now the Nezinscot Stream in Turner. Awards include the 2006 LL Bean Beans Best, the 2011 Auburn YMCA Volunteer of the Year, the 2011 Kaplan University Deans Award, and the 2012 Kaplan University Presidents Cup."

Jane Meade
Bucksport

P.S. TALK ABOUT HEROES!

Somewhere in "Still Mill" should be mentioned the fact that the men who worked at the mill, many of them were volunteer firemen before there was what we have now - people hired full time. These men would leap out of bed in the wee hours of the morning, regardless of the fact they had to report to work at the mill for their 8 to 4 shift; or fight fires all day and still get to their evening shifts. Remember the obscene, not to mention frightening sound of the alarm at one a.m.? My father would be out of the house in two minutes when that thing sounded. Talk about heroes!

Editor's note:

Jane Harvey Meade grew up on Central Street. A member of the Bucksport High class of 1958, she was editor of the yearbook and a champion varsity debater, winning multiple county and Penobscot Valley Conference "best speaker" awards. She has stayed involved as a class officer, reunion planner, and other town efforts.

Terry Grasse
Lisbon Falls

COMBAT PAPER: "GRAND PA"

dedicated to the legions of Veterans of U.S. Armed Forces
who worked at the Bucksport Paper Mill through the years
and their families

HI GRAND PA
CAN I SIT ON YOUR KNEE?
GRAND PA, PAPA SAID YOU
WERE IN THE "GREAT WAR"
DID YOU HAVE A UNIFORM?
AND A STEEL HELMET?
WAS IT GREEN?
DID YOU MARCH GRAND PA?
WITH BIG BOOTS?
WAS IT FUN?
DID YOU SHOOT A GUN?
HOW BIG WAS IT?
GRAND PA DID PEOPLE DIE
IN THE WAR?
WHAT WERE THEIR NAMES?
WHAT WERE THEIR NAMES
GRAND PA?

Given to the STILL MILL *collection, including the* Bucksport Area Poetry Route *preview exhibit and archive, by Maine artist and poet,* **Terry Grasse** *of Lisbon Falls, this poem was written on paper made from combat soldier's fatigue trousers. A Vietnam Veteran, the poetry of Mr. Grasse focuses on war and recovery from the trauma that war generates. He is active in Peace and Justice efforts and coordinates an annual* Memorial Day Poetry Reading *with fellow* Service Veteran Poets *from the* Combat Poets Writing Group *at the Lewiston, Maine Veterans Center. A participant in the* Warrior Writers *organization, he has attended* "Combat Paper" *workshops at Haystack School in Deer Isle for several summers.*

Author note: "Thanks for your interest in Combat Paper and thanks for the opportunity to send poetry and paper for sharing. Hope this helps in your endeavors."

* * *

Instructions for making Combat Paper, courtesy of Terry Grasse:
1. Deconstruct the uniform with scissors and tearing
2. Beat the scraps into a pulp using a Hollander beater
3. Form sheets by hand by pouring slurry through a screen using a mould and deckle
4. Turn the drained pulp onto a flat absorbent surface
5. Press and dry the finished paper

Donna Smith
Bucksport

JUST WHAT YOU DID IF YOU HAD A TRAIN CLOSE BY

Hope this fits the bill for mill stories.

My story is not so much about the mill itself as it is about the trains coming and going, bringing needed supplies to what was known to me, from birth to adulthood, as St. Regis Paper Co., and returning, loaded with the best-made printing paper available, on its way to the many weekly magazines that kept the mill lucrative. The story, as told to me by my Mom and Dad, really began in the early 1900's, in Orono, where they were both born and raised. Back then, seeing a train go by was about the most exciting thing that would happen in a child's day, and my Mom and her family were lucky enough to have one traveling almost through their back yard. And although the tracks weren't nearly as close to my Dad's house, he still had plenty of contact with that train. So both of my parents learned early on how much fun you could have waving to the train. To my Mom and her family, however, it was almost as important as their religion, and they used to flock to the tracks to wave to the train every time it went by—every time, and every time, the men on the train waved back—every time. This wasn't unique to my Mom's family though; "It's just what you did if you had a train close by." You were on a first-name basis with the train men; you knew if someone was missing or if there was somebody new, and they knew the same about you. Friendships were made and thrived.

Time passed and my Mom and Dad grew up and got married. It was the 1930's and a new paper mill had opened in Bucksport. It was called the Maine Seaboard Paper Company (later to be re-named St. Regis) and my Mom had landed a job there. Later on my Dad would do the same. So they pulled up stakes and moved to Bucksport, along with a lot of other folks from all over the area. They lived on Broadway for a while; then in the Fall of 1939, they bought a three-room log cabin on the River Road, just a mile from the mill, and moved in with my brother, who was six months old. A gift came with that tiny log cabin, train tracks, about fifty feet behind it. So, the waving began again, with my brother now a part of the ritual. They waved every morning as the train went to the mill, and again every afternoon as it traveled back up the line, because "that's just what you did if you had a train close by." The best part though? The train was the same one that had passed through my Mom's back yard in Orono a few years before, with many of the same old friends aboard. Old friendships were rekindled.

Once again, time marched on. It was 1945, and my Mom had given up her job at the mill two years earlier due to illness. She was going to have a baby in November, specifically, me. She was still waving religiously to the train twice a day, and I was learning how while still inside the womb. A doctor was called on an afternoon in mid- November, and I came into the world right there in that little log cabin.

348

The following morning, it was deemed not such a good idea for Mama to be out of bed yet; but if she wasn't there waving, the guys on the train would wonder what was wrong, because Mama was always there to wave. So here is how my Dad announced my arrival to the guys on the train. He went out on the back steps, formed his arms into a cradle, and as the train came, he made rocking motions as if he were cuddling and rocking his newborn daughter, until the day he could hold me up for real. The guys on the train then knew why Mama wasn't there and that all was well. They cheered and clapped, and I soon grew into a strong and happy toddler, waving to the train every chance I got, because I was born knowing "that's just what you did if you had a train close by."

Once again weeks, months, and years crept by. It was the 1960's, and I had emerged as an adult (or at least, that's the fantasy world I enjoyed living in). I married, and in late December of 1966, gave birth to a terrific baby boy, who spent a lot of time with his Mimi in that little log cabin close to the tracks. He, too, learned very early on about waving to the train, because "that's just what you did if you had a train close by." He made friends with the guys on the train, and one day, with permission asked and given, they even gave him a ride on the engine; a little boy's dream-come-true and never to be forgotten.

In the early 1980's, my husband and I bought and moved into the house next door to the little log cabin, with the son who had been waving to the train since before he could remember. We just automatically took up where we had left off. There was more than just one train a day now, so each of us probably waved at least once during any given twenty-four hour period. Sometimes there was a train in the middle of the night (which we did not wave to), but got so used to it, we rarely even awoke. So three generations of my family have waved to the trains that made their way to and from our now-silent mill.

Time has passed once again. That's what time does. The need for the trains at the Bucksport mill no longer exists. Once in a while, I see a short train pass my house (I still live by the tracks), pulling a few empty cars, and days later, it returns, loaded with debris from the demolition of our mill. If I'm lucky enough to be outside, I still wave because "that's just what you do if you have a train close by." In all the years I have been waving to trains, the guys on the trains have never failed to wave back. It was fun to wave to the trains as a child, and it still is, as a senior citizen.

I miss my trains, but understand that as time moves on, lives and things change. Some are tucked safely away in memory, giving opportunity for the new to arrive. I am looking forward to seeing how we, as a town, will meet the new challenges that must be met in order for our wonderful, picturesque hometown to continue to thrive, because Bucksport is a great little town and community. I, for one, realize how lucky we are to have chosen Bucksport to live in.

Recipe for Pot Roast
(Better known in our house as "Smileys Favorite")

Just a quick explanation—Smiley is the family nickname for my brother. I was almost in high school before I knew that "Smileys Favorite" was actually known to the rest of the world as Pot Roast.

1 four to five-lb. chuck roast, seasoned with salt and pepper, and browned in a heavy-bottomed kettle or cast iron Dutch oven.

Add at least 2 onions, 2 potatoes, and 2 carrots per person, turn down the heat and let simmer for 3 or more hours. Add water if necessary. Serve with its own juice (or make gravy, if you prefer-I do). Serve with hot biscuits.

See why it's "Smileys Favorite"?

Wilbur Smith
Huntersville, NC

TWO SMELLS, SULPHITE AND MY MOTHER'S COOKING

Just some unarranged thoughts. Two smells, the sulfite odor and my mothers cooking, the smells of which would meet me as I walked over the hill on the River Road coming home from track practice. Unless the weather were very cold she always had the southern windows open on the cabin and the wind always out of the north west and I would be salivating when I got home.

Of course, the mill put me and hundreds of others through college, although it didn't pay for everything, and I was on my second tour in Vietnam before I paid off my college loan. Nonetheless, summer work in the mill was wonderful, and I always felt that I had been part of the paper making team when I went back to school.

Do with this anything you want. If it comes out good, I will take the credit. If it's terrible, I will blame you.

Your friend, Donna's brother "Smiley".

Wilbur "Smiley" Smith was born in Bucksport in 1939 "in a 18X18 log cabin on the River Road where I grew up. No running water til I was about 15 – when it's minus 20, you don't go to the outhouse to read. Bucksport schools until 1957 then U of M. Thrown out for poor grades after one year. Had the St. Regis Scholarship. Complete embarrassment. I have a natural bent for laziness, so a year of work in the mill encouraged me to go back to school. Majored in German – easiest for me – don't forget the laziness comment. Out in '63. Commissioned 2nd LT = Germany '64–'67, '67–'69 1st Cavalry Division Viet Nam, '69 Ordinance Officer Career Course, Aberdeen, MD – meet future wife, Miriam. '70–'71 Columbus, Ohio National Guard Advisor, '72 Command and General Staff College Fort Leavenworth, KS. '73 Civilian, begin work National Defense Stockpile, Baltimore. '80 move to DC, same job, more money. Retire 1995 to pursue career as sloth. Received two Bronze Stars–Air Medal– and was member of two European Championship Military Pentathlon Teams (1965–66). Memberships, Sigma Chi fraternity and VFW (Veterans of Foreign Wars)."

Pearl Mattson
Surry

A BASKET OF BOUNTY

Hometown Americana has been portrayed so beautifully by artist Norman Rockwell. What a "heyday" he would have had if he had brought his brushes to our hometown of Bucksport, Maine. It is a town where people conversed at regular intervals, while retrieving mail from their Post Office boxes. They "keyed in" on local politics or events of the day while discarding the "junk" mail into the large waste container. People, gingerly carrying packages wrapped in brown paper and tied up with string to be sent "far away", did business at the post office window. Mr. Rockwell's canvas would depict life where middle class predominated in a small rural town in the 20th century. It is a town where prosperity was dependent on the quality of the publication paper produced in the St. Regis Paper Company. The scenario would not have been so unique in many ways, unless Mr. Rockwell had happened by the paper mill at the change of shifts.

Uniformed Security Guards stopped traffic allowing workers the "in" and "out" right-of-way to cross Route 15. In the crook of each elbow the hourly employee of St. Regis Paper Company carried a wicker picnic basket. Depending on their destination, that basket was either empty or holding a lunch. No small tin pails, nor fancy "Swingers" nor brown paper bags for these men working 'round the clock in 8 hour shifts. No, indeed, these men needed to be fortified!

My father-in-law worked 42 years to make the buyers (*Sears & Roebuck*, *Life*, *Better Homes and Gardens*, *Readers' Digest*, *Playboy* etc.) happy with Bucksport produced paper. In those 42 years, many a lunch was carried to and fro in nothing less than a wicker picnic basket. Yes, that was the carrier of choice.

In my husband's family, the dinner meal of the day was prepared for noon. As the kids walked (1 m ile) home from school, they could depend on a hot meal to strengthen them for the hike back to school and an afternoon of classes. Consequently, a hot meal for Dad was bundled into the picnic basket along with a cloth napkin, a thermos jug of coffee, and a bit of sweet. (There was a rare instance when Mum grabbed a square (desert sweet) from the freezing unit of the ice box. When Dad arrived home, with the square untouched, Mum was informed that at dinner time (at the mill) the treat had not yet "come alive". By this he meant that it was still frozen.

The loaded picnic basket was hefted into the family vehicle and delivered to the mill security gate. there, multiple baskets awaited a trip, in a wheel barrow, to the various sections of paper production. The identity of these iconic baskets was easily recognized by the colors and placement of necessary mending tape. As the baskets were often passed down from father to son, all had soiled handles – handles dirtied by hard working hands and food. A clean handle was indicative of a "Newbie".

Thus, when the noon whistle sounded, the crews gathered to eat and swap tales. I expect the shifts bonded as a unit during these quick repasts. That same mill whistle signaled 8:00 a.m. (time to get serious about the day), a 4:00 p.m. shift change and a 9:00 p.m. curfew. It screeched, also, to notify the town of school closings and to announce a local fire. The Morse Code type of broken whistles indicated the location of the fire. Each town resident referred to an information card that was distributed with the phone book.

Paper making was the backbone of Maine industry. The occupation gave Hancock County people (and Maine people, in general) gratifying and stable employment. Turning out rolls of paper was crucial to Bucksport's well-being. For 84 years, the opportunities of the town's "Mill" provided families a substantial standard of living, supported good schools and was respected in business.

Today, the mill has closed its security gate, the train cars sit on a deserted track, and Route #15 traffic flows unimpaired into a small town struggling to fill its store fronts and restore prosperity.

The picnic baskets of those faithful workers are now stored in damp basements and atop attic shelves. Some are varnished, some are rickety. Some contain the cloth napkin recycled, washed and intact. The basket's uniqueness will be remembered for a generation or two. As we closed Dad's home, there, hanging from a hook in the garage, was the food bearing receptacle. A symbol of loving times. A reminder of practical times.

Today, if Norman Rockwell had fresh paints in front of him he might depict the paper mill's tall stacks, which will remain as a monument to a forgotten era. In front of those stacks he would paint a bustle of workmen threading through the front gate. The marquee in front of them would be lit up announcing, "THROUGH THIS GATE PASS THE WORLD'S FINEST PAPER-MAKERS!"

Previously published by Todd Blair's Hometown Memories, L.L.C. in "Harvest Recess and Picker Shacks", *2016.*

Pearl Robinson Mattson *was raised in Bucksport where her father was a 35-year employee of the paper mill. She graduated from Bucksport High School (class of 1961) and the University of Maine/Orono (class of 1965). "My career as a Marketing Agent for the Maine Dairy Council was enjoyable but second to the fulfillment of my life as a homemaker. The part I have played in a 50-year marriage and raising 3 successful children are my proudest accomplishments." Pearl and her husband, Perry, "are blessed to reside on the Bay in Surry, Maine."*

Jane Harvey Meade
Bucksport

BACK AND FORTH, DAY AFTER DAY, YEAR AFTER YEAR BY DAD'S SIDE

THE LUNCH BASKET

The mill is gone, but my father's brown wicker basket is still here. It sits in my dining area. We've filled it with a flower arrangement. Sometimes it's on our high mantle over the pantry; sometimes it just sits on the floor by the hutch. When it's there on the floor, it appears more weary, as if it's about to buckle from all the shift work; for all the years that my dad, John W. Harvey, carried it faithfully on the 4 to 12, midnight to 8, and 8 to 4 shifts. He had come to Bucksport with his whole family when his father, Ozro Saunders Harvey, heard that a mill was being built in this town. The Harveys moved to Verona Island, and Dad first went to work for Alton Grindle as a butcher at his market on Main Street.

During those early days in town, Dad poured over books on electricity in his off hours and became a licensed electrician. As a result, he was hired as a switch room operator at Bucksport's St. Regis Paper Mill. What a blessing that mill was to all the families who grew and thrived because of the opportunity it provided. Dad went on to acquire a real estate license, become a notary public, a volunteer fireman, and even a selectman for awhile because shift work offered him enough hours in the week to accomplish other goals and pursue his and my mother's other interests; to build their family a house and send their two children to college. Mama (Agatha Dyer Harvey of Dexter, Maine) substituted in the Bucksport schools after we were born, and helped Dad run his real estate and insurance office. She did secretary work for him and answered the phone, etc. Her assistance was important especially when he was working the day shifts or sleeping in preparation for the midnight to eight rotation – I can remember Mama warning that "Dad's sleeping; he has to go to work at 11:30."

I also have a vivid recollection of both of them at the big steel desk in the office, she's typing and he's dictating a letter, or both of them pouring over ledgers at the end of the month or maybe during tax season.

All the while, that basket traveled back and forth, day after day; year after year, by Dad's side. I keep it to look back and remember my father's hard work, and now to remember to be thankful for a town and an industry which provided such a stable way of life for its families.

Yes, the mill is no longer humming in the background of our lives, but every day we see what it has left us: a solid, reputable public education system, a vital health care facility, a theater that is becoming an historical museum and keeper of our past, a library, elegant in design and filled with cultural treasures, a well maintained 9-hole golf course (What other town the size of Bucksport has such a feature?), our well-built homes and our cherished families. They, like my father's lunch basket, are to be honored and cared for and will help us to remember how blessed we have been as we move forward.

Jane Harvey Meade: "As for my biography, it is long, but I am old with a long portfolio. Growing up, I loved writing and the English language. In junior high, I found my favorite English teacher and role model in Rena Gray who inspired my bent for poetry and English. By the time I was in high school, I was teaching my younger brother and his friends about grammar and how to diagram sentences whenever I could inspire them to sit still in my makeshift garage 'classroom.'" When the local newspaper, "The Free Press" *advertised for a high school student columnist, someone who would do a column each week about interesting items for young people, Jane submitted a sample column and got the job. Her* "Teen Talk" *became a weekly part of Bucksport's newspaper. "For a while, I thought I had discovered what I would do with my life - become a journalist, but my high school English teacher discouraged such a profession for a 'nice young lady.'" After graduating with the class of 1958, then four years at Gorham State, Jane became a teacher instead, following her mother's devotion to education. She taught sixth grade in Casco, Maine, her first year, after a year in a junior high setting in Limerick, Maine before she moved to Binghamton, New York and taught sixth grades there and in neighboring Johnson City. After my daughter was born, I did substitute teaching for a while. One of my most memorable positions was as a multi-graded teacher in Binghamton. Three days a week, I was in partnership with a retired teacher who conducted the class on the other two days. It was an experimental arrangement that worked out flawlessly. The youngsters in the multi-graded classroom were labeled troubled children who found a mother figure in the older, retired instructor and a big sister in me. We communicated by phone to keep the instruction flowing smoothly. I remember it as one of my most rewarding teaching experiences. Following New York, I spent one year in Auburn, New Hampshire where I taught in an open classroom setting, a phase that became briefly popular in the late 60's and early 70's. After that year, Needham, Massachusetts sought me out for a sixth grade position, and I stayed until retirement in 2000. During my work with Needham, I went with the town's changing configuration of grades into a middle school facility, went on to gain a Master's degree plus 45, and taught summer school, becoming the elementary director of the summer school program for the district. In all, I logged 38 years in education, retiring at age 60." In 2005, "after the untimely death of my brother from non Hodgkins Lymphoma," Jane and husband, John Meade, moved back to her hometown where they put an addition on the family home now owned by her daughter and husband, Keith and Lisa Parker. "A funny thing happened about that time. I became a published author, self-publishing a book,* "Remembering Peter," *which documented the life of my uniquely talented brother, Dr. Peter Harvey, who was a college dean at Hart College in Connecticut as well as a successful entertainer across the country, gaining fans from Hawaii to California to Maine with his humor and rich tenor voice. At the time of his death, he had performed every lead role in every major opera, starred in many musicals in the Hartford area, been the director of the Simsbury Theatre, and director of Hartford's St. Joseph's Cathedral choir for twenty years, to mention just a few of his abundant accomplishments. At the urging of my daughter, I began polishing some of the novels that I had been creating during my busy working years." Jane began her*

355

formal publishing career with Maine Authors Publishing in Rockland. Currently, she is working on her sixth book, "Something About the House" *to be launched in the spring of 2017. Her first novel,* "The Summer of the Disco King," *is "a mystery mixed with lots of humor and a smattering of romance." Her second publication was "a novelette, 'Glimpses,' a collection of true stories about unexplained occurrences of ordinary people." She hopes to do a sequel to this book soon after her next novel is launched." Jane's third book is "a serious novel about spousal abuse called,* 'The Season in Between.' *It was given rave reviews by the world-renowned review service, 'Kirkus.'" She has also published a poetry book called,* "Piper's Song - My Life in Poetry," *which is dedicated in the memory of her sixth grade teacher, Rena Gray, of Bucksport. "From a young age, I have written what totals about one hundred songs, many in partnership with Peter. I hope to include a book of songs in my repertoire of publications before I conclude my 'second life' as an author."*

Larry Leach
Skowhegan

SO LUCKY, SO MANY GREAT MEN

I started at the mill in August 8, 1970, fresh out of Bucksport High School. It was a huge eye-opening experience being around such massive equipment and I remember the heat was very oppressive. After my first night of unloading a rail car full of clay I wondered if this was what I wanted to do for the rest of my life but with some encouragement from my father who had been in the mill many years I decided to stick it out. After I spent a few years bouncing around in different departments I eventually settled in the stock prep department. I was so lucky to be surrounded by so many great men in this dept. I would like to name some that come to mind. My boss was a wonderful person. Charlie Wentworth. One thing that comes to mind for me was I had 1970s shoulder length hair that required me to wear a hairnet. This resulted in many comments from many WWII and Korean War vets and some nicknames as well. Keep in mind it was in a light-hearted way. But this served me well throughout my career with a thick skin. Names that I would like to drop of people I had tremendous respect for – Ralph Robshaw, Linwood Robshaw, my dad Lloyd Leach, Bill Austin, Earl Cunningham, Russ Merithew, Jimmy Burgess, Freddy Drew, Ed Arey, Jimmy Stone, Orin Flagg, Froggy Hanson, Dickey Varnum, Don Peet, Fran Serafin etc etc. and so many more, too many to name. These guys not only taught me how to make paper but they offered so many life lessons. I was at the Bucksport mill for 12 years and left to work for SD Warren and Sappi for the next 27 years. I will say that paper mill life is pretty much the same no matter where you go. Same people with different names and faces but many parallel stories. I will never forget my time at St Regis and I find it kinda spooky when I drive by and see it being torn down.

Larry Leach *was born in Castine in 1952 and was brought up on Verona island. "I was in the class of 1970. Bucksport High. I enjoy coaching youth baseball and coaching my 9-year-old son, yes I have a 9-year-old son. I enjoyed hiking for years and have hiked the Grand Canyon and just completed my 2nd trip up Katahdin last fall."*

Through the years, coolers became a popular choice as lunch and dinner carriers among some workers.

357

Barbara Tilley
Prospect

A WOMAN WORKING IN THE PAPER MILL

In 1973, the Mill was dominated by the men in the work force. That changed and woman started working there in the Production. In the past women worked on the roll wrapper but had been phased out by a mechanical wrapper.

The decision to add another Paper Machine, Super Calendar and Winder required more people, men and women, so a Spare Pool was formed to be available for whatever job they needed to fill on a daily basis. After limited training (one shift with Operator) they might be a winder helper, broke helper, rewinder helper, supercalender helper or tearing up logs and cleaning. In time the management realized they had to make change for women. They built a new locker room on the ground level by the Supercalender Foremen's Office with flushes and showers and also made changes on the winders to help people load up the winders with heavy cores and shafts and improving methods for unloading winder and moving heavy rolls. They installed a conveyer that ran from No. 8 winder straight out to the core room, some distance away which carried the manufactured rolls to be wrapped and labeled for the customer and sent to the train shed to be shipped.

There was no discrimination against women in the work force as long as they could perform their duties. St. Regis merged with Champion and it brought along some new ideas and a change in the management. Work days had been eight hours but then the idea of working 12 hours, 4 days a week with one week off a month was appealing to the younger employees and so voted. This was harder on older people and also the beginning of eliminating some helper jobs. This meant less time with your family but the lure of the one week off a month sealed the deal.

Most of the workers will agree that the ownership, St. Regis then to Champion, was the best of times. After Champion came International Paper and then Verso with stricter work rules that did not cause a good relationship with the workers. Finally, Verso pulled the plug on a Paper Mill that made money and a good paying job for the employees. Many careers have been rooted up, leaving only the memories of past years of good friendships. God Bless them all.

RELATIVES JOINING THE WORK FORCE

Back in the past of St. Regis, it was common for a child of a father, uncle or grandfather working in the Mill to be able to have summer employment and after graduation, they would apply for steady employment, resulting in the beginning of relatives joining the work force.

Women worked wrapping rolls of paper but in 1973, production lines were opened to women resulting in several husbands and wives working there at the same time.

I went to work at St. Regis in 1976 as a spare and worked around many different machines and occupations, finally settling for the Supercalendar Dept. and spent 18 ½ years there on shift work, followed by 4 years of working in the Shipping Dept. for Production Control. In the Supercalendar Dept. I was a helper on various machines then--a Rewinder and Winder Operator. I became a Spare Foreman while working in the Supers and then offered the chance to become the first woman foreman in the Production Department. The twenty-two years of working there, we became a family.

My father-in-law, Louis Bill Tilley was night Superintendent of Ground Wood and later was named Night Super of the entire Mill, his son, my husband, Paul C. Tilley worked as a pipe fitter there for 33 years, his brother Dick Tilley worked in the Accounting Dept. for many years. I had many members of my family work there also. My brother, Harold Haley was a Paper Inspector and then a QCC. Two of my sons-in-law worked in the Kraft Plant, Tim Webster and Thomas Valenoti, so we had quite a few relatives working there at the same time.

This Mill provided a very nice income to all and the working conditions were improving all the time and there was nowhere else that could offer the wages and benefits that we enjoyed.

Ardeana Hamlin, *Hampden*
with Geremy Chubbuck, *Orono*

THE DEATH OF A CULTURE

This interview was conducted by Ardeana Hamlin of Hampden on April 13, 2015, with mechanical engineer Geremy Chubbuck of Orono, who worked from 1993 to 2003 at the Champion – International Paper mill in Bucksport:

Where did you grow up?
Enfield, which is another mill town. My grandfather and father both worked in the paper mills. I envisioned myself working in the automotive industry or going in the military, or being a design engineer with dreams to do amazing things, but that's not the reality of life. My junior year in college, there was an opening at the mill in Bucksport, a co-op job the summer of 1992. I stayed with my grandparents in Stockton Springs that summer. After the co-op experience, my course was set. I enjoyed the experience [of working in the mill] and fortunately, I was offered a fulltime position at mill beginning in May 1993. I graduated from the University of Maine on Saturday and the following Monday I began work at the mill as an entry level project engineer.

What is your educational background?
I majored in mechanical engineering at the University of Maine and graduated with a bachelor's degree in mechanical engineering. In 2000 I became a licensed professional engineer.

What years did you work at the Bucksport Mill?
The last month I worked at Bucksport was February 2003.

What was it called then?
It was International Paper. Champion International ceased to exist in 1999 when International Paper did a hostile takeover of Champion. It was a huge culture shock.

What was your position at the mill and did you have a title?
Project engineering, water service and eventually mechanical maintenance.

Describe your duties.
At the outset, I was an early career project engineer, did improvements, small projects and miscellaneous duties including optical precision alignment on the paper machines. I really enjoyed it. I also gave tours of the mill - I think, looking back, we [engineering department guys] were asked to do the tours because our department had the most available time to do the tours. Then I was responsible for capital

investment projects up to $200,000. Through attrition and retirements I eventually became a senior project engineer. I was also responsible for the water service which consisted of four bodies of water and four dams. Water is the blood of a paper mill. Water service was truly an operation - I was on call for operational things - to maintain fishways and monitor and maintain lake levels, monitor and track water levels for land owner needs, coordinate with town officials and the state Department of Marine Resources and Maine Emergency Management Association. I did that concurrently for the remainder of my career at the mill. Eventually, I progressed to maintenance – Area 3 foreman - for the last three years that I was at the mill.

How many people were in your department?
As foreman, I was responsible for two shops, and 24 people. In this position, the next oldest person to me was 15 years older. On day one I told the crew they had a unique opportunity to mould me the way they wanted a supervisor to be. They were a great group of folks and I really miss those people. They were great to work with.

What did you like about your time at the mill?
I really enjoyed working on the gas turbine, gas generator project - I was very involved with that - it was one of the highlights of my career. I was able to travel to many different places in United States, as well. Texas, Minnesota, Michigan, Connecticut - I went to many of the mills in Maine on behalf of Champion - I was able to see a lot of the country. With Champion I received the very best maintenance education available at the time. Champion really invested in their people - it was an excellent company. The company was very successful – the Bucksport mill made $10 million a month - month after month after month in the mid-1990s - then we made $9 million and it was like a depression had set in. People felt they hadn't met the goal, that they hadn't done their jobs well – a difficult thing to imagine these days. Champion shared with its employees. I learned a lot about people, how to manage people and crews. The company really invested in their employees. That's rare these days. It wasn't all easy, it was hard work and it was a mill environment, but it was honest work. Ultimately, everyone pulled in the same direction.

What was the downside of your job and working at the mill?
It's easier to remember the good than the bad, but many of my difficult memories occurred during the time that International Paper owned the mill. The culture shock was dramatic because IP had a very different way of doing business. They had a different workplace philosophy. I also remember long days and nights at the mill during shutdowns.

When you worked at the mill did you have a family to support and did you live in Bucksport?
Yes, I was married in 1993 and in 1996 my son was born. For me, it was a tremendous period of change in a very short timeframe - I graduated from college, bought a house, got married, began a career, had elderly grandparents who needed help and support - it was a bit of a whirlwind. All this was not company related, but Champion was supportive of my personal needs - they expected a lot, but they provided a lot. I have not worked for another employer since who was as supportive as Champion was.

When you think about your years of working at the mill, what did you take away with you when you moved on to another job?

Some of the training that I learned at profession development school - recruitment and assessment skills, management styles, personality sets - has proven to be invaluable. Basically, it was my first professional job. I had worked since I was in seventh grade in non-professional roles. I learned a great deal about unions - it was my first real exposure to them. Other valuable assets were the maintenance schooling, and contacts I made in the paper industry and the vendor industry.

What made you decide to take another job?

In 2003, I became disenchanted with IP, I didn't agree with their method of management. I realized that the company wasn't going to change so I had to. I didn't want to leave Bucksport. When IP began the takeover, Champion gave us all a book on dealing with significant change, "Who Moved My Cheese," [a motivational tale written by Spencer Johnson]. It was their way of telling us to get ready; your life is going to change. With the closure of mills in the state, such as Bucksport, we're seeing the complete death of a culture - people walking in and out of work with pack baskets [filled with their gear and lunch], or men wearing welding jackets [a thin fireproof garment worn when doing hot work] and bandanas on their heads. You don't see that much anymore, it was culturally common - little nuances like that are now gone from our society. It's not coming back.

What do you think contributed to the closure of the mill?

My time at the mill was just over a decade in length and coincided with the height and end of the Champion International era. Champion went through several recession and recovery eras when paper prices dropped then rebounded. From 2003 until the end of the mill, I am told that Bucksport wasn't able to get one single price increase for its product to stick. In the paper industry, if you raise the price, orders will drop offl, but eventually the orders should come back. When I began working at Bucksport in 1993, more than 1,400 people were working at mill. When the mill closed its doors, I'm told there were only 550 people working at the mill. The paper industry as a whole has been really disadvantaged by NAFTA - North America Free Trade Agreement. I feel that this has contributed very significantly to the demise of the paper industry in our state. Again, it's the death of a culture in our society. When the company and worker can no longer make money - it's all connected.

Ardeana Hamlin *works for the* Bangor Daily News *as a copyeditor and writer for* The Weekly. *She is the author of the novels "Pink Chimneys," which references Bucksport in the age of sail, and "Abbott's Reach." A third novel, "The Havener Sisters" was published in October 2015. She grew up in Bingham on the banks of the Kennebec River in the 1950s and early 1960s, a mill town where veneer and Bristol boats were manufactured. As she grew up, she lived by the mill whistle - 7 a.m., 11:30 a.m. and 5 p.m. Her father worked in the woods for S.D. Warren Co. as a bulldozer operator. The pulpwood that was trucked out on the roads her father built was shipped by train to the paper mill in Westbrook. Her Uncle Don Hamlin was one of the workers who "juggled pulp" into the boxcars. Recently she learned that a Bingham resident, Albert Bushey, grandfather of a woman she grew up with, built one of the "towers" at the Bucksport mill, thus bridging, in a manner of speaking, the paper mill on the Penobscot to the veneer mill on the Kennebec.*

Barbara A. Tilley
Prospect

MILL FAMILY MEMORIES, THE GOOD AND THE HARD

Camping at Masthead on the Shore of Hancock Pond

For many years summer was marked by campers pulling into Masthead and setting up in the same place as they had in the past.

Bob and Annette Valenoti were the owners and when Bob was back in N.Y. working for the Postal Dept., Annette was assisted by Frannie Grindle. My daughter Debbie Herbest has been married to their son Thomas so there was a relationship between us.

Masthead was a family orientated camping ground with sensible rules of quiet after 10:00 PM, keeping your area cleaned up and watch your children. Visitors to your site were welcome but if a big crowd was expected, the owners wanted to know how many, when and for how long.

Many of the campers stayed there all summer long and worked daily, to return to the campgrounds to enjoy "the community".

Masthead had the basics, showers, water, bathrooms, horse shoe courts, dump station for the trailers, big center area with picnic tables, electricity, running water and a main wood pile and each lot had a fire pit. We had our own wood as Paul would get the cull wood from St. Regis and bring it out and stack it between two trees. Many people thought he was taking it from the main pile but he didn't. The wood made a beautiful fire as it had water in it and what beautiful flames it made. We enjoyed ours every night and people would gather around and laugh, eat and drink while the kids were at someone's camp playing spoons or other games. One night my husband Paul threw a package of fire crackers in the fire which caused me to come all unglued and jumped into the air and came back down on the recliner I was on and flattened it.

If someone called for you, Annette would holler for you until you came to the office. This was before cell phones and what a help that would have been.

There were occasional pot luck suppers in the main area and just about everyone would attend and bring something to eat and eat we did. We also had horse shoe tournaments that would bring not only the campers but relative and there would be trophies and a lot of yelling. On days off, I would spend time on the court along with friend Olla Reynolds trying to improve my game but to no avail. Did have fun though.

One of the rules were no fireworks but every 4th of July, you would see Bob and Annette sitting on the shore watching the fireworks being shot off from a float in the pond with the fireworks stored in a canoe alongside. One night they had a close call as one of the rockets went up in the air and came down into the canoe causing everyone to abandon the float and swim as fast as they could for shore. This slowed down further celebrations.

Our dog, Lobo was kept tied to a big tree across from our camper and everyone thought he needed nourishment I guess as many would bring their leftover meat for him. He loved it and occasionally

363

would chew his rope and get lose to mosey around the campground until someone corralled him and tied him back up.

There were people camping there that worked at the Mill: Paul Reynolds and family, Bobby Verge and family, "Stubby" Stubbs and family and others that would come for a week or just to visit.

The last summer of good times ended in tragedy when on the night before the 4th of July, two Gilbert sister's died in an explosion in their camper caused by a leaking propane tank inside the camper. That day had seen all the kids riding their bikes around and playing and having a good time and at night when I went to work for the 12-8 shift, people were sitting around their camp fire and talking. When I got to work at the Mill I was told about a fire at Masthead which I couldn't believe as I had left there about 20 minutes before and there had been a tragedy. When I got there in the morning after work there were hardly any campers there as the men had stayed up all night getting everyone packed up so they could be out of there before morning. They did not want their children to see the area. The camper involved was just about 20 feet away from ours and it melted some of the vinyl siding on ours. Never a 4th of July comes I don't think of the girls and their family.

The memories of Masthead will always remind me of happy times and wonderful people. Both Bob and Annette are gone now but their hard work provided a great place to camp. They are missed.

Sharon Bray
Orland

WHEN WE WERE KIDS IN MILL-TOWN TIME

"thinking about old days of changing the clocks around here"

November 1, 2015

At this time yesterday, the clock said, "Noon." Over Saturday night we fell back into standard time, gave up saving daylight for afternoons. But now school buses can pick up kids in pale morning instead of pitch dark.

When we were kids in mill-town time, families waited until Sunday to change their clocks (though some churches did and some didn't) because work shifts for the week started Sunday night. We barely knew what the rest of the country was doing with these time games.

Back then, too, the time changes were in October and April. Parents and school teachers told us the change from Eastern Daylight to Eastern Standard time were developed to make best use of longer days during growing season. Later, daylight saving became more of an electric lights and energy issue. Every year, now, newspapers carry stories about who wants to stay on daylight savings year round.

Since our mill closed, shift work has become more of an issue for circadian rhythm experts; less for out-of-work mill laborers.

Since I no longer go to church, I can give up worry about what time to leave home the first Sunday morning of a new time zone.

Russell Buker
Alexander

NO

No chance for meditation
with
an audience of one

patient
shaming my anger
large

white flakes land on
scare
crows damp mimic

shoulders
molding to the board
as I

wish you a Leonid
star path
among those you were

unable
to lift your head to see
so

when we're both
gone
ravens will no longer

steal
tufts of straw from
our

beckoning ears for

nesting
purposes or curse

how
beautiful, tipsy, glowing
silent

Teacher and writer **Russell Buker**'s connection to the Bucksport mill is one of solidarity with relatives in the mills of Jay and Rumford, Maine, and neighbors where he lives near the Woodland pulp mill "with their uncertainties." "*Making connections is an important part of my understanding of history. The connection between Weld and Wilton is much like the connection between Alexander and Woodland. How many of our ancestors moved from Alexander to Woodland to work in the mill? Now with better roads and cars, people are moving back to the rural communities and commuting to their jobs. My ancestors settled in Weld and lived in that mountainous western Maine community for several generations. Then the mills of Wilton called my grandfather to Wilton, and that is where I had my earliest memories of Maine.*" Russell is recently retired from Shead High School of Eastport where he taught English and Creative Writing. He has also coached for many years: football, baseball, basketball and tennis. Russell has had numerous poems accepted in many publications in the U.S. and in Canada including:* The Antigonish Review, The Windrow Anthology, The Cape Breton Collection, Pottersfield Press, Goose River Anthology, Germ Magazine, Portland Press Poetry Section, The Aurorean, Felt Sun, The Aputamkan Review, River Muse, Page & Spine, Maine Writes Anthology, Stoneboat, Crack the Spine, *and* Axe Factory Press. Russell has also served on the board of editors and written book reviews for Off the Coast Review. *His latest collection is* 9XXX The Best of Myself (Just Write Books), *about which the award-winning poet, Annie Finch, has said, "Russell Buker has a distinctive voice, wry, capacious, and apt. From 'the white now of winter' to 'the bang-getty-bang of leaping summer,' this book hums with charm, and leaps with good surprises."*

Doug Gross
Bucksport

YES I WALKED THE PICKET LINE IN 1979

I was raised right here in Bucksmills. I graduated from Bucksport High with the Class of 1969 and I raised my children in Bucksmills and Bucksport. Margaret and I and now our children and grandchildren continue the tradition of farming in Bucksmills. However, this enterprise often requires additional resources in order to exist. This is where our Mill came into my life.

To support my three children, Margaret, and the farm, I went to work at the Paper Mill on April 13, 1971. I went on to staying at the Mill for 32 years. The 32 years went by much faster than one could imagine. I was fortunate to experience several positions within the mill culture. In the early years I worked Union jobs such as laboring. Driving truck, running heavy machinery, etc. Yes, I walked the picket line in 1979.

I was promoted to a management position in 1980. I worked as a foreman and department supervisor for approximately 10 years. The last 12-13 years of my career I worked just as an Organizational Development Consultant.

The experiences that the mill provided were invaluable. My growth as a person and a manager were very much connected with the experiences of the mill culture.

As I start to call on the OLD memory banks, there are just too many stories for me to put on paper. However, I can share with you a typical day that reflects a culture that has been LOST.

A Typical Day:
Get to work and the lunch room is full of "the guys'" laughter, smell of fresh coffee yes, the occasional argument and the thunderous roar of the machinery starting up. Most people thought we all smelled like Christmas trees.

Moving on to the scale house where the drivers and scalers are having your review of last night's news and politics. Yes occasionally they even talk about the scale and wood quality. Rarely, but in reality occasionally there was an unhappy customer that I got to deal with. However, this was usually a fun, cooperative environment to visit.

Now for the walk to the Mill. The clank of the wood conveyor and the pounding of the wood going to the Mill was a very prominent noise. The noise of the "canteen area." Guys razing each other, fresh coffee, local news. Local sports, busy people interacting with a short period of time to do it in.

Now to the Grinder Room, where solid pieces of wood are ground into fiber that holds your sheets of paper together. The sweaty brows, people with wood mallets, and Pick Poles. The thunderous sound of that raw power that vibrates the floor under your feet.

Now on to the Production Meeting. To get there you have to walk by 1 & 2 Paper Machines. The thunderous noise has now changed to a high-pitched shrill! The guys are sometimes just sitting in their sweat. When those paper makers are sitting it's a good thing! The smell has changed from Christmas trees to hot vapor, chemicals, and PAPER (Yes, it has a smell). As those rolls come off the machine you can see the pride in those faces. The best lightweight coated paper makers in the world....DID IT AGAIN!

As we all say from time to time, change has to happen. It did! A new owner brought some operating principles that were challenging my whole work force, NO LONGER was was the best the priority. Money became the measure of success. Formulas that were successful for many years were cast aside in order to improve efficiency.

The laughter, community, pride, cockiness were all being replaced with insecurity, frustration and anger. No longer were community and school topics the focal point. It was "How much longer will we be here?" The strain of this change was evident to all of those who took the time to observe. We all know the story from this point forward. It's with sadness that we have lost a manufacturing location that provided wonderful standards of living for thousands of people. It's sad that all the confidence and pride will not be experienced by the next generation.

Well, for me I took an early retirement in 2003. The wonderful experience and education I received while in Organizational Development allowed me and my family to start a business that is still operational today, and treating us very well. However, most importantly I'm still in Bucksmills, the Farm continues to grow, and my Family are all part of that! Bucksmills is as fun, wholesome, and therapeutic as it has been my entire life.

Well, its haying season, the grandchildren are preparing the cattle for another Fair Season. And it's just generally busy. I'm writing this as I enjoy a Ritz cracker and peanut butter sandwich, by the way my Mill favorite food. I consider myself the luckiest man alive, life is good. I know all those wonderful people that were at the Mill will also find their way and they will also be able to say "Life is good."

My granddaughter just came in and wants to borrow some money to buy a boat and motor so they can go fishing. I'm luckier than I thought.

Raymond (Chuck) Bishop
Bucksport

THE PAPER MACHINES ARE HAYING

I started working for the St. Regis Paper Mill in June of 1976. The first job that I had (like most of those who started in the mill) was working in the magazine room pulling pulp wood. During that time the number 5 paper machine was just getting ready to come on-line and there were openings in both the Super Calendars and the Paper Machines. About six months later, I received a job working in the Super Calendars Department where I worked for the next 14 years.

I worked with a great group of people who became like a second family. In that fourteen years, I built a home, got married, and started a family in the Bucksport area. The mill provided a good living for a lot of people. While working in the supers a lot of friendships were made. Camaraderie was spread throughout the mill. You would work all week together and then on your days off you, your co-workers and your families would often go hunting, fishing, canoeing and camping together.

When the paper machines were having a hard time getting paper on the reel that's what we called "the paper machines are haying" and when all the back log was caught up we would have a little competition like foot races, standing broad jumps, arm wrestling, etc. and the losers usually bought the coffee or soda.

Working on number seven winder, Mike (R.) Gray and I would compete often. Number 7 winder was the new winder that ran the paper from the number 5 paper machine. It would wind paper by about 7,000 feet or more per minute. It had air driven slitters that cut the paper to size. These slitters were like little jet turbines and the operators could press a button to get these slitters to speed up faster while you were threading the machine. They sounded just like a jet engine, they really whistled and it would drive you crazy. You'd have had to have been there to know the noise. Some operators did it more than others.

While I was working in the Supers, I started doing woodworking. Like my father, I started with little figurines, garden ornaments, like a farmer and cow and a lady bent over weeding her garden. I also carved my name into my lunch box lid. Soon many co-workers started asking me to carve various things into their lunch box tops. I carved everything from a frog for Dick Theriault, a roadrunner for Mike (R.) Gray, a snowmobile and a cabin for George Ames and various others. From there, I started carving signs.

Champion took over St. Regis while I was in the Supers. Things were never the same after that. Through the years, first we lost Sunday double time and a half. Then Sunday time and a half. Then we only got time and a half over 40 hours.

I took a job in the Power Plant when my oldest daughter started kindergarten where I worked alongside another great group of people, a few that I graduated from high school with. We often put together "feeds"– pot luck meals – in the department and went snowmobiling, fishing, and hunting outside the mill together.

While working in the Power Plant, we went to 12 hour shifts, working 4 days then 3 days off and I got a lot of woodworking done. I worked my way up from Utility Worker to Operator in the Fuels Area earning my 2nd Class High Pressure Boiler license. I continued with my woodworking hobby on the side, making furniture for my family and friends, blanket chests, window freezes, hutches, bedroom sets, entertainment centers, and gun cabinets.

While in the Power Plant, International Paper took over and things began to change even more. They didn't treat the workers and the mill with the same respect and the equipment and product soon took a turn for the worse.

14 years later I decided to take a job in the Stores Department where I stayed for 7 years working alongside another great group of people before I returned to the Power Plant. During that time, I started building kitchen cabinets and continued making custom woodworking projects for others including a dresser/changing table, a three-in-one crib, toddler bed, and full-size bed for my grandson. Verso Paper took over while I was in the Stores Department and started shutting paper machines down and from there curtailments began.

When Verso announced that they were closing the mill it was definitely a shock. It was sad to see it go. It had supported a lot of families from truck drivers and wood cutters to the papermakers. That's something you don't see as much of anymore. People who relied on the mill for a living were left wondering how they would move on. Myself, I was able to use my woodworking ability as a way to earn a living. My wife and I still reside in Bucksport in the community of Bucksmills where I have my woodworking shop.

We wish all of the workers who worked at the mill the very best.

***Raymond Charles Bishop** grew up in Bucksport with the Class of 1975. He values his childhood participation in the Bucksmills Busy Bees 4-H club and as an adult, the Snowmobile Club whose clubhouse across the road from his place he helped build. His chief interest, woodworking, began with a bathroom vanity he made from a wood-working course in high school. He and his wife, Leah, have raised two children in the house they built on family land on the banks of Stubbs Brook. His grandfather, Eddie Bishop, helped cut off land for the creation of Silver Lake and his Uncle Charlie went into the mill to work on the papermachines. His older sister, Susanne, worked in the Purchasing Dept. summers during* *school and full time for some 40 years, retiring before the mill closed. A storehouse of historic memories, one of Chuck's most vivid is "a photograph on an office wall of men working barefoot with their pants rolled up, it was so hot on the papermachines."*

First custom-made cover for ash lunch baskets designed, carved and painted to order in the mid-nineteen eighties by Chuck Bishop, Supercalendar Winder Operator of #2 or 3, after the one he carved with his own name. Owned by Dick Theriault who worked in the mill lab. Carved of pine, the frog stands for Dick's nickname, "Froggie" signifying his Franco heritage which, with the St. Regis logo, adorns the little shirt. In the background can be seen miniature features of Dick's lab desk, and in the forefront the conveyor carrying a processed roll just coming off the winder that Chuck had just built for Dick's inspection, headed for the roll wrapper. Chuck figures he made seven or eight personalized designs at the request of other mill men depicting their jobs, pets and hobbies. Photo courtesy of Chuck Bishop.

Greg Wilson
Bucksport

YOU CAN SLEEP WHEN YOU'RE DEAD, WORKING THE FARM AND THE MILL

I started working in the mill in July 1984 and of course it closed down and we all walked out Dec. 2014. I had 30 plus years working there with most of the time in the Train Shed (Finishing and Shipping Dept.) This is where the paper rolls are loaded into railcars and tractor trailers. Part of this dept. also handled the cores to wind paper onto. I also operated the roll wrapper machine, putting the final covering on the rolls before shipping.

My grandfather, Don Wardwell worked in the boiler room and retired after 35 years of service. My father, Wilbur Wilson retired out of ground wood after working there for 34 years. My great grandfather, Frank Wilson, worked sharpening saws during construction of the mill which was originally known as Seaboard.

My father passed away on May 30, 1999 unexpectedly at 56 years old. Up to that point my wife Leslie & I were raising our two children, Cody & Cassi, just across the field from the farm. We spent most of our summers camping. The four of us were in karate, all achieving our black belts over the course of several years plus many other school related activities like many other families. When dad needed help during haying we were there. On occasion he would need help with cows or equipment and I would always give him a hand.

When he passed away there were things that needed to be done, the hay was standing tall and almost ready to be mown, the cows needed to be taken care of and it just seemed like a natural progression. I had never mown hay before or baled; it was always dad's job. So off on the tractor I went, not knowing what I was doing. There were a few tears and a few prayers to dad to help me out.

I have to say the farming community has a great bunch of people. If it weren't for the offers of help and advice from my father's friends, it would have been a much bigger struggle. Whoopie Atwood, Dwight Sargent, Floyd Clement all offered their advice and the "call anytime." It was so greatly appreciated. But I have to say that I relied heavily on Doug Gross; everything from why was dad breeding with this bull or that cow to "are you mowing hay today and when should it go in." I will always be grateful for that shoulder to lean on when I had no idea what I was doing. But this is what farming is all about, Community & Family. I never knew it was going to be such a huge part of my life.

On our farm we have 25-35 head of Lowline Angus cattle, pigs (most of the time,) eggs and meat birds. Working a 12-hour rotating shift is hard on a person. Chores before work on the day shift was 3am and off to work at 4:15am, home at 5pm and back in the barn for night chores. After the night shift you come home tired and really just want to go to bed but no, it's chore time! Chores are done 14x a week no matter what.

Haying is a big part of farming. Vacation time is taken in order to get it done. Getting time off at Verso was frustrating. Dealing with the weather was frustrating; getting time off with good weather was always a hit or miss. Farming is a good life. Raising my kids on the farm was the best, they had so many life lessons; Hard work, responsibility, friendships, competition, compassion and even life and death.

We showed cows at a few fairs. We had cows, camper and kids and off we would go. Vacation time came into play here as well. This was always concerning because if the weather didn't cooperate on the planned vacation, we would have to adjust. Hopefully it left enough time off to do the fairs which were important as well. The sun, moon and stars need to line up with a little luck added in!

I really enjoy the farm. It's a lot of hard work and dedication. Unfortunately, there isn't enough income to make a living so working a full-time job is necessary. So actually you have two full-time jobs, off the farm and the farm. There isn't a lot of free time because something always needs to be done but as one of my farmer neighbors said, "You can sleep when you're dead!"

The mill was a great living. We made great paper up until the end. Be it known that we closed due to corporate greed. We were making a great product. Lack of common sense and poor managers created a lot of stress for the workers. The workforce and product were WORLD CLASS.

My wife & I consider ourselves lucky that the mills closed when it did. Our children are grown and on their own. Sports and sporting events cost money and following them around to their events could be expensive. Health insurance for them, things they needed and yes, things they wanted all cost money. It would have been a real struggle had they still been home. It sounds awful but we were lucky that our mill closed first, I believe most people that lost jobs are employed. If we had been one of those other mills I don't know that we would be so lucky to find jobs. Here's hoping those millworkers find employment.

A lot of people had told me that there is life after the paper mill and they were right. I found a job at Maine Maritime Academy in Castine a month after I lost my job. If I got a call tomorrow saying I could have my job back at the mill I would say no way, you can keep your job.

It was a good journey, a good job & a great bunch of people. But I'm happy and I've moved on.

Greg Wilson *was a member of the Bucksport High School Class of 1981.*

Editor's note:
Greg and Leslie Wilson's Beechwood Farm markets Registered Lowline Angus, beef and pork by the side and "call for hay availability" c/o www.mainelowlines.com and wilsonlowlines@aol.com.

Garret McAllian
Bucksport

A VERITABLE MUSEUM OF 20TH CENTURY INDUSTRIAL TECHNOLOGY

Growing up in a mill town like Bucksport and having many relatives who worked in the mill, there came a time in my childhood where I decided that I wanted to work in the mill when I grew up. My grandfather, Tommy Gross, worked there many years, while simultaneously operating the family farm in Bucksmills, a neighborhood about four miles out of town on Central Street. I have been fortunate enough to come into possession of the family farm, due in large part to the income provided by the mill. I still live here to this day and in 2019 the farm will have been in the family for 100 years!

I started working in the mill in 1987, after getting my associates degree in electronics from Eastern Maine Technical College in Bangor, but didn't get into the Electrical and Instrumentation Department for a couple of years. I spent a good part of that time throwing 4-foot-long pulp logs into a hole in the floor, to be ground into paper pulp on the lower level of the building. This was the hardest job I ever had, working shift work. We worked the "southern swing" shift which was 7 straight day shifts, 8 hours, from 7 a.m. to 3 p.m. This was followed by 2 days off and then starting 7 straight 3 p.m. to 11 p.m. Followed by 2 days off. Then came the midnight shifts, 7 straight 11 p.m. To 7 a.m. shifts. This part was most brutal. I always got sick toward the end of the graveyard shift. It was grueling, but the $11.00 an hour was better than the $5.00 an hour I had been making fixing microwave ovens at Brown's Appliance in Ellsworth.

I'll always remember my grandmother, Mary Gross, putting up my grandfather's "dinnah bucket," as she called it, for work, complete with 2 packs of Camel non-filter cigarettes – Grampa's brand. When I first got into the mill, people smoked everywhere, all the time. By the time the mill closed, smokers were restrickted to little homeless style shacks erected on the outskirts of the mill property or in dark corners tucked away out of sight.

Grampa's "dinnah bucket" was an icon of his generation, a small version of the iconic picnic basket everyone remembers. I watched the transition from these baskets to the plastic "igloo playmate" coolers so common today.

I eventually got into the Electrical and Instrumentation Department in 1989. Being an E & I tech gave me a unique perspective of the inner working of the mill machinery. Built in 1930, the mill was a veritable museum of 20th century industrial technology, and seeing, working, and understanding the evolution of this technology is something few people experience. I've often thought that the mill would be a great place to work if it wasn't for all the people. Being a gadget geek, I loved working on all the electrical and mechanical equipment. I like fixing things. Most of the irritation and aggravation about working at the mill was caused by interpersonal relations, be it management vs. workers, operations personnel and maintenance personnel, or mill workers and outside contractors. I now realize that this is true no matter where you are.

Over the years, I watched the rift between the management and the workers grow. The mill was a much friendlier place in my early years there. Bosses deserved and received respect and they reciprocated that respect. Near the end, the supervisors had become inhuman, unfeeling, malicious, corporate zombies. Governor LePage got it right when he called VERSO management "bottom feeders," and who would know better than him.

Garret McAllian *graduated with the Bucksport High School Class of 1983. Another generation of the Cole-Gross family that settled Bucksmills, an outback community named for the Buck family which ran a barrel stave on Stubbs Brook, he credits his job at the mill for being in a position to hold on to his family's ancestral ground, the Tom Gross place, built by Moses Buck. He has raised his family there where his children and grandchildren continue to keep and pass on the land. He and they enjoy "rock hounding" visiting quarries and mines, as well as fishing, paddling, and Katahdin climbing. In addition to being a great story teller, Garret is known as an avid amateur explorer, historian and geologist. He has transformed his experience as an electrician at the mill into establishing a new business,* BUCKSPORT ELECTRICAL SERVICE, Licensed and Insured Master Electrician.

Patricia Ranzoni
Bucksport

WHERE ONE MAINE USED TO BE COME SEE

Someday, a paper maker cried, all that used to be Maine
will be found only in museums. He wrote and raved
over the roar of the machines and other voices
and the factories went on closing and the festivalization
of Maine rolled on. Funds for preservation not severance.
For celebrations of the way some will never know
how it was. Monies for humanities but for humans
watch Hathaway Shirt convert. "Let's Talk About It"
programs in libraries here's the money let's talk about it
in quaint towns where Mainers die to museums
how Maine used to be how Maine used to be used
how Mainers are used if only they'd agree to pose
for those talks and tours how it used to be One big trail
of history come see how Maine used to be one trail
without tears you will ever hear no one there this is where
it was this is where the money is this big festival Maine
this big museum Maine instead of being us any more
this is how we used to be this big tour and up north
this treacherous bridge not a cent to make safe no near
shelter their blood on Maine's map come see where
in hidden forest plantations. . . these sweet brown men
      (*los hombres marrones dulces*
      tendran ellos un signo / will they have a sign
      un relicaro situado al borde de la carretera / a roadside shrine
      los angustiosos tienden / heartbroken ones tend
      catorce los alientos estallan / their fourteen breaths burst
      en Guatemalteco, Hondureno florece / into Guatemalan
                    and Honduran flowers
      en la nieve de pino / frozen forever in pine snow)
for our museum oh our highways widening not for them,
sacrificial trees chopped to make safer and faster your tours
to where Maine used to be watch Hathaway convert
and look in vain for those worn women making the best
shirts in the world – *history* – see Hathaway convert
and over there that poet who made that paper that made

that mill in 'round the clock 'round their life shifts pleads
for fifteen minutes managed care for his suffering wife
with the Franco name that earns her nothing
where she used to live with the snowsuit of papermachine felt
the way Maine used to be route that culture trail 'round here
save her house if not her give her a sign.

Translations by scholar and educator, Robert Robles, used gratefully with his permission.

Author note:

Written in honor of Rumford, Maine's **Jacqueline Thibodeau Fallon (1940 – 2012)** *and her devoted husband,* **Tom Fallon**, *retired paper mill worker and union man, distinguished writer and performer of prose, including plays, poetry, and what he has named "anti-poetry," and innovator of literary forms drawn from his experiences, the natural world, human struggles, the visual arts, and music, without limits. He is remembered as one of the founders of Maine Writers & Publishers Alliance, for being a life-long advocate for Maine voice, and for being both a working class and experimental poet, proudly confessing to "reading and writing on the job." Widely published in collections of Maine writing, and beyond, Tom is recognized as the only 20th century writer and publisher of Maine paper mill short stories based on experience. It was my privilege to appear with him at one of my first invitational public readings, for the* Live Poets Society *in Rockland, which I count as one of the most influential of my writing life, the way his unforgettable voice boomed from the Rumford paper machines he was writing from and about, giving me permission to write my own knowledge of my father's mill. I hadn't realized yet that industrial papermaking could be the stuff of poetry. It shocked, thrilled, and taught me. Tom Fallon is respected as a distinguished American author without whose work Maine literature would be incomplete. Publications in which his writing is included can be located on the internet and through Maine libraries and book stores.*

David Brainerd
Old Town

MILLS REMEMBERED

in solidarity

once american dreams
shimmered like white rayon
under clear lights
in the humid weave room
we slid loom to loom
with grease and adjustments
serving machines

shuttles go faster than vision
fast as thoughts in fixers' minds
we creeled and wove and doffed and packed
but the shuttles wavered and jumped their tracks

power and payroll cut
looms ripped from the floor
some other place
they weave
and dream
here it freezes and thaws in the empty hall
we wait for the mortar to crack
and the bricks to fall

Previously published in The Binnacle, *journal of the University of Maine, Machias.*

Author note:
"What a tragic and disturbing situation, the closing of the Bucksport mill, made especially sickening by the disposition of the machinery as scrap metal! 'This is the way the world ends, not with a bang but a whimper,' as Eliot said, and this is the way the economy ends, too, along with much of the structure of our society. Your project should, at least, provide a bang that will echo for many years, in the aftermath of this particular ending. My sympathy to you and all the folks in your area who will continue to

be affected by this closing. The situation has reminded me of that period, in the late 1970s and 1980s, I guess, when the textile mills in New England started to close, along with the shoe factories. Back then, the big companies were consolidating their operations in the Southern U.S., and pulling out of the North where our wage levels tended to be higher (though maybe not so much in Maine) and they had the additional cost of heating their facilities in the winter. Compared to what has happened to our economy since then, that regional shift seems almost benign. But, as I'm sure you remember very well, the local impact was devastating. Of course, it was just the beginning of the process that is continuing today on an international scale. In the mid-1979s, I worked for a while at the Machias Mill. It was owned by Milliken, and we produced rayon cloth then. I worked there less than a year, and, a few years later, when Milliken closed the place, though I was not directly affected, I wrote this poem. I keep thinking about the similar circumstances, so am sending it along as a sort of sympathy card and a token of solidarity."

David W. Brainerd *was born in 1952 in Massachusetts and grew up in a small town in the foothills of the Berkshires. "Married and divorced twice, I have four daughters and one son (including stepchildren), all from the first marriage, and nine grandchildren. The first time I ever went to Maine, in 1975, my first wife (Susan McNerney) and I put a one-dollar down payment on a house in Whitneyville. We bought the place for $4500, and it was while living there that I worked at the Machias Mill. I earned a B.A. from the University of Massachusetts and a MDiv. from Bangor Theological Seminary. I have learned a great deal in academia, and even more from my own reading and experiences. My work history is a tapestry of blue and white-collar jobs, and I have engaged in writing since childhood, getting my first poem published at the age of 14. My poetry, news articles, and essays have been printed in a variety of magazines and newspapers, and I have self-published two chapbooks of poetry. In recent years, my poetry has appeared in* Echoes *and the* Aurorean, *and, online, in Dana Wilde's* Parallel Uni-Verse. *I was a regular contributor to* Small Press Review *from 2011 until it ceased publication in 2015. Since making the dollar down payment in Whitneyville, I have lived in a few different places in Maine, and even, for about five years, in New Hampshire. From 2002 to 2016, I lived off the grid in Howland, but, a year ago, my daughter, Jessy, and I bought a two-family house on French Island in Old Town. From that vantage point, the aging poet and jack-of-all-trades works in his gardens and keeps an eye on the Penobscot River as it makes its way to the Atlantic." In the winter of 2014-15, Brainerd wrote: "With my Social Security, I have won the game of life in the USA, as far as I can tell. I'll probably continue to do odd jobs once in a while, but I shouldn't actually need to. I have long maintained that I have too much work to do to waste my time at a job, anyway. I continue to write regularly for* Small Press Review, *and to write poetry, though I must say the volume has been somewhat limited as of late. My Christmas card poems are brand new ones, though. It is a bit sobering to look at how the stacks in my woodshed have already shrunk. And the way we keep getting rain mixed in with the snow! Ice storms used to be a pretty rare occurrence, as I recall, but, these past few years, they've become quite frequent. But it can't be global warming, because, as I heard someone say, as long as the temperature in Rush Limbaugh's back yard is about the same as it was last year, that proves that global warming is a hoax! Oh, well, it's still a beautiful world. Even the ice is beautiful when it clings to the trees. Peace & Love."*

Paula Kee
Bucksport

LATE BLOOMER

Many of us came late to the mill town.
Business was still pretty good and the town was busy still on Main Street.
From away, this small town life felt warm and safe to me.
One from away can only imagine how it was to grow up here
When the mill was going full speed ahead.

The sense of security.
The sense of community.
The sense of forever it will be so.

The tide turned and things changed.
Merchants suffered as their customers sought the big bargains.

Then the suits took over.
The "demand" for our paper waned – so they said.
Did their corporate raiding policies steer us that way?
Too late to know.

But we know we are all left here in our town.
And we care still.
And we will make it.
And we will prevail.

Because we are this town
And these people
And we are good in our hearts.

*Born and raised in Richmond, Virginia, "with the gift of gab," **Paula Kee** moved to Bucksport in 1982 "after a checkered marital career which was continued by marriage to David Kee the following month. Success!" She has been a legal secretary, national sales representative, restaurant manager, retail* *salesperson, buyer and merchandizer, and "of late" an event planner and fundraiser. "I am a proud step-mom and grandmother of THE most fabulous kids, lover of gardens, theatre, music, animals and birds, and a happy reader of many books. And I am the grateful recipient of the friendship of many wonderful women." Also, an "enthusiastic resident of Bucksport with visions of future projects for the benefit of the town, 'fair to middlin' cook', and rabid liberal."*

Editor's note:
Of the award-winning *Wednesday On Main* (WOM) program, Paula Kee says it really was "an idea in my head before the mill closure at the end of 2014, but as soon as that was announced, I decided to try to put it together. The goal was to bring people downtown to not just enjoy our programming, but to linger, spend some money with our local merchants, enjoy the waterfront and get to know Bucksport. We needed then, and still do, new faces, ideas, families, young professionals, retirees – the full spectrum of what makes a community tick, to keep our town viable going forward. I think that's happening to some degree, and *WOM* is just one of the excellent summer events on tap now that keep putting Bucksport's name out there as an arts and culture destination. This is a tremendous turn for our town, and the logical place for us to go." *WOM* was the recipient of the 2016 Downeast Acadia Regional Tourism Award for Innovation and Creativity, "which was wonderful. Our first year was grant funded by the Maine Community Foundation, along with support from local banks and the Town."

Patricia Ranzoni
Bucksport

WELCOME!
WE'VE BEEN WAITING FOR YOU A LONG, LONG TIME

We've all followed the rich smells of evergreens and mudflats
north and south, east and west, to this province believing
how lucky, choosing it, of all the corners of the world, to settle,
visit, and touch stones. Felt drawn to this place and there have
been signs. The people have built bridges, after all. After canoes
and ferries. Horses, railroads, motor vehicles. Landing strips. Sails
all along. Councils and chambers. How could we not feel welcomed?

When we saw the bay and its valleys between mountain quarries
and formations, the River still surprised us rounding the bend
in its power and glory. We'd heard of its historied narrows, battles,
survivors rising above the sorrows of its waters right here.

*Oh, remember the taste of our pressed fruits and roast game,
our fish shelled or not,* we say as was said to us when ancestors
feasted on the shore and in the clearings, asking, *Is it true
what's said of the abundance here? The good people? The comfort
they take in their work and arts?* We feel what we lost in our mill
and found – inviting performers to make us smile, hum, tap,
and applaud again. Musicians to pipe the spirit of what abides.
Our sound, that we may still be known by our presence.

So that when, come June, under the same moon rising on us all,
a young man with dawn, Wabanaki, Orono, and Cold Stream
in him follows his way home, bringing Cree and Nashville,
and raises flutes carved by masters, maybe birch, maybe cedar
sometimes two at once – we on the riverbank notice how
the moon's phases might be fingered holes for playing Creation's
breath flowing over us in celestial vespers. How the last quarter,
like tonight, and the first, later in the month, are harmonic notes
under crescent finger-stops. Watch how the new moon and

the full, their next times around, look capable of wholeheartedly
open tones, blown through, full of the ancient strains of this
place on earth, sighed for more than ever.

Thank you for coming! We're glad you're here!
We've been waiting for you a long, long time.

Previously published in the electronic journal, *e*lix*ir.*

Author note:
The composition and introductory reading of this poem was inspired by the appearance of award-win-
ning Native American Flute player, Gareth Laffely, at the June 10, 2015 "Wednesday on Main" series.
From Gallatin, Tennessee, young Laffely is of Mi'kmaq/Cree descent with generational ties to Maine.
The greeting of honor was intended for him, for Penobscot Nation guests, and for all in attendance.

Paul Averill Liebow

Bucksport and Great Cranberry Island

OUR ONCE AND FUTURE RIVER

In olden days the Penobscot was a waking dream
of coral reef abundance and diversity.
Vast spring migrations of riverine life mirrored
the plaintive honkings of ducks and Canada Geese overhead.

Salmon magically returning from Greenland and Icelandic seas
spawned in silence and privacy all the way up
from the Narramissic River, Marsh Stream,
and Sunkhaze Meadows to shady groves near Canada.

Uncountable alewives surged silver in full flower moonlight,
while a billion tiny elvers set out to find their way
home from the sinking vortex of the Sargosso Sea
where their parents had set their eggs adrift.

Huge stripers cavorted well up beyond Bangor,
two million shad played in the bright waters of May,
and pink petals of shadblow floated on the wind –
spring plum blossoms from ancient Chinese poetry.

Prehistoric ten–foot sturgeon cruised the depths
of the lower channel on red October days,
so powerful that Winterport sports had themselves
towed around like whalers on a "Nantucket sleigh ride".

Then for several neglectful generations, the river choked
and steamed brown – a stinking cadaver of industrial shame.
Mercury and chemicals, dams and the politics of greed
killed so many noble creatures from The Maker's Dominion.

A Log Pond smirked down by the mill in Bucksport
where people snickered and winked or sighed
about what was permitted to seep or be thrown in –
but never dared let their kids swim in the water.

(continues)

I vividly remember the Great Green Bridge to Verona
from my childhood on the way Downeast to Gramp's
but too few would look beneath its swirling tides or into
the secrets of its hidden heart, deep in the Great North Woods.

Now all our dignity and hard work have been sold overseas,
the grumbly old mill, that gave our town its life,
is a huge pile of scrap metal and weeping cement,
and we struggle once more to find our future in the river.

But the river does smile up again, at a new Great Gray Bridge,
whose Maine granite sings in the eternal flames of JFK,
sways with the lines of the Washington Monument –
and sleeps in winter–camp with our soldiers in Fort Knox.

Its towers look back down to Mosquito Mountain and Waldo,
out on Katahdin's shimmering cerulean blue northers,
the Sun's golden lily pad cupping the islands of the bay,
the fish and their river returning home to the Penobscot People,

the People of the Dawn, because so many care.

Published in an earlier version in *Narramissic Notebook #10*, 2009.

For more than forty years, **Paul Averill Liebow** *and his family have lived on the Penobscot just upriver from the Bucksport paper mill where the original property deed included "salmon weir rights on the Penobscot." He is the son of Averill Abraham Liebow, who escaped the Nazis "with just the shirt on his back" and returned to Germany on behalf of the U.S. Army forty years later with the protocol rank of 2nd Star General to inspect U.S. hospitals. As a ranking member and youngest member of the Atomic Bomb Casualty Commission he wrote* Encounter with Disaster *about the medical effects of the atomic bomb on Hiroshima and Nagasaki. His mother, Carolyn Booth Gott, from Southwest Harbor, Maine, served as a Captain in the U.S. Army Nurse Corps in the South Pacific during World War II where they met. Paul, who at age two was called "Little Doctor Liebow," is a board-certified ER "doc" with a lifelong dedication to emergency medicine and environmental issues. A prolific writer of Op Eds and Letters to the Editor, studies position papers, and contributor of medical protocols and guidelines, many of which have been widely adopted, he was moved in midlife to begin expressing his knowledge and vision in the form of poetry. This accelerated "after I had to retire from medicine following a very successful heart transplant on President Obama's first election eve." Paul graduated in 1964 from Amity Regional High School in Woodbridge, Connecticut with highest scholastic and athletic honors. He received his B.S. in biology from Yale University in 1968, "where I played rugby next to two guys named Bush", and his M.D. From the University of California at San Diego Medical School in 1972 followed by residency years at Roger Williams and Peter Bent Brigham hospitals. Paul served as an*

Emergency Room doctor at Eastern Maine Medical Center in Bangor for 30 years, advising and serving on the boards of many local and state groups, for which he has received numerous medical and civic awards. He was appointed a citizen member to the bi-partisan Commission to Rewrite the Maine State Disaster Protocols after 911 which were unanimously approved by the Legislature, and as an Ambassador to the exemplary Penobscot River Restoration Project. A founding member of State Taxpayers Opposed to Pollution (STOP) which evolved into the Coalition for Sensible Energy, he remains active in ongoing efforts to preserve and improve the Great Pond Mountain Trust lands, including the addition of 4200 acres of undeveloped land between Bucksport and Ellsworth to their holdings where he has advocated for children's gardens in the wildlands based on Richard Louv's Last Child in the Woods: Saving Our Children From Nature-Deficit Disorder *(Workman Publishing, 2005). Paul was recognized as an "outstanding communicator on environmental issues" in a documentary photo feature in the National Wildlife Federation Annual Report of 2003, and was Maine Representative to the Federation for two years on behalf of the Natural Resources Council of Maine. "My interests continue to include photography as well as trying to show people the hidden paths through our medical 'care' system." Paul's poems have been published in and beyond Maine including the Maine Poets Society's 2005 anthology,* Coming Home Twice. *Several of his works can be found on internet web-sites. "Having missed the usual chapbook ['cheapbook' paperback] train to publishing, I envision a hardback first and soon, working with a superbly qualified poet, editor and adjunct professor at* WriteByNight *and quietly in the background with several nationally known Maine poets and writers. The title may be* Red Rock Cranberry Dreaming *or possibly* Some Canticles from Licbowicz."

Author note:
Many Mainers call me "doc" and always have – cops, Emergency Medical Services, fire fighters, kids I grew up with on Cranberry, and often I've helped them through the mysterious medical system – one of the things I'm most proud of. To me it connotes way more respect than "doctor" because it means I'm available and listen. It once took me under a minute to diagnose a neighbor who was still a mystery after x-rays, a CT scan and gall bladder studies – literally! And he is still better!

Hans Krichels
Bucksport

PAPERMAKING REFLECTIONS

My father was a papermaker down in Massachusetts, where I grew up.
A chemical engineer from Germany, he made specialty papers – hundred
percent rag content. He even made stationery for the Pope at one point
with Keys to the Kingdom for a watermark. He told us, his children,
about the first papermakers, the wasps, and the Chinese after that. I
remember Sunday morning romps at his mill, the great, airy rag loft
where I and my sister and brothers thrashed about in mountains of
cotton remnants, rags just waiting their turn in the beaters below.
Later in the day, the family would walk along the river, waters red
from dyes and chemicals at the mill, father so proud of his children,
the papers he was making, the river, HIS river, so red at our feet.
That was back in 1952.

In 1971, I came to Bucksport with my own little family. (Those so
inclined viewed that as a return to the papermaking culture of my
childhood.) We built a home, raised our children, Nubian dairy goats,
chickens for eggs, organic vegetables. Often we'd sit on the hilltop at
Fort Knox and watch the shift change at the mill across the river –
files of workers, each carrying his wicker lunch basket covered with a
checkered cloth. On those same streets, robed priests from the Oblate
Seminary strolled, breviaries in hand. And dark-skinned sailors from
tankers at anchor explored the various shops and after-dark
establishments of our town.

The town was a culture unto itself, proud, self-sufficient, poised on
the banks of the mighty Penobscot River – sacred water, sacred grounds
to cultures before our own. Millions of tourists passed over nearby
bridges, heading for quainter surroundings with shoppes, sidewalk
cafes, and colorful boutiques. Our town had history, character,
magnificent vistas – but none of it was for sale.

Except now, our paper mill has shut down, become a thing of the past.
And we find ourselves emerging from the shadows, shaken a bit, charting
a new course for our future. Perhaps our original papermakers, the wasps,
offer us our best guide: chew slowly, blend thoroughly, construct meticulously
according to the finest schematics and wisdom of those who came before.

Hans Anthony Krichels *left the academic world and came to Bucksport in 1971. "In the years that followed, I and my young family built our home, raised goats and organic vegetables, worked in various writing and teaching capacities, sat on the board of the remarkable New Alderbrook School and became deeply involved in Bucksport's self-evaluation of its public school system. Years rolled by. I continued writing and worked with troubled teenagers at a residential treatment center in Ellsworth, coordinating community service programs and developing a Forestry program in collaboration with the Great Pond Mountain Conservation Trust in Orland. More recently, six years ago, I purchased a small home on Elm Street in Bucksport, where I live happily with Nancy, recently retired from the Center Street School in Orrington." Hans has been involved in bringing the Schoodic Sculpture to our waterfront and is currently active on the Comprehensive Planning Committee. "I have deep respect for Bucksport's history and high hopes for its future."*

Editor's note: Hans donated heirloom rag papers – including Early's Famous Authors watermarked series, made in the 1950s by his father, Engelbert Krichels's Hurlbut Paper mill in So. Lee, Massachusetts – to the STILL MILL preview exhibit and archive.

Lisa Miller Joy
Bowdoin

MILLER'S GIRL

All told in naming
Generations of Millers
Grandfather in coating
Old timer remembers
Daddy working winders
Sweat beads on brow
Mumma home making
Twenty years gone now
Home in mill town
Entered life schools
Young woman of men
Milked off paper spools
All grown from seed
Vocation planted
Engrained by spirit
Conscious relented
Trade of learning
Hard work desired
Groundwood pulp
Along paper wires
Recession played
Fresh tune of heart
Off rolled mill town
Brand new start
Traveling on through
Finished for press
Passages of living
Always lead back

Author note:
"It is wonderful that the *Still Mill* anthology will memorialize the heritage of the mill. Standing tall in Bucksport, the mill was a thread in the fabric of our lives. It wove through generation after generation who made a living and raised families while working paper machines and winders – my grandfathers,

father, uncles, and cousins. And here, my career began with an education bought and paid for by a currency of groundwood pulp, on hands and sweat beads, on brow, coursing through and changing me forever. So yes, it is here, in this mill town, where I will always be 'Miller's Girl'– a proud papermaker's daughter."

LISA MILLER JOY *was born in Massachusetts but grew up in Bucksport, Maine, graduating with the Class of 1987. Receiving several Pulp and Paper Foundation scholarships, Lisa earned her Chemical Engineering degree at the University of Maine. While studying the papermaking process, Lisa was fortunate to gain valuable experience at the Bucksport paper mill as a Groundwood Pulp Tester and then as a Co-op Engineer. When the recession hit, Lisa reluctantly moved away from the paper industry but stayed in Maine to begin her career as an Environmental Engineer for the Department of Defense. Now serving over a decade as an Environmental Director, Lisa has been honored with two Navy Meritorious Civilian Service Awards and has been a part of stellar environmental programs recognized with numerous awards and accolades.*

Ryan Pickoski
Bucksport

FROM GRANDMOTHER'S ATTIC, SIGNS OF OUR 4-GENERATION MILL FAMILY

"I would wake up with my hands curled into the shape of my pick pole!"

While cleaning out my grandmother's attic I came across my great grandfather's 25-year service award from St. Regis. The date on the award was from 1955, which means he started at the mill in 1930. His name was Aaron LaBree. He had a son and a daughter. His son Aaron Labree Jr. worked in the mill as well as an electrician until his retirement. He has since passed away. His daughter (my grandmother) Mary Ward worked as a secretary in the mill for a number of years. She too has passed away. Mary's husband (my grandfather) Les Ward worked in the mill on the re-winders until his retirement. He too has passed away.

On the other side of my family, my grandfather, George Pickoski, was a foreman on number 4 paper machine until his retirement. He was hired from a papermill in Canada to come and help start up number 4 paper machine. He moved his entire family from Canada to the US and remained Canadian citizens here in the US on permanent visas. He has also passed away.

Two of George's four children also worked in the mill. His son, David Pickoski (my father), worked there for 20 plus years until taking a buy-out. George's other son, Mark Pickoski (my uncle), worked there in the coating plant 20 plus years until medical issues forced an early retirement.

I started working there in April of 1999 as a fourth-generation mill worker. I worked in the pulp mill up until the last day the mill was open. Just about 15 years. This is a brief history of my family in that mill. I will try to expand on this with some of my memories from my time there.

As I sit back and reflect on my 15 years at the Bucksport Paper Mill, I realize how fast the time really does go. I remember my first day and last day like they both were yesterday. My very first day in April of '99, when I heard that I was going to work in the Magazine Room, I honestly thought that it must have something to do with putting the finishing touches on magazine type paper! Come to find out, I was way off. I will never forget the smell of the Magazine Room, the thousands of chords of spruce pulp wood mixed with hot steam coming from the magazine vents. There were 24 magazines and was I shocked to see those guys were loading all of them by hand with a pick pole and because I was a small guy I never thought I would be able to do it. Somehow I managed to survive and although the work was very physically demanding, I came to enjoy loading magazines. I remember after working a long stretch of shifts, I would wake up with my hands curled into the shape of my pick pole!

I ended up spending all 15 of my years in the pulp mill, with 13 of them right in the magazine room, despite having numerous opportunities to leave. There are moments during my time there that I will never forget and are ingrained in my memory forever. The hot sweaty summer shifts that would lead to water fights, listening to the Red Sox come back from a 3-0 deficit in a dark corner of the magazine room on cheap FM radio, hearing about the Columbine shooting on that same radio, the 24-hour shifts were you felt like you could sleep standing up, the work ethic of my co-workers that inspired me to want to do better, laughing so hard I cried on more than one occasion, sharing in the joy of co-workers welcoming new babies and the grief of losing loved ones, taking my breaks out on the roof so as to enjoy the cool fall nights, the click clack of the chain bringing wood over from drum de-barking, the team work that was used to accomplish any task, accidentally spray painting a co-worker, too many pranks to even mention, co-workers who left this life far too early, but most of all I remember being part of a team that put out some of the best damn paper products for over 80 years.

From the age of 21 til I was 36 I worked in the Bucksport Paper Mill and often times I spent more time with my co-workers than I did with my family. Some of those friendships will last a lifetime and some of those friends have become my family. The Bucksport Mill was more than just a place to work, it was a community and a family, with a long-standing tradition of hard work, integrity and an ability to produce the highest quality paper in the industry!

Ryan Pickowski lives in the vintage mill housing development in Bucksport known as the Town Site. He was born in Germany in 1977, and grew up in Bucksport, graduating with the Class of 1995. He has been a student and chaperone of the Bucksport High School Outing Club since 1992 and still leads students on trips across the country. He spent three years in the Air Force where he was stationed in Phoenix, Arizona. "In addition to my work at the mill, I have enjoyed playing ALL sports and am in basketball, softball, flag football, volleyball, dodge ball and kick ball leagues. I love to hike and have hit almost all the National Parks in the U.S. And I am an avid reader and read ALL the time." Ryan is a licensed Maine skull and skeleton mount taxidermist. His company is called "Bare Bones." "I take care of all of the University of Maine's skull and skeleton collection." Ryan is a recent graduate of Eastern Maine Community College with a 4.0 in Fire Science Technology, and where he was named Student of the Year.

While some mill workers carried traditional ash and tin lunch and dinner baskets, pails, and buckets until the end, Chuck Bishop was among those who adopted modern backpacks for food and personal items.

OVER

I was hired in 1983 when we were still St. Regis. As the saying goes, "I started at the bottom" delivering and sorting the mail, moving to switchboard operator, payroll, shipping and receiving, maintenance secretary and then to Human Resources (HR) where I started as an Administrative Benefit Specialist, then HR Generalist.

I have so many memories. During all my time I have to admit that I have always helped people in one way or another, from transferring calls to helping people with their pay to working with benefits. The other most important memory are the friends that you make and the stories and experiences that you have with them. I have heard the saying that your high school friends are your friends at the time but your college friends are for a life time. Well my experiences and friendships that I have had at the Bucksport mill are REALLY your friends for life as they become your "other" family.

Some of my most memorable times at the mill were when we had the opportunity to develop our own health care program. This was a time where one member from each of the unions along with 2 salaried people worked together to develop a medical plan for all the Bucksport Mill employees. I started as an hourly Office and Professional Employees International Union (OPEIU) representative and worked very closely with the other 4 locals – United Steel Workers (USW) 1188 and 261, International Brotherhood of Electrical Workers (IBEW), and International Association of Machinists (IAM). I can't say that this was an easy job but it was very rewarding as we were the ones that made the choices of how our plan was to work. When issues arose, we were the ones that made the decision as to how it needed to be handled within our plan restrictions. Working with the different unions during this period of time is when I feel that I gained much respect from the different unions as well as from many employees. A trust developed which stayed even after I became a salaried employee, which doesn't always happen.

Once the move to becoming a salaried employee, I continued to work with benefits of all aspects (short and long-term disability, workers' compensation, and health benefits (medical, dental, Employee Assistance Program). As the mill started downsizing I remained as the person that people could come to for assistance in helping with their medical bills, starting disability for an illness or just talking through problems that they needed to vent to. My door was "always open".

Once it was announced that the mill was going to close, it had to be one of the most difficult times of my life as well as every employee's life. However I still had to stay strong due to the fact that everyone came to my office as to what were their benefits going to be like, how they were going to get insurance, how they could get their retirement (every aspect of benefits). At times, I know that they knew it deep down, but really didn't always realize that I was losing my job too. As stressful, difficult, emotional as this time was, I still felt the need and desire to help my fellow employees/friends.

December 17, 2014 will always be a day that I will never forget. Everyone saw how the community responded to the mill closing that day, but on the inside, earlier in the day, it was my responsibility to meet with the employees as all hourly employees were scheduled in group-type meetings to get the necessity of information completed. Having groups of 50-60 people in every meeting, I explained how their benefits and pay would be distributed through the end of the year and answered their questions.

After all the hourly employees left and machines had been shut down it was then that the rest of the mill shut-down really began. With just a minimum crew of people all aspects of the mill was shut down, boxed up and shipped out. During this time, I continued to meet with the salaried people now doing the exact same thing as I did with the hourly until it was my turn.

During this point in time, all files needed to be packed, coded, numbered, and organized. Most of my time was only packing and organizing the HR files due to all the severances and union issues that were still on my plate.

However, May 15, 2015 was my actual last working day. At this point I was the last salaried Bucksport employee as anyone else still there was considered a corporate employee. As I said goodbye to fellow Verso employees at other locations, I decided that it wasn't over until "the fat lady sang" (as the saying goes) and I guess she might have been singing that day because it is over.

Over the past year since the mill closed, I still continue to help past employees and their spouses answering questions and assisting them if necessary. It is very seldom that more than a few weeks go by without the phone ringing or running into someone that still has some sort of question or just wants to talk about either what they are doing or wanting to know what I'm doing. Even though my job at the mill no longer exists, my job as "mama bear" continues as I still have all my cubs to help as they grow past the mill. I was extremely lucky to have all the opportunities to grow during my time at the mill and not only did you make many friends but they become your family. As I hear people's stories I am very pleased to know that from going back to school, getting another job or just retiring, most of the Bucksport employees are thriving and moving forward. As the saying goes, we are Bucksport Strong and how people have been able to keep their memories (good and bad) but at the same time being a different chapter in their lives, is a success story.

Ann Calderwood Remick lived in Thomaston, Maine until the 4th grade and then moved to Union. She attended Medomak Valley High School in Waldoboro, then went on to the University of Maine at Machias where she received an Associate Degree in Secretarial Science. "My parents grew up and attended school in the Union and Appleton area. My mother is still living in Union and my Dad, who sold cars for over 35 years, died in 2007. I have one brother Randy. Once our family moved to Union, we lived across the street from our grandparents where my Grandmother taught me how to cook and sew and my Grandfather taught me the love for card games and music. Over the years I have always enjoyed sports. I have also enjoyed music from my Mom and Grand-father. As a child my Mom, brother and I played at American Legion Hall dances with Mom on the piano, Randy on the drums and I on the clarinet or saxophone. I continue to play the sax today in church usually during holidays and special occasions. I met Pete at the University of Maine at Machias and we were married shortly after he graduated. We resided in Bucksport during our first six years and then moved to Orland where Pete started his pastorate with area United Methodist Churches which he continues to serve. I started working in Bangor for the first year of our marriage then was fortunate enough to start my career at the mill in 1983." The Remicks have one child, Christopher, who lives in Bucksport and is married with a son of his own. Pete's dad, Ralph, worked at the mill in the Supercalendar Department for many years as did his grandfather and several other relatives also work for the mill. Currently, in addition to working full time at the University of Maine System in the HR / Benefits area, Ann serves as Chair Person of the Board of Directors at the Bucksport Regional Health Center.

Patricia Ranzoni
Bucksport

FAREWELL FORCE ~ An Unapologetically Sentimental Tribute

Alas, we'll all be okay.
– Marie Duplessis, Administrative Assistant, 26 years, Bucksport Paper Mill

Our eyes are blurred with slush this season that shall not come again.
December fourth, they say, will be the day Verso goes quiet and
the papermakers go home from this *once upon a history*. Our history.
The labor force they've been, our men and women, will gather their
dinner pails, baskets and coolers for the last time as a shift of personnel
devoted to creating something of consequence together, head out the gate
and cross to the lots for their bikes, pickups, and rides. A work force
capable of skills only certain people on earth will have known how to do.
Their jobs -- turning tons of trees into tons of world class paper and
their families' livings. Traffic up and down the River Road will stop
in salute as for troops, knowing what is passing. *Farewell, workers
of wonder through the years, meaning no disrespect calling you dears,
rather, all the more.*

Farewell, dear materials coordinators, mill controllers and mill managers.
Off machine coater operators and helpers. And you, fuels area operators.
Oh, and numbers 1, 2, 4 and 5 paper machine tenders, clothing specialists,
machine tenders, third hands, stock prep operators and coordinators,
fourth hands, operating spares, production spares and coordinators,
water technicians and printers. *The sounds of your jobs are poetry to us.*

Dear line coordinators, winder operators and helpers, spare wood
processors, coaters, groundwood and steam spares. Dear general mill
services including laborers and temps, fieldsmen and operators 1st, 2nd,
3rd and 4th class and journeymen. *Fare well, all, on your journeys!*

Farewell, dear accounting specialists, fiber administrators, specialists
and managers, air conditioning technicians, area managers, operators,
coordinators and supervisors. Dear maintenance planners, boiler tenders,
broke operators, business analysts, managers and buyers. Lab technicians
and coating operators. Farewell, communications managers, cost analysts,
document controllers, drive technicians, dry end line testers. And dear
administrative assistants, environmental performance managers, fuels

fieldmen and finishing operators. Dear general mill service providers and supervisors, and grinder operators. Farewell, dear human resources staffs. Dear inspectors, system specialists, kraft operators, payloader families, maintenance clerks, power and pulp planners. *Our relations, classmates and neighbors, towns around.*

Farewell, dear process and project engineers and interns. Maintenance, power, paper, pulp and utilities process managers. Dear production control coordinators, purchasing leaders, quality control coordinators and reliability managers. *Thank you for all you've made and made possible here.*

Farewell, raw materials and utilities coordinators, roll grinder operators and journeymen. Dear roll tracking technicians and safety performance managers. Supercalender 5, 6, 7 and 8 operators, schedulers and coordinators. Dear screen deck operators and journeymen, senior magazine loaders and operators. Shipping clerks, environmental engineers, stock prep additive mixers, supervisors and proportioners. *You are awesome to us.*

Farewell storekeepers and stores coordinators and supervisors. And summer helpers. Woodyards team leaders, process engineering technical leaders, thermal mechanical pulp operators and tour electrical and instrumentation technicians and journeymen. Farewell, traffic clerks and woodroom operators and helpers, and winder and salvage operators. Dear wood processing loader and log processing families, cutters, haulers, product storage operators and families, and waste water treatment lab operators and specialists. *We are listening for your stories and promise to save your lives.*

(Farewell blessings, dear unions, for looking out for them, us, through the years. *Soon the roar of the machines will no longer drown out your songs.*)

While they have you cleaning and mothballing, keep this in your hearts -- *we refuse farewell to the respect and admiration we hold for your strength as a one of a kind force*, already legend. Ask Danny Wentworth and the generations of those who grew up here now conducting a celebration of honor across the internet of this changed, changing world, wishing only to hear the 4 o'clock whistle governing lifetimes here one last time. Tell the way we mill families and towns were, dears. We know we shall not see the likes of your brother-and-sisterhood again but are all the richer because we did, bidding you *happily ever after.*

Author note:

"Farewell Force" owes its realization to Marie Duplessis who returned calls to the mill during a time when others did not. Thanks to her, the poem documents the work force responsible for the last paper made at the Bucksport mill. It should be noted that jobs and their titles changed and/or disappeared through the years and that there will be those who worked there back along whose jobs do not show up in the last personnel list. Further, employees of the steam plant that kept operating after the mill closed may not be included. After going out with a call for submissions over George Van Deventer's Maine-based network of writers, artists and musicians, this poem was invited for publication by the Episcopal Diocese of Maine as part of their fund drive to benefit the former Bucksport mill workers. "A few weeks ago the Episcopal Diocese of Maine launched its 2014-2015 Advent Campaign to support former employees of the Verso mill by opening an online donation portal that gives donors the option of giving to the Washington Hancock Community Agency's Bucksport Mill Crisis Fund, Waldo Community Action Program, Penquis Community Action Program, or to the Good Shepherd Food Bank to benefit any one of the five food pantries in the region (Bucksport, Searsport, Ellsworth, Blue Hill and Orland). This week Bishop Stephen Lane is sending out another request to each Vestry at our 60 congregations across Maine. I was wondering if we might include a copy of your poem - with attribution, of course - in with our request and as a link from our online donation page (episcopalmaine.org). I found it really moving as I read the names of each position an employee might hold. Somehow that humanizes the work and the impact of real people in a way that saying "579 employees" just can't do. Poetry is powerful that way. So far, we've raised more than $13,500. to be distributed among the agencies. We believe the agencies we've identified are better poised to assist the former employees. The Diocese is covering all transaction fees so that 100% of each donation will go to the agency a donor designates." (Heidi Shott, Canon for Communications and Advocacy, Episcopal Diocese of Maine). With permission, the Diocese sent copies of "Farewell Force" to members of their Maine congregations and posted it on their web site. Upon last report, they were up to $17,000. in donations for the four organizations. A signed, framed presentation copy was given Marie at the passing of the mill's last shift on December 17, 2014. Another was given on behalf of the Bucksport papermaking family to playwright Monica Wood between acts of her play "Papermaker" at its premier by the Portland Stage Company in May, 2015. She reported that she read the poem aloud to the cast following their performance. This news is celebrated in the poem, "Papermakers, Please Stand."

REST IN PEACE, PAPERMAKING

Buycsport entering post-paper era

Mill machines to go idle today

<u>The Bucksport Enterprise</u>   **<u>December 4, 2014</u>**

The making of quality paper has a very long, very proud history in this town and in this area, home to so many talented folks who've devoted most of their working lives–and, often, their entire careers–to one thing: turning wood into paper.

We don't know if we're talking about billions or even trillions or even more pages of the stuff, all we know is that this is one sad day for anyone who's made paper here and those who've known and loved them.

We'll not join the chorus of harsh comments and even curses that go with the end of such an industrial era in the very heart of our community. We'd prefer to celebrate the many people in the many crafts that, day after day, hoisted their lunch baskets and went off to do what they knew how to do so well.

Morning, noon and night the mammoth papermaking machines functioned, and when one of them didn't, the chances were better than good that someone instantly was on hand to make the behemoth come alive once again. From those who designed whatever it took to keep the original machine that dated from 1931 functioning to the small "R & D" contingent that tried to find new uses for such a commonplace product, we salute you.

To those who labored in the background, doing the personnel and myriad other paperwork chores, to the mill nurses and the long-since retired telephone operators, the warehouse people, and to those mill managers who through the decades truly cared and knew that only dedicated workers could produce the largest amount of quality paper, we salute you all.

For the moment, we'll stay away from the financial machinations of some of the mill owners, past and present, those who sought profits without knowing much, if anything, about what it takes to produce a ton of usable paper that meets the customers' specs. The folks at far-away Apollo Management and those at the top of the Tennessee headquarters of Verso, the firm spawned by Apollo, will have to decide for themselves what's best for them.

But, as for our neighbors, who soon will be passing the security shack at the entrance to the mill for the final time, we say, "Hold your heads high! You've met the needs of your families, and you've done your jobs well and with dignity. Nobody can ask for more."

As for Bucksport, we–like those who toiled in the mill–will survive and, in time, we will prosper (at least by Maine standards!). We–and you–should believe in the Bucksport area, for those who live and work here know what truly matters. In the days and weeks ahead, we can collectively figure out where our community wants to go from here.

– Don Houghton, Editor

Patricia Ranzoni
Bucksport

PAPERMAKERS, PLEASE STAND

after the play, "Papermaker" by Monica Wood premiered by Portland Stage Co., May 22, 2015

Papermakers, please stand.
The playwright wants you to take a bow.
She has put your story on the stage.
From all over we've come to see.

The playwright invites you to take a bow.
Trembling, being papermaking families
from all over come to see,
we shudder to the shocking roar.

Trembling, being papermaking families,
alert to the ear-hurting sound effects,
we shudder to the shocking roar
she took the actors to her town's mill to hear.

Alert to the ear-hurting sound effects –
recorded papermachines with the deafening reel
she took the actors to her town's mill to hear real
you know what it is and how it makes you feel.

Recorded papermachines with their deafening reel –
no wonder the audience wants you to stand.
You know what it is and how it makes you feel –
the fear, pride, strikes, jokes, pain.

No wonder the audience wants you to stand
being the last of our kind. Beribboned,
(knowing the fear, pride, strikes, jokes, pain)
I gave her our "Farewell Force" in your names.

Being the last of our kind, beribboned,

she called it "beautiful ode to the Bucksport mill"
(our "Farewell Force" poem written in your names)
and read it to the cast after the show.

"Beautiful," she wrote, "all extremely moved."
"Stunning, the incantatory nature of all those jobs..."
(she read aloud to the cast after the show).
So, Papermakers, won't you please stand?
She has put your story on the stage.

Previously published on Dana Wilde's electronic journal *Parallel Uni-Verse, poetry from Maine, and worlds elsewhere.*

Author note: This poem presented itself as a local and modern variation of an old Malaysian *pantoum* form, relying as it does on a particular pattern of repetition in which the second and fourth lines of each stanza serve as the first and third lines of the next, and with the first line being repeated near the end.

Shawn Mercer
Orland

THE CALLING

to your best self

(Up beat reggae)

```
 F                      Dm
I open up my heart to the feeling
      F              Dm
Of a world that's falling apart
 F                    Dm
I cry for my part in all the killing
       F                       Dm
But I'm helpless not knowing where to start
      F                     Dm
I'm helpless not knowing where to start


Dm
My friend, my friend she told me how
       F            C
They tried to block her way
Dm
She broke down all the barriers
       F          C
They put up in her way
Dm
She knows they'll keep crossing over
        F          C
What path may lie ahead
Dm
But she'll keep on a lovin'
        F                 C
All the more than they can hate, and she cries
F    C     Dm
Oh,   oh,     oh (repeat 4x)


Dm
My friend, my friend I told her how
 F              C
I walked the easy way
```

403

```
    Dm
By privilege and promised land
 F           C
I am now here today
     Dm
The trouble and the trying times
    F           C
In truth I'd have to say
     Dm
Are only things with my own hands

F           C
I laid in my own way, and I cry

F    C     Dm
Oh,  oh,    oh (repeat 4x)

       ^F                    ^Dm
I've got blood in my hands and it changes
      ^F                    ^Dm
My perception of my place in the matrix
       ^F              ^Dm
My complicity in all that is wasted
  ^F                      ^Dm
I'm waking up to answer the calling
     F           C
It's happening, it's happening
Dm
No more time for questioning
     F           C
It's happening, it's happening
    Dm
Do what your love is demanding
     F           C
It's happening, it's happening
Dm
Consciousness awakening
     F           C
It's happening, it's happening
Dm
Answer your own calling, and you'll cry
F    C     Dm
Oh,  oh,    oh (repeat 4x)
```

```
       Dm
So we hold the pain together now

    F         C
For all the poison rain
    Dm
For all the brothers crying out
    F         C
And sister's silent pain
    Dm
As all the tears come pouring down
 F            C
Behind the pain there lies
  Dm
A love for all creation
        F          C
That's the truth behind the lies

F    C    Dm
Oh,  oh,   oh (repeat 4x)

    F                    Dm
We open up our hearts to the feeling
    F              Dm
Of a world that's falling apart
    F                  Dm
We cry for our part in all the killing
        F                  Dm
But we're moving now following our hearts
      F                  Dm
We're moving now following our hearts
      F                  Dm
We're answering the calling of our hearts
      F                  Dm
We're answering the calling of our hearts, and we cry
F    C    Dm
Oh,  oh,   oh (repeat 4x)
```

*Like many of **Shawn Mercer**'s compositions, "this song speaks to being your best self in difficult times, and of following your heart to find what is right for the self, others, and the planet." The Mercer family's connections to the mill "go all the way back to the time of the beginning of operations. Both of my paternal great grand-fathers worked for the mill, and at times through the generations, my grandfather, father, cousins, and uncles also found employment there". Shawn grew up in Bucksport, the son of Bob and Jean Mercer, with his siblings Todd and Cara. He attended school here, "from New Alderbrook Nursery School all the way up through graduation from BHS in the class of 1991." After receiving a degree in Elementary Education from the University of Maine, he came back to Bucksport to teach 5th and 6th grade. He went on to teach in Belfast, the Alaskan bush, and the Cloud Forest School in Costa Rica before leaving the teaching profession in 2011. He now works full time as co-owner and operator of The Nancy Place Homestead & Hostel with his wife Molly and their children Ella, Maizey, Ivy, and Jeb. "My interest in creating a better world isn't limited to my work on the farm." Shawn participates in "the revisioning of Bucksport" by helping with and participating in community events that promote music and the arts. A singer songwriter who performs regularly in the area, Shawn has released two CDs of his original music--* Boondock Blues, *2006 and* Reflections, *2010. "You can find more information about my music, work, and The Nancy Place at* www.thenancyplace.co

Patricia Ranzoni
Bucksport

THIS YEAR LET'S SEARCH FOR CURVED BRANCHES

Arm length. Rounded.
Shaped by the weight of what threatens to break. Because Sarah
sent this card.

Because Sarah sent this card, my snowfolk and I
will never be the same. No more straight out sticks
stuck in old ways, unable to reach round. No!

Because Sarah sent this snowman card all sparkly and scarfy
I see something new. The possibility of bending arms encircling
in that ancient way humans dance turning our rounded arms
into lifted suns, our fingers sparking with what runs through us
when we touch.

Because Sarah sent this card my snow people will still
sport buttons and eyes of stones I pry from the icy drive
and, you bet, smiles. And each carrot, oh, tipped high
and back, not straight out, *no, nosier than that*, the better
to see the cardinals lit in its twiggy hands overhead.

This year when it snows our sculpting kind of snow here
I promise I will stretch for this joy Sarah sent. This new way
of dreaming. Of making and showing.

Wherever we are, through whatever tears, won't you watch
for this spirit with me, and *wave*?

Author note:
Upon being invited to introduce the February 5, 2015 *Pecha Kucha Bucksport, What's Next?* event, I
composed this poem for performing with fluttery, fringed, red satin wing-like finger puppets. According to its web site, *Pecha Kucha*, Japanese for "chit-chat," is "the art of concise presentations, devised
in Tokyo in 2003 as an opportunity for young designers to meet, network, and show their work in
public" is now in hundreds of cities around the world.

Naomi Graychase
Bucksport

A TIME TO DREAM

from the February 5, 2015 "Pecha Kucha Bucksport, What's Next?" Alamo Theater event

1) Good evening. I'm Naomi Graychase. My ancestors on both the Chase and the Gray sides were among the first families to venture to America in the 1600s. In fact, there is even some evidence that the first woman to step ashore at Plymouth Rock was my ancestor on the Gray side.

2) My family are Grays and Chases, Sawyers, Sopers and Hutchings. I can trace my family back on both sides to the War for American Independence and I am proud to say that I know of four Patriot ancestors who fought on the right side of the Revolution.

3) I was born on June 27, 1972. Part of the 9th generation of Grays to call Hancock County home. I grew up in Orland and Bucksport and graduated from Bucksport High School, just like my mom, my dad, my maternal grandmother, some aunts and uncles and lots and lots of cousins.

4) I share my birthday with my hometown. On June 27, 1792, the town of Bucksport was incorporated as Buckstown. Some of my ancestors had already been in the area for more than 30 years at that time.

5) What brought the Grays to this part of the world was the French and Indian War. In 1759, my 6th great-grandfather Reuben Gray was stationed at Fort Pownall. He helped to build the fort at the site we now know as Fort Point in Stockton Springs.

6) But, times have changed. That fort is long gone. So this fall, when some of the 8th, 9th, and 10th generations of Grays and Graychases visited that same spot, we didn't build a fort and we didn't think about wars. We did what *we* do, instead: yoga.

7) My family was here long before Bucksport was a milltown; we cut trees; we cut ice; we built ships and sailed them. In fact, my great-great grandfather, Albina Sawyer helped to build Admiral Peary's great ship, The Roosevelt, which he launched from Verona Island.

8) Admiral Peary sailed that ship all the way to the North Pole and back. Imagine the enormity of that dream—106 years ago men here, right here—dreamt of building a ship that could reach the North Pole for the very first time. And they did it! It takes courage, tenacity, and imagination to dream that big.

9) When it came time to build the mill, my family was there, too. In fact, sadly, one of my ancestors on the Sawyer side, who had also helped to build the WABI tower, was electrocuted while working on the new powerhouse at Seaboard Paper Company.

10) As we ourselves consider what to build in our future here, in Bucksport, I find it helpful to remember that we have a long history of adapting to change. Where once there was a ferry, oil tankers now dock. Where once there was no bridge, the very first long-span suspension bridge in Maine was conceived and built.

11) And while it's not an exaggeration to say that members of my family gave their lives to the mill, it is also true that my 87-year-old grandfather, Richard Chase—who worked as the personnel manager at the mill for 36 years—has managed to outlive the mill. When I asked him if he ever thought he'd last longer than the mill he said, "No." And then he added, "…everyone thought the mill would live long after them."

12) There are other fixtures in Bucksport that have changed, as time has passed and the need for change arose. I, for one, miss that distinctive 1960s façade at Bucksport High School. But even that had to change.

13) A few years ago, I addressed the graduates at BHS and I told them that no matter where they went, this is always where they would be *from*. I left Bucksport High and went to college and became a magazine journalist.

14) I never worked in the mill, but my life, it turns out, was also tied as directly to demand for coated paper as it was for the millworkers. And just as the Waldo Hancock Bridge crumbled and a new bridge was dreamt of and built in its place

15) So, too, did I build a new bridge. When I was laid off in 2011, I dreamt of a completely different life. I imagined the possibility that maybe I could become a yoga teacher—and a firefighter! Which is how, four centuries after my ancestor took a leap of faith and stepped off a ship in Plymouth, I came to be doing this.

16) The mill wasn't always there. But someone had an idea, and they built it. And like Fort Pownall and the Waldo Hancock Bridge, and the ferry, and my career in journalism, each one was built and mattered and was essential—and then each one met its end.

17) My parents and grandparents and I, we grew up in a milltown. But my niece—part of the 10th generation of Hancock County Grays--she's only 11. And for her, Bucksport will mean something other than a mill. It's up to us to decide what that will be for her.

18) When I look out at this town, what I see is its place in a long arc of history that is defined by bold exploration and creative problem-solving, hard work, and clever engineering. I see the same grit and determination and capacity for adaptation that built ships and forts and bridges and, yes—even a nation.

19) What we know in yoga, is what we know in Bucksport—every ending creates room for a beginning. Every exhale creates room for another breath. And every sunset heralds a necessary darkness, a time to rest, to regroup—and then…

20) …a time to dream.

Naomi Graychase *is a writer, teacher, animal communicator, healer, and interior firefighter. She grew up in Orland and Bucksport and is a graduate of Bucksport High School (1990), like her parents (1970) and her mother's mother (1950) before her. She graduated* cum laude *from Smith College (1994) with a degree in American Studies and a minor in Secondary Education and spent much of her twenties and thirties working as a journalist and living "away," in San Francisco and Western Massachusetts, returning home to Maine in 2009 to fulfill her dream of home ownership. "The organizing principle of my life is "Seva" (the yoga of selfless service) and I feel most fully myself when I am being of service to people, animals, and the green and growing things of this world. My heart opens into my service, which these days is mostly as a volunteer firefighter and as yoga teacher, especially for children with special needs, women with PTSD, and cancer patients and survivors." Naomi makes her home in Bucksport with her partner and five rescued cats. She runs two small businesses, "Yoga with Naomi" and "Peace, Fellow Mammals", and works part-time at the Beth C. Wright Cancer Resource Center in Ellsworth. Her writing has appeared in the* New York Times, *on* National Public Radio, *and in dozens of business and consumer magazines, newspapers, and websites. Her most recent true stories can be found in* Down East *magazine in the archives of community radio station* WERU. *"I keep myself very busy gardening, telling true stories, volunteering with the Orland Fire Department where I am Public Information Officer, teaching, and working as a fire instructor with Maine Maritime Academy, but even amidst all this busy-ness, I still make time every day to dream."*

Editor's note: It is heartwarming, remarkable, and challenging to realize that, to the best of our knowledge, a dozen or more of us who've contributed to STILL MILL descend, with Naomi, from the Gray brothers who put down roots along the Castine peninsula and Penobscot shores after serving in the seventeen hundreds in the French and Indian War at their Fort Pownal which became Fort Point, with only the location in Stockton Springs remaining.

Patricia Ranzoni
Bucksport

HANCOCK COUNTY BALLAD

Where her dad's mill roared
the poet labors for words
so do the woodsmen

where the mill is done
the potter burns through blizzards
keep heart prayer gems

while the mill still heaves
its bare bones go up for sale
musicians lament

when the mill quiets
fishermen compose their songs
moaning with the tides

when mill people leave
children ask where friends will be
teachers planting seeds

while the mill turns ghost
families who built it cry
see how they, too, fade

where the mill is sold
pipers pipe and dreamers dream
the flower shop blooms

where mill echoes sound
the river wakes and exhales
farmlands refeel hope

where the millfolk grew
old and young meet to question
believing in spring

when the mill trembles
the long and new here feel it
yogis stretch and sigh

where the mill is lost
cartographers go to work
here's your town! right here!

where the mill was. . . clears. . .
soil, river, and air breathe free
leaders sleep again

where heirloom halls lean
saviors propose new life
oh   what do you see?

Previously published by the electronic journal, *e*lix*ir.*

Author note:
These glimpses are inspired by presenters at the February 5, 2015 "*Pecha Kucha* What's Next for Bucksport?" program hosted by Brooke Ewing Minner at the Alamo Theater, and efforts underway on many fronts by elders to youngsters to honor, save and rejuvenate our town and greater community. Names of participants, reflected in the individual stanzas along with realities of community actions and reactions to the mill's closing are, in addition to the poet laureate, David Weeda of Williams Pond Lodge; Naomi Graychase, Yoga with Naomi; Jim LeClair, Belfast Smart DataMap Services; educator Laurie Brooks, Wilson Hall advocate; Asha Fenn, artist and poet; Shannon Grimes of Maine Farmland Trust; and Ben Sprague, Bangor councilor and municipal visionary.

Michael W. Shaw II
Bucksport

I AM A PAPERMAKER

Because I love the feeling of shredded muck
mixed between my fingers

Because the patience it takes is highly rewarded

Because of the feeling of water that is not
like water but goo in my hands and pot

Because I enjoy creating shape,
I enjoy pressing down on the goo

Because I love the satisfaction of water
dripping from the screen, letting this
goo turn into soft paper

Because the long days of letting paper
dry excite me

Because to be able to create is a treasure
on its own

Because watching the long work of chewed
substance turn to pulp turned into art
is my pleasure

Because my father and his father before
him worked hard everlasting days in paper
mills creating paper for all of the state and
all of the world

Paper made by hand of recycled paper and petal fibers by Michael Shaw II.

Patricia Ranzoni
Bucksport

PAPERMAKERS STILL

> *now that the mill is hushed*

Because is was in our trees
Because it was in our air
Because it was in our waters and fire
Because it was in us heart to bone
Because it still is

Because all fibers might be pressed
Because tea leaves can be read
Because pulp can be shredded and beat
Because petals can be dried and spread
Because threads can be felted and paged
Because the papermakers' sons
                    and daughters still are
Because it is in our hands

Previously published in the electronic journal, *e*lix*ir*.

Patricia Ranzoni, *Bucksport*
Bernard Vinzani, *Whiting*

RISING ABOVE
Two Words & A Master Hand Papermaker

Photograph by Hans Krichels, as exhibited in the Alamo Theater poster case for the Bucksport Area Poetry Route anthology preview. Collage by the author.

Author note: The word "Mill" and its action, inspiring this collage, presented itself as a "concrete" or "shape" poem because its form is as important as its text, showing as it does, visually, the message of the whole. As the mill literally tumbles down, the text draws from within itself transforming to the word "Will", thereby rising above the destruction of the mill and its culture, and illustrating the way the people have found it within themselves to transcend what has befallen us.

          – Patricia Ranzoni
          Bucksport Poet Laureate

Artist note: The fleck bit paper is all recycled from the university throw-away pile, the cream-colored paper that is smooth is conservation paper with cotton muslin and flax fiber, and the rough paper is abaca fiber. It is really about text, image, craft and art, all hand in hand.

          – Bernie Vinzani, Professor of Book Arts and
            Interdisciplinary Fine Arts
            University of Maine at Machias

Bernie Vinzani lives in Whiting, Maine where he runs his own paper mill for making paper by hand. Renowned as a master papermaker and esteemed teacher, he generously donated these examples of his work to Bucksport's *Still Mill* project. Please see The Artists.

THE END / THE BEGINNING

VII. MORE

Of Our Voices

VIII. AUTOGRAPHS

Of Papermaking People Who Shall Not Come Again

IX. APPENDIX

CALL FOR SUBMISSIONS

I would be grateful to receive donations of small pieces of handmade papers from around the world to fill out an exhibit on the theme of our mill closing in which vintage industrial and handmade papers are being paired with original poems and song lyrics previewing our anthology in progress, *STILL MILL*. Note card size fine. All shapes, fibres, welcome.

The exhibit, which is being mounted along storefronts of Main St. businesses and gathering places and out into country communities, will run through fall before being archived with the Bucksport Historical Society.

All contributions to the collection will be cited.

Appreciatively,
Pat Ranzoni
289 Bucksmills Rd.
Bucksport, ME 04416

Mill Anthology Project Receives Grant

February 5th, 2015

Bucksport Poet Laureate Pat Ranzoni has been awarded a $1,000 grant from the SpiritWords Fund of the University of Maine Foundation to support her proposal for an anthology titled *STILL MILL, Poems, Stories & Songs of Making Paper in Bucksport, Maine, 1930–2014.* The grant will help fund the cost of the book's publication and distribution. Ranzoni will compile and edit the collection without compensation as a gift to her hometown. Proceeds from the book beyond the costs of production and marketing will be donated to the Bucksport Historical Society for locating, protecting and exhibiting material documenting the Bucksport mill, further addressing the fund's mission.

"This generous grant, for which we are exceedingly grateful, makes a huge and hopeful difference to our vision," says Ranzoni. "To have our voices believed in and respected in this way, not just locally but statewide, shows us that the work of our lives is valued beyond the scrap heap we've heard it might become."

The SpiritWords Fund was established in 1996 to discover, support, honor and preserve the full breadth of poetic expression that grows out of a long and intimate relationship with the state of Maine and its rich and various cultural traditions. It seeks to recognize and honor those voices whose memories, dreams and imagination inhabit this homeland and whose work remembers and renews the significance of place and community.

The call for submissions, announced after the mill's closing, has brought about a dozen poems, two songs, a half dozen stories, even cartoons. The collection includes a "treasure-trove" of verses and drawings of mill and regional life by "The Papermill Poet" Owen K. Soper (pen name, Fuller Clay), whose work appeared in the *Seaboard Bulletin*, a publication about the mill's early identity in Bucksport. "Many of us old mill families have wealth such as this in our records," says Ranzoni, "and we have promises from third- and fourth-generation mill workers for more."

March 1, the collection will be reviewed to determine if additional resources are needed for the project. Rather than a totally romanticized account, the project seeks recollections, including the pride and the problems, along with the details and reality of industrial papermaking in Bucksport that only those affected by it can know.

Authentic submissions from all are welcomed regardless of age or schooling, including traditional and experimental treatments. All subjects and perspectives, from all time frames will be considered. Previously published work with standard rights and permissions may be submitted. All submissions will be copyright protected and all contributors will receive a copy of the book.

Send typed or handwritten submissions, with a few lines about your relationship to the Bucksport mill, its people and/or place, to pranzoni@aol.com or c/o Pat Ranzoni 289 Bucksmills Rd., Bucksport, ME 04416; enclose a self-addressed stamped envelope for a reply.

PHOTO: The sun sets on the last papermaking shift at the Verso paper mill in Bucksport. December 4, 2014. Photo by Ernie Smith

DIRECTORY

An Exhibit of Poems & Papers honoring our papermakers and

papermaking heritage and

Previewing

STILL MILL,

Poems, Stories & Songs

from Making Paper in Bucksport, Maine

1930 – 2014

Poetry & Paper Displays	*Locations*
Small Town America, song lyrics, Chris Soper, Orland	Information case, Bucksport waterfront
This is What Was Bequeathed Us, Gregory Orr, Virginia	" "
At the Four O'Clock Whistle, Hazel Smith Hutchinson, Kansas	Bucksport True-Value storefront
Halfway, Minnie Bowden (1915–2000), Orland	Orland Community Center
The Woods, Rick Doyle, Bucksport	Bucksport Golf Club
Maine Real, Part I, John Campbell, Dedham with paper made	
by Ed and Pat Ranzoni	Dr. Tom Gaffney, office window, Main
My Little Mill Koan, Frank Berry, Bucksport	Fellows, Kee & Tymoczko, LLC, Main
Stone Ones, Pat Ranzoni, Bucksport	Bucksport Hannaford display case
Landscape of Our Lives, Lynne Findlay, Verona Island	Fort View Variety, Verona, newsstand
Prospect, Gary Lawless, Nobleboro, paper made by Georgeann Kuhl	Th'Pit Stop, Prospect, counter
Combat Paper & Poems made by Terry Grasse, Lisbon Falls, and	
from Making Maybaskets by Pat Ranzoni	Information case, Bucksport waterfront
Welcome! We've Been Waiting for You a Long, Long Time, Pat Ranzoni	Buck Memorial Library and Bay Area Chamber of Commerce

Farewell Force, Pat Ranzoni, with last Verso Co. papers   Buksport Town Office upstairs

Paper, Anne Stevenson, Northumberland, UK, with papyrus and
      Krichels famous-author watermarked papers   Bucksport Town Office downstairs

Who Will Bear Our Ancient Marks?, Leslie Linder, Penobscot   "   "

Papermakers, Please Stand, Pat Ranzoni   "   "

from The Man On The Moon, Tom Fallon, Rumford   "   "

Papermakers Lament, bagpipe air lyrics, Ernie Smith, Bucksport   MacLeod's Restaurant storefront, Main

Handmade Books, Sharon Bray, Orland   BookStacks storefront, Main

That Clear First Morning, Philip Booth (1925–2007), Castine   Jed Prouty Assisted Living, Main

A Hancock County Kind of Haiku, Pat Ranzoni   Community Pharmacy storefront, Main

from Our Present and Future River, Part I, Paul Liebow, Bucksport   Rosen's storefront, Main

Shutting Down Paper Machines 2014, Sharon Bray, Orland   "   "

The Pulp Cutter Speaks, Rick Doyle, Bucksport   Rosen's storefront, Main

Gigantic Mill, Tom Gaffney, Bucksport and Stockton Springs   "   "

Bucksport ~ What Abides, Pat Ranzoni   "   "

Welcome! We've Been Waiting for You a Long, Long Time, Pat Ranzoni   "   "

The Mill; Dennis, Hannah Varnum, Mrs. LaLonde's 4th Grade   "   "

Mill, Hannah Mantsch, Mrs. LaLonde's 4th Grade   "   "

Mill Town (acrostic), Kelsea Gaff, Mrs. LaLonde's 4th Grade   "   "

Paper Mill (acrostic), Hannah Mantsch, Mrs. LaLonde's 4th Grade   "   "

The Bucksport Mill Was (acrostic), Marissa Brown, Mrs. LaLonde's 4th Grade "   "

Good-bye Mill, Meg Morrison, Mrs. LaLonde's 4th Grade   "   "

How It Feels, Mary Elsa Theobald, Mrs. LaLonde's 4th Grade   "   "

from Our Once and Future River, Part 2, Paul Liebow, Bucksport   Former H & R Block storefront, Main
      with paper made by Richard Lee (1933–2008)

The Woods, Rick Doyle, Bucksport   "   "

These are the days..., Pat Ranzoni, with paper made by Diane Hebert   "   "

Where This Bell Was~This Green Bell~Hundreds of Green Bells,   "   "
      Pat Ranzoni

Comes back a dark / before the four o'clock shift lets out...   Talk 'n' Shop storefront, Main
      Pat Ranzoni

Miller's Girl, Lisa Miller Joy, Bowdoin   Daffodil Flowers, window, Main

Rising Above, Pat Ranzoni, with papers made by Bernie Vinzani   Alamo Theater entrance case, Main

from Shiftwork: A Sequence (III), Paul Corrigan Jr., Millinocket   Marina, then Harbor View Grille, Main

He Worked at the Mill His Whole Life, Anne Smallidge, Blue Hill   Frank Dunbar's Barber Shop, Main

Maine Real, Part II, John Campbell, Dedham   Gold Star Laundromat, Main

Shut Down of the Verso Paper Co., Linda Smith, Bucksport	Edward Arey Bldg. entrance, River Rd.
Today, Too, Pat Ranzoni	Municipal boat landing, Silver Lake,
	under small rock on boulder
Outback Ball, Pat Ranzoni	Roadside pine, P.D. and Jean Smith lot,
	Millvale
The Pulp Cutter Speaks, Rick Doyle; *When the 4 O'clock Whistle*	Bucksmills Rod & Gun Club
Blows, Ernie Smith; and *Maine Real*, Part II, John Campbell, Dedham	
Two Forts, Pat Claus, Orrington	Knoxview Apartments, lobby
St. Regis Mill, 2012, Sharon Bray, Orland	Gardner Commons, lobby
Patent Leather Prayer, Pat Ranzoni, with paper by Rebecca Goodale	Jewett Community Ctr., Bridge St.
Miller's Girl, Lisa Miller Joy, Bowdoin, and *Today, Too*, Pat Ranzoni	Bucksport High School, Broadway
When the 4 O'Clock Whistle Blows, Ernie Smith, Bucksport	Senior Citizens Ctr., Broadway

PLEASE NOTE: Vintage machine and handmade papers from around the world are paired with the poems throughout the exhibit, though only the handmade and heirloom papers are cited in the directory and only once. Thanks to makers, donors, and lenders, acknowledged on each of the 55 broadsides, for honoring our people and archives with these gifts.

Exhibit will remain up through the end of November for viewing by homecomers and photographic documenters.

Wholehearted gratitude for your participation and interest, Patricia Smith Ranzoni, Poet Laureate

LETTER OF THANKS

TO THE EDITOR:

Please permit me to convey gratitude for all who contributed in any way to the realization of the recently concluded Bucksport Area Poetry Route previewing our *STILL MILL* anthology in progress. What a privilege to be entrusted with your precious voices, proof that we are transforming our cultural shock into an historically important document witnessing survival, pride and celebration of the life and death of our paper mill. The exhibited poems and songs are just a few of hundreds of writings, including prose, being gathered in the book.

Bucksport thanks you authors, youngsters to elders. Especially Milissa LaLonde for involving her 4th graders resulting in their soon-to-be first publication in a book. And the paper makers and collectors for their gifts adding to mine to our Town's archive honoring the history of papermaking here and world wide: master Maine hand papermakers, Rebecca Goodale and Scott Vile, Diane Green-Hebert, Georgeann Kuhl (donated by Gary Lawless), Richard Lee (loaned by Trudy Chambers Price), and Bernie Vinzani. Charylene Stubbs Gilbert for the loan of Egyptian papyrus. Hans Krichels for his donation to the Bucksport collection of his father's heirloom industrial rag paper with famous author watermarks.

Thanks to the welcoming businesses and building hosts and keepers of the keys, not least, our Town Clerk, Kathy Downes, who facilitated access for Town displays so respectfully. And Pearl Swenson for keeping a protective eye on the installations, helping with the tending.

Gratitude, of course, to Ed Ranzoni for helping to get the broadsides installed throughout Bucksport to Orland, Verona and Prospect and collecting them for their journey to the Bucksport Historical Society.

Bucksport thanks Hans Krichels for his assistance as a media liaison and most especially for his masterful photography creating a priceless visual archive which we look forward to visiting on a dedicated website, and his helper Nancy Minott.

We thank *The Enterprise* for printing news of each installation of poetry and paper pairs as they unfolded through summer and fall, and our final calendar notices.

And *The Ellsworth American* and *Bangor Daily News* for their splendid recent features, assigning reporters to come see what we've been up to.

To all who helped spread word, looked them up, tarried in thought and respect, our paper making families and towns thank you. What an amazing thing we did together!

Cheers for the holidays and new year before returning to the completion of the book,

Pat Ranzoni
Bucksport Poet Laureate

Submissions still welcome c/o pranzoni@aol.com or 289 Bucksmills Rd.

X. THE ARTISTS

Harriet Fisher Hill COVER: Emily Newell photograph of oil on board painting, worked from a 1964 photograph, by esteemed Maine artist, Harriet Fisher Hill (1915–2004), and loaned by Bucksport artist and businessman, Larry Wahl. Born in Arizona, Hill attended Winterport and Bangor, Maine schools and was active in the art community, including the Bangor State Fair Art Show. For years, she and her husband, Marion "Pop" Hill, ran Hill's Newsstand and soda fountain, complete with juke box, on Main Street. She was a member of the Bucksport Historical Society.

George Danby *(DanbyInk.com)* grew up in Bangor and Portland. He spent the summers on Phillips Lake and "enjoyed the coast from Bar Harbor to Bucksport." Danby free-lanced at the *Bangor Daily News* while in school. He worked in New York, New Haven, CT and Providence, RI as a cartoonist before returning to Bangor as staff cartoonist for the *Bangor Daily*. He became nationally syndicated in 1981. His cartoons have appeared in the *New York Times, Time, Newsweek, The National Review, The Washington Post, USAToday, DownEast, The Chicago Tribune* and *The Funny Times*, to name a few...including - appearing in 500 weeklies. He has won numerous state and New England awards for his daily editorial cartoon. Danby published his first book, *The Essential Danby* with Islandport Press in 2014, during a huge reception at the Bangor Public Library. "I enjoy playing tennis, kayaking on Green Lake and breathing. I also enjoyed spending time with my two amazing children, Nick and Sarah."

Edward DesJardins, 80, donor of his railroad station and bridge sketches, called "The Boy from Bucksport," by the *Georgetown* [MA] *Record* in a recent feature on his retirement from their Historical Commission, "was raised in Bucksport, Maine, a small town along the Penobscot River, which even today has fewer than 5000 people." After graduating from Bucksport High School with the Class of 1955, Ed served in the U.S. Air Force, then studied Architecture in Boston. "I went to Harvard and learned from the chairman of the Department of Architecture, Benjamin Thompson." He joined Thompson's Cambridge-based architecture firm and "went on to enjoy a thriving career in architecture, working with Thompson on Boston's Faneuil Hall markets, the South Street Seaport in New York and Colonial Williamsburg, and embarking on a thriving architecture career," which, "kind of got me into historical perservation," which he has done for close to a half century." In what spare time he has, Ed makes sketches of buildings which he sells and gives away. Through the years, he has been a generous benefactor of his home town where he is remembered with mutual pride. For example, he donated dozens of his drawings of Bucksport to the Buck Memorial Library to be sold to raise money for its restoration. According to the *Record*, "he has spent more time researching buildings, cemeteries and other quiet standing monuments to history than most people could imagine. The work of a preservationist isn't easy or simply a hobby. He's channeled his passion and expertise to secure grants to save and refurbish properties [throughout New England] that otherwise would have crumbled into oblivion or been torn down." "People don't realize," stresses Ed, "that once these are gone, they're gone forever. You can't bring history back. So you try to capture some of that." He and his wife, Jeannine, lived in Georgetown from 1967 to 1976, in Byfield from 1976 to 1994 and in Rowley from 1994 to 2005 where he co-wrote a book, "Images of America: Rowley." In 2005, Ed and Jeannine returned to Georgetown and in 2014 he was honored with the Massachusetts Historical Commission Preservation Award. "Now, I want to spend some time with my kids on the West Coast and my grandchildren."

Editor's note: Upon the death of their mother, in her honor, Ed and the Des Jardins family established "Helen's Kitchen" Community Assistance Fund of Bucksport Community Concerns to provide assistance to those in need with rent, medical, electrical, car repairs needed for work, special needs clothing, and more.

Lawrence Robert Wahl, loaner of the Harriet Hill painting of the Bucksport paper mill for our cover, and creator of the documentary series of lunch carrier sketches throughout the book, was born December 18, 1945, and brought up on a farm in upstate New York. He attended Williamson Central School, class of 1963, where he was editor of the yearbook, providing most of the layout and artwork. After serving six years in the Army Reserve, he was honorably discharged in 1971. Larry held a variety of jobs, leaving a management position with XEROX in 1977 and moving to Bucksport/Orland where he worked construction for 20 years while owning "The Dairy Port" since 1981.

His interests are globes and maps, local history and architecture, designing spaces, the outdoors, and ice cream. In addition to designing the Dairy Port sign, props and logo, he created the logo for "Heart & Soul" (the Orton Foundation's presence in Bucksport), the letterhead for the Bucksport Sculpture Committee, his home, garage and camp addition.

He is often seen around town checking on various buildings and projects to which he is devoted, being involved with four of the nine buildings in town that are on the National Register of Historic Places – Buck Memorial Library (Trustee), Old Railroad Station (Historical Society Director), Heywood House (owns), and Wilson Hall (efforts to save) – also the historic Spofford House on Federal St., circa 1810 (owns, not on register), and the "Little Yellow School House" which is.

Larry is chairman of the Board of Trustees of the Buck Memorial Library; on the Board of Directors for the Bucksport Bay Area Chamber of Commerce (BBACC), Bucksport Area Cultural Arts Society (BACAS) and the Bucksport Historical Society; serves on the Comprehensive Plan and Economic Development Committees; and is a member of the Bucksport Garden Club, Friends of Fort Knox, Great Pond Mountain Conservation Trust (GPMCT), and Northeast Historic Film.

Larry has been the recipient of the Tourism Award from Bucksport Bay Area Chamber of Commerce (BBACC), 2007; "Super Supporter" Award from BBACC, 2014; Business Person of the Year Award from BBACC, 2015; 93.7 'The Wave', "Every Town Has a Story" Honor for Volunteerism, 2015; and in 2016 received recognition by the State of Maine Senate and House of Representatives for "Volunteer Efforts in Promoting Community Economic Development and Recovery Following the Closure of the Verso Paper Mill."

He says his present goals are "to save Wilson Hall, promote the arts, help Bucksport flourish and become <u>all</u> that it can be. 'Get your wiggle on' Bucksport!"

All of this co-operative work, including his artful contribution to this documentary, and in addition to serving mill workers and their families at the Dairy Port through the years, has constituted a remarkable relationship for which his community is immeasurably grateful.

For more than twenty-five years, **Bernard G. Vinzani,** master hand papermaker and distinguished teacher has lived and worked at his paper mill, Vinzani Papermakers, in Whiting, Maine., making paper professionally for book editions and artists. He is Professor of Art and Book Arts at the University of Maine in Machias where he directs the Book Arts Studios which house letterpress and papermaking facilities and where he is also Director of the UMM Book and Art Galleries. "The art of making paper is what Bernie Vinzani celebrates, but on a very different level. Vinzani makes paper by hand as part of the process of making books by hand." (From *"Mill closures remind us of Maine paper's power/Mainers remain attached to a product that seems to be crumpling into memory."* Ray Routhier, Portland Press Herald, Oct. 26, 2014.) Vinzani holds a Master of Fine Arts degree in Printmaking from Indiana State University. A member of the Washington County, Maine Flat Bay Artists Collective, he has exhibited his work nationally and internationally in such venues as The VI International Print Biennial, Cracow Poland; ARC Gallery, Chicago; Das Papier, Duren, Germany; Paperworks, Caracas, Venezuela; and the Maine Invitational, Portland, Maine. He has taught work-shops at the Penland School of Crafts, North Carolina, Haystack School, Maine, Anderson Ranch Arts Center, Colorado, The Southwest Craft Center, Texas, and the International Paper Conference, Boston. He has made paper for and collaborated with such artists as William Wegman, Red Grooms, Claire Van Vliet, Robert Natkin, John Cage, Robert Rauschenberg, and Ansel Adams. Vinzani's work has been featured in such publications as *Hand Papermaking Journal, The Book of Fine Paper, American Craft Magazine, Art New England,* and now, *STILL MILL, Poems, Stories & Songs of Making Paper in Bucksport, Maine 1930 – 2014.*

XI. THE EDITOR

Patricia Smith Ranzoni was born in 1940, upriver in Lincoln-Enfield territory, to a young Canadian-American woodcutter and hauler from Webster Plantation and a farm girl from Castine who brought her and her sister down to Bucksport in the hope he would find work at the paper mill upon returning from W.W. II. His Navy skills earned him a position with the riggers crew where he worked as long as he could while working several small subsistence farms, dealing in cattle and antiques, providing for his wife and five children. Many of Pat's uncles, cousins, nephews, classmates, neighbors, friends, and students worked at the mill through the years as did her mother, briefly, wrapping, until childcare became a problem during the war.

Pat began earning her way as a bean and strawberry picker in the truck farms of Hancock County at about nine, then as a babysitter, mother's helper, farm hand and (Crosby's) diner cook and server. She worked her way through a Bachelor's degree in education at the University of Maine as a summer island hotel waitress, laundress, seamstress, university office clerk, faculty babysitter, AVON Lady, Co-op dorm cook and housekeeper. Marrying as university students, she taught first grade in Orono (Asa Adams) while she and Ed finished their studies. Following his work out of state for several years, they soon returned to Maine to keep one of the subsistence farms of her youth in the family and raise their children in Bucksport where they co-founded New Alderbrook farm nursery school and kindergarten, having tested their Alderbrook model at their country place in North Yarmouth on the way home to Bucksport.

She taught first grade in Bucksport (Luman Warren) while homesteading with Ed and children Gina, Joseph and Daniel; and co-founded The Children's Garden therapeutic early childhood school at the Counseling Center in Bangor where she became Director of Child Development Services. Continuing to integrate family with professional interests, she earned her Master's degree and a Certificate of Advanced Studies at UMO until health troubles caused a change in direction, turning her towards writing which she had always enjoyed and done plenty of. While doing limited free-lance writing for the mill retirement program and other area organizations she was recruited to consult to the Maine Independent Living Center which she did as long as she could. In 1994 the Hancock County Children's Council presented her with the Nancy Gentile Award "In recognition and appreciation of her dedication and caring service to the benefit of children" and her advocacy on behalf of children and families with disabilities.

Unschooled in the literary arts, she found herself drawn naturally to poetry, in her people's way, as a means of documenting their culture, which she saw slipping away, and began teaching herself to submit her work with the vision of publication. In addition to articles on the work she had done in education, mental health, and disabilities studies being published in the journals of her profession, her poetry found acceptance in literary journals in and beyond Maine, across the country and abroad. Her writing is being

431

acquired by archives of Maine history and writing, and is drawn from for Maine studies, especially Maine women's writing and working class studies at the University of Maine, has been used for Colby College's "Many Maines" course, and has been included in anthologies representing writers of Maine. Her books are available through Maine libraries and bookstores and her work can be found on the internet as well as along the waterfront in Bucksport.

In 2014 Pat was named the Poet Laureate of Bucksport "for as long as she shall live." *STILL MILL* is a more than two-and-a half-years-in-the-making gift to her town and her people, whose voices she loves.

Also by Patricia Ranzoni:

A PLACE FOR ME, A PLACE TO BE, A Workbook for People Who Live With Children (published with grant from National Association for the Education of Young Children); *CLAIMING, Poems* (Puckerbrush Press); *SETTLING, Poems,* (Puckerbrush Press); *LEAVINGS, Poems,* cooperative chapbook (Bay River Press); *ONLY HUMAN, Poems from the Atlantic Flyway* (Sheltering Pines Press); *Take Me Back To Sebec,* chapbook (Author-sewn through OneWater Press); *Patricia Ranzoni's Greatest Hits* (Pudding House Publications' Invitational *Gold* Series); *FROM HERE, Poems from Being Born in Lincoln, Maine* (Author-sewn through OneWater Press); *HIBERNACULUM & Other North-natured Poems* (Author-sewn through OneWater Press); and *BEDDING VOWS, Love Poems from Outback Maine* (North Country Press). Also edited by Patricia Ranzoni: *SCATTERINGS FROM OFFNECK, Heirloom Poems & Photographs of Old Castine from Jean Young Smith of Dunc's Meadow* (OneWater Press).

Still Mill editor Patricia Smith Ranzoni, with University of Maine faculty, as recipient of 1976 scholarship for graduate studies in educational administration from International Paper Company Foundation.